ESSENTIAL

STUDY SKILLS

As part of Houghton Mifflin's ongoing commitment to the environment, this text has been printed on recycled paper.

ESSENTIAL
STUDY SKILLS

LINDA WONG
LANE COMMUNITY COLLEGE

HOUGHTON MIFFLIN COMPANY   Boston Toronto

Geneva, Illinois   Palo Alto   Princeton, New Jersey

Essential Study Skills is dedicated to my son, Kailee, for his patience and support throughout this project, to my parents Robert and Mary Wallace (both deceased) who always placed a high value on education, and to the many students at Lane Community College who make teaching and learning a priceless experience.

Sponsoring Editor: Mary Jo Southern
Senior Development Editor: Barbara Roth
Associate Project Editor: Nicole Ng
Production/Design Coordinator: Jill Haber
Senior Manufacturing Coordinator: Priscilla Bailey
Marketing Manager: George Kane

ACKNOWLEDGEMENTS

The authors are grateful to the following for granting permission to reprint excerpts from their works:

Barnwell, William and Robert Dees, THE RESOURCEFUL WRITER, Second Edition. Copyright © 1991 by Houghton Mifflin Company.

Bernstein, Douglas A., Edward J. Roy, Thomas K. Srull, and Christopher D. Wickens, PSYCHOLOGY, Second Edition. Copyright © 1991 by Houghton Mifflin Company. Used with permission.

McKay, John P., Bennett D. Hill, and John Buckler, A HISTORY OF WESTERN SOCIETY, Fourth Edition. Copyright © 1991 by Houghton Mifflin Company. Used with permission.

Ober, Scott, CONTEMPORARY BUSINESS MANAGEMENT. Copyright © 1992 by Houghton Mifflin Company. Used with permission.

Osborn, Michael and Suzanne Osborn, PUBLIC SPEAKING, Second Edition. Copyright © 1991 by Houghton Mifflin Company. Used with permission.

Pride, William M., Robert J. Hughes, and Jack K. Kapoor, BUSINESS, Fourth Edition. Copyright © 1993 by Houghton Mifflin Company. Used with permission.

Cover photo by Scott Morgan. Cover design by Harold Burch, Harold Burch Design, New York City

Student Edition ISBN: 0-395-64396-1

Instructor's Edition ISBN: 0-395-69107-9

123456789-B-97 96 95 94 93

CONTENTS

EXERCISES

PREFACE

Essential Study Skills is a worktext that presents an array of practical study skills strategies, enabling students to select, refine, and adapt the techniques that will serve them best.

Recognizing that each student is an individual with a unique way of learning, the book helps students identify and understand their personal learning styles, strengths, and attitudes. As students progress through the text, their understanding of the concept of studying and the process of learning broadens; they come to view academic learning as a product of a set of skills and behaviors that they can comprehend, acquire, customize, and implement effectively.

Essential Study Skills is appropriate for all post-secondary students. Its encouraging tone, clear rationales, step-by-step approach, versatile exercises, and ample feedback make it ideal for students considered at risk, students with specific learning disabilities, adult students returning to school, students who have experienced difficulties in school, and students in developmental studies programs.

Content and Organization

The information in *Essential Study Skills* is organized into four parts. Part I, "Setting the Stage for Learning," equips students with knowledge about themselves as learners and about how best to absorb the information presented throughout the book. Chapter 1 points out the many **resources** available to college students and includes a comprehensive questionnaire that identifies each student's preferred **learning style**. Chapter 2 encourages students to set both **academic and personal goals** and to **manage time** week by week in order to achieve those goals. Chapter 3 offers practical tips and exercises for **improving concentration**, from arranging a distraction-free study area to preparing one's mind for receiving information to applying the technique of concentrated listening. Chapter 4 establishes the underpinning of the rest of the book: that by understanding how we learn new information, we enhance our ability to learn. The chapter walks students through the **information processing model** and presents a set of twelve **memory principles** that helps students learn more efficiently.

Part II, "Selecting and Processing Information for Memory," applies the information processing model and memory principles directly to learning from textbooks and lectures, emphasizing the rationale for the steps and the significance of the strategies for promoting stronger memory skills. Chapter 5 tells how and why to **survey textbooks**. Chapter 6 presents **SQ4R**, a proven method for thorough textbook reading and comprehension. Chapters 7, 8, and 9 cover the varying techniques for **taking notes** in textbooks, from textbooks, and from lectures.

Part III, "Rehearsing and Retrieving Information from Memory," encourages students to develop creative, original study tools that emphasize their learning strengths and make learning an exciting, active process. Chapter 10 shows how to make and use vocabulary sheets and flash cards for learning general and course-specific **vocabulary**. Chapter 11 shows how to create and study from **visual tools** including mappings, hierarchies, category grids, and timelines. Chapter 12 shows how to create and study from **multisensory tools**—visual, auditory, and kinesthetic—and offers compensatory measures for learners with weaker skills in each area. Chapter 13 shows how to create **mnemonics** for academic and general use.

Part IV, "Testing Your Skills and Your Memory," provides students with strong test-taking skills, which will reduce students' test anxiety and increase their test scores. Because many students need test-taking skills early in the term, several basic skills are introduced indirectly in the chapter review questions throughout the book. Part IV teaches the skills thoroughly. Chapter 14 examines **test anxiety** and presents methods for **taking control of stress**, thereby reducing the effects of anxiety on students' performance. Chapter 15 offers strategies for answering **objective test questions**. Chapter 16 provides **educated guessing** strategies to be used selectively—and only when all else fails. Finally, Chapter 17 teaches strategies for answering **recall questions** (fill-ins and listings) and **recall-plus questions** (definitions, short answers, and essays).

By providing strategies that increase students' self-esteem, confidence, learning potential, and success, *Effective Study Skills* equips students with learning tools for their college courses and beyond.

Special Features

Each chapter of *Effective Study Skills* includes eight features designed to raise students' self-awareness, highlight important information, and provide practice.

- The *visual mapping* provides an overview of the chapter, literally at a glance. At the end of the chapter, students expand the map to include supporting details that will help them recall the content.
- The *profile* allows students to assess their attitudes and behaviors. Students complete each self-evaluation twice, once before reading the chapter and again at the end of the term. By recording the scores on the Master Profile Chart in the Appendix, students generate before and after "academic portraits" that show their strengths, weaknesses, and progress.
- *Boxed information* throughout the chapters highlights key points. Students will benefit from previewing this information, referring to it as they take notes, and reviewing it in preparation for tests.
- *Exercises* throughout the chapters provide guided practice in applying the skills to material from an array of academic disciplines. The exercises can be used in a variety of ways: as homework assignments, as material for class discussion, and as partner or small group activities.
- The *chapter summary* reviews the main points in succinct lists, which students can consult for a quick review of the chapter content.
- *"Personalizing What You Learned"* activities encourage students to tailor the chapter information to their own academic needs. In *scoring the chapter profile*, students identify the skills they already use and those they need to develop. In *expanding the visual mapping*, students dig into the chapter, identifying key terms and supporting details and arranging them in a meaningful, visually memorable way. In *creating vocabulary lists or flash cards* for the key terms printed in color, students compile their own glossaries for further reference and study.
- *Review questions* at the chapter end assess students' progress in learning the strategies and in applying them to course content. The questions can be assigned as homework, answered in class, or completed with partners or in small groups.
- *Writing assignments* promote reflective, critical, and creative thinking about the chapter content and its applications.

Instructor's Resource Manual *Essential Study Skills* is accompanied by an Instructor's Resource Manual. Part I of the IRM provides complete answer keys and teaching tips. Part II contains twenty-two additional exercises and eight transparency masters. Part III provides tests (with answer keys) for each of the four parts in the student text that assess students' retention and integration of material across the chapters.

Acknowledgments I extend my appreciation to the reviewers, who provided valuable recommendations for *Essential Study Skills*. Teaching is an art, and the instructors who reviewed the drafts generously shared their art—their ideas and expertise—to enable this book to meet the needs of students throughout a wide range of post-secondary programs and institutions.

Terry Bayless, Study Skills Consultant, WA
Judith Schein Cohen, University of Illinois, Chicago
Jerry Cross, Diablo Valley College, CA
Michael E. Ericson, Monroe Community College, NY
Wanda Harris, Henderson State University, AR
Dawn Leonard, Charleston Southern University, SC
Dorothy Martinez, Austin Community College, TX
Michael T. Moore, Georgia Southern University
Susan L. Neste, University of North Dakota
Harry Rosemond, Ventura College, CA
Ann K. Schafer, Sacramento City College, CA
Maureen P. Stradley, Community College of Allegheny, PA
Ron Williams, The Pennsylvania State University

L.W.

TO THE STUDENT

Essential Study Skills is designed to provide you with skills that will unlock your learning potential. By consistently using the skills presented in this book, you will learn information more thoroughly and remember it more easily. This section tells you how to get the most out of *Essential Study Skills*.

How to Start Each Chapter

For the best results, prepare your mind before you read each chapter.

1. Read the paragraph on the first page for a glimpse of the skills you will learn in the chapter.
2. Study the visual mapping that follows the first paragraph. This mapping is a picture form of the main headings in the chapter.
3. Answer the chapter profile questions on the second page of the chapter to become aware of your current study habits and attitudes.
4. Preview the chapter for about ten minutes. Read through the chapter headings, subheadings, summary, and review questions, and look at the visual aids and the key terms printed in blue.

Now you are ready to begin the process of thorough, accurate reading.

How to Use the Chapter Features

The special features in each chapter will help you learn and apply essential study skills.

Visual Mapping This overview shows the big picture of the chapter, that is, the most important information and how it fits together. The chapter title is in the middle of the map. The main headings branch out from the title; read them clockwise, beginning from the 11:00 position.

Profile You will discover your current strengths and weaknesses by completing this self-evaluation honestly. During the term, you will learn strategies and techniques for bolstering your weaknesses. At the end of the term, you will answer the questions again to assess your progress.

Boxed Information During your chapter previews and reviews, pay special attention to the blue boxes throughout the chapter. Read each box carefully; then read the following text, which discusses each point in detail. A review of the boxes will be especially useful when you study for tests.

Summary For a brief list of key points in the chapter, turn to the summary. Read it during your preview and again after you have read the chapter thoroughly. By expanding the summary's points with additional details you have learned, you can make it a helpful review tool.

Personalizing What You Learned When you do the three activities in this section, you begin to make the material your own.

Scoring Your Profile Return to the profile that you completed at the beginning of the chapter. Based on the skills, techniques, and strategies presented in the chapter, decide whether "yes" or "no" is the best answer for each question. Then check your answers with the Profile Answer Key in the Appendix (p. 311). If your initial answer matches the correct answer, you are already using an effective study skill. If your initial answer does not match the correct answer, *circle the number of that question* as a reminder to learn to use the skill it involves. Count the number of questions that are *not* circled. This is your score. Record your score in the correct column on the Master Profile Chart in the Appendix (p. 307).

Expanding the Visual Mapping   To make the visual mapping on the first page of the chapter a customized study and review tool, expand it by adding key words and details. Here's how to expand the mapping:

1. Copy the mapping onto a sheet of paper.
2. Return to each main heading in the chapter. Locate key words or concepts discussed under the heading. These words will remind you of the important details you need to learn.
3. In a clockwise order, extend outward from each heading. Write your key words at the ends of the lines. To keep the mapping uncluttered and quick to read, do not write complete sentences.

Visual mappings allow you to express your creativity and individuality. Don't be alarmed if your mapping looks different from someone else's. The chapter information can be expressed in various ways, so there is not just one "correct" way to map it. (See Chapter 11 for more about mappings.) The following visual mapping is an example of one way to map the "To the Student" section you are now reading.

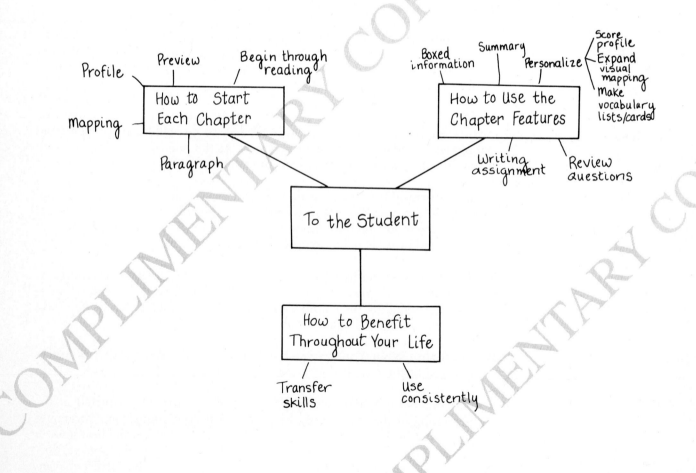

Making a Vocabulary List or Flash Cards Learning vocabulary is essential for understanding the foundation of any course. You can practice by learning key terms in this book. Skim through the chapter to locate the key terms, which are printed in blue. On a sheet of paper, list these terms and write their definitions beside them. Or, if you prefer, write the words on index cards, putting a term on the front of each card and its definition on the back. Review the list or cards frequently. Chapter 10 provides additional ways of learning important terms.

Review Questions The questions at the end of the chapter will help you check how well you have learned and applied the chapter's study skills. You should be able to complete the questions without looking back at the chapter or at your notes. Be sure to read the directions carefully before answering the questions.

Writing Assignments Organizing your ideas and expressing them in writing is an extremely valuable skill that requires practice. The writing assignments give you the chance to practice while you think further about the material you have just learned. Even if your instructor does not require you to do the assignments, you will benefit by completing them independently.

How to Benefit from These Skills Beyond College

Essential Study Skills provides you with valuable skills that become a part of your approach to learning. Rather than simply learn *about* study skills, your goal is to learn *to use* those skills consistently in your academic life and beyond.

Learning, after all, is a lifelong enterprise. Each time you are faced with a new learning situation—whether at school, at home, or at work—you can draw upon the skills you have learned in this book. Apply the skills of goal setting, time management, and concentration, as well as methods for processing and remembering new information to any new task at hand. Now prepare to experience the rewards of success.

L.W.

PART

I

Setting the Stage for Learning

*T*he process of learning places many demands on your mental abilities. To meet the challenges you will encounter as you learn new information in your courses, a solid foundation for learning is essential. The first four chapters of this textbook include the skills necessary to set the stage for effective learning and success in college.

Chapter 1 encourages you to use the many resources that are available to you. Chapter 2 focuses on setting goals and organizing your time so you can work efficiently. Chapter 3 provides you with an array of techniques to expand your ability to concentrate. Chapter 4 shows you how new information is processed in your memory system. The skills you develop through these chapters will help support the additional study skills you will learn later on for in-depth learning.

1 *Using Your Resources*

*Y*ou already have available four kinds of resources that can help you set the stage for learning. Determine which resources you are familiar with and already use by answering these questions. What are some of your best qualities? What is your preferred way of learning? Do you remember more when you read information, hear information, or use a "hands-on" approach? What campus and classroom resources have you not tapped into yet? This chapter explores ways to utilize the many resources that are readily available.

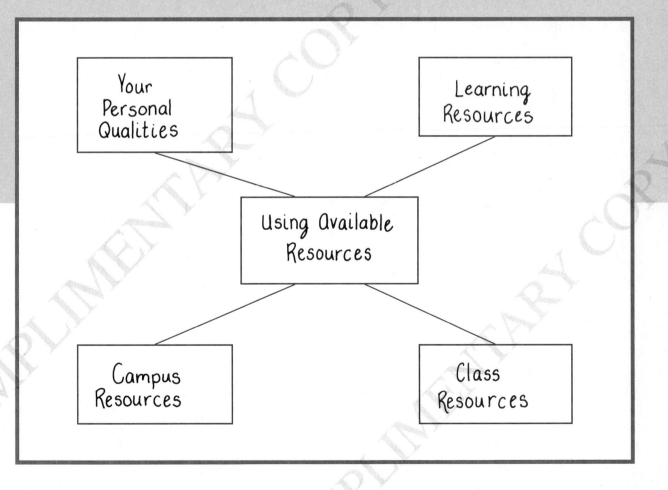

Resources Profile

Answer honestly each of the following questions about your current attitudes and study habits. Your answers should reflect what you *do*, not what you *wish* you would do.

After you read each statement, check YES if you do this *always* or *most of the time*. Check NO if you do this *seldom* or *never*.

YES   **NO**

1. I know some of the personal qualities that I already have for success in college.   _____   _____

2. I know my learning style or learning preference.   _____   _____

3. I often take a negative attitude toward new situations or changes.   _____   _____

4. When things get difficult, I tend to blame others for the situation.   _____   _____

5. I have a system for organizing my notebook so that I can easily find information and papers.   _____   _____

6. I know the times during the day when I am more mentally alert.   _____   _____

7. I know where to find counselors, the library, computer labs, and the student health office.   _____   _____

8. I know all my teachers' names.   _____   _____

9. I am unsure how my grades will be calculated in at least one of my classes.   _____   _____

10. I sometimes forget to do assignments because I don't remember where I wrote them down.   _____   _____

11. I know how to use available resources to solve problems or meet challenging situations.   _____   _____

12. I am willing to contact a counselor, an instructor, or a tutor to get extra help.   _____   _____

Your Personal Qualities

You already possess **personal qualities** that are important **resources** for success in college. You are here in college, so you have already shown:

- a desire to expand your knowledge
- a willingness to aim for a new direction in your life
- courage to begin something new

Personal Qualities of Success

Many additional personal qualities contribute to success in school and in your field of interest for future employment. The following qualities reflect the approaches and attitudes that successful people often show. These qualities can be difficult to obtain, and many people continue to learn and apply them throughout life. You can consult your school catalog for classes offered by the counseling department that focus on developing and strengthening these personal quality skills.

Know Your Strengths, Weaknesses, and Values You can work at your optimum level when you use your strengths and recognize your weaknesses. In this textbook, you have the opportunity to learn more about yourself. You can learn to use your strengths to advantage. And by recognizing your weaknesses, you can keep them from getting in your way and even learn how to overcome them.

The choices that you make for yourself in your courses, in your classes, and as you study reflect your personal values. They provide you with many opportunities to use personal values such as work hard, be honest, be determined and responsible, and show respect and concern for others. You may identify some new values that you have not had in your life but would like to develop.

Take a Positive Approach Toward Life You can look at most situations from at least two points of view: the positive and the negative. Learning to see life as a positive, exciting process leads to less stress and greater personal happiness. The positive person sees each "problem" as a challenge and as an opportunity to learn and grow. So when you find yourself using negative talk, either to yourself or to others, look for ways to turn the negative into the positive.

Be Flexible and Willing to Change Learning is a lifelong process. To acquire new information, learn new skills or new values, or grow as an individual, you have to embrace change instead of resist it. Develop a positive, flexible attitude that shows you are willing to try something new. Recognize that change is not always smooth or easy and that feeling a little unsure, frightened, or hesitant is natural when you are moving through a transition stage into something new.

Be a Risk-Taker To be flexible and willing to change also requires you to gather up your courage, take risks, and move outside your comfort zone into new territories. A **comfort zone** is a position or situation that is familiar, safe, and comfortable to you. This zone is enjoyable because it usually contains less stress and fewer challenges. Making a change usually means leaving a comfort zone to venture into an unfamiliar zone. Nevertheless, moving out of a comfort zone can be very rewarding, for when you do learn new information or skills or make the changes you desired, your personal satisfaction can be enormous.

Feel Confident, Competent, and Resourceful Transition periods can be uncomfortable. A good way to get through them is to focus on your strengths, your values, and your past successes. When you do, your confidence level rises. Self-confidence brings a feeling of competence—you recognize that you are capable of performing the tasks that you have set for yourself.

When you do encounter challenges, feel doubts, or have difficulties learning something new, use your resources. When you are resourceful, you activate your problem-solving abilities. You recognize a challenge (or a problem) and begin to look for solutions. This chapter encourages you to be resourceful by using campus resources and by seeking help from counselors, teachers, and tutors.

Develop Passions in Your Life Passions are strong desires that motivate you to achieve specific goals. Passion to work in a specific occupation, to complete a specific program, or to finish a lifetime goal gives a genuine reason for spending the time and effort that are often required to be successful. When you have specific passions that motivate you, you often have a strong sense of purpose. Feeling your life has a purpose helps you move toward success; it also gives you the belief that your life is valuable, satisfying, and a contribution to your world.

Take Responsibility and Charge of Your Life Successful people know that choices exist but that definite outcomes are not necessarily guaranteed. However, these people are willing to take charge of situations, accept responsibility for their decisions, and analyze and learn from their choices. They also realize that blaming someone else for what is happening in their lives or shirking responsibility for their decisions results in loss of personal power and the sense of being in control. Practice using your personal power by recognizing your options, making decisions, and taking responsibility for outcomes. Avoid blaming others or feeling that you have no choices. If the outcomes are not as you wished, analyze the events that took place and explore alternative choices.

Exercise 1.1	**Recognizing Your Personal Qualities**

Everyone has personal qualities that contribute to personal success. How would you describe yourself? Circle all the words below that apply to you. If you have additional strong points that do not appear in the list, add them to this list.

eager	enthusiastic	motivated	goal oriented
honest	curious	sincere	willing
positive	powerful	confident	flexible
competent	productive	efficient	organized
healthy	relaxed	brave	fun
happy	playful	creative	friendly
loving	kind	compassionate	gentle

mature	successful	attentive	achievement oriented
talented	bright	smart	intelligent
fair	trusting	loyal	patient
forgiving	dependable	determined	responsible
helpful	cooperative	polite	dedicated
sensitive	persistent	lovable	generous
thoughtful	considerate	supportive	independent

All the qualities you circled are personal qualities that you can use as resources. These qualities are an important contribution to your success.

Personal Qualities Appropriate for the Classroom   The classroom offers you the opportunity to share ideas and use your personal qualities. If you have not been in the classroom for many years, or if you have had problems in school in the past, you may not always recognize what is an appropriate or acceptable way to act in the classroom. The following exercise clarifies classroom expectations and guidelines for working effectively in groups.

Guidelines for Group Work

1. Encourage each person to participate by giving ideas.
2. Accept all ideas as possibilities.
3. Respect others' views, even if you don't agree.
4. Respond to each person and each answer in a positive way.
5. Help the group stay on task to complete the assignment.
6. Use your positive personal qualities as needed.

Exercise 1.2   Clarifying Classroom Behaviors

Use the *Guidelines for Group Work* as you do this exercise.

1. Work in groups of three to four students. Your instructor will let you know how much time you have for this activity.

2. Your group will be assigned *one* of the following tasks:
   a. List classroom behaviors that reflect positive qualities of a successful student.
   b. List classroom behaviors and personal qualities that are ideal for learning.
   c. List classroom behaviors that are characteristic of a struggling, frustrated student.
   d. List classroom behaviors that annoy other students and/or the teacher.

3. Record each person's answer. Everyone in the group may take notes, or the group may select one person to jot down responses for everyone.

4. Your group will be asked to share its answers with the rest of the class.

Learning Resources

Learning resources focus on you and the ways you learn best. A strong foundation for learning thoroughly and effectively is made when you:

- know your learning style or learning preference
- use learning strategies that work best for you
- pay attention to your body's natural cycle of alert times

Identify Your Learning Style

Learning styles are the general ways people most easily learn and remember new information. These styles fall into three general groups, which are called **modalities:** 1) *visual*, 2) *auditory*, and 3) *kinesthetic*.

Visual learners learn best by seeing information. They are able to remember information that is presented in pictures, charts, or diagrams. Visual learners often have strong visualization skills. They can look up or close their eyes and "see" the information they have learned. Visual learners benefit by copying or writing information so that they can see it in their own handwriting. Visual study tools (Chapter 11) can help visual learners organize and recall information.

Auditory learners learn best by hearing information. They can remember information that is explained to them orally better than information they have seen or read. Auditory learners are able to follow conversations or lectures and remember the details. These learners often have strong language skills and are usually able to express their ideas clearly when they speak. Because they benefit by hearing information, they do well making their own study tapes and participating in study groups. When they study, they tend to remember more if they recite (talk out loud) to themselves as they read or review notes.

Kinesthetic learners learn best by doing—by working with their hands, working with objects in hands-on experiences, and involving larger body movements as they study. Kinesthetic learners can often concentrate better when they walk or use large muscle movements such as when they write on a chalkboard, or dance. Because typing involves the use of many different muscles, typing notes and information to learn is beneficial for these learners.

Children often learn to use one modality much more effectively than the others. As they mature, they become more and more capable of using all modalities. By adulthood, most people have developed a preference for one modality over the others, but they are able to work in all modalities if needed. This integration of modalities occurs over years and enables adults to learn in a wide variety of situations. For example, you may prefer to have written directions from your supervisor about a new office procedure you are expected to follow. However, if the directions are given verbally instead, you can still follow them.

Students with specific learning disabilities may not be able to function adequately in all three modalities because of neurological impairments. For example, if an individual has a visual processing deficit, the information from his or her eyes does not travel clearly or efficiently to the brain. This individual's auditory processing system, however, may be average or above average. Adults with learning disabilities are certainly able to process information; they do, however, need to know which modality works best for them so that they are drawing on strengths, not weaknesses.

This book provides all students, including students with learning disabilities, with strategies that focus on learning-style preferences and strengths. If, for example, you think you are a kinesthetic learner, when you can, select study tools and methods that are kinesthetically based. Remember, however, that kinesthetic strategies may not work for all kinds of learning situations or may not always be available. This is also true for visual and auditory strategies. Being flexible and willing to shift to strategies based on other modalities can help you greatly when you study. Chapters 11 and 12 provide you with strategies to use for all three learning styles so that you can develop the flexibility required for effective learning.

Learning-Style Preferences

1. Visual learners prefer to work in the *visual modality* and should select visually oriented study tools when possible (see Chapter 11).

2. Auditory learners prefer to work in the *auditory modality* and should choose auditory-oriented study tools when possible (see Chapter 12).

3. Kinesthetic learners prefer to work in the *kinesthetic modality* and should use kinesthetically oriented study tools when possible (see Chapter 12).

Exercise 1.3   Discovering Your Learning Style

This informal survey helps you identify your own learning styles.
Read each statement carefully. Check YES or NO as it relates to you. Your first reaction to the question is usually the best answer.

	YES	NO
1. I like to listen and discuss work with a partner.	____	____
2. I learn by hearing my own voice on tape.	____	____
3. I prefer to learn something new by reading about it.	____	____
4. I often write down the directions someone has given me so that I don't forget them.	____	____

	YES	NO
5. I enjoy physical sports or exercise.	_____	_____
6. I learn best when I can see new information in picture form.	_____	_____
7. I am able to visualize easily.	_____	_____
8. I learn best when someone talks or explains to me.	_____	_____
9. I usually write things down so that I can look back at them later.	_____	_____
10. If someone says a long word, I can count the syllables that I hear.	_____	_____
11. I have a good memory for old songs or music.	_____	_____
12. I like to discuss in small groups.	_____	_____
13. I often remember the size, shape, and color of objects.	_____	_____
14. I often repeat out loud the directions someone has given me.	_____	_____
15. I enjoy working with my hands.	_____	_____
16. I can remember the faces of actors, settings, and other visual details of a movie I saw in the past.	_____	_____
17. I often use my hands and body movement when I'm explaining something.	_____	_____
18. I prefer to practice redrawing diagrams on a chalkboard rather than on paper.	_____	_____
19. I seem to learn better if I get up and move around while I study.	_____	_____
20. If I wanted to assemble a bike, I would need pictures or diagrams to help with each step.	_____	_____
21. I remember objects better when I have touched them or worked with them.	_____	_____
22. I learn best by watching someone else first.	_____	_____
23. I tap my fingers or my hands a lot while I am seated.	_____	_____
24. I speak a foreign language.	_____	_____
25. I enjoy building things.	_____	_____
26. I can follow the plot of a story on the radio.	_____	_____
27. I enjoy repairing things at home.	_____	_____
28. I can understand a lecture when I hear it on tape.	_____	_____
29. I am good at using machines or tools.	_____	_____

	YES	**NO**

30. I find sitting still for very long difficult. _____ _____

31. I enjoy acting or doing pantomimes. _____ _____

32. I can easily see patterns in designs. _____ _____

33. I need frequent breaks to move around. _____ _____

34. I like to recite or write poetry. _____ _____

35. I can usually understand people with different accents. _____ _____

36. I can hear many different pitches or melodies in music. _____ _____

37. I like to dance and create new movements or steps. _____ _____

38. I enjoy activities that require physical coordination. _____ _____

39. I follow written directions better than oral ones. _____ _____

40. I can easily recognize differences between similar sounds. _____ _____

41. I like to create or use jingles/rhymes to learn things. _____ _____

42. I wish more classes had hands-on experiences. _____ _____

43. I can quickly tell if two geometric shapes are identical. _____ _____

44. The things I remember best are the things I have seen in print or pictures. _____ _____

45. I follow oral directions better than written ones. _____ _____

46. I could learn the names of fifteen medical instruments much easier if I could touch and examine them. _____ _____

47. I need to say things aloud to myself to remember them. _____ _____

48. I can look at a shape and copy it correctly on paper. _____ _____

49. I can usually read a map without difficulty. _____ _____

50. I can "hear" a person's exact words and tone of voice days after he or she has spoken to me. _____ _____

51. I remember directions best when someone gives me landmarks, such as specific buildings and trees. _____ _____

52. I have a good eye for colors and color combinations. _____ _____

53. I like to paint, draw, or make sculptures. _____ _____

54. When I think back to something I once did, I can clearly picture the experience. _____ _____

Ignore the NO answers above. Work only with the YES column. For every YES you checked, find the number in the box below and circle it. When you finish, all the numbers in the boxes will not be circled. Count the number of circles for V, A, and K. Write the totals on the lines below the boxes.

V	**A**	**K**
3, 4, 6, 7, 9,	1, 2, 8, 10, 11,	5, 15, 17, 18, 19,
13, 16, 20, 22, 32,	12, 14, 24, 26, 28,	21, 23, 25, 27, 29,
39, 43, 44, 48, 49,	34, 35, 36, 40, 41,	30, 31, 33, 37, 38,
51, 52, 54	45, 47, 50	42, 46, 53

Total: _____   Total: _____   Total: _____

The V in the above chart represents visual skills. If you have more circles in this box than in the others, you have strong visual skills and a preference for visual learning. If you have more circles in the A box, you have strong auditory skills and an auditory learning preference. If you have more circles in the K box, you learn well kinesthetically.

If you don't notice a sharp difference between the number of circles in two boxes or among all three boxes, you have integrated your ways of learning; you don't have strong preferences, but you can probably learn in two or all three ways. If you have a box with very few circles, you have identified a learning style that is not effective for you unless it is strengthened.

Identify Your Body's Natural Cycle   Even though clocks on the wall may work on a twenty-four-hour cycle, your body may not. Even though clocks move at a consistent rate, your body does not. Everyone has a **natural cycle**—times during the day where she or he is more alert and times when she or he is in a "slump." Being familiar with your own patterns of high energy and **peak alertness** as well as with your low-energy slumps is important because you can use that knowledge to your advantage. Whenever possible, schedule your study times during your high-energy, peak-alertness times of the day. Save routine tasks such as running errands or completing household chores for the time of day where your mental performance is lower.

Many studies are available that show the energy and alertness patterns that many people experience throughout the day. If you are interested in exploring this subject further, check your library's database or magazine index for recent research articles on the subject of *circadian rhythms*, which is the term for your body's natural patterns or rhythms.

Your body may follow the patterns reported for many individuals, or you may have your own cycle. No one knows as well as you when you feel energetic and when you feel low-key.

| Exercise 1.4 | **Discovering Your Peaks and Slumps** |

The following chart shows typical hours of a day. In the left-hand column is a list of activities. Decide when during the day you prefer to do each activity. Write the activity on the chart in the correct time slot. You may place an activity in more than one time slot.

■ When would you prefer to

1. concentrate on memorizing
2. work on hard math problems
3. sit and relax
4. take a nap
5. do creative writing
6. do household chores
7. sit and talk with a friend
8. give a speech or a class presentation
9. exercise or work out
10. do easy review work
11. do problem-solving kinds of homework
12. type or copy notes
13. move around and stretch
14. eat
15. sleep

5:00 A.M. – 7:00 A.M.
7:00 A.M. – 9:00 A.M.
9:00 A.M. – 10:00 A.M.
10:00 A.M. – 12:00 noon
12:00 noon – 1:00 P.M.
1:00 P.M. – 3:00 P.M.
3:00 P.M. – 5:00 P.M.
5:00 P.M. – 7:00 P.M.
7:00 P.M. – 9:00 P.M.
9:00 P.M. – 11:00 P.M.
11:00 P.M. – 1:00 A.M.

What patterns do you see?

Class Resources   Using the **resources** available in your classes will help you begin your term in a confident and organized way. The following skills learned early in the term can easily be continued throughout the term to bring you positive results:

■ Understand your course syllabus.
■ Organize your notebook.
■ Get extra help when needed from teachers and tutors.

| **Exercise 1.5** | **Recording Your Classes This Term** |

1. Complete the following chart for your classes this term.

Reg. #	Course Title	Credits	Days	Time	Room	Instructor

2. Lightly shade in the areas to show when you are in class. Add the names of your classes (or labs) to this schedule.

	Monday	Tuesday	Wednesday	Thursday	Friday	Saturday	Sunday
7–7:30 A.M.							
7:30–8 A.M.							
8–8:30 A.M.							
8:30–9 A.M.							
9–9:30 A.M.							
9:30–10 A.M.							
10–10:30 A.M.							
10:30–11 A.M.							
11–11:30 A.M.							
11:30–12 P.M.							
12–12:30 P.M.							
12:30–1 P.M.							
1–1:30 P.M.							
1:30–2 P.M.							
2–2:30 P.M.							
2:30–3 P.M.							
3–3:30 P.M.							
3:30–4 P.M.							
4–4:30 P.M.							
4:30–5 P.M.							
5–5:30 P.M.							
5:30–6 P.M.							
6–6:30 P.M.							
6:30–7 P.M.							
7–7:30 P.M.							
7:30–8 P.M.							
8–8:30 P.M.							
8:30–8 P.M.							
9–9:30 P.M.							
9:30–10 P.M.							

3. Which classes do you think you'll enjoy the most? Why?

4. Which classes do you feel will be the most difficult for you? Why?

5. Check the reasons you used to select your classes this term.

    _____ Recommended by placement tests

    _____ Recommended by a counselor

    _____ Recommended by an instructor

    _____ Recommended by a friend

    _____ Chosen because of my own special interest

    _____ Other:

6. List the positive feelings you have about this term.

7. List the concerns or fears you have about your courses, instructors, or workload this term.

8. Refer to your schedule. Check the following areas that are true for you this term.

    _____ I have breaks between each of my classes.

    _____ I have two classes that are "back to back" without breaks.

    _____ I have three or more classes without breaks in between.

    _____ I have one or more evening classes.

    _____ I have one or more weekend classes.

    _____ I have classes only two or three days a week.

    _____ I have classes five days a week.

9. Which of the following best describes how you feel about this term's schedule?

    _____ The schedule will be easy.

    _____ The schedule will be manageable.

    _____ The schedule will be somewhat difficult.

    Explain your answer:

Your willingness to share this information with your instructor will help your instructor begin to know you as a person. You may wish to schedule an office time to discuss some of these ideas or some of your concerns with your instructor.

Understand Your Course Syllabus   The course **syllabus** is a handout that provides you with valuable information about the course.

Syllabus Information

1. The teacher's name, office number, and office hours
2. The objectives for the course
3. The attendance policy for the course
4. The method used to calculate grades
5. The policy about late work or late tests
6. The possibilities for extra credit work

All of the syllabus information is important for you to know. If the course syllabus does not include some of the areas just outlined, ask the instructor for the missing information. Many instructors appreciate the opportunity to clarify course expectations that are not clearly stated on the syllabus.

Your Teacher   Learn each of your teachers' names. The little effort it takes to do so goes a long way. When you need to fill out a form, talk to a counselor, discuss class with friends, or make contact with the instructor, knowing his or her name is important. In addition, taking the time to learn a person's name reduces the distance between you and that person.

Most instructors hold office hours to meet students individually, provide extra help, and answer questions. It is always to your advantage to let your teachers know you as an individual; contact outside the classroom setting is most easily accomplished through an office visit. If you are a student with learning disabilities, the office hour time should be used to discuss your learning disability, your needs, and appropriate accommodations. The course syllabus usually states the office location and office hours. Politely ask for this information if it is not printed on the syllabus.

Course Objectives   The course syllabus generally states the objectives for the course and the goals you can accomplish by completing the course. An outline of the course that lists the topics and chapters to be covered and reading assignments for the term may also be included. At the end of the term, review the syllabus to see if the course objectives were covered and if you accomplished the goals for the course. If you are asked to complete a course evaluation, refer back to the syllabus goals and objectives before you write the evaluation.

Attendance Policy   Attendance policies vary greatly from one instructor to another. Some policies are set by the college, and others are determined by individual instructors. It is your responsibility to know all these policies. Make a determined effort to attend every class so that you receive the information and the assignments. Good attendance leads to feeling a part of the class and "tuned in" with other students. If your instructor has no attendance policy, do not assume that attendance is optional. Make sure you know the following:

- Will your grade be affected after a certain number of absences?
- How can you contact the instructor to arrange for make-up work or to discuss assignments?
- Will your instructor excuse a medical absence if you provide a doctor's note?

Keep a list of names and phone numbers of several students in each class. If you are absent, take the time to contact a student to learn what was covered, what was assigned, and if that student can give you a copy of his or her notes.

Grade Calculations   Grades can be based on tests, papers, homework assignments, class participation, discussions, labs, and attendance. Each instructor has a different set of criteria for calculating your final grade. It is your responsibility to understand how your final grade will be determined. If the syllabus is vague, ask what percentage of your grade will be based on the different course requirements.

Late Work or Tests   Some instructors do not accept late work. Others do accept late work up to a specific date, or they accept late work but give a lower grade. If you use good time management principles, all your work can be done on time (see Chapter 2). However, if something occurs to prevent you from having work turned in on time, it is usually better to turn work in late than not at all. Instructors appreciate a brief note explaining why your work is late.

Instructors do not always apply the same policy to tests as they do to final exams. Some instructors allow you to take a test late, especially if you were absent on the day the test was given. Find out in advance if your test grade will be lowered for taking a test late and what you have to do to schedule a make-up test. For final exams, many instructors do not allow them to be given early or late; finals must be taken on the assigned date and time. If you simply cannot take the final exam on the assigned date, discuss your situation with the instructor as early as possible to see if other options are available.

Opportunities for Extra Credit   The course syllabus may indicate if extra credit projects will be available during the term. If an extra credit project is available, plan time to complete the project. You will have the opportunity to learn more from the project, and you will be able to boost any low grades you may have received during the term. Your interest and effort in completing extra credit projects demonstrate that you are willing to get as much as possible from your course.

| Exercise 1.6 | **Examining a Course Syllabus** |

The following information is important for you to know about each of your classes. Select a syllabus for one of your courses. Use the syllabus to answer these questions. If the syllabus does not have the information, ask your instructor.

1. Course name:_____

2. Instructor's name: _____

3. Office location:_____ Office hours: _____

4. What are the objectives for the course? _____

5. What is the attendance policy for this instructor?

    _____

    _____

6. How will your grade be calculated?

    _____

    _____

7. What is the policy for late homework?

    _____

    _____

8. What is the policy for make-up tests?

    _____

    _____

9. Will extra credit be available?_____

    If yes, what is the project and when is it due?

    _____

    _____

10. Check the expectations that are appropriate for this course.

_____ I am expected to have my own book.

_____ I am expected to participate in class discussions.

_____ I am expected to take notes in class.

_____ I am expected to turn in homework assignments.

_____ I am expected to attend a lab.

_____ I am expected to write a paper or a report.

_____ I am expected to type/computer print writing assignments.

_____ I am expected to take tests.

_____ I am expected to take a final exam.

_____ I am expected to arrange a conference with the teacher.

_____ Other: _____

Organize Your Notebook   Take a look at your notebook. Does it have any of these characteristics?

1. Papers are randomly shoved in.
2. Wrinkled papers are sticking out from all sides.
3. Class notes and assignments are buried within.
4. Graded work is missing or difficult to find.

If so, the following suggestions can help you select and organize a notebook so you won't waste valuable classroom time and study time searching for what you need.

Types of Notebooks   Notebooks come in many sizes and shapes. Choose a three-ring notebook that is large enough to hold dividers for each of your classes. If you are taking too many classes or are likely to have too many notes, handouts, and homework to fit into one notebook, you may want to use more than one notebook. For instance, you can use one notebook for your Monday/Wednesday/Friday classes and a second notebook for Tuesday/Thursday classes. Or you may prefer one notebook for morning classes and another for afternoon classes. Although a separate notebook for each class may seem a good idea, you'll soon discover the awkwardness of carrying four or five notebooks.

Separate folders or spiral notebooks do not lend themselves well to being organized. If you use folders with pockets, you may have trouble finding papers when you need them because it's so much easier to misplace or lose them. Spiral notebooks have many of the same disadvantages. There are no convenient ways to organize and keep track of loose papers, rearrange notes, or hold papers that need to be turned in for grading.

Once you have selected your notebook or notebooks, the next step is to organize them.

Organizing Your Notebook

1. Place a complete class schedule in the front of your notebook.

2. Place a master assignment sheet behind the class schedule.

3. Use dividers to show sections for each class.

4. Include a list of names and phone numbers for at least three students and the instructor.

5. Place notes and handouts chronologically in each section.

6. Keep returned papers or assignments in each section.

7. Place extra notebook paper in each section.

Class Schedule   You are wise to keep a schedule of classes (such as the one on p. 14) in the front of your notebook. If your college provides you with a printed schedule that lists your classes, times, and room numbers, place this in the front of your book.

Master Assignment Sheet   Do you sometimes jot down assignments and then forget where you put them or even that you have them? A **master assignment sheet** is an easy-to-use system that can provide you with a quick method of knowing what assignments were given and when they are due. Each week, place a master assignment sheet in the front of your notebook. (A form is available in the Appendix. Make enough copies so that you have one for each week of the term.)

Notebook Dividers   Now that the front part of your notebook is organized with your class schedule and your master assignment sheets are ready to be used, divide your notebook into sections, with one section for each class. Use dividers with tabs, and label each divider with the name of a class. Organize the dividers in the sequence you attend your classes—that is, the first class of the day is the first divider and so on. Organizing your notebook can be done before the term begins.

Important Names and Numbers   Place a list of the names and numbers of your instructor and two or three members of your class in the front of each section of your notebook. If you are absent or have questions about assignments, then you can easily refer to these names and numbers.

Class Notes and Handouts   Handouts often include information that you are required to know. When you receive a handout in class, write the date on it and add it to your notebook with the notes for that day. Your handouts are then readily available when you need them as you study.

Returned Papers and Assignments   Be sure to save all your returned papers and assignments. Sometimes you are asked to refer back to them during class discussions or lectures, and you need them when you review for tests. If an instructor forgets to record one of your grades, you will have proof that the work was completed and graded. You may want to look at the date on

HOW TO USE THE MASTER ASSIGNMENT SHEET

1. Place the master assignment sheet in the front of your notebook.

2. Write the dates for the week on the top line.

3. List your courses in the left-hand column. Begin with the first course of the day.

4. Write the assignment in the box as soon as it is given. Use abbreviations if they help.

5. Most assignments are due by the next class. If there is a different due date, write it next to the assignment.

6. If no assignment is given, use this time to review the material you've just learned.

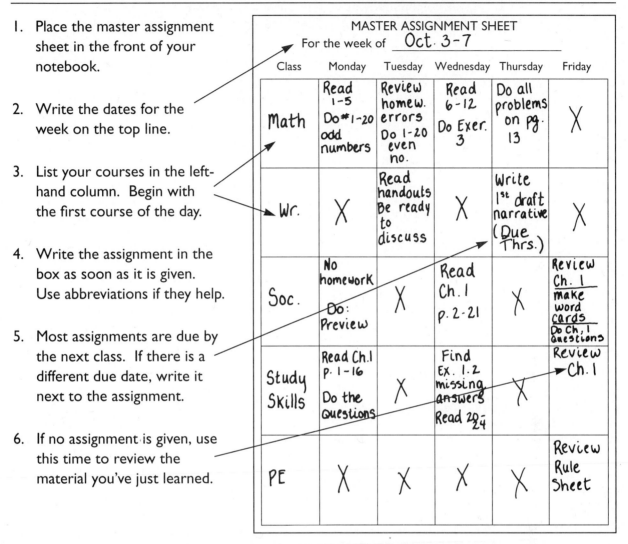

MASTER ASSIGNMENT SHEET
For the week of Oct. 3-7

Class	Monday	Tuesday	Wednesday	Thursday	Friday
Math	Read 1-5 Do #1-20 odd numbers	Review homew. errors Do 1-20 even no.	Read 6-12 Do Exer. 3	Do all problems on pg. 13	X
Wr.	X	Read handouts Be ready to discuss	X	Write 1st draft narrative (Due Thrs.)	X
Soc.	No homework Do: Preview	X	Read Ch.1 p. 2-21	X	Review Ch.1 make word cards Do Ch.1 Questions
Study Skills	Read Ch.1 p. 1-16 Do the Questions	X	Find Ex. 1.2 missing answers Read 20-24	X	Review Ch.1
PE	X	X	X	X	Review Rule Sheet

the assignment and place the assignment next to your other notes for that date. Or you may prefer to keep all your returned papers together at the end of each notebook section.

Notebook Paper   Keep plenty of notebook paper available in each section of your notebook. You do not want to be in the position of interrupting another student to ask for paper.

All these suggestions will help you have a neatly organized, efficient notebook for the beginning of the term. By the middle of the term, you may find that your notebook has become too full to turn the pages you already have or to add new ones. If this happens, you can remove pages of notes, handouts, and returned assignments from the beginning of the term. Place these items in file folders at home. Label each folder according to the class and the contents. Store the file folders in a drawer or box so you can locate them when you need to study for midterms or final exams.

Get Help from Teachers and Tutors   Your teachers are one of your primary resources at college. Teachers set aside office hours to help students with coursework in whatever way possible. If you ever become frustrated with a course, confused, or overwhelmed, schedule an office appointment with the teacher. The following suggestions will help you go into your teacher's office with a plan and a positive attitude:

1. Try to identify your point of confusion, frustration, or difficulty. Up to what point were you understanding and following the information? What was introduced or done that caused the confusion?
2. Explain this to the teacher. "I understood when you talked about . . . , but as soon as we started studying . . . , I got lost."
3. Listen carefully to the teacher's explanation. If you have questions while she or he explains, ask these questions freely. Questions show a real interest and an alertness, so don't hesitate.

You may also want to ask if there are *alternative materials* available that might help explain the information in another way that you can understand more easily. Audio cassettes, videos, interactive videos, computer software, or books may be available. If your instructor recommends alternative materials, take the time to investigate these materials. If they are in the school library, the librarian can help you locate them.

Many schools have *tutors* available for writing, math, and particular subjects. Students with learning disabilities may be eligible for tutors, too. Ask your instructor about the availability of tutors, how to arrange tutorial time, and how to work with tutors. Even though most tutors have been well trained, you can make their jobs easier by telling them how much you understand and by identifying the point where you started getting confused, frustrated, or lost.

Campus Resources

Campus resources include a wide variety of programs and services for students. Becoming aware of and using your campus resources can increase your chances of success at college. Getting comfortable on campus and becoming familiar with its layout make you feel more at ease. After all, you will be spending many hours in this "home away from home." Gaining a sense of belonging begins with having knowledge about your environment.

Increasing Your Awareness of the Campus

1. Know the locations of main offices and departments that provide special services for students.

2. Know what organizations and clubs exist on campus.

3. Know what support groups are on campus and how to join them.

4. Know the calendar of important dates for the term.

Locations of Main Offices and Departments

Tuition and student fees often cover special services that many students fail to use because they do not know these services exist. If you are not familiar with the following offices and services, take the time to explore your campus. Consult your school's catalog for more specific details about the functions and special services of each.

- Student health clinic—for sicknesses, emergencies, physicals
- Legal services—for basic legal counseling and assistance
- Services for students with disabilities—for assistance, advising, and accommodations
- Veteran's center—for assistance, counseling, and financial benefits for veterans of the armed forces
- Vocational rehabilitation programs—for advising, training, financial assistance, and program coordination for injured workers or dislocated or displaced workers
- Counselors' offices—for advising, counseling, and information
- Financial aid office—for applications, assistance, and information for financial aid programs
- Financial services—for paying fees and cashing checks
- Student records office—for transcripts and address changes
- Work-study office—for work opportunities on campus
- the library—for research material, books, tapes, videos, reference materials, and study location
- Resource or tutor centers—for extra help with coursework
- Administration office—for campus administrators
- Student activities or student government office—for a wide variety of information focused on students' needs (child care, housing, transportation, fees, campus participation)

Organizations and Clubs

Joining organizations and clubs is an excellent way to make new friends, increase your interest in school, and heighten your enjoyment of life. The beginning of the term is an ideal time to join since many other "newcomers" will also be getting involved. For information, check your school's student activities office or student government office. Counselors, teachers, the school catalog, and the school newspaper are also resources for more information. Why not share your special interests and put your talents to use?

Support Groups

Balancing personal life and school life is difficult for some people. Pressures, concerns, anxieties, or excessive stress can sometimes occur as students strive for balance and success. Special support groups on campus can offer the support, encouragement, and understanding that make the difference between success and failure. If you are dealing with specific stresses, personal challenges, or physical or learning disabilities, or you are in a recovery program for addictive behaviors or substance abuse, go to a counselor when you need some help, or consult your campus catalog to learn about available support groups. If you feel a need for a support group that is not organized on campus, discuss your interest with a counselor. Perhaps you could be the spark that gets a new group started on campus.

School Calendar

Being familiar with your school calendar is vital to your success in college. A calendar for the term should be available in your class schedules or catalogs. It is your responsibility at the beginning of the term to know the following important dates for the term:

- Deadlines for paying tuition and fees
- Deadlines for changing grade options or classes
- Deadlines for withdrawing from school
- Dates of holidays and other special events
- Dates of final exams

Exercise 1.7   **Increasing Your Campus Awareness**

Work in groups of three or four to answer as many of the following questions as possible. You may use your school catalog or class schedules to help with answers if necessary.

1. Are campus tours available? _____

    If yes, whom do you contact and where do you make arrangements for a tour?

2. Where are the following offices located?

    Counselors' offices: _____

    Student health: _____

    Registrar's office: _____

    Financial aid office: _____

    President's office: _____

    Financial services (pay fees): _____

    Student newspaper office: _____

    Student activities office: _____

    Cafeteria: _____

    Campus security: _____

    Library: _____

    Lost and found: _____

    Computer labs: _____

    Bookstore: _____

3. Which of the following are available on your campus? Where is each located?

    Veteran's office: _____

    Tutors: _____

    Work-study office: _____

    Women's center: _____

    Career counseling: _____

    Clothing exchange: _____

Disabled student services: _____

Bus passes:_____

Legal aid services: _____

4. What organizations or clubs on campus may interest you? Why?

_____

_____

_____

5. What support groups are organized on campus? What department or person can be contacted for more information?

_____

_____

_____

6. Use the school calendar to answer these questions. Give dates.

When is there a holiday this term? _____

When is final exam week this term? _____

When is the last day to change grade options?_____

When is the last day to pay fees without a penalty?_____

When is the last day to drop a class?_____

When is the last day to withdraw to receive a W grade?_____

7. Answer the following questions.

Is the school on the semester or quarter system? _____

How many weeks are in this term?_____

Where are transcripts ordered? _____

What does an *incomplete* grade mean?_____

What grade options are available?_____

How many students attend this college?_____

How many faculty members are there?_____

SUMMARY
- College resources exist for one purpose: to help you achieve academic success.
- You can learn more readily when you draw on your personal qualities, such as knowing your strengths, weaknesses, values, and personal characteristics.
- Your choice of effective study skill strategies can be based on your learning styles: visual, auditory, or kinesthetic modalities.
- The time of the day can affect your energy level and your ability to learn.
- Learning to use class resources involves familiarity with class schedules, syllabi, methods of obtaining extra help, and the organization of your notebook.
- Special programs, services, and people on your campus are valuable resources for obtaining the information and support you need to reach your educational goals.

PERSONALIZING WHAT YOU LEARNED

1. Score and record the score for your chapter profile.
2. On your own paper, expand this chapter's visual mapping.
3. Make your own vocabulary list of all the terms in this chapter that are printed in color.

"To the Student" (p. xv) provides you with more detailed directions for completing these activities.

Review Questions

True-False

To help keep your mind focused, underline the key words in the True-False questions before you answer them.

Write *T* if the statement is TRUE. Write *F* if it is FALSE.

_____   1. You can work at your optimum level when you put all your attention on your strengths and positive qualities.

_____   2. Seeing a problem as a challenge or an opportunity to grow is an example of using a positive approach.

_____   3. A flexible person finds the transition time needed to make changes to be difficult.

_____   4. A person who refuses to take risks continues to remain in his or her comfort zones.

_____   5. A successful person does not need to make choices or accept the outcomes of poor decisions.

_____   6. Auditory learners do well typing notes and making pictures or charts of important information.

_____   7. Most adults are able to work with tasks that require the use of different modalities.

_____   8. The best way to approach an instructor is to say, "I am lost and don't understand anything."

_____   9. A course syllabus states course goals, objectives, and policies.

_____ **10.** There is no reason to use an instructor's office hour if you are not having problems.

_____ **11.** You should ask about important course information if it is not included on the syllabus.

_____ **12.** Support groups on campus are designed to give all students financial support.

_____ **13.** A school calendar gives important dates for changing grades, holidays, class tests, and final exams.

_____ **14.** When you work in a group, you should encourage every group member to contribute ideas.

_____ **15.** The best place to keep an assignment sheet is in the front of each section of your book.

Definitions

Use two or three sentences to explain each of these terms.

1. Learning style _____

_____

_____

2. Kinesthetic learner _____

_____

_____

3. Auditory learner _____

_____

_____

4. Syllabus _____

_____

_____

WRITING ASSIGNMENTS

1. Write a few paragraphs to share what you learned about yourself as you worked through this chapter. What are your personal qualities? Your learning style? Your peak-energy or mental alertness times?
2. Discuss the campus resources that you learned about in this chapter. Explain how you can benefit from the information you learned.

Setting Goals and Managing Your Time

*T*ime management, perhaps the most essential of all study skills, is an organized method for planning the use of your time to reach goals. Do you set realistic goals and use steps to achieve your goals? Does a lack of time create stress in your life? Do you have too little time for family or friends? Does time control you, or do you control time? Do the patterns of your weekday and your weekend make you feel as if you are on a roller coaster? Do you have to cram to get ready for tests? This chapter teaches you strategies to set obtainable goals, manage your time, and create a more fulfilling balance in three important areas of your life: school, work, and leisure.

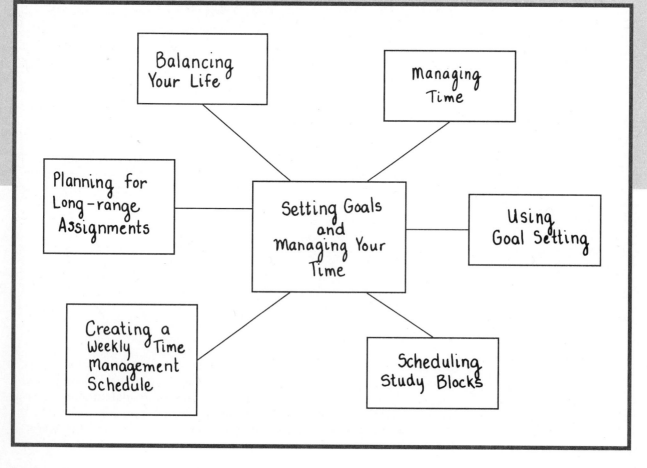

Goal Setting and Time Management Profile

Please answer honestly each of the following questions about your current attitudes and study habits. Your answers should reflect what you *do*, not what you *wish* you would do.

   After you read each statement, check YES if you do this *always* or *most of the time.* Check NO if you do this *seldom* or *never.*

		YES	**NO**
1.	I set goals for myself every week.	——	——
2.	My study blocks are at least four hours long.	——	——
3.	I schedule specific times to study during the weekend.	——	——
4.	I often choose to spend time with friends instead of studying.	——	——
5.	I set target dates to reach goals.	——	——
6.	I try to make each scheduled day different so that I don't get bored.	——	——
7.	I avoid time management because I like to be spontaneous.	——	——
8.	I visualize myself reaching my goals, and I use positive statements to motivate me toward those goals.	——	——
9.	I often try to study at certain times even though I know those times are my low-energy periods of the day.	——	——
10.	I break long-range assignments into smaller steps and set goals and time lines for each step.	——	——
11.	If my assignments are done, I use my study time for social activities.	——	——
12.	I have a positive attitude toward goal setting and time management.	——	——

Balancing Your Life

As a student, you need to continually balance three main areas in your life: school, work, and leisure. The figure that follows shows these three areas that, when balanced, can result in greater happiness and less stress.

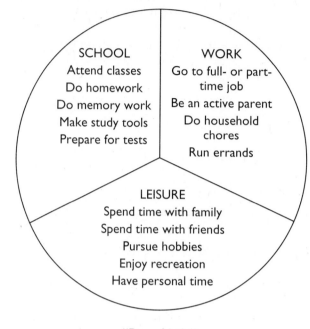

"Pie of Life"

It is not likely (or desirable) that your "life's pie" will be divided into three equal sections. How the pie is "sliced" will differ from one person to another. Your goals, needs, and interests will shape your choices in each of these areas. Feeling confident, challenged, satisfied, fulfilled, happy, and in control can be signs that you have done well in balancing the three main areas of life. Frequent bouts with negative feelings, emotional responses, and resentments can be signs that the three areas of life need to be examined and rebalanced.

Exercise 2.1   **Dividing Your Life's Pie**

1. In very general terms, draw your life's pie. Divide it into three sections to show approximately what percentage of your waking hours you spend in the three areas of school, work, and leisure.

2. At this point in the term, do you feel the amount of time you spend attending classes and studying is comfortable, too little, or too much? _____

Explain: _____

_____

3. At this point in the term, do you feel the amount of time you spend working is comfortable, too little, or too much?_____

Explain: _____

_____

4. At this point in the term, do you feel the amount of time you spend on leisure and social activities is comfortable, too little, or too much? _____

Explain: _____

_____

Use the Increase-Decrease Method

You have only so many hours in a day. If one of your areas of life does not have enough time, you need to take time from somewhere else in the pie. If you have too much time in an area, you need to use time differently or give it away to one of the other areas of the pie. This time management technique is called the **increase-decrease method.**

Too Little Time for Family

1. Reduce other kinds of leisure to find more family time.
2. Reduce or change work hours (employment) if possible.
3. Reduce the hours spent doing chores by seeking more help from other household members or by completing chores more efficiently. Goal setting can help.
4. Reduce school time by taking fewer classes or by learning study techniques so that you can use less time and accomplish more.

Too Little Time for School

1. Reduce social time. Since success in school should be your primary goal, some "less significant" social or leisure time may have to be given to studying time. Do not end *all* social time; social and leisure time are always important for a sense of well-being and enjoyment of life.
2. Reduce work time. Perhaps you need to reduce the amount of time spent on chores or on a job. If you are employed full time, financial aid, grants, or loans may make it possible for you to attend school and work fewer hours.
3. Reduce the number of classes. If you do not have enough time to complete assignments and study for the number of classes you are enrolled in, you may have a combination of classes that requires too much time and energy for one term. Consider dropping a class; look for an alternative class if you need to maintain a specific number of credits for the term. Discuss this with an instructor or a counselor.

Too Much Leisure Time

1. Increase school or work. Find new ways to use your spare time: Add another class, volunteer your time, or seek part-time employment.
2. Use leisure time differently. Find a new hobby to pursue. Get involved with new groups or organizations. Set new goals for yourself while you have time to work on them.

Now that you have identified areas that could be adjusted for a better balance in your life, the questions then become How do I get started? Where can I find time to do all these new things? How can I find time to accomplish my goals? You can find answers in setting goals and using time management to balance the three areas of life more comfortably.

Managing Time

You have already become familiar with the advantages of using time management. You can begin to benefit from these advantages by generally organizing your time. The following guidelines are the beginning of a more balanced, productive, and positive life pie.

General Time Management Strategies

1. Aim for balance.

2. Create strong patterns in your schedule.

3. Include time for your goals.

4. Include time for good nutrition, exercise, and sleep.

5. After three weeks, make adjustments and occasionally allow yourself to "trade time."

Strive for Balance

As you develop a schedule for studying, check that you have included enough time for work/chores and leisure/social activities. Your schedule should show a commitment to important goals, such as school, but it should also reflect the need for social, recreation, and leisure time.

Follow Patterns

Your schedule will be much easier if it follows consistent patterns. Instead of having each day of the week be different, you might try creating some similarities among the days. The following examples show several kinds of consistent patterns that make following a schedule easier:

1. Study for a specific class the same time each day or the same time on alternating days (MWFS).
2. Plan peak-energy times as study periods every day.
3. If you are on a Monday/Wednesday/Friday and a Tuesday/Thursday schedule for classes, try to have M/W/F look the same and T/TH look the same.
4. When possible, include similar time blocks each day for family, exercise, hobby, and other goals.
5. Plan meals at about the same time each day.
6. Go to bed and wake up about the same time each day.

Include Time for Your Goals   Whenever you make a time management schedule, give some thought to your goals. You may even want to list them on paper. Recognize your goals for school; schedule sufficient time to better assure you will reach your goals. Also pay attention to your personal goals and work/chores goals. Your commitment to your goals should be reflected in your schedule.

Establish Good Health Habits   To keep your energy high and your emotions positive, do not neglect your health. Remember to include time for health-related areas such as nutritional meals and adequate sleep. Plan to go to bed early enough each night so that you can get the amount of sleep you need. Schedule time to slow down, relax, and enjoy three nutritious meals. Plan time in your schedule for exercise. Adequate sleep, meals, and exercise all contribute to a healthier, well-functioning body.

Make Adjustments   At first your schedule may seem difficult to follow because it is new and may require a type of self-discipline that you have not used in the past. Try to use your schedule for at least three weeks. If you find then that some activities simply are not successful in certain time slots, adjust your schedule.

After you have tried following your time management schedule for three weeks, you can occasionally **trade time.** Trading time means that you can switch activities. For example, if an unexpected social event appears, but you had planned to study, look at your schedule for that day, choose another time that was scheduled for social or leisure, and trade times. By trading time, you are still able to meet the commitment of studying and enjoy the company of friends; the two activities simply exchange time slots. Trading time gives flexibility, but it must be used with caution. If you begin trading time too frequently, you will no longer have a schedule, and you will not be strengthening your self-discipline to say "no" to every appealing activity that comes your way.

Using Goal Setting

Goals are well-defined plans aimed at achieving a specific result. Students, teachers, athletes, and businesspeople commonly set goals. Successful goal setters

1. Want to obtain specific results
2. Design plans to help them reach goals
3. Are willing to put effort into their plans
4. Know when they have successfully accomplished a goal

Motivation, the feeling, emotion, or desire that moves a person to take action, is a key to successful goal setting. Motivation helps you make changes, learn something new, perform at a higher level, and end procrastination. Motivation can also help you stick to a goal even when you feel frustrated or discouraged.

Use Steps for Writing Goals   Is there something new you would like to learn (to play the guitar, speak a foreign language, grow herbs)? Are there some skills you have that you would like to perform on a higher level (swim twenty laps a day, increase sales 10 percent this month, read two books for leisure a month, learn twenty new words a week)? Are there some tasks you need to complete but tend to avoid (cleaning a closet, weeding a garden, organizing tax records, organizing your notebooks)? Regardless of the kind of goal you wish to achieve, the following steps can be used to plan and achieve your goals.

How to Write Effective Goals (STSR)

1. Be **S**pecific, clear, and realistic.
2. Set a specific **T**arget date for achieving the goal.
3. Identify the individual **S**teps involved in meeting the goal.
4. Plan a **R**eward for yourself when you reach the goal.

Be Specific   When your goal is clear, specific, and realistic, you have an exact picture of what you wish to achieve. To simply say, "I will do better," or "I want something new" results in vague goals whose achievements are not easily measured. To say, "I will be a millionaire tomorrow" is not realistic for most people. Before you commit to a goal, evaluate if the goal is clear, specific, and realistic for you.

Set a Specific Target Date   Procrastinators (people who put off doing something) seldom achieve goals. You can reduce or eliminate procrastination by setting a specific target date (deadline) and even a specific time to finish the steps involved in reaching your goal. The target date works as a form of motivation to keep you moving forward and on time.

Identify Steps   Careful planning of the steps involved makes it possible for you to allocate enough time for each step to complete it. Take time to think through the individual steps required. List these steps on paper. If several steps are involved, list specific target dates for completing each step. When you use this method of breaking one large goal into smaller ones, a goal that extends over a long period of time can be treated as a series of smaller goals to be accomplished on their own time lines.

Plan a Reward   You can celebrate the completion of a goal with a reward. You can also use that same reward as an incentive, a motivation, to meet your goal. There are two kinds of rewards you can include in your goal setting plan: extrinsic rewards and intrinsic rewards.

Extrinsic rewards are material things or activities that you will give yourself after you reach your goal. The following rewards are examples of extrinsic rewards: buy a tape, buy a new shirt, go to a movie, go out to dinner, plan a short trip.

Intrinsic rewards are the emotions or feelings you know you will experience when you reach a goal. Many people can be motivated just by recognizing that when the goal is reached they will enjoy feelings such as increased self-esteem, pride, relief, joy, higher confidence, or immense satisfaction.

A reward is a strong motivator only if you use it *after* you reach the goal. You must also withhold the reward if you don't reach the goal. For rewards to work as motivators, select rewards that truly represent what you *want* and can look forward to receiving.

Follow Helpful Hints for Reaching Goals   Have you ever started working toward a well-planned goal with great enthusiasm and conviction only to find yourself quitting before you reach the goal?

Many distractions and options can become barriers for reaching goals. The following tips can help keep you motivated and get you back on track when you begin to encounter difficulties achieving your goals. The term **EVA, BAT** is a memory aid to help you remember each of the six tips. Each letter represents one of the key words for each tip.

*H*ow to Reach Goals (EVA, BAT)

1. **E**valuate your goals from time to time.
2. **V**isualize yourself reaching your goals.
3. Make **A**ffirmations to strengthen your convictions.
4. **B**reak larger goals into a series of smaller goals.
5. **A**sk for help, guidance, or suggestions when needed.
6. **T**ell your goals to others when this seems appropriate.

Evaluate Your Goals   If you are having difficulty with a specific goal, examine whether it is still important or relevant. Goals can become outdated. If the goal is no longer of value to you, abandon it. However, do *not* abandon a goal for the wrong reasons. Do not abandon a goal because it is more difficult than you thought it would be or because you feel frustrated or doubt your own ability to reach the goal. If you truly still desire the end results, do not throw the goal away; use the following techniques to help you continue to move toward your goal.

Visualize Your Goals   Visualizing is the process of picturing or imagining information or events. Close your eyes and try visualizing yourself achieving your goal. How do you feel? How are others affected?

If you have great difficulty visualizing yourself achieving the goal, this particular goal may not be realistic or right for you. Ask yourself, Who actually set this goal? Why did I choose this goal in the first place? Am I trying to do this for myself or to please someone else? Is this really what I want? Again, if you can explain why this goal is no longer appropriate for you, abandon it.

Use Affirmations   Affirmations are positive statements used as motivators. Many psychologists believe affirmations help change your basic belief systems and your self-image. When you write affirmations, use the following guidelines:

1. *Use positive words and tones.* Avoid using words such as "no, never, won't." Say, for instance, *I complete my written work on time,* not *I will never turn in a late paper again.*
2. *Write in the present tense.* Present tense in verbs gives the sense that the behavior already exists. When you think and believe in present tense, your actions begin to match your beliefs. Say, for example, *I am a nonsmoker,* rather than *I will stop smoking soon.*

3. *Write with certainty and conviction.* Say, for instance, *I exercise for thirty minutes every day,* not *I want to exercise more every day.*
4. *Keep the affirmation short and simple.* Brief, simple affirmations are easier to remember and repeat.

Break Large Goals Down   Any time a goal seems too overwhelming, think about it as a series of individual steps. Focus on completing one step at a time. As you accomplish one step, motivation increases to begin on the next.

Ask for Help   You do not need to reinvent the wheel. If you have difficulties with part of your goal or feel stalled, seek help and information from knowledgeable people or books. Be resourceful; asking for advice is an effective shortcut.

Tell Your Goals to Others   If there are some people in your life who would be supportive of your desire to reach a certain goal, tell them about it. They can help motivate and encourage you to stay on track.

Scheduling Study Blocks

The following seven guidelines are very effective whenever they can be incorporated into your schedule. Because of other goals, commitments, or obligations, you may not always be able to follow all these guidelines. Nevertheless, for an effective schedule, aim to follow as many of these guidelines as possible.

Study Schedule Guidelines

1. Estimate your study time needed for each subject.
2. Study during your alert times of the day.
3. Study the hardest, least-liked subjects first.
4. Study right before or right after a class if possible.
5. Use fifty-minute study blocks with ten-minute breaks.
6. Have at least one study block every day of the week.
7. Do not study for more than three hours in a row (avoid marathon studying).

Estimate Your Study Time

To estimate how many hours you need to study, use the **2:1 ratio.** According to this ratio, for every hour you are in class, plan to study two hours per week outside class. For example, if your class meets for three hours per week, expect to study six hours per week.

At first glance, you may think the ratio gives too many study hours per week. However, studying in college only begins with reading the assignments and finishing homework. Memorizing, reciting, making study tools, comprehending, pondering, and reviewing college-level material require additional time. Planning your time using the 2:1 ratio provides you in most cases with the extra time needed to use the new study skills you will be learning. For difficult courses, you may find that you will need to plan even more hours to study than suggested by the ratio.

Use the ratio as a starting point to estimate the number of hours per week to study; adjust the study hours upward or downward after you have given careful thought to the expectations and demands of each course.

Study During Your Alert Times

In Exercise 1.5, you discovered your peak-alertness times during the day. To get the greatest benefit from your study blocks, try studying during these times.

If some of your available time for studying is during your low-energy periods, be an active learner. Use the strategies you learn in this book—such as notetaking, reciting, making study tools, reviewing or making study tapes—to help keep you active and involved in the learning process.

Tackle Your Hardest, Least-liked Subjects First

Your normal tendency is probably to save the hardest or the least-liked subjects for last; unfortunately, this is when you may be too tired or too uninterested to give these subjects your full attention. When you are planning your schedule, try to begin studying your hardest or least-liked subject first in the day or when you are more alert. If you run into difficulties with the assignment, you will have the rest of the day to contact the instructor or other students. Beginning your day of studying with the challenges reduces the tendency to **procrastinate,** put things off for another time. Once you have studied the hardest or least-liked subjects, the study blocks for the rest of the day will feel easier and more enjoyable.

Study Close to Class Times

If you are taking a class that involves discussions or your active participation (such as a language class), try to study for that class right before it meets so that you can review the work for the day and get yourself into a "mindset" for the class. If you are taking a class that consists mainly of lectures, schedule a study block right after the class so that you can make additions or corrections and review your notes while the information is fresh in your mind. If you have questions, ask the instructor shortly after class while the lecture is still fresh in his or her mind, too.

Focus on Fifty-Minute Blocks

Your time management schedule will show one-hour blocks. Plan to study one subject steadily for fifty minutes and then enjoy the reward of a ten-minute break. A **fifty-minute block** provides sufficient time to create a mindset for the subject so that your thoughts stay focused on the process of "thinking math," "thinking writing," or "thinking" whatever subject you are working to comprehend for memory. If your concentration skills need to be strengthened to achieve the fifty-minute study block, strive to lengthen your attention span by using active learning techniques and concentration techniques (Chapter 4).

Once you finish the reading and homework assignments, use the remaining time to begin "memory work." Recite and review the information. Think about it, its significance, and how it relates to other material. Make study tools such as flash cards, review sheets, tapes, or notes.

Plan at Least One Study Block a Day

School is a form of mental work that requires commitment, time, and energy. Some students try to use a roller-coaster approach—they study hard Monday through Thursday and then drastically change their lives to a social/leisure scene for the weekend. Better results occur when at least one hour of studying is scheduled for each day of the week. An ideal way to end the weekend is with a Sunday night study block in which you review the previous week's work, get organized for the upcoming week, preview upcoming chapters, and prepare a time management schedule for the week.

Avoid Marathon Studying

Marathon studying, which is studying for more than three hours at a time, usually does not produce good results. When you try to study in these large time blocks, even with ten-minute breaks, you probably will not remember the information you studied last. You may find yourself spending several hours reading mechanically, not really comprehending what you are reading. The mind seems to respond best when learning is spaced over time. It would be far better to study for two hours, take a one-hour jog or bike ride, and then return to study for two more hours.

There is one major exception to this rule: If you are working on a project that requires a great deal of creativity (creating a sculpture, writing a term paper, building a model), it may be better to continue as long as you are not fatigued. Such projects can be difficult to return to with the same creative flow or motivation.

For most types of studying, however, marathons are ineffective. Manage your time wisely by spreading your studying out over time, throughout the day, and throughout the week.

| **Exercise 2.2** | **Planning Study Time** |

1. In the first column, list all the classes you are enrolled in this term.

2. In column 2, list the grade that you would like to receive for each class and that you feel you could earn with good effort.

3. In column 3, estimate the number of hours per week that you think you will need outside of class time to study for this class.

4. Ignore the last column, New Hours, for now.

	Class	Desired Grade	Hours Per Week	New Hours
1				
2				
3				
4				
5				

5. Read the section Estimate Your Study Time on p. 36. Return to this exercise after reading.

6. Complete the following chart, which uses the 2:1 ratio for each class.

Class	Hours in Class/Week	x 2	Study Hours Needed/Week
1		x 2	
2		x 2	
3		x 2	
4		x 2	
5		x 2	

7. In the New Hours column, write a more realistic estimate of the number of hours that you will need to study for each class. Remember that most classes will require the 2:1 ratio; you can use fewer or more hours than the 2:1 ratio if needed.

Creating a Weekly Time Management Schedule

Each Sunday spend a few minutes planning your schedule for the upcoming week. Keep this schedule in the front of your notebook with your weekly assignment sheet. Refer to this schedule whenever you wish to make new plans or set up appointments. By using the following steps to create your **weekly schedule,** you can feel confident that you have allotted enough time for studying, enjoying social activities, and completing necessary work. (See p. 41 for a completed schedule.)

Creating a Weekly Time Management Schedule

1. Write in all your fixed activities.
2. Write in your fixed study times for each class.
3. Add several flexible study times.
4. Add times for specific goals.
5. Add times for other responsibilities.
6. Schedule time for leisure, social, and family times.

Write in Fixed Activities   **Fixed activities** are activities that do not change from week to week or special appointments that cannot easily be rescheduled. Class times, work, meetings, meals, and sleep are all fixed activities. Begin your weekly schedule by filling in all your fixed activities.

Add Fixed Study Times   Use the strategies discussed for the best times to study. Refer back to the estimated hours needed for each class. Remember, if you have completed all your assignments, these study blocks are for review, memorization, creation of new study tools, or preview of the next work to be covered. On your weekly schedule, write enough study time throughout the week to study for each class. Specifically name the subject that you will study in each time block.

Add Flexible Study Blocks   In addition to your regular study blocks, schedule a few study blocks that say "flex." These are safety nets to use in case you have an unexpected assignment or underestimated the amount of time needed to study. You can use this **Flextime** as needed. If you do not need it for schoolwork, convert the flextime into free time.

Include Time for Goals   Schedule time to work on any goals you have that are not school related. If you have a goal to clean the garage, exercise three times a week, do leisure-time reading, and so forth, plan time to work on these goals. If you don't have time set aside, you will probably not find the time to work on these goals.

Plan for Other Responsibilities   If you have any other responsibilities, such as household chores, schedule time to complete these tasks. Your schedule can show specific time for the chores that you need to do.

Include Social/ Leisure/Family Time   You can schedule all the remaining time blocks for friends, family, and yourself. Write specific plans or events on your schedule. Having social and leisure time is important; if you do not have enough time on your schedule, look for ways to reduce other areas so that you can find a comfortable balance.

| **Exercise 2.3** | **Creating Your First Weekly Schedule** |

Use the form on page 304 in the Appendix to develop your weekly schedule. Follow the steps just presented. Add color coding if you wish. In the Appendix you will find another blank form to copy so that you can make a new schedule for each week of the term.

Use Other Time Management Helpers   Three additional helpers can lead to your success managing time. The first helps you evaluate the effectiveness of your weekly schedule. The last two can be used in addition to the weekly schedule.

Check Your Weekly Schedule   Mentally walk through each day on your schedule. Is your schedule realistic? Have you allotted enough time between activities so that they can happen on time? Have you allowed time for commuting? Have you included consistent patterns from day to day and week to week so that your schedule will be easy to learn? If you cannot "see" yourself

WEEKLY TIME MANAGEMENT SCHEDULE

For the week of ___Oct. 10 - 15___

TIME	MON.	TUES.	WED.	THURS.	FRI.	SAT.	SUN.
12–6 A.M.							
6–7:00	←———————— SLEEP —————————						SLEEP
7–8:00	←— WAKE UP, EAT, COMMUTE —→					SLEEP	EAT, GET READY
8–9:00	←—— STUDY PSYCHOLOGY ——→					Laundry	CHURCH
9–10:00	PSY. CLASS	STUDY PSY.	PSY. CLASS	STUDY PSY	PSY. CLASS	House-	
10–11:00	COMPUTER CLASS	COMPUTER LAB	COMPUTER CLASS	COMPUTER LAB	COMPUTER CLASS	Cleaning	
11–12:00	←——— LUNCH ———→					FREE	BRUNCH
12–1:00	ALGEBRA ←CLASS	←——————————————→				LUNCH	
1–2:00	STUDY ALGEBRA	P.E.	STUDY	P.E.	STUDY	FREE	GO
2–3:00	COMMUTE	Class	ALGEBRA	Class	ALGEBRA	FREE	FISHING
3–4:00	REVIEW ANTHRO.	HOOPS	FLEX	HOOPS	FLEX	STUDY	
4–5:00	EARLY DINNER	←——— SHOOT HOOPS ———→				ALGEBRA	
5–6:00	COMMUTE	←————— DINNER —————→				FLEX	DINNER
6–7:00	ANTHRO.	←— FAMILY TIME —→				DINNER	STUDY
7–8:00	CLASS	T.V.		T.V.	SOCIAL	SOCIAL	ANTHRO.
8–9:00			BOWLING		TIME	TIME	FLEX
9–10:00	T.V.	STUDY ANTHRO.	LEAGUE	STUDY ANTHRO.			PLAN WEEKLY SCHEDULE
10–11:00	T.V.	SLEEP		SLEEP			SLEEP
11–12:00	←——— SLEEP ———→						SLEEP

getting through the day as you have it scheduled, adjust your schedule before you begin the week.

Consider Using Daily Reminder Lists Before you go to bed each night, you may want to take a few minutes to make a list of the planned events for the next day. This **to do list** can be more specific than your weekly schedule. For study times, you can set goals for what you plan to study during each study block. If you have time planned for errands, list the errands in a priority order so that you can check them off as you complete them. If you plan to do household chores, list them in order. Be as specific as necessary to help you organize your day.

```
TO DO WED. :
8-9:00   Study PSY.
         Read + notes for
         pages  95-116.

CLASSES...Regular Schedule

1-3:00   Study Algebra
         -Redo Ex. 6 #2-5.
         - Do Ex.7 Odd Numbers
         -Make study flashcards

3:00-4:00 FLEX - Use if
         Psy. or Alg. not done
         If really done....go
         shoot hoops
```

Try Calendar Planners   Look in your bookstore or a stationery store to see what other kinds of calendar planner books are available. You may find one that complements your weekly schedule. There are many calendar planners on the market, so look carefully to choose one that meets your needs.

Planning for Long-Range Assignments   Some instructors assign a project at the beginning of the term that is not due until the middle or the end of the term. Many students get a false sense of time; rather than start right away, they begin the assignment too close to the due date. Unnecessary stress is added, plus study times for other classes often have to be neglected so that the project can be finished. As soon as you are assigned a long-range project, begin planning a schedule for that project.

Planning a Long-Range Assignment

1. Break the assignment into individual steps.

2. Estimate the time needed for each step.

3. Double the amount of estimated time.

4. Use a calendar to map out due dates.

5. Begin right away.

Identify the Individual Steps   What are the actual steps you will need to work through from the beginning of the project to the end? Analyze the project carefully until you can identify all the individual steps involved. List these steps on paper. The example that follows shows how to use these steps with a research paper. You may want to ask your instructor to check the steps you have identified and to give additional suggestions.

Example: estimating a research paper

Steps	Estimated Hours	Doubled
1. Choose a topic.	1	2
2. Find out what's available in the library.	3	6
3. Read chosen references; take notes.	15	30
4. Organize notes into an outline.	5	10
5. Write the first draft on the computer.	6	12
6. Proofread and revise.	3	6
7. Add bibliography and cover.	1	2

Estimate the Time Needed

Next to each step, estimate the number of hours you feel will be necessary to complete the step. Base this estimate on your past experiences with similar projects.

Double the Estimate

You do not want to run out of time. To avoid any tendency to underestimate the amount of time you will need, double your estimate. In this way, you are giving yourself extra time in case you run into unforeseen problems or find that you have to change directions.

Write Down Due Dates

Use a calendar that covers the term. Consider the amount of hours needed for each step and the study block times (and flextimes) you have available on your weekly schedules. Set a goal to complete each step by a specific date. Each week when you make your weekly schedule, check this term calendar. Add due dates for steps to the weekly schedule, too.

If you finish a step ahead of schedule, it is because you did not need the "doubled time" you allocated. Begin the next step immediately. If you finish your project ahead of schedule, you will have time to revise it again if you wish, and you will be able to breathe a sigh of relief!

Begin Right Away

Don't delay or prolong the beginning of the project. In the preceding example, the student will need to find seventy hours throughout the term to complete the research paper. If the student waits too long to begin, seventy hours will not be available.

For each step of the project you are able to complete on time or ahead of time, you will gain a feeling of satisfaction and accomplishment. This feeling of success becomes greater motivation to move ahead to the next step. Your ultimate goal is to finish on time or, better yet, ahead of schedule.

SUMMARY

- Learning to become a time manager can reduce or eliminate worrying, procrastination, slackening off, and cramming. Managing time also leads to greater self-discipline and a more balanced, enjoyable life.
- Time management involves goal setting. You can use the STSR method to write effective goals.
- The memory phrase *EVA, BAT* can help you remember the six tips for staying motivated and on track to achieve your goals.
- You can organize your time by creating weekly time management schedules.

1. Write your fixed activities.
2. Write fixed study times. Use the 2:1 ratio and follow the recommended strategies for studying.

3. Add flex study times in case you need more time.
4. Add time to work on specific goals.
5. Add time for other chores or responsibilities.
6. Schedule leisure, social, and family time.

■ You can also plan your time for long-range projects.

PERSONALIZING WHAT YOU LEARNED

1. Score and record the score for your chapter profile.
2. On your own paper, expand this chapter's visual mapping.
3. Make your own vocabulary list of all the terms in this chapter that are printed in color.

"To the Student" (p. xv) provides you with more detailed directions for completing these activities.

Review Questions

True-False

To help keep your mind focused, underline the key words in the true-false questions before you answer them.

Write *T* if the statement is TRUE. Write *F* if it is FALSE.

_____   **1.** The three areas of life that need to be balanced are school, leisure, and studying.

_____   **2.** Procrastination increases when you use time management.

_____   **3.** The increase-decrease method states that every time you increase sleep, you decrease productivity.

_____   **4.** The amount of time spent on social or leisure activities should always be more than the total hours for work.

_____   **5.** A time management schedule should show time set aside for three meals a day, adequate sleep, and exercise.

_____   **6.** Visualizations, affirmations, intrinsic rewards, and extrinsic rewards can help you achieve goals.

_____   **7.** All college courses require you to use a 2:1 ratio for studying.

_____   **8.** A schedule with consistent patterns is easier to follow and to remember.

_____   **9.** If a personal goal is to write letters once a week, letter writing time should be planned on your weekly time management schedule.

_____   **10.** As soon as you try using time management, you should experiment with trading time so that you know how it works.

_____ **11.** Always begin by studying your favorite subject first so that you can get motivated.

_____ **12.** Study blocks should be converted to free time blocks if you have finished all your reading and homework assignments.

▬▬▬▬▬▬▬▬▬▬▬▬

Short Answer

1. A friend of yours does not know how to develop a weekly time management schedule. You are going to help your friend by explaining step-by-step what needs to be done. List the steps needed to make an effective weekly time management schedule.

2. Your friend also does not know how to write effective goals. You decide to explain the STSR steps so that your friend can also become an effective goal setter. List the four STSR steps for writing effective goals.

WRITING ASSIGNMENTS

1. Discuss specific time management strategies and the goal-setting strategies that you feel will work well for you. Tell why you feel these strategies are important for you to use.

2. What are your long-range educational goals? Discuss the steps and the time periods involved in reaching your final goal. End your writing by explaining the rewards you visualize yourself receiving when your goal is achieved.

Improving Your Concentration

Concentration is a mental process of directing your thoughts to one subject or issue at a time. Does your mind wander when you read textbooks or listen to lectures? Can your concentration be easily broken by people, things, or events around you? Do you waste precious study time trying to start concentrating? Is your attention span short? This chapter helps you train and discipline your mind so that your level of concentration and the length of your attention span can be increased to produce better results.

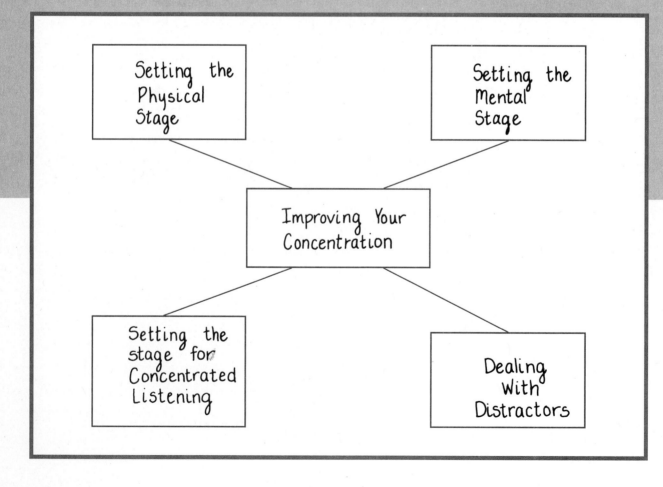

Concentration Profile

Please answer honestly each of the following questions about your current attitudes and study habits. Your answers should reflect what you *do*, not what you *wish* you would do.

 After you read each statement, check YES if you do this *always* or *most of the time*. Check NO if you do this *seldom* or *never*.

		YES	NO
1.	I tune out when a speaker is boring.	_____	_____
2.	I often feel tense and unable to relax.	_____	_____
3.	My study area is often cluttered or disorganized.	_____	_____
4.	I am able to picture myself successfully concentrating while I study.	_____	_____
5.	I have all the necessary supplies readily available at my place of study at home.	_____	_____
6.	I know what distracts me, and I use techniques to reduce distractions.	_____	_____
7.	I use a system to let others know when I do not want to be interrupted or disturbed.	_____	_____
8.	Because my mind wanders to problems or worries, concentration for more than fifteen minutes is difficult for me.	_____	_____
9.	I am able to keep my mind focused on studying most of the time.	_____	_____
10.	I am often distracted by thoughts of tasks that I feel I have to get done.	_____	_____
11.	When I feel overwhelmed, I break large tasks down into smaller, meaningful units.	_____	_____
12.	I turn on the radio, the television, or the stereo when I study.	_____	_____

Setting the Physical Stage   Careful attention should be given to the place you choose for studying because your physical environment can directly affect your ability to concentrate. The **ideal study area**, whether at school or at home, has few or no distractions to break your concentration. Begin your search for an ideal study area at school or at home that has as many of the following qualities as possible.

The Ideal Study Area

1. The noise level is appropriate for concentration.

2. The table and the chair are a comfortable size.

3. The work surface and surrounding walls are uncluttered.

4. Two or more sources of lighting are present.

5. Necessary supplies are readily available.

Noise Level   Studying, comprehending, and learning are activities based on thought processes. A physical environment filled with noise conflicts with thought processes; the brain is forced to tune in, tune out, tune in, and so forth as it tries to take in sounds and handle thinking processes. Some students believe that they can concentrate just as well while they listen to loud music or television, but when they adapt to a quieter environment, they are surprised at how much faster they can comprehend and memorize information.

How much noise is acceptable without being distracting? The level of tolerable noise varies from person to person. People with attention span deficits often need a very quiet and motionless environment. Individuals with fairly strong concentration skills are able to stay completely focused even when minor noises or movement occurs in the physical environment.

When you are selecting a place to study, begin by considering the amount of noise (and movement) present. On campus, look in the library, lab areas, student areas, or even empty classrooms to find a suitable location for studying. Reserve the lounges, lawns, cafeterias, and coffee shops for relaxation, coffee breaks, and socializing. Seldom do these locations have the qualities of an ideal place to concentrate and study.

Furniture   A cozy couch, an overstuffed chair, or a bed is not conducive to effective studying. These pieces of furniture are too comfortable and can induce naps instead of studying. In addition, holding a book, taking notes, or writing papers is extremely awkward, if not impossible, with this furniture. Studying is work, and it requires an appropriate work environment. The starting point is a supportive chair, a table or a desk with an adequate work surface, and enough room to spread out your books, notebook, paper, and necessary supplies.

If you are studying at home, use a table or desk reserved only for studying, if possible. Each time you sit down at this table or desk, your mind associates the location (the table) with the task (concentrating to learn). If you are using a kitchen table or area that serves dual purposes, remove all the items unrelated to studying. This breaks the association with that location and its other purpose (for example, a kitchen table associated with meals).

A large desk at home is ideal. If you don't have a desk available, consider making one by placing a large piece of wood (or an old door) on sawhorses or cement blocks. You will spend many hours in your study area, so give careful consideration to its location and organization.

Few Surrounding Distractions   Clutter on your work surface or on the walls surrounding you can easily become distractions. Interesting pictures, objects, a stack of someones else's materials, or a pile of bills can send your mind in a whole new direction. Remove unrelated items, and select places that have limited visual stimuli.

Two or More Sources of Light   Proper lighting is important in any study area. If you have too little light, your eyes can easily become strained and tired. Some lighting can create shadows or glare on your books. To avoid many of the problems created by poor lighting, have two sources of light in your study area. This may include an overhead light and a desk lamp or two lamps in different locations. Two sources of lighting may seem like a minor detail, but sometimes ignoring small details leads to big problems.

Necessary Supplies   Having all the necessary supplies with you when you study at school is often difficult. However, think ahead and plan to have basic supplies with you.

At home, you can give more attention to equipping your study area with necessary supplies; you do not want to interrupt your schoolwork to look for these supplies. Organize your study area at home by using file folders for important papers and small boxes or trays for other useful items.

Use the following checklist to equip your study area at home.

_____   **1.** Lead and colored pencils, pencil sharpener, erasers

_____   **2.** Pens, felt-tipped pens/highlighters

_____   **3.** Paper clips, rubber bands

_____   **4.** Stapler, staples

_____   **5.** Calculator (and possibly a spell-checker)

_____   **6.** Ruler, compass, hole puncher

_____   **7.** Scissors

_____   **8.** Dictionary (perhaps a thesaurus)

_____   **9.** Notebook paper, blank white paper

_____   **10.** Index cards

_____   **11.** File folders for papers, handouts, notes

_____   **12.** All your textbooks and notebooks

_____   **13.** Course outlines, syllabuses, assignment sheets

Exercise 3.1	**Analyzing Your Study Area**

This exercise is designed to analyze your physical learning environment. Answer each question as accurately as possible.

1. Select *one* place you frequently study on campus. Write the name of that place in the second column of the chart that follows. Select one place you frequently study at home. Write the name of that place in the third column.

Question	Place:_____	Place:_____
What is the average level of noise here?		
What furniture is here?		
What kinds of clutter are often found here?		
What kinds of lighting are usually found here?		
What supplies are readily available here?		

2. Which of the following describes you and your tolerance of noise?

_____ I work best in total silence.

_____ I can't concentrate when there is total silence.

_____ I can concentrate with minor noises around me when the sounds are consistent and familiar.

_____ I can't concentrate when a variety of minor noises that I don't expect or recognize occur.

_____ I can't concentrate when I hear people talking.

_____ I can't concentrate when there is movement around me such as people walking by.

_____ I can concentrate when there's soft, classical music playing in the background.

_____ I can't concentrate when I hear a radio or a television set is turned on, even if it is in another room.

3. Answer each question about your study place at school and at home.

   a. How could your study place at school be improved so that it is more ideal for studying? _____

    _____

    _____

   b. How could your study place at home be improved so that it is more ideal for studying? _____

    _____

    _____

Setting the Mental Stage

After you have set the physical stage for concentration, you can turn your attention to setting the mental stage. Since concentration is a mental process, you have to let the mind know that it is time to begin serious work.

RAVES is a memory word that represents five important techniques for creating the ideal mental stage for concentration. Learning to use these five techniques enables you to set a mental stage for strong concentration.

Techniques for Mentally Preparing to Study (RAVES)

1. Use **R**elaxation techniques to calm your mind.
2. **A**rrange your goals and priorities for the study block.
3. **V**isualize yourself capable of full concentration.
4. Remember the **E**motional *E* words related to success: effort, enthusiasm, energy, eagerness.
5. Use positive **S**elf-talk to set a positive attitude.

Use Relaxation Techniques

Concentration is difficult to achieve if your body is tense and your mind jumps from one subject to another. Relaxation techniques can help slow down your body's systems (heartbeat, blood pressure, muscle tension). When in a more relaxed state, your mind becomes more receptive to new information. If you check any bookstore or library, you will quickly realize that there are numerous relaxation techniques available. The following techniques are appropriate for your learning situation because they are easy to do and require very little time. These techniques can be practiced each time you sit down to study, arrive to class a few minutes early, or are preparing to begin a test.

Soothing Mask   Close your eyes. Place your hands on the top of your head. Slowly move your hands down your forehead, down your face, and to your neck. As you do this, picture your hands gently pulling a **soothing mask** over your face. This mask removes other thoughts, worries, fears, or stresses from your mind. Keep your eyes closed for another minute. Feel the soothing mask resting on your face. Block out thoughts or feelings that are not related to your soothing mask. As you practice this technique, you will be able to do it without using your hands. Your imagination can take you through the same process of pulling the mask over your face.

Relaxation Blanket   Sit comfortably in your chair. Close your eyes. Focus your attention on your feet. Imagine yourself pulling a soft, warm blanket up over your feet. Continue to pull this blanket up over your legs, lap, and chest until the blanket is snuggled around your shoulders and against your neck. Feel how your body is more relaxed now that it is covered with the blanket. This **relaxation blanket** feels as if it is a security blanket keeping you warm, confident, and comfortable. Keep your eyes closed for another minute as you enjoy the warmth and comfort of the blanket.

Breathing by Threes   This technique can be used with your eyes opened or closed. Inhale slowly through your nose as you count to three. Gently hold your breath as you count to three. Exhale slowly through your nose as you count to three. Repeat this several times. Often you can feel your body begin to slow down and relax when you **breathe by threes**

Deep Breathing   Take a deep breath to fill your lungs. You may think your lungs are full, but there's room for one more breath of air. Inhale once again. Now slowly exhale and feel your body relax. Repeat this **deep breathing** several times. If you feel lightheaded or dizzy after trying this exercise, you may want to select one of the other options.

Perfect Place   This technique combines breathing with your imagination. Breathe in slowly. As you breathe in, start creating a **perfect place** in the world where you feel relaxed, confident, safe, happy, and comfortable. Breathe out slowly and keep imagining this perfect place. Continue the process of breathing and imagining for a few minutes. The goal of this technique is to get your emotions relaxed and your mind in a positive state. When you have achieved that goal, whisper a friendly "farewell" to your safe place ("later," "thanks," or "bye"). Now that your mind is in a calm state, you are ready to begin working.

Arrange Your Goals and Priorities

Goal setting and time management have already introduced you to many of the planning techniques that set the mental stage for concentration. Use the techniques you have already learned with these additional techniques.

Saying No   You have scheduled a block of time to study. Studying during this block of time is your priority. If friends call or stop by, **say no** to their suggestions for other activities. Be firm when you tell them that you have made other plans. Let them know the times that you are available to get together with them. Saying no also applies to television and the stereo; these will distract you from your schoolwork. Your mind cannot concentrate if you require it to shift from one activity to another. The words and actions on television will disrupt your focus on your books. The words and rhythms from the stereo will also break the focus. Use your self-discipline (and self-talk if necessary) to say "no."

Setting Goals for Studying   As you are about to begin your study block, identify what you want to accomplish for the first fifty minutes. You may want to read and take notes on a given number of pages or work on memorizing a section of facts from your notes. If you have a large assignment, break the assignment into smaller parts so that you can focus on one part at a time. Plan a reward for yourself when you finish.

Doing Warm-ups: Review and Preview   Begin your concentrated studying with tasks that gradually move you into the subject. Reviewing the information covered the last time you studied is an effective way to "warm up your mind" to the subject. Look over your last set of notes. Glance through any homework that was returned. Preview the work that you are about to begin. If you are going to be reading a new chapter, glance over the contents of the chapter. (This is discussed further in Chapter 6.) If you have a new homework assignment, glance at the assignment and the directions given in class. Even though reviewing and previewing activities last only five or ten minutes, they create the "mental set" for your study block.

Visualize Yourself Concentrating   **Visualizing** basically means using your imagination to create a picture in your mind. Some people are able to close their eyes and visualize easily. Others can visualize clearly by just looking up (often up and to the left). The first technique that follows is designed for those who have difficulty "just seeing pictures." The second technique is useful for everyone.

Framing   Most pictures have some type of frame, so experiment with the following ways to find the frame that works best for your pictures. If you enjoy watching television, movies, or plays, close your eyes and picture the screen or the stage. If you enjoy art, picture a large canvas. If you enjoy photography, picture yourself looking through the camera and focusing the lens on a well-composed scene. Each of the methods of framing can include vivid colors. Once you have done this **framing**, you can then proceed with a particular visualization exercise.

Seeing Success   Close your eyes and picture yourself successfully doing what you are ready to begin (this technique is called **seeing success**). See yourself sitting at your desk with all your books, materials, and supplies readily available. Picture yourself knowing exactly where you will begin, what you will work on, and how much you will accomplish. Picture yourself reading, writing, memorizing, reciting, and remembering information. Become a part of your story. Smile at the feelings of confidence, success, pride, relief, and joy that greet you at the end of the study session. Open your eyes and begin working just as you saw in your picture.

Remember the Emotional E Words Many words related to success and motivation begin with the letter *E*. Developing strong concentration skills involves *effort*; concentration does not usually occur "naturally." Feel *excited* and filled with *enthusiasm*, with the idea that you are learning to discipline your mind. Approach your study block *energetically* and *eagerly*. Your attitude toward any task can affect the outcome, so remember that **emotional *E* words** are necessary for *effective* concentration.

Use Positive Self-Talk **Self-talk** is the little comments you say to yourself quietly or "inside your head." These comments can be negative or positive. If you ever hear "a little voice" telling you something negative about yourself, you are hearing "old tapes" or statements based on old belief systems that do not necessarily remain true today. Negative self-talk is often related to what you saw in the past as failures, disappointments, doubt, guilt, embarrassment, shame, or pain. As soon as you hear negative self-talk, "hold up a big stop sign." A negative self-talk statement such as "I know I'll fail this test even if I try" can be counteracted with positive self-talk—"I am ready to do well on this test."

Positive self-talk involves using statements that show optimism, confidence, determination, a sense of control, and your positive qualities. You can make positive self-talk statements by using "I" or by using your name. Examples of positive self-talk may be statements such as

> "Okay, Sam, you listened in class, so you can do this."
> "I know I can handle this because it's almost like the last chapter."
> "All right, Janice, you are an intelligent woman. With your patience you can figure anything out."
> "Come on, I can do anything now that I am willing to take the time that's needed."

You do not need to encounter negative self-talk to use positive self-talk. Some people seldom have that nagging inner voice making negative statements. As a part of your regular routine for setting the mental stage for concentration, do a short relaxation technique, identify your goals, visualize your success, recognize the positive emotional *E* words, and then give yourself some positive self-talk related to the task that you are about to begin. If you are working on specific concentration goals, your positive self-talk could even be used as an affirmation to be repeated throughout the day. (Affirmations are discussed in Chapter 2.)

Exercise 3.2   Learning to Relax

Select another person in class to be your partner. Then refer to the relaxation techniques in this chapter.

1. Choose one technique that you would like to try. Tell your partner the name of the technique. Have your partner do the same.

2. Practice reading the technique that your partner chose.

3. Begin by reading your partner's technique out loud while she or he follows the directions to complete the relaxation technique.

4. Now your partner reads your technique, while you do the exercise.

5. Discuss the following with your partner:

   a. Did you enjoy using the technique? Why or why not?

   b. Could you benefit from learning to include relaxation techniques in your daily life? Why or why not?

| **Exercise 3.3** | **Writing a RAVES Review** |

RAVES stands for five general ways you can mentally prepare to concentrate. Label each of the headings given by the capital letters. Under each heading, write important points related to the heading. You may refer back to your book.

1. R _____

    a. _____

    b. _____

    c. _____

    d. _____

    e. _____

2. A _____

    a. _____

    b. _____

    c. _____

3. V _____

    a. _____

    b. _____

4. E _____

    a. _____

    b. _____

5. S _____

    a. _____

    b. _____

Dealing with Distractors   Distractions (also called distractors) are any occurrences that break your concentration. **External distractors** are caused by things around you (noises, people, television, weather). **Internal distractors** are disruptions that occur within you (daydreams, worries, depression, sickness, hunger, any other emotions). The first step in improving your concentration is to recognize your own common distractors.

Exercise 3.4   Identifying External and Internal Distractors

Work in a group with three or four people. On your own paper, write the names of the people in your group.

1. List as many external distractors as you can. If you run out of ideas, think of a time when you were trying very hard to concentrate, but "things" going on around you broke your concentration. Add these distractors to your list.

2. List as many internal distractors as you can. If you run out of ideas, think of a time when you were studying alone, but you just couldn't concentrate because of things going on "inside you." Add these distractors to your list.

3. Circle all the distractors on your lists that frequently break your concentration. These are your personal distractors. As you work through this chapter, pay extra close attention to techniques that can help you control or eliminate your personal distractors.

Even when you have carefully selected and prepared the physical stage and the mental stage for concentration, you may find yourself distracted while you are studying. Knowing a variety of techniques to use while you are studying enables you to deal with distractions quickly and effectively. Notice that many of the following techniques can be used for more than one kind of distractor.

Mental Storage Box Technique   Picture a box (a cardboard box, a trunk, a wooden crate, a plastic box, a tool box, a safe) in which you can store your personal items. This is your **mental storage box.** Before you begin studying, identify any concerns, worries, or emotions that might interrupt your concentration. Place those thoughts inside your storage box and close the lid. Gently push the box out of sight. Now your internal distractors are stored temporarily out of sight and out of mind. You can return to the box and work with the issues at a more appropriate time.

Red Bow Technique   People are one of the major external distractions you will face. The people around you need to understand your priorities and learn to respect them. Find a big red bow and place it outside your door when you want privacy to study. If you are studying at a kitchen table, place the bow on the table. Explain to the people around you that the bow signals a time when you want to be able to work without being interrupted. Use your **red bow** system consistently.

Take-Charge Technique   If the neighborhood is extremely noisy when you want to study, or a group of students in a study area can't seem to settle down, or the air conditioner stops working on a sweltering day, you may be inclined to blame everyone else for your inability to concentrate. Don't fight the conditions around you; **take charge** and move to a better place to study. If your friends keep calling you even though you told them you were studying, take charge—turn on the answering machine and turn off the ringer on the phone if possible, unplug the phone, or move it into another room for someone else to answer. If your desk is too cluttered for you to find anything, take charge and schedule a block of time to clean up the mess. You can take charge in creative ways; in doing so, you are also taking responsibility.

No-Need Technique   Imagine yourself studying in a library. The room is relatively quiet, but there is a lot a movement as people walk by, take books off shelves, go in and out of doors. Or imagine yourself studying near a window outside of which is a tree. A branch keeps moving each time a bird perches. If you continually look up at minor movements, your concentration will frequently be interrupted. When you know what the movement or the soft sounds are around you, when they are predictable, there really is **no need** to look up. Force yourself to keep your eyes on your work. Quickly say to yourself, "no need," and get your mind back to the task at hand.

Checkmark Technique   This technique can be used for almost any kind of internal or external distraction. Start with a goal to reduce the number of times you let yourself be distracted. Have a "scorecard" on your desk. Each time you let yourself be distracted, give yourself a **checkmark**. Count the number of checkmarks at the end of your study block. Your goal for the next study block is to end the study block with fewer checkmarks. You can make a bar graph to show your progress. The bar graph will go down steadily if you are motivated and determined to reduce the number of times you let distractions interfere. (Notice how helpful the no-need technique would be to keep the total number of checkmarks low.)

Tunnel Vision Technique   The **tunnel vision** technique can be used when your internal distractors are on your mind. If your mind keeps turning to pleasant thoughts (daydreams, anticipation, fond memories) or to unpleasant thoughts (personal problems, worries, fears, anger), your goal is to catch these thoughts as soon as they begin and bring them to a halt. Picture yourself at the beginning of a tunnel with a yellow line right down the middle of the tunnel. A light shines at the opening at the other end of the tunnel. As you move through the tunnel, you want to walk on the line in the middle of the road. If you move too far right or left, you will collide with the wall. As soon as your mind starts to wander, flash on the picture of the tunnel, and tell yourself to stay in the middle. There's no room to move left or right; the safest route is in the middle. With practice, you can use this mental technique quickly. As soon as you are off course, see the tunnel and adjust your direction.

To Do List Technique   If you have many responsibilities and duties, one of your internal distractors may be remembering things that have to be done, even if they are not necessarily related to studying. Make a **to do list** before you begin studying or as these responsibilities pop into your mind while you are studying. After you finish studying, set a time to deal with the items on your list.

Chunking Technique   Sometimes when you study, you may feel panicky, frustrated, or doubtful that you will complete the assignment. The feeling of being overwhelmed can become a tremendous internal distraction that wastes your time and energy. Analyze the task that you face and break, or **chunk**, it into smaller units. (This concept is discussed in Chapter 2 for goal setting.) Your goal is to regain a sense that your assignment is indeed possible to do. Plan now to work on only one step at a time. As you complete each step, you can move with more confidence and less pressure to the next step.

Active Learning Technique   Passive learning means that you let learning "happen to you" instead of being actively involved. For example, trying to read a textbook nonstop for several hours is passive learning; the process becomes mechanical, and you remember little of what you've read. If you feel sleepy (even though you got enough sleep the night before) or you feel bored, this may be a result of passive learning. To greatly increase your level of concentration, be an **active learner**

There are many ways to be an active learner:

1. Take notes as you study. Have a pen in your hand, and use it as you read.
2. Talk out loud to yourself as you study. Reciting keeps you actively involved and participating with your own learning.
3. Use a wide variety of study techniques. Experiment with the methods you learn in this book until you find the ones that improve your concentration and comprehension.
4. Walk around as you read or recite. If you have difficulties sitting, you can move around the room and still stay "on task."
5. Quiz yourself. Write good test questions for yourself. Recite possible answers. (These test questions could also be used as a warm-up the next time you sit down to study.)

Physical Checkup   You can have difficulties concentrating if you are physically ill or have chronic pain; check with your doctor for recommendations. If you have constant hunger (but are eating), you may have a nutritional problem that needs medical attention. If you try very hard to concentrate, but your attention span is very short, discuss your situation with a doctor. Some medications, prescription and nonprescription drugs, alcohol, or caffeine may be lowering your ability to concentrate and shortening your attention span. If you are trying with sincere effort to improve your concentration, but nothing seems to be working, don't rule out the possibility of a physical condition that can be detected and treated by a physician. A **physical checkup** may be in order.

Exercise 3.5   Choosing Your Techniques

Each individual needs to learn to combat those internal and external distractors that affect concentration. A wide variety of techniques are available to help in this battle.

On your own paper, list at least three *external distractors* and three *internal distractors* that affect your concentration. After each distractor, list possible concentration techniques that you could use to reduce or eliminate the distractors.

Evaluation of Your Progress   After an effective study block, take a few minutes to make a list of any concentration techniques you were aware of using. Include your reaction to each technique. As you experiment with all the techniques in this chapter, you will find the ones that are best for you. Continue to use the techniques whenever you need them.

Setting the Stage for Concentrated Listening

Well-developed listening skills are valuable in the classroom as well as in life outside school. Being able to concentrate in the classroom is essential for listening and understanding lectures, taking accurate notes, following discussions, and communicating effectively with others.

You may think that as long as you have ears that work, you can listen. If your auditory channels are functioning, you can *hear*, but that does not necessarily mean that you are *listening*. Listening requires more than taking in the sounds and being aware that words are being spoken. Listening requires that you understand information as it was intended. **Concentrated listening** occurs when you use effective listening technique and a focused mind. The memory term **DATE IAN** represents seven ways to achieve concentrated listening. Each letter of DATE IAN represents a key element of concentrated listening.

How to Achieve Concentrated Listening (DATE IAN)

1. Eliminate **D**istractions so that you can concentrate effectively.

2. Pay **A**ttention to the development of ideas.

3. Stay **T**uned in even when information is difficult, unfamiliar, or uninteresting.

4. Monitor your **E**motions.

5. Create an **I**nterest in the topic being discussed.

6. **A**sk questions at the appropriate times.

7. Be **N**onjudgmental about the speaker's appearance, mannerisms, and speech patterns.

Eliminate Distractions

To be an effective, skillful listener, you must be able to concentrate. Concentration requires you to block out distractions such as people walking by outside the classroom, standing by a classroom window, or speaking or laughing loudly. In the classroom a student rummaging through a book bag, eating a candy bar, or chewing gum loudly can be a distraction. Even someone's personal appearance, either because of the person's uniqueness or beauty, can cause the mind to wander. Use the techniques on pp. 56–58 to block out distractions.

Pay Attention to Ideas

Many students feel that details are the most important points to remember and understand. Although knowing details is important, details by themselves are not enough. Details belong to a larger picture, a chain of thoughts and interrelated ideas. As you listen to details, try to connect them to the larger ideas that are being presented. Good listeners can follow how a speaker is developing ideas and how the details are used to support the main ideas.

Stay Tuned In

Concentrated listening is much easier when the topic is interesting, easy to understand, and familiar. However, you will be in many situations where the opposite is true. The natural tendency is to tune out the speaker as soon as the information becomes technical, difficult, unclear, or boring. When this occurs, force yourself to focus even harder. You may not be able to understand everything being said, but you will be able to pick up some general trends, a sequence of information, and some important details. The more you concentrate, the more the topic begins to make sense. If you tune out the speaker and then try to begin listening again, you will feel even more lost and confused. Staying tuned in when the information is difficult requires mental discipline; however, the more you practice, the easier it will become for you to follow even the most difficult lecture or conversation.

Monitor Your Emotions

Letting emotions interfere with your listening can create barriers to understanding because then your attention shifts from the speaker to yourself. Emotional responses can occur when you strongly disagree (or agree) with the speaker, when a controversial issue is being discussed, or when a remark triggers the memory of a past experience. Rather than interrupt the speaker with a spontaneous reaction, write your reaction on the side of your notes and continue listening. As the speaker develops his or her ideas, you may gain a new perspective or change your initial reaction in some way.

This listening technique asks you to monitor your emotions, which does not mean that you must become a zombie. Accept your emotions as they surface, but suspend judgment. Return to your reaction after the speaker has finished expressing his or her ideas. Monitoring your emotions and putting them "on hold" are not easy to do, but if you hold on firmly to your emotions and convictions, you will miss, or misinterpret, what the speaker has to say.

Create an Interest in the Topic

The attitude you bring with you to a listening situation greatly affects your success as a good listener. When your interest level is high, you are curious to learn more and eager to compare ideas or participate. This genuine interest is ideal because then listening requires less effort. When, however, the topic is not especially fascinating, you must create an interest. Find *something* about the topic that makes you curious, generate some questions about the topic, or consider how much knowledge the speaker is sharing with you. Genuine interest or created interest makes a difference in your listening abilities, so work to develop some enthusiasm for newness.

Ask Questions

Good listeners spend most of the time listening, not interrupting with endless questions. Be sensitive to each speaker; speakers will often indicate when it is best to ask questions. If the speaker encourages questions at any point in the lecture or discussion, ask questions that are specifically related to the points being discussed. If the speaker requests that questions be saved for later, each time a question pops into your mind, write it down on paper. If the question has not been answered by the end of the lecture or speech, ask it at the appropriate time.

Be Nonjudgmental

A speaker's clothing, physical appearance, mannerisms (body language), speech patterns, dialect, or accent can become distractions. Focusing on and criticizing the speaker for these features create another barrier between you and the ideas being presented. Even though it is always good to make eye contact and focus on the speaker, if these physical distractions are too difficult to ignore, focus on the speaker's forehead. If the situation requires notetaking, you can look more at your note paper as you listen for ideas and information.

Exercise 3.6	**Practicing Concentrated Listening**

Select one of the following to listen to:

    a. A documentary film on television
    b. A panel discussion on television
    c. A speech given on campus or in your community
    d. A church sermon
    e. A lecture on campus for a class you are not enrolled in
    f. Other: _____

Preview the following questions before you begin listening to the "event."
Answer these questions on your own paper.

1. Describe the event you listened to for this assignment.

2. What <u>distractions</u> did you notice around you as you tried to listen to the speaker?

3. Write one or more of the main ideas that you heard the speaker develop when you <u>paid attention</u>.

4. Explain what you did to <u>stay tuned in</u> when the information became too technical, difficult, unfamiliar, or uninteresting.

5. What, if any, <u>emotions</u> surfaced as you were listening? How did they affect your ability to concentrate?

6. Was your <u>interest</u> in the topic genuine? Why or why not? If no, were you able to create an interest?

7. What questions did you want to <u>ask</u>?

8. What features of the speaker annoyed or distracted you? Were you able to be <u>nonjudgmental</u>?

9. On a scale of 1 to 10 and using the seven techniques for concentrated listening, how would you rate yourself as an effective listener for this exercise?

SUMMARY
- Concentration requires that you set a positive mental and physical stage conducive for maintaining a mental focus.
- A positive physical stage includes an ideal study area that deals effectively with noise level, furniture, clutter, lighting, and supplies.
- The memory word RAVES helps you set a positive mental stage.

    1. Use relaxation techniques.
    2. Arrange your priorities.
    3. Visualize your success at concentration.
    4. Recognize the importance of the emotional *E* words.
    5. Use positive self-talk to create a positive attitude.

■ Select appropriate techniques to reduce or eliminate internal and external distractors.

■ The memory phrase DATE IAN can help you obtain concentrated listening, a skill frequently required in college classrooms.

1. Eliminate distractors.
2. Pay attention to the development of ideas.
3. Stay tuned in to difficult or uninteresting material.
4. Monitor your emotions.
5. Create an interest in the topic.
6. Ask questions at appropriate times.
7. Be nonjudgmental.

■ Select techniques from this chapter that will help you increase your concentration while studying and listening in class.

PERSONALIZING WHAT YOU LEARNED

1. Score and record the score for your chapter profile.
2. On your own paper, expand this chapter's visual mapping.
3. Make your own vocabulary list of all the terms in this chapter that are printed in color.

"To the Student" (p. xv) provides you with more detailed directions for completing these activities.

Review Questions

True-False

To help keep your mind focused, underline the key words in the true-false questions before you answer them.

Write *T* if the statement is TRUE. Write *F* if it is FALSE.

_____ **1.** Concentration is the ability to focus on two or more things at one time without being distracted.

_____ **2.** An organized desk, a supportive chair, and two sources of lighting help concentration.

_____ **3.** Caffeine and nicotine can reduce some people's ability to concentrate.

_____ **4.** Active learning can be used to overcome boredom.

_____ **5.** RAVES is a formula for solving external distractions.

_____ **6.** Relaxation techniques can help your mind become more receptive to learning.

_____ **7.** Using "say no" shows that you are committed to your own goals and priorities.

_____ **8.** The desire to concentrate can be strengthened by planning positive rewards for yourself.

_____ **9.** You should never walk around while you study because it always creates distractions.

_____ **10.** A person with good concentration uses all the concentration techniques every time he or she studies.

Matching

Read through the items in the left column.

Begin with the first item in the right column. Try to match it to an item in the left column. If you see the match, write the letter on the line. Cross off the item on the right so that you do not use it again.

If you do not see the match right away, skip the question. Go back to it after you have made all the matches that you are sure are correct.

_____	**1.** Concentration	**a.**	techniques to set a mental stage for concentration
_____	**2.** RAVES	**b.**	a technique to signal other people not to interrupt you
_____	**3.** Visualization	**c.**	a technique used to analyze tasks so that you can work on one part at a time
_____	**4.** Mental storage box	**d.**	a relaxation technique that gently covers your face
_____	**5.** Red bow technique	**e.**	a technique to get you to participate in a nonpassive way
_____	**6.** Tunnel vision	**f.**	the ability to focus attention on one idea or subject area at a time
_____	**7.** Chunking	**g.**	a technique used to record the number of distractions on a scorecard
_____	**8.** Active learner	**h.**	the ability to use your imagination to picture things
_____	**9.** Warm-ups	**i.**	the ability to use good listening and concentration techniques
_____	**10.** Soothing mask	**j.**	a technique that keeps your thoughts in the middle of the road
_____	**11.** Checkmarks	**k.**	a technique used to store thoughts until later
_____	**12.** Concentrated listening	**l.**	a method that involves reviewing and previewing when you begin studying

Multiple Choice

Read each question carefully with all the options. Cross out the options that you know are incorrect. Select the best option that remains. Write the letter of the best option on the line.

_____ **1.** Which of the following could reduce concentrated listening?

    a. asking inappropriate questions during the lecture
    b. writing emotional responses on your paper
    c. creating an interest in the subject
    d. being nonjudgmental about the speaker

_____ **2.** Good listeners

    a. criticize the speaker's appearance.
    b. see how details relate to the big picture.
    c. let their minds wander when the topic is boring.
    d. have short attention spans.

_____ **3.** Mental self-discipline is needed to

    a. stay tuned in to a speaker.
    b. monitor emotional reactions.
    c. block out distractions.
    d. all of the above.

CHAPTER 4

Understanding How You Process and Learn Information

*T*he workings of the human mind have fascinated people for centuries. What is involved in learning new information? Are you sometimes certain you've learned new information only to find you can't recall it? Do your study techniques give you feedback to let you know how you are doing? Do you remember main ideas or details more readily? How do you organize information for your memory? This chapter shows you ways to strengthen your ability to process and recall important information.

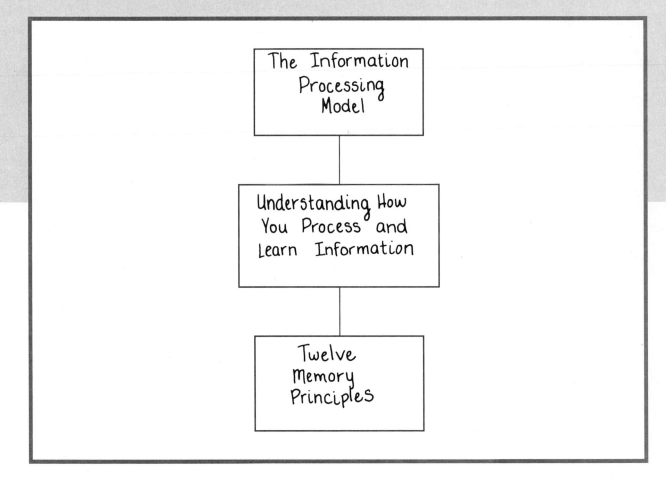

The Information Processing Model

Understanding How You Process and Learn Information

Twelve Memory Principles

© 1994 by Houghton Mifflin Company

65

Information Processing Profile

Please answer honestly each of the following questions about your current attitudes and study habits. Your answers should reflect what you *do*, not what you *wish* you would do.

After you read each statement, check YES if you do this *always* or *most of the time*. Check NO if you do this *seldom* or *never*.

		YES	**NO**
1.	I use study methods that give me feedback so that I know if I am learning.	_____	_____
2.	I have problems studying new information when it is not an area of genuine or natural interest for me.	_____	_____
3.	I recognize that learning does not just happen; I am willing to put forth the effort that is required.	_____	_____
4.	I have problems identifying and pulling out the information that is important to study.	_____	_____
5.	I rearrange information into meaningful units or clusters so that it is easier to learn.	_____	_____
6.	I wait until close to test time before I practice the information that I have put into memory.	_____	_____
7.	I talk out loud to myself as I study because reciting seems to help me learn.	_____	_____
8.	I use the same method of learning information for everything I need to study.	_____	_____
9.	I spend almost all my studying time memorizing specific details.	_____	_____
10.	I make movies in my mind about the information I am learning.	_____	_____
11.	I take time to relate or associate new information to information I already know.	_____	_____
12.	I use methods to concentrate when I study.	_____	_____

The Information Processing Model

Psychologists frequently use the **Information Processing Model** to help explain how we receive, process, and learn information. The Information Processing Model consists of six main parts. While each part has its own distinctive functions, the parts do not work independently. Each part has an important role to move information through your memory system as you learn. Refer to the following diagram of the model as you read about each of its parts.

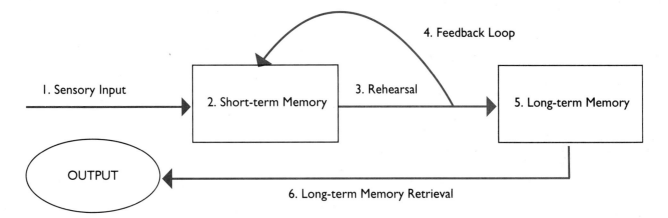

The Information Processing Model

1. Our senses take in information, or sensory input.

2. Our short-term memory receives the information and holds it briefly.

3. We rehearse the information we want to learn.

4. If we get feedback that we aren't learning what we rehearse, that information goes through the feedback loop.

5. Information that is adequately rehearsed moves into our long-term memory.

6. Information stored in long-term memory is accessed through long-term retrieval, and the output shows that we have learned.

Sensory Input   We receive information through our five senses (sight, sound, smell, taste, and touch); this information is called **sensory input.** Such input comes in the form of **sensory stimuli,** which can be letters, numbers, words, pictures, and sounds.

Short-Term Memory   **Short-term memory** is a temporary storage center that is very limited in time and capacity. Sensory input first moves into short-term memory and remains there for a few seconds. Within that time, a "decision" is made by the person receiving the stimuli either to pay attention to the information and begin to learn it or to let the information go and forget it. This decision is not always made consciously. The following examples show how short-term memory works:

- On your way to school today, you probably passed many different cars. However, you probably cannot accurately remember how many black cars you passed; there was no reason to remember such information. This is true for a vast amount of information taken in by your senses. Information that seems unimportant simply drops out of short-term memory and is forgotten.
- You begin to leave for the grocery store with a short list of groceries in mind. Two members of the household call out a total of eight more items for you to pick up at the store. If too much new information is given rapidly, your short-term memory probably overloads; you forget some of the items when you are shopping.
- At school, you ask for someone's phone number. You repeat it several times as you head for the phone. You are interrupted by a question from another student. By the time you reach the phone, you have forgotten the number.
- At the end of class your instructor says, "Be sure to review page 10 because it will be on the test Friday." You instantly receive the information and decide it is important. If you don't write down the information, it may be forgotten hours later.

To help your short-term memory work best, recognize the importance of the following:

1. Pay attention to sensory input. You must consciously decide which information is important to learn.
2. Take a positive attitude toward incoming information. If you label it as boring, dumb, too complicated, or not important, you will likely "dump," or forget it.
3. Remember that the information you identify as important to learn will begin its journey along the rehearsal path.

Rehearsal   Once a learner decides that particular information must be learned, that information moves into the **rehearsal** stage. The learner now selects effective study techniques to get information into memory. The following examples show how rehearsal works:

- Say that you need to learn five math formulas. You make flash cards for each formula and begin to practice and recite the information; you check your accuracy with the answers on the cards.
- In a literature course, you are instructed to read a short story. You know that you will be asked about the main characters, the setting, and a sequence of events. You make a list of the important information and begin memorizing it. You practice writing answers to questions that you have posed for yourself about the story.

The following points are important to know about the rehearsal step:

1. Your choice of rehearsal activities is important. Select strategies that use your strengths. If, for example, you know you learn best auditorally, create study activities that help you learn through your auditory channels.
2. Use a variety of rehearsal techniques. You are more likely to recall information that you have practiced in more than one way. In the literature example above, the student made lists, wrote questions, and wrote answers.
3. Emphasize understanding what you are practicing. Avoid rote memory in which little understanding is attached to the information.
4. Recognize that this stage involves practice. Time and effort are required to learn the information accurately and thoroughly.
5. Feedback should be included so that you know whether you are learning the information. Feedback can include reciting, writing, discussing, drawing, or demonstrating the information.

Feedback Loop When you rehearse and find out that you do not understand or know new information, you receive **feedback** that more rehearsal or practice is required. You need to route the information once again through short-term memory and along the rehearsal path.

For example, if you try reciting your math flash cards and find that you can explain only three of five formulas, you immediately know that you have not learned two of the formulas. You need to rehearse them again until you have practiced them enough to recite them. You might choose another method to practice the information such as reading the cards out loud, having a friend quiz you, or writing the information several times.

Positive feedback also occurs, signaling that you understand the information and can move on to new material. In the case of the preceding literature example, let's assume that you could write answers to your own questions about the characters, setting, and events of the short story. The new information that you have learned then moves to the next stage, your long-term memory.

The following points are important to remember about the **feedback loop:**

1. Pay attention to the feedback you receive during rehearsal. If you don't know the information, do not skip over it or move on. Try a different way of practicing the information.
2. Avoid doing the same learning activity again and again; you may wind up recycling through the feedback loop without showing any progress. Use a different method to help move the information to long-term memory.

Long-Term Memory **Long-term memory** is an enormous storage system that "files away" information. So that new information can be located when it is needed, long-term memory often stores it in clusters of related information called **schemas.** The more knowledge you acquire, the greater are the size and the number of schemas in your memory system.

For example, in sociology you are learning about different forms of family structure. What are your current knowledge and definition of family? Your answer indicates what information is already in your schema for "family." As you learn about nuclear families, extended families, and families that practice different marriage partnerships, the new information links up with the information you already know. Your early "bank of knowledge" may now be expanded as you study cultures that practice polyandry (more than one husband) and polygyny (more than one wife). As you rehearse the new information about family structures, your schema for the concept of family broadens, and you have an easier time learning additional new information about families.

Think of your brain as a filing system with many different files and many different drawers. Your brain, like a filing cabinet, has numerous sections; each section stores different kinds of information. If information is put into memory carefully, thoroughly, and accurately, it will be placed in the correct file. Thus, if you are asked about the word *polygyny*, you will not give unrelated information such as "It's the name of a game."

The following points about long-term memory are also important to know:

1. The information that has been processed along the rehearsal path is carried to long-term memory by impulses.
2. Information that enters long-term memory is **imprinted** into brain cells. Impulses mark the information on the brain.
3. Because information is imprinted, long-term memory is considered permanent memory. The information has been placed in long-term storage.

4. Long-term memory has unlimited capacity; new information can continually be received and added to existing information.

Long-Term Retrieval   **Long-term retrieval** is the process of accessing, or finding, information stored in the long-term memory system. When information is retrieved, it is pulled back through short-term memory and you are then able to show what you have learned through some form of "output." Output may mean that you are able to respond correctly by talking, explaining, writing, drawing, demonstrating, or applying the learned information in one or more ways. Practice and use keep information accessible. By reviewing information on a regular basis, you strengthen the retrieval path so that you can use the information you worked hard to learn.

Learning a foreign language is a good example of the necessity to practice retrieval. You spent time learning a foreign language but have not practiced it for many years, so you probably no longer speak that language fluently. You may remember the sentence structure, but you have probably forgotten the vocabulary needed to express your ideas. If you do not retrieve information for years at a time, you will no longer have access to that information in memory. However, by "brushing up" with a few lessons, the vocabulary may return to you fairly quickly. You will definitely "relearn" the language faster than you learned it the first time.

The following points are important to remember about long-term memory retrieval:

1. To readily access information stored in long-term memory, you must review that information regularly and frequently.
2. When you search your memory for information that you have learned, think in terms of related categories.
3. Practice retrieving information by several methods. This can include reciting it, summarizing it, drawing or reproducing it, or seeing the relationships that it has with other information.

Exercise 4.1   Understanding the Information Processing Model

Without referring to your notes, draw and label the six parts of the Information Processing Model.

Which part of the model does each of the following describe? Write your answer on the line.

_____   **1.** Requires ongoing review to work efficiently

_____   **2.** Should include some form of feedback so that you know if you are actually learning

_____   **3.** Should emphasize understanding what is being practiced

_____   **4.** Requires that you pay attention to the incoming stimulus

_____   **5.** Results in successfully showing some form of output that demonstrates your knowledge

_____   **6.** Is organized around clusters or schemas of information and concepts

_____   **7.** Provides you with a second chance to learn the information more accurately

_____   **8.** Should include a variety of learning methods to work with the material

_____   **9.** Is very limited in time and capacity

_____   **10.** Involves taking in information through the senses

---

Exercise 4.2	**Understanding What's Happening**

Work with a partner or in a group of three or four people. Read the following situations carefully. In each case, the student has problems learning because she or he is not using one part of the Information Processing Model efficiently. Identify which part is not being used. Write your answer on the line.

_____   **1.** Manuel has twenty new vocabulary words to learn. He reads through them quickly and is surprised to find he can't remember any of the definitions.

_____   **2.** Teresa spent many hours studying her biology notes for a test that was scheduled three weeks later. She got involved with many other activities and did not review before the test. She figured that she had already learned the information; her test scores showed that she hadn't.

_____   **3.** Leon repeated several math formulas again and again. He is good at rote memory. On a test, he was not able to answer questions about the formulas because they were presented differently from the way he had memorized them.

_____   **4.** Cindy needed to associate fifteen writers to the time periods in which they produced their work. She practiced matching the writers to their works. On the test, she could recall which author wrote which book but not in which period.

_____ **5.** Kim made flash cards for all the important terms she had to know in her psychology class. She recited the information on her cards. If she missed some definitions, she continued on until she could find ones that she knew.

Twelve Memory Principles

Learning, as you have seen, is a complex process. Many mental processes are involved in moving information into long-term memory and then retrieving that information when it is needed. The following **twelve memory principles** can help you process information more efficiently through all the stages of information processing. These principles, when used consistently throughout the learning process, result in a stronger, more efficient memory. The memory words **SAVE CRIB FOTO** will help you remember all twelve principles; each letter in the words represents one of the memory principles.

Twelve Memory Principles (SAVE CRIB FOTO)

1. Use **S**electivity when you study.
2. **A**ssociate the new information with what you know.
3. **V**isualize what you are learning.
4. Recognize that learning requires **E**ffort on your part.
5. **C**oncentrate when you study.
6. **R**ecite information as you study.
7. Create an **I**nterest if genuine interest isn't there.
8. See the **B**ig picture and the little pictures.
9. Provide yourself with **F**eedback to check your progress.
10. **O**rganize information into meaningful clusters.
11. Use **T**ime to your advantage.
12. Use **O**ngoing review to practice retrieval.

Selectivity   Learning everything—every detail, every example, every word—is not possible and is certainly not reasonable. You as the learner must continually strive to pick out the significant information. Parts II and III of this book help you improve your selectivity skills as you learn to survey, underline, take notes, and make study tools. In each of these essential skills, your job is to learn how to pull out the main ideas and the important supporting details.

If you answer "yes" to either of the following questions, you can benefit from learning to be more **selective:**

- Do you spend a lot of time studying but seem to study the "wrong information" for a test?
- Do you get frustrated because everything seems important?

Association

Information moves more readily into long-term memory when you already know something about the subject. By associating new information with old information, you learn more quickly and completely. So it is wise to take the time and make the effort to relate new information to information you already know. Ask yourself, What do I already know about this subject? Have I seen something similar to this before? How does this fit with what I previously learned? Such questioning allows you to activate and connect to an existing schema that is already established in your long-term memory.

In addition, look for connections between ideas. For example, you want to remember the meaning of the word *insubordinate*. The prefix *in* can mean "not," as in incorrect. *Sub* means "under," as in subway. *Ordinate* sounds as if it comes from "order" (and it does). By making these associations, you can more easily remember that insubordinate means "the person under the authority is not following orders."

When you link new information to something you already know, the old information works as a "retrieval cue." **Retrieval cues** can help you locate information needed from long-term memory. Retrieval cues can be words as well as pictures. For example, if you are trying to learn the difference between "positive correlations" and "negative correlations" (which are research terms), create a graph that shows the difference so that you have a strong association between the words and the picture of them.

If you answer "yes" to any of the following questions, you need to practice **associating** new information with information you already know:

- Do you memorize facts or ideas in isolation? If you do, you are probably using rote memory techniques.
- When you try to recall information you have studied, do you feel "lost" because there is no direct way of accessing it in your memory?
- Do you feel that you are memorizing lists and lists of information but don't understand what they mean or how they are connected?
- Do you "go blank" when a test asks for information differently from the way you studied it?

Visualization

Visualizing is the process of making pictures in your mind. It is a valuable skill for several reasons. Information that is mentally pictured is easier to comprehend. And long-term memory is strengthened when two sensory channels (such as auditory for reciting and visual for visualizations) are processing information. Also, mental pictures are stored in one side of the brain (the right hemisphere) and words in the other (the left hemisphere). Using visualizations to aid in processing information activates your entire brain. The result is better memory skills.

Learning to **visualize** clearly and accurately takes practice. There are three ways you can strengthen your skills. First, visualize *individual objects*. If you are learning about an ancient tool or a specific geometric angle, look at the object for a few minutes. Close your eyes. Try to see the object "on the inside of your eyelids." Add color to your picture. Open your eyes. Get feedback by seeing if the object you pictured matches the actual object. Now look up toward the ceiling. Picture the object again (size, shape, color) with your eyes opened. Get feedback by comparing this picture to the original object.

Second, visualize *larger pictures*. Use the techniques just described to visualize larger pictures, such as maps, graphs, and charts. Once you see the "whole picture" (the skeleton), go back through it and focus on the individual parts. When you begin looking at the parts, you "zoom in" to work on one part at a time. Of course, you can verbalize or recite as you focus on each part.

Third, create *stories or movies* in your mind. This visualization process focuses your attention on units of meaning. Begin by reading a sentence. Then close your eyes and let the inside of your eyelids be a television screen for that sentence. Watch the information you just read move across the screen as if it were a movie. After you are able to visualize sentences, apply the same methods to creating movies of concepts, paragraphs, sections of your textbook, or complete chapters.

If you answer "yes" to any of the following questions, you are wise to develop your **visualization** skills:

- When you finish reading, do you have difficulty remembering what the paragraphs were even about?
- Do you remember seeing a chart written on the chalkboard but are not able to create a mental picture of the details?
- Do you enjoy daydreaming? (Daydreaming involves visualizing.) Can you use the same kind of visualizing skills with your schoolwork?
- When you try to recall information, do you have to rely mainly on words rather than on pictures?

Effort   Effort, driven by motivation and determination, is needed throughout information processing. Taking information in, rehearsing it, and retrieving it all require effort. Many of the study tools you will use to help you boost your memory will not necessarily be seen by teachers or graded. You are the one who decides whether such study tools will help you learn; you create your own learning activities for yourself, not because they are "required." By applying effort to your learning, you will be rewarded with more thorough learning, a greater sense of satisfaction, and better grades.

If you answer "yes" to any of the following questions, you are probably in need of using more **effort:**

- Do you take the "easy way out" or look for shortcuts when you study?
- Do you feel it is a waste of time to create study tools that are not assigned by the teacher?
- Do you consider studying to mean "Do the assignments" and then you are finished?

Exercise 4.3   Using the SAVE Principles

The expression *SAVE CRIB FOTO* is a memory phrase designed to help you learn the twelve principles of memory. Copy the following on your own paper. Complete each line to name the first four principles.

S_____

A_____

V_____

E_____

Do the following exercises on your paper.

1. A lot of information is given in every class. You need to *select* the details and ideas that are important to learn. List three main ideas or important details presented in this class that you need to learn. Be specific.

2. Write one term that you must be able to define. Explain or show how you can *associate* this word and its meaning to something you already know, a similar word, or a picture.

3. Open any one of your textbooks. Read any paragraph in the current chapter you are studying. Describe the "movie" that you can *visualize* as you think about this information.

4. List several things you are doing as a student that show you are applying *effort* to learn information in your courses.

Concentration You have already learned important techniques for setting the physical stage and the mental stage for good concentration (see Chapter 3). Being able to control your concentration enables you to create the ideal setting for receiving sensory information and moving it through the stages of information processing. Your mind has to be alert and focused on the task at hand. Internal and external distractors should be blocked out or eliminated.

If you answer "yes" to any of the following questions, your concentration requires strengthening:

- Do you get easily distracted or find your mind wandering?
- Are there so many interruptions that at the end of your study time you are not sure what you really accomplished?
- Do you miss important information as you listen or read because your mind has difficulty staying focused?

Recitation Reciting information is the process of verbalizing what you are learning or have already learned. Effective reciting can be the result of several techniques. First, use your own words to speak in complete sentences to explain the information as clearly as possible. Second, imagine that you are trying to explain the information to a friend who is not familiar with the subject. Third, pay attention to areas that seem a little "fuzzy." Go back to the sources of your information to check for accuracy and additional details.

Some students are uncomfortable with reciting because they are not used to talking out loud to themselves and so feel that others will think they are "weird." Nevertheless, an increasing number of teachers and students recognize the value of reciting and encourage this process of verbalizing. Reciting is valuable in studying because it provides you with immediate feedback so that you know whether you are really understanding information. As you recite, you activate your auditory channel, which strengthens the path to your long-term memory. Reciting keeps you actively involved; active learning leads to better concentration and comprehension. And as you recite in your own words, your focus is on understanding rather than on rote memory. You are personalizing the material.

If you answer "yes" to any of the following questions, increase your **recitation:**

- Are your auditory skills weak?
- Do you have difficulty expressing ideas on paper? Could this be because you spend little time trying to state information clearly in your own words?
- Do your methods of studying lack a form of immediate feedback that lets you know if you are learning?

Interest

Learning new information about areas that you "love" is usually easy; you have genuine interest working for you. Unfortunately, you will be required to take some courses in which you have no natural interest. Your task, then, is to generate an interest so that your learning is more enjoyable and less stressful.

You can create an interest by looking for a value or a purpose in knowing the information, by using new study techniques to learn the information, or by asking another student or several students to join you in a study group so you can learn together. You can also locate someone who is knowledgeable or works in the field that you are studying and ask that person what draws him or her to this field. Checking out books, videos, or cassettes that are related to the topic you are studying may give you a new, more appealing perspective on the topic.

On a more personal level, you may wish to examine your attitude toward the subject to see if your dislike or lack of interest is related to a previous experience or a past incident in the class. Meanwhile, identify what you do like about the subject. Emphasize and strengthen the positive aspects rather than focusing on the negatives.

If you answer "yes" to any of the following questions, you probably have to create some **interest:**

- Do you label the class or the book as boring, dumb, useless, or a waste of time?
- Do you dislike going to class?
- Once you are in class, do you resent being there and tend to tune out whatever is going on?
- Do you find it difficult to complete homework assignments because you just can't get interested in the subject?

The Big and Little Pictures

Learning based on understanding requires you to use at least two levels of information. One level is the "big picture," which is the general concept or category of information. For example, the subject of concentration is a big picture. To really understand the concept of concentration, however, you need to know another level of information, the specific details, or the "little pictures," that together create this concept. These details include a definition, the uses of concentration, its effects, how it works, and specific strategies.

To get a sense of these two levels of information, draw a circle in the center of your paper. This circle represents the main idea or the general category of information. (This is a schema.) Surround the circle with details that are related to the topic in the center of the circle. The details can be written randomly, or lines can be extended from the circle to create a visual mapping. You can also make a list of all the important details you are gathering and learning for a topic. At the top of the list, in large capital letters write the category name. In either case, frequently ask yourself how details relate to each other and what big picture is created when all the details are grouped together.

This principle of big picture–little pictures is sometimes also referred to as the "forest and the trees." If you focus only on seeing the forest, you miss the meaning and the beauty of the individual trees that grow there. If you focus only on a few individual trees, you do not see that all the trees create a much larger group, the forest.

Learning new knowledge is similar to the idea of the forest and the trees. If you place too much emphasis on the details, you may fail to see their relationships to each other and to larger concepts. If you focus only on finding the main ideas, you are left without the specific details that support or prove the main idea.

If you answer "yes" to any of the following questions, your sense of **big and little pictures** could use some strengthening:

- Do you have problems finding the main idea even though you are able to understand the individual details?
- When you are asked questions on tests, do you understand the general idea but have problems recalling specific names, dates, definitions, or supporting facts?
- Do you seldom take time to relate details to each other and then to a larger idea?

Exercise 4.4   Using the CRIB Principles

Work with a partner to complete each part of this exercise.

1. The first letters of memory principles five through eight spell the word *CRIB*. Write the names of these principles on the following lines:

    C _____

    R _____

    I _____

    B _____

2. Discuss answers to the following questions.
    a. What concentration strategies do you use to pay attention to important information as you receive, rehearse, and practice retrieving it?
    b. How do you use reciting when you study?
    c. What subjects do you have a natural interest in learning? What subjects do you need to create an interest in?

3. Read the following information. Write the category, or the big picture, inside the circle. Surround the circle with important details that support the big picture.

    Even when the twelve principles of memory are used, some information may be forgotten. Decay Theory applies to short-term memory when the stimulus that is received is too weak; the information simply decays or fades away. Displacement Theory also applies to short-term memory; if too much information comes into short-term memory too rapidly, it shoves aside or displaces some of the information before there is time to process it. The Interference Theory applies to long-term memory; new information gets confused with previously learned information, so new and old information interfere with each other. The Incomplete Encoding Theory applies when information being rehearsed is only partially learned, so all the information does not get processed and imprinted in long-term memory.

The Retrieval Failure Theory applies when enough attention is not given to how the information is organized. When you search for the information you learned, you can't find it even though you know you learned it. The information is not attached or associated to a strong information schema.

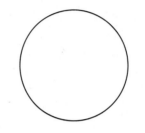

Feedback   The feedback loop can be activated only if you incorporate study techniques that include self-checking or self-quizzing. If you are involved in marathon studying or cramming, you do not have sufficient time for feedback. The main feedback from cramming comes *after* you have taken a test. Feedback should occur frequently *before* test time.

Several study techniques can provide feedback as you are learning. *Reciting* is the most frequently used form of feedback. Reciting can be used after you read a paragraph, underline, take notes, practice from flash cards, or use other visual study tools. *Writing summaries* can be effective feedback. At the end of a section in the chapter and at the end of the entire chapter, practice writing summaries of what you have read (and underlined or placed in your notes). For this to be true feedback, attempt to write your summaries without looking at your notes or your book. After you have finished writing the summary, check your accuracy by comparing the summary to your notes or the book.

You can also *draw mappings or pictures* without looking at your notes or the book. Compare your drawings to the original ones. Check your accuracy, and add any details you missed when you drew from memory. This same process can be used to reproduce the visual mappings found at the beginning of each chapter in this book. Finally, as you work through a chapter, *write*

your own test questions. Once you have finished with the chapter, quiz yourself. This gives you feedback that is similar to the feedback you receive during tests. If the chapter has chapter questions, sample exercises, or quizzes, complete these sections even if they are not assigned. This extra effort will provide you with feedback that can help you focus your attention on areas that need additional work.

If you answer "yes" to any of the following questions, you need to include more **feedback** as you study:

- Do you use tests as your main means of getting feedback about whether you have learned the information?
- Do you keep taking in new information without stopping to see if you are trying to learn too much too fast?
- When you are rehearsing, do you ignore the times when the feedback you get clearly lets you know you don't completely understand information?

Organization

If you sit at a computer keyboard and begin punching in random commands and information, the computer will not accept what you have just typed. The mind works in much the same way. The information you want to put into your long-term memory must be organized in a meaningful, logical way if you want to access it later. When you try to retrieve information from long-term memory, your mind searches through the different "files" of information you have stored. If you "threw everything into your memory" without filing it properly, or without associating it to clusters of information, you will have difficulty locating the information you thought you learned.

This principle of organization explains why rote memory of small, individual facts is not a very reliable memory. Rote memory involves repeating a fact or detail in the exact words each time. Information learned through rote memory may be in your long-term memory but may be difficult to find. If a teacher asks you a question that is stated differently from the way you memorized the information, you will not be able to use the memorized detail effectively. You may not even recognize that the question and what you learned are related.

However, there are ways to logically organize information as you process it for storage in long-term memory. One way is to organize information chronologically. Rearrange your information so it is listed in the proper time sequence that shows the order of occurrence. A second way is to group information into meaningful categories. Work with facts and concepts to identify the ones that "belong together" because of common characteristics. Clearly label each category. A third way is to make a visual mapping or a picture of the key points of the information that you are trying to learn. Selectively identify the key ideas and then look for how they are related. Group the ideas that belong together. Add these to your mapping or picture.

If you answer "yes" to any of the following questions, your **organizational** abilities require some attention:

- Does the information you learn in class and from your textbook seem disorganized?
- Do you have difficulty remembering the sequences of important events?
- Do you have problems seeing how information from class and information from the textbook or information from several chapters are related?
- Do you spend most of your time using rote memory to learn important details?
- When you try to recall or retrieve information, are you unable to find it in your memory?

Time   To keep from overloading your memory system, you need time to learn new information. You also need time to rehearse information, run it through the feedback loop if necessary, and to associate it to information already in long-term memory.

Planning your study time effectively is essential; the most effective study blocks are fifty-minute blocks of concentrated effort. In addition, studying a subject for an hour or so each day is more effective than studying all on one day for several hours in a row. Using the strategies presented in Chapter 2 for effective time management provides you with ample time to process information carefully and thoroughly.

If you answer "yes" to any of the following questions, the way you manage **time** needs to be adjusted:

- Do you often have to cram before tests?
- Do you get tired when you study because you are trying to study too much all at one time?
- Does information get confusing because you are taking in too much information in a short period of time?

Ongoing Review   Ongoing review, or practicing what you have stored in long-term memory, makes that information much more accessible than it would otherwise be. As a result, long-term retrieval occurs more readily, information remains active and fresh in your mind, and you can avoid last-minute cramming.

If you answer "yes" to any of the following questions, you need more **ongoing review:**

- Once you have completed the work on new information, do you put it aside until close to the time of a test?
- Do you have trouble retrieving or recalling information several weeks later even though you know you learned it?
- Does your mind go blank when you try to recall learned information?

Exercise 4.5   Using FOTO Principles

1. The last four memory principles begin with the letters in the word FOTO. Write the names of the principles on the following lines:

F _____

O_____

T_____

O_____

2. Answer the following questions on your own paper:
   a. Where does feedback occur in the Information Processing Model?
   b. What can you do to get feedback when you are studying?

c. How can you organize the following list of information so that it is meaningful and therefore easier to learn?

California	San Francisco
Louisiana	Baton Rouge
Portland	Oregon
Orlando	Florida
Houston	Texas
New Orleans	Miami
Salem	San Antonio
Los Angeles	Austin

d. Evaluate your own management of time. Do you feel that you allow enough time to learn information thoroughly and accurately? Why or why not?

e. When was the last time you reviewed information that was presented in Chapter 1 of this book? Chapter 2? Are you using ongoing review on a regular basis?

Exercise 4.6   Reviewing the Memory Principles

1. List the twelve principles of memory.

S _____

A _____

V _____

E _____

C _____

R _____

I _____

B _____

F _____

O _____

T _____

O _____

2. In the space to the right of the twelve principles, draw a picture that will help you remember SAVE CRIB FOTO. Be creative!

3. Practice naming each principle without looking. After you name the principles, practice reciting what you know about each.

SUMMARY   ▪ The six-part Information Processing Model explains how information is learned.

1. Sensory input is received from stimuli in the environment.
2. Short-term memory briefly stores the information.
3. Information moves along the rehearsal path, where it is practiced.
4. Information that is not yet learned is rerouted through the feedback loop.
5. Effectively learned information is stored in long-term memory.
6. When learned information is needed, it is pulled out of long-term memory and moved along the retrieval path.

▪ The memory phrase *SAVE CRIB FOTO* is a way of remembering the twelve principles that can be used to strengthen your memory.

1. Selectivity	7. Interest
2. Association	8. Big picture–little picture
3. Visualization	9. Feedback
4. Effort	10. Organization
5. Concentration	11. Time
6. Recitation	12. Ongoing review

PERSONALIZING
WHAT YOU
LEARNED

1. Score and record the score for your chapter profile.
2. On your own paper, expand this chapter's visual mapping.
3. Make your own vocabulary list of all the terms in this chapter that are printed in color.

"To the Student" (p. xv) provides you with more detailed directions for completing these activities.

Review Questions

True-False

To help keep your mind focused, underline the key words in the true-false questions before you answer them.
    Write *T* if the statement is TRUE. Write *F* if it is FALSE.

_____   **1.** All sensory stimuli are imprinted in long-term memory.

_____   **2.** Long-term memory stores information for a brief period of time.

_____   **3.** Practice is needed in the rehearsal and the retrieval stages.

_____ 4. Information that is well organized in long-term memory is believed to be organized around clusters of related information.

_____ 5. The principle of ongoing review is needed in the retrieval stage of the Information Processing Model.

_____ 6. The principle of effort is used in more than one stage of the Information Processing Model.

_____ 7. Writing summaries is an activity recommended to strengthen short-term memory.

_____ 8. When you visualize objects, try to see the shape and color.

_____ 9. Relating new information to old information involves the principle of association.

_____ 10. The principle of time recommends that you space your practice over several different time periods.

Short Answer

1. In the following examples, students in a psychology class are successfully learning new information. Examine the techniques used in each situation. Identify at least one major memory principle being used in the study technique. Explain specifically why you chose this technique.

   a. Marsha is learning that different regions in the brain receive information about different senses. The occipital lobe receives visual information. The temporal lobe receives auditory information. The parietal lobe takes in information from the skin. Marsha drew a picture of the three lobes and paired the pictures with pictures of eyes, ears, and skin.

   Principle: _____

   Explain: _____

   _____

   b. Damon knows he learns best when he can discuss information with others. A midterm is scheduled in two weeks. Damon asks other students in class to join him in a study group. Because of his enthusiasm and enjoyment of the subject, many students ask to be a part of the study group.

   Principle: _____

   Explain: _____

   _____

   c. Elena has found that using flash cards helps her tremendously. She writes psychology terms on one side and definitions on the other. She works with all her cards for the course at least once a week. She very conscientiously sorts the cards by the ones she knows and the ones she needs to study further.

   Principle: _____

   Explain: _____

   _____

2. Use your own piece of paper. Draw and label the 6 main parts of the Information Processing Model. Below the model write a short description of each part of the model.

WRITING ASSIGNMENTS

1. Identify two or more memory principles that you have *not* been using on a regular basis when you study. Discuss ways you can start to incorporate these principles more consistently when you study.

2. Now that you have finished studying this chapter, you have become aware of the complex processes involved in learning new information. Write your reactions to what you have learned about the way memory is described through the Information Processing Model.

II

Selecting and Processing Information for Memory

*I*n Part I you learned to use resources, set goals, manage time, improve concentration, and understand how memory works. Now that the stage is set for learning, Part II helps you learn how to select and process textbook and lecture information.

Chapter 5 familiarizes you with your textbooks. Chapter 6 presents a system for reading textbooks. Chapter 7 helps you learn to select appropriate textbook information for underlining and taking marginal notes. Chapter 8 introduces you to the Cornell notetaking system for use with your textbooks. Chapter 9 focuses on using the Cornell notetaking system to select and process information presented in lectures. By learning to use the skills presented in Part II, you will be able to select the essential information from textbooks and lectures that you want to process into your memory.

Surveying a Textbook

Surveying, which is the process of previewing, helps you become acquainted with new information before you begin reading. Are you familiar with the different parts of your textbook? Do you proceed through a term without ever reading the book's introduction? Do you spend needless time trying to locate information in a book by searching through chapters trying to find the specific topics you need? This chapter helps you become familiar with the eight important sections of a textbook that immediately provide you with helpful information you can use all term.

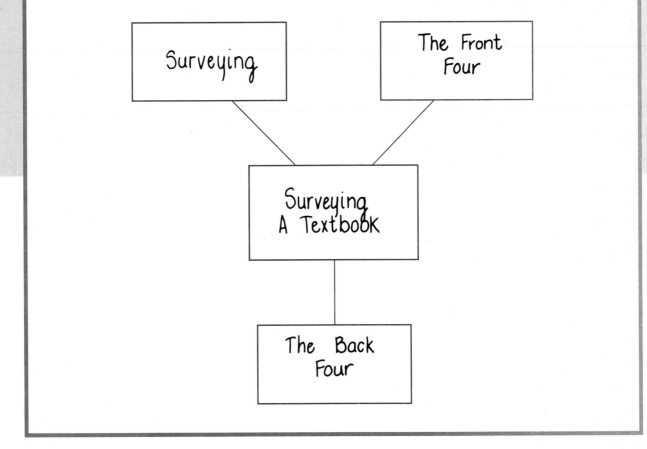

NAME_____ DATE_____

Textbook Surveying Profile

Please answer honestly each of the following questions about your current attitudes and study habits. Your answers should reflect what you *do*, not what you *wish* you would do.

After you read each statement, check YES if you do this *always* or *most of the time*. Check NO if you do this *seldom* or *never*.

	YES	NO
1. If the teacher mentions the author of my textbook, I recognize the author's name.	_____	_____
2. I know how current the information in the textbook is because I have looked at the copyright date.	_____	_____
3. I have a general idea about how the chapters in my book are organized.	_____	_____
4. I skip reading the preface or introduction because they are not part of my reading assignments.	_____	_____
5. Unless the teacher tells us, I don't know anything about the author or his or her purpose in writing the textbook.	_____	_____
6. I understand the purpose of bibliographies or references in the textbook.	_____	_____
7. I use the table of contents to get a general idea of the topics and chapters I'll be studying.	_____	_____
8. When words are in special print, I look them up in the glossary.	_____	_____
9. When the teacher mentions a specific topic or assigns a writing topic, I use the index to locate pages throughout the text that discuss this topic.	_____	_____
10. I know if my textbook gives answer keys or extra exercises in the back of the book.	_____	_____
11. I begin the term reading the chapters and look at the other parts of the book only if they are assigned.	_____	_____
12. I spend several hours surveying my textbook properly.	_____	_____

Surveying The term **surveying** means to preview, overview, or look through information. The purpose of surveying is to help you become acquainted with a book's organization, content, and features. This knowledge enables you to use the book effectively and efficiently throughout the term. Because the information you learn from surveying is helpful all term, plan to survey your textbook as soon as possible—even before your first class.

A textbook can often be surveyed in less than thirty minutes. When you survey, you look at each part and notice certain features, but you don't read thoroughly. The time spent surveying, whether it is thirty minutes or fifteen minutes, is time well spent because you will use the knowledge you gain throughout the term as you study.

The Front Four Four important parts of a textbook are in the front of the book and should be examined during the surveying process.

The Front Four Parts of a Textbook to Survey

1. Title page—name of book, author's name, textbook edition, publishing location

2. Copyright page—date of publication, printing history, publisher's address, Library of Congress ISBN number

3. Table of contents—titles of units and chapters, page numbers

4. Introductory material—information about the author, purpose of the book, special features, acknowledgments

Title Page The **title page** appears first in the front of the book. Many books are revised or updated every few years. If there is no "edition" information under the title, the book is a "first edition." If the book has been revised or updated, the edition number is stated under the title.

The author or authors' names appear next. An author's affiliation to an organization, a university, or a corporation may be mentioned below the name. If the author frequently quotes studies or gives information about an organization, university, or corporation, knowing that he or she is associated with that organization, university, or corporation helps a reader determine if the author shows bias or favoritism.

The page ends with the name of the publishing company and the cities where it is located.

Copyright Page The **copyright page** is on the back of the title page. The copyright date indicates when the book was published. This date is important when you need to know if the material in the book is current. If you are doing research work and two pieces of information seem to contradict each other, knowing the copyright dates of both sources enables you to determine which is more current.

The copyright page also states the publisher's policy for copying or reproducing information in the book. Books that are copyrighted are on file with the Library of Congress. The Library of Congress catalog number is given on this page, as is the **ISBN** (International Standard Book Number). This number can be used to order books from the publisher or from other libraries.

Table of Contents

By surveying the **table of contents,** you get an overview of the topics that are included and the way these topics are organized. By looking at the chapter titles, you may able to tell if the chapters are arranged in a chronological order or if they are arranged according to another pattern. Reading the chapter headings and the subheadings introduces you to the scope of information included in the book.

Page numbers in the table of contents can be used to quickly locate chapters, headings, or special features within the book. The lengths of the individual chapters can also be determined by examining the table of contents.

Introductory Material

The **preface** (pronounced prĕf'ĭs, not prē-fāce) or the introduction tells you the purpose of the book and provides you with information about the author. Introductory material gives you background information about the book, why it was written, why it differs from other books, how it is organized, and what features are included to help you use the book more effectively.

The introductory material is the most important section to read in the front of the book. You can learn to use the book effectively when you read about the organization and purpose of the special features. Special study techniques may also be included to help you read and understand the textbook more thoroughly.

Exercise 5.1   Surveying Introductory Material

When you survey the front parts of a textbook, you *look at* the title page, the copyright page, and the table of contents. You *read carefully* the introductory material.

Read the introductory material for this textbook. Answer the following questions on your own paper.

1. What is the purpose of this book?

2. What are the special features of this book?

3. What did you learn from this introductory material that will help you use this book more successfully?

Exercise 5.2   Surveying Tables of Contents

The first part of the table of contents of two books follows. Work with a partner. Examine each table of contents. Answer the questions following each table of contents.

Contents in Brief

1. Do you think these chapters are organized chronologically? Why or why not?

2. What time period is covered in Chapter 3?

3. When did the Classical Period occur?

1. What are the first three headings for Chapter 1?

2. What page gives you a list of key terms for Chapter 1?

3. What five goals are discussed under the Goals of Research?

The Back Four   After you survey the front parts of a textbook, take time to survey the back of
the textbook for the many extremely valuable parts that will assist you as you
study. Textbooks may vary the information in the back of the book, so as you

survey the following four parts, you may also encounter additional parts not listed here. The following are the four most common parts in the back of the textbook.

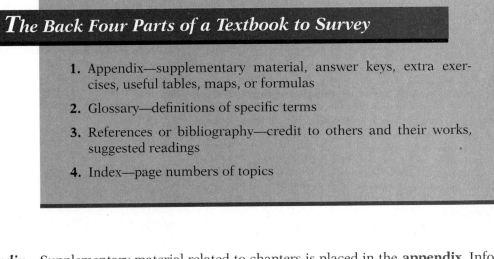

The Back Four Parts of a Textbook to Survey

1. Appendix—supplementary material, answer keys, extra exercises, useful tables, maps, or formulas

2. Glossary—definitions of specific terms

3. References or bibliography—credit to others and their works, suggested readings

4. Index—page numbers of topics

Appendix

Supplementary material related to chapters is placed in the **appendix.** Information that is useful but would break the flow of the chapter or disrupt the reading of the chapter material is placed in the appendix. In a history textbook, for example, the Bill of Rights and the Constitution are important documents, but because of their length, they are better placed as supplementary material in the appendix.

The appendix can contain a wide variety of materials. Answer keys to exercises, additional exercises, practice tests, and additional readings may be found here. Math, science, and social science textbooks often include tables, graphs, charts, or maps in the appendix. If there is a large variety of material placed in the appendix, the author may help keep the information separated by using more than one appendix. Appendix A, Appendix B, and Appendix C may each contain a different type of supplementary information.

Glossary

Survey to see if your book has a glossary. The **glossary** is a mini dictionary. Key terms used in the chapters are clearly defined in the glossary, and these definitions are specifically related to the way the words are used in the textbook. Definitions are not as detailed as those you would find in a standard college dictionary.

Most textbooks use bold print, italic print, or underlining to help you know which words are in the glossary. When you see the special type, take time to review the glossary definitions. You may want to make flash cards or study sheets with key terms and their specific definitions; these vocabulary study tools can help you get ready for tests.

If your textbook does not have a glossary, build a personal glossary of key terms and definitions. Your glossary will be a valuable study tool to help you learn information and prepare for tests.

References or Bibliography

References provide you with the names of the books, magazines, or articles that the author used to write the textbook. If you are working on a research paper or speech, you can check with your library for the books or magazines

listed at the back of your textbook. If you find a topic that is of special interest, you can use this list to expand your knowledge.

The term **bibliography** is sometimes used instead of *references*. (*Graphy* means written record and *biblio* refers to books.) If your textbook does not have a section at the back called References or Bibliography, the information may be found within the chapters.

Small numbers called superscripts may appear after some words or quotes within the chapters. These numbers indicate that the source of the information is cited in a note. Look at the bottom of the page, at the end of the chapter, or in the bibliography in the back of the book to find that source.

Index The **index** is an alphabetical listing of important names, terms, events, and concepts found throughout the textbook chapters. The index is one of the most important sections in the back of the book. You can quickly locate pages throughout the textbook that contain information about a specific topic. If the teacher is talking about a topic and you don't quite understand it, you can use the index to find the pages in the textbook where the topic is discussed. If the teacher assigns a paper or indicates that a particular topic will be on an essay test, the index can help you find pages with information about the topic.

The topic you look up may be found in more than one place in the index. First, look up the word or the topic itself. For example, if you want to find pages for the topic "short-term memory," look in the alphabetical listing for *S* until you find short-term memory. If it is not listed, ask yourself what larger category or subject short-term memory belongs to. The larger category is memory. Look in the *M* section to find the topic "memory." When a word is listed in more than one place, the word is **cross-referenced,** meaning it is listed at least twice in the index.

Your textbook may have more than one index. If many authors are used throughout the textbook, or if there are numerous illustrations or pieces of art, you may, for example, find a second index that lists authors or illustrations. Once you know the types of indexes that are available, you can use them to quickly locate any type of information that you need.

Exercise 5.3   Surveying a Textbook

Select any textbook you are using for a course this term. Survey the front four and the back four parts of the textbook. Answer the following questions.

1. What is the name of the book?_____

2. Who is the author?_____

3. What, if any, university or organization is the author affiliated with?

    _____

4. When was the book published?_____

5. How many chapters are in the book?_____

6. Name three important points you learned by reading the preface or the introductory material.

_____

_____

_____

7. What information is given in the appendix?

_____

_____

8. Is there a glossary?_____

If yes, copy one term and its definition.

_____

_____

9. Is there a bibliography or reference section?_____

10. Name one term you have recently discussed in class:_____

List all the pages where this term is found in the book:

_____

SUMMARY
- Take twenty to thirty minutes at the beginning of the term to survey each of your new textbooks.
- By surveying, you familiarize yourself with the purpose and organization of the eight important parts of a textbook:
  1. Title page
  2. Copyright page
  3. Table of contents
  4. Introduction
  5. Appendix
  6. Glossary
  7. References
  8. Indexes

PERSONALIZING WHAT YOU LEARNED
1. Score and record the score for your chapter profile.
2. On your own paper, expand this chapter's visual mapping.
3. Make your own vocabulary list of all the terms in this chapter that are printed in color.

"To the Student" (p. xv) provides you with more detailed directions for completing these activities.

Review Questions

Matching

Decide which parts of the textbook would best be used to find the desired information. Write the number or numbers of the textbook sections on the blank next to each statement.

---

1. Title page	**5.** Appendix
2. Copyright page	**6.** Glossary
3. Table of contents	**7.** References
4. Introductory material	**8.** Index

_____   **1.** Where would you look to see if answer keys are given?

_____   **2.** At the beginning of the term you want to get an overview of the topics and learn how the topics are related. Where could you look?

_____   **3.** You remember reading about the Pacific Rim countries in several different places. Where would you look to find the pages to review on this topic?

_____   **4.** Some of the information in the textbook no longer seems accurate. Where would you look to see if it is outdated?

_____   **5.** Where would you look to discover the organization of chapters and subheadings?

_____   **6.** You need to get a clearer definition of an important theory. Where would you find it?

_____   **7.** Where would you find the beginning page for the chapter on kinetic energy?

_____   **8.** You want to get a sense of who the author is and what his or her philosophy is regarding the subject of the textbook. Where would you look?

_____   **9.** Where will you find a list of books or articles the author used to write the book?

_____   **10.** Which part of the book clearly shows the name of the author, the publisher, and the edition of the book?

Short Answer

1. What benefits can you gain by taking twenty to thirty minutes to survey a textbook at the beginning of the term before classes begin?

2. Which *two* sections of a textbook do you feel are the most valuable for you to use throughout the term? Explain why (give reasons) these two are the most valuable.

3. Look at the index in this textbook. On the line, identify *all* the pages where you will find the following information.

a. Information about auditory learners _____

b. Howard Gardner's seven intelligences _____

c. Kinds of accommodations for students with learning disabilities _____

d. A special mnemonic device called loci _____

WRITING ASSIGNMENTS

1. Down the left-hand side of your notepaper, list the eight basic parts of a textbook that should be surveyed. After each item, briefly describe the kind of information provided by that section of the textbook.
2. Survey this textbook for the eight basic parts of a textbook. Indicate which parts you find easy to use. If there are parts that are not easy to use, explain why. If there are parts omitted, discuss if you think those parts would strengthen this book.

Using a Reading System

*T*he process of reading college textbooks requires you to comprehend and learn large amounts of information. Does the amount of information in some chapters overwhelm you? Do you sometimes spend time reading and then not know what you have just read? Do you want to know how to condense the information into notes? Do you skip over some words because they are unfamiliar? Do you have difficulty finding the important details to learn? This chapter provides you with a six-step reading system and techniques for improving your comprehension and remembering larger amounts of information.

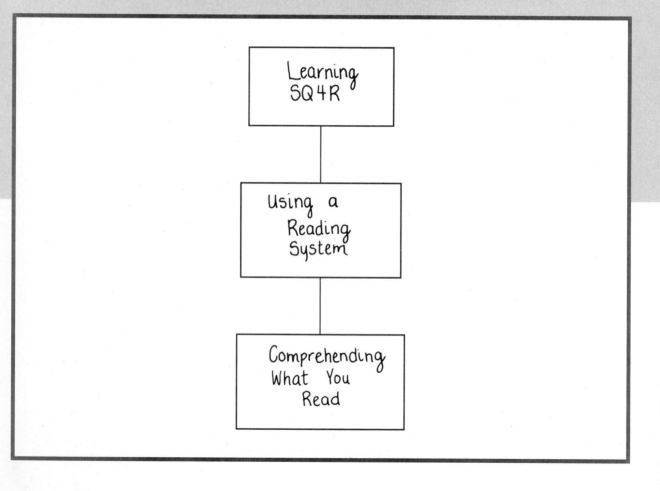

Learning
SQ4R

Using a
Reading
System

Comprehending
What You
Read

Textbook Reading Profile

Please answer honestly each of the following questions about your current attitudes and study habits. Your answers should reflect what you *do*, not what you *wish* you would do.

    After you read each statement, check YES if you do this *always* or *most of the time*. Check NO if you do this *seldom* or *never*.

		YES	NO
1.	When I begin reading a new chapter, I open the book to the first page and read straight through to the end of the chapter.	_____	_____
2.	I read the chapter review questions before I begin reading the chapter.	_____	_____
3.	I write my own study questions for each heading and subheading in the chapter.	_____	_____
4.	I read all the information under one complete heading before I stop to think about what I've read.	_____	_____
5.	I often finish reading a chapter only to find out that I remember very little of what I have just read.	_____	_____
6.	After I read a short section, I stop to highlight, underline, or take notes.	_____	_____
7.	When I study, I am quiet because I do all my practicing or reviewing in my head.	_____	_____
8.	I skip over unfamiliar words as long as I understand most of the other information.	_____	_____
9.	When I don't understand a paragraph, I skip it and hope the next paragraph is easier.	_____	_____
10.	I look for the topic sentence in each paragraph.	_____	_____
11.	I am aware of the general level of my reading skills.	_____	_____
12.	I use a consistent system for reading textbook chapters.	_____	_____

Learning SQ4R   One of the first textbook reading systems, SQ3R, was developed by Francis P. Robinson in 1941. This system acquired its name by using the first letter of each step in the system: survey, question, read, recite, and review. Other systems have been developed for reading textbooks, but they all basically contain the same essential steps found in SQ3R. The **SQ4R system** in this chapter is based on SQ3R with a fourth R added for the "record" step. The SQ4R system thus becomes a six-step approach to reading and comprehending textbooks.

*T*he Steps of SQ4R

1. *Survey* the chapter.

2. Write *Questions* for each heading and subheading.

3. *Read* the information one paragraph at a time.

4. Select a form of notetaking to *Record* information.

5. *Recite* the important information from the paragraph.

6. *Review* the information learned in the chapter.

Step One: Surveying the Chapter   When you first open the book to a new chapter, do not dive right in and begin reading from the beginning of the chapter straight to the end. Instead, learn to use the process of **surveying.**

As you walk through the chapter, there are nine features in the chapter that should get your attention. Some of these features should be read carefully, and some can be glanced over for familiarity.

*H*ow to Survey a Chapter

1. Read the title of the chapter.

2. Read the introduction carefully.

3. Read the chapter objectives carefully.

4. Read the chapter headings and subheadings.

5. Look at the visual aids.

6. Read any marginal notes.

7. Glance at terms in bold or italic letters.

8. Read the chapter study questions.

9. Read the summary carefully.

Title   The topic for the chapter is stated in the title. Read the title and take a moment to relate this topic to the previous chapter or chapters. Do you understand how the chapters are fitting together to form a larger picture or concept?

Introduction   The introduction is a key to understanding the contents of the chapter. It highlights the main ideas and may give you organizational clues about the relationship of ideas. For this reason, read the entire introduction carefully and thoroughly. The introduction may be in the form of a paragraph or a list.

Chapter Objectives   Chapter **objectives** state the goals of the chapter, what the author intends for you to achieve from your reading. These objectives may be in the form of a list or an outline. Read them carefully and thoroughly.

Chapter Headings   The **headings (and subheadings)** appear in a larger or an italic print. Begin moving through the chapter by glancing over the headings and the subheadings. These show you the "skeleton" structure of the chapter.

Visual Aids   When you come to **visual aids,** such as graphs, charts, or pictures, look at them long enough to get a general idea of their content and how they relate to the topic. Read the information printed beside or below them.

Marginal Notes or Insert Boxes   **Marginal notes** are brief comments written in the margins. They may include important terminology or short summaries of main ideas. Inserted boxes may highlight key points or give other information related to the topic. Since they are usually brief, read them carefully.

Terminology   Most textbooks contain many terms and definitions that are important to the content. Words that you should know how to define are often shown in color, in bold print, in italic print, or in underline. Glance at the terms, but do not stop to read the definitions. If you stop to read the definitions, your surveying will become lengthy, and you will be moving into the reading process itself.

Chapter Study Questions   The questions found at the end of the chapter help you review the information the author feels is important to learn. Read these questions carefully. When you begin the reading process, you will have some foresight on the key points to learn in the chapter.

Chapter Summary   The chapter summary should also be read carefully because it highlights the main ideas of the chapter. The summary, like the introduction, helps you identify the main ideas you should be familiar with before you begin your thorough reading.

Surveying the nine features of most chapters takes less than twenty minutes. Surveying the complete chapter gives you an overview of the full chapter contents. If only a portion of a chapter has been assigned, you have the option of surveying only the assigned sections. If the chapter is unusually long, you have the option of surveying only the portion that you plan to study during your study block.

Surveying works to your benefit in several ways:

- Surveying is a warm-up activity that gets your mind focused and prepared for serious work. You will not waste time procrastinating or stumbling through your books and notes trying to find a starting point.

- It increases your motivation, interest, and confidence in learning new information. You may find areas in the chapter that look interesting, stimulate your curiosity, or make you realize that the chapter is not going to be as difficult as you first thought.
- It helps you set goals and manage your time. You will get a general idea about the level of difficulty of the material and the length of the chapter so that you can set goals for the amount of material to cover in a study period.
- It stimulates the learning process by laying a foundation for comprehending the chapter. You will gain insight as to how the chapter is organized and how information is grouped.

| **Exercise 6.1** | **Surveying a Chapter** |

Survey this chapter, and answer the questions on your own paper. Keep track of the time it takes to survey.

1. How long did it take you to survey this chapter?

2. Did you carefully read or just glance at each of the following parts? Copy this list on your paper. On the line, indicate if you read or glanced at this section.

_____ Title

_____ Introduction

_____ Objectives

_____ Headings and subheadings

_____ Visual aids

_____ Marginal notes and inserted boxes

_____ Terms

_____ Chapter study questions

_____ Summary

3. Which of the preceding parts helped you gain an overview or understanding of the contents of the chapter?

Step Two: During the **question step,** you formulate a question for each heading or sub-
Questioning heading in the chapter. The amount of time needed to complete this step varies depending on the number of headings and subheadings in the chapter. Generally speaking, the questioning step requires less than fifteen minutes.

Return to the first heading in the chapter. In the margin of your book or on separate paper, create a question by using one of these question words: *who, what, why, which, when, where,* or *how.* If you write your question on

notebook paper, make a 2¹/₂" margin on the left. Write the question in the left margin. Leave the right side of the page blank. Do not spend time during this step trying to write an answer. Move through the chapter creating your own set of questions for each heading.

Writing your own study questions has several advantages:

- The questions give you a purpose for reading. Natural curiosity then leads you to read so that you can answer your questions.
- Your curiosity can help you concentrate on what you are reading.
- With increased concentration, you gain increased comprehension.
- Your questions help prepare you for future tests. You can prepare for a test by answering your own questions during the review step of SQ4R.

Exercise 6.2	**Writing Questions**

Begin with the first heading in this chapter. Write a question for the heading. Remember, there are two options: Write the question next to the heading in the book, or write the question in the left margin on a piece of notepaper.

Continue through the chapter. Write a study question next to each heading and subheading.

Step Three: Reading Carefully

Some students feel that they should be able to "read fast" to get through the chapter. Others read the chapter only to find at the end of the chapter that they don't remember much of what they have just read; consequently, they find it necessary to reread at least one more time. The **read step** of SQ4R encourages you to read *carefully*. For most textbooks, you should read paragraph by paragraph so that you can concentrate and comprehend one section of information at a time. With careful reading, you will not need to spend valuable study time rereading and rereading chapters.

If the textbook is written on an easy-to-read level and does not contain large amounts of details in each paragraph, you can read more than one paragraph at a time before you stop for the next step. For a very difficult, technical textbook, you may find that you need to read and stop after several sentences rather than at the end of the paragraph. Reading carefully requires this flexibility; the amount you read at a time should be determined by your reading skills and the level of difficulty of the material.

The reading process is also a thinking process. After you have read one paragraph, stop and think about what you have just read. Ask yourself: What did the author just say? What is the main point of the paragraph? What details are important to know?

This process of reading a paragraph, stopping, asking questions, and thinking about the information helps you in several ways:

- Your mind stays focused on the information. Reading too quickly or carelessly puts your mind into **"automatic pilot,"** where little or no information registers in your memory.
- By keeping a stronger focus, you can attain accuracy and higher levels of concentration. The result is better comprehension.

- This approach gives your memory time to process new information before you start demanding that it take in even more information. You also have time to think about information and understand it with greater accuracy.

Step Four: Recording Information

Reading comprehension involves finding main ideas and recognizing important supporting details. This chapter and the next one show you how to locate this information. After you read a paragraph carefully, it is time to **record** into notes the important information you will need to learn. You have four basic choices of notetaking or recording systems to use for the important information:

1. Underlining or highlighting (see Chapter 7)
2. Writing notes in the margins of the book (see Chapter 7)
3. Using the Cornell format to take notes on paper (see Chapter 8)
4. Making hierarchies or visual mappings (see Chapter 11)

After you learn to use all four options, you may find that you prefer one or two of them. If the textbook you are reading is not too difficult, usually one form of notetaking is sufficient. You may find, however, that you prefer to use a combination of two or more systems to help you study and learn. Your goal is to learn how to use all four options and apply them as you feel is most appropriate for the situation.

Recording can benefit you in several ways:

- It gives you a reduced or condensed form of the information that you need to learn.
- Because writing is involved, you are actively involved in the learning process. Your automatic pilot, a passive form of studying, does not have the opportunity to work.
- The writing process also involves fine motor skills, which form another channel into your memory system.

Step Five: Reciting

Before you move on to the next paragraph, stop and recite the information you wrote in your notes. When you **recite,** speak out loud and in complete sentences.

Reciting, one of the twelve memory principles, is valuable for these reasons:

- Reciting requires you to explain the information clearly.
- Reciting provides you with important feedback. If you are not able to recite the information, then you know that you did not understand it very well. Glance back at your notes for clues.
- Reciting leads to active learning, which increases your level and length of concentration.
- Reciting activates the auditory channel to your brain. The more senses you can use in the learning process, the stronger the paths will be to your memory.
- Reciting in your own words helps you avoid rote memorization. You are giving meaning to the information by using your own words.
- When you finish the **read-record-recite cycle** for the paragraph, you have the paragraph's ideas fresh in your memory. You can then connect these ideas to the new information that you will be taking in as you read the next paragraph.

Once you have finished reciting the information just covered, continue to move through the chapter by reading the next paragraph (or section) carefully, recording main ideas and important supporting details, and reciting the new information. As you move through the chapter with this method, you gain a greater understanding of the information, its relationships, and its important points. Your reading is thorough, detailed, and accurate. Your mind is alert, challenged, active, and focused. By devoting time and effort to this careful method of reading, you do not need to reread the chapter again. When you have completed this cycle for the entire chapter, move on to the final step of SQ4R.

Step Six: Reviewing

After you have finished surveying, questioning, reading, recording, and reciting, you take the last step—**reviewing.** Reviewing can be accomplished in a variety of ways. The following activities are helpful for immediate review and ongoing review:

1. Answer the questions in the chapter.
2. Answer the questions that you wrote in the question step.
3. Study and recite from the notes that you took in the record step.
4. Write a summary of the information in the chapter.
5. Personalize the information by asking yourself additional questions: How can this information be used? How does the lecture from class fit in with this information? Why is this important to learn?
6. Create additional study tools such as vocabulary flash cards, study tapes, or visual mappings. (These are discussed in Chapters 10–13.)

Reviewing is a vital step for several reasons:

- An immediate review of information summarizes what you just learned. It provides you with the big picture supported by important details.
- The process of memory involves putting information into your long-term memory and being able to retrieve it from this memory storage when needed. To be able to retrieve information efficiently, you must practice it by reviewing it frequently.
- Frequent ongoing review keeps information fresh in your memory. You have less need to cram or feel unprepared for tests. Also, you can more easily associate new information to information in your memory.

Exercise 6.3   Knowing the Six Steps

Work with a partner. Write the first step of the SQ4R system on the left side of your paper. Across from the name of the step, with your partner list as many important points as you can about the first step without looking back in your book. Repeat these directions for all six steps.

Comprehending What You Read

If you read a paragraph and are not able to understand what the author is saying, taking notes and reciting are impossible. The following techniques can be used in any order to help you comprehend a paragraph that is difficult to understand.

Strategies for Comprehending Paragraphs

1. Assess your reading skills.

2. Read the paragraph out loud.

3. Find definitions for unfamiliar words.

4. Find the topic sentence with the author's main idea.

5. Look for supporting details for the topic sentence.

6. Discover the organizational pattern used for the details.

7. Review your notes for the preceding paragraph.

Assess Your Reading Skills

College level reading requires strong decoding skills (reading multi-syllable words), comprehension skills, vocabulary skills, and critical thinking skills. If you find reading college textbooks to be difficult, you may need to strengthen your reading skills. Check with your school's developmental education department, study skills department, or remedial programs. If reading courses are offered, seriously consider enrolling in one. A struggle with reading can be reduced through reading skills instruction.

If you answer yes to one or more of these questions, you would benefit from reading instruction:

- Do you find that many of the words in your textbooks are unfamiliar?
- Do you often skip words because you can't read them?
- Do you have difficulty sounding out longer words?
- Do you read word by word rather than phrase by phrase?
- Do you frequently have difficulty figuring out what the author is saying?

Read Out Loud

Active reading can be enhanced by reading the information out loud. By saying the words and hearing the words, you give yourself extra assistance in understanding a difficult paragraph. When you read out loud and when you speak, you usually group information into natural phrases, which make the information easier to understand. When you use this technique, read out loud slowly, enunciate clearly, and concentrate on hearing the words. Repeat the process several times.

Find Definitions for Unknown Words

Many readers have a tendency to skip over unfamiliar words. If you skip some words or read words but do not know their meanings, your lack of understanding of a paragraph may be tied to its vocabulary. Specialized vocabulary (or course-specific words) or general vocabulary words may be the source of the problem. If a word is in bold or italic print, that word is specialized vocabulary. You can find the definition several ways:

1. Reading carefully to see if the word is defined within the paragraph. (Chapter 10 discusses specific methods of finding definitions within the context.)
2. Checking for a definition in the glossary of the book. The word will be defined with a definition that matches the way the word is used in the text.
3. Using the surrounding sentences to help you predict a general meaning.
4. Looking up the word in a dictionary.

| **Exercise 6.4** | **Reading Out Loud to Find Definitions** |

1. Read the following paragraph out loud.

> Paleolithic peoples also nourished themselves by gathering nuts, berries, and seeds. Just as they knew the habits of animals, so they had vast knowledge of the plant kingdom. Some Paleolithic peoples even knew how to plant wild seeds to supplement their food supply. Thus they relied on every part of the environment for survival.

   a. Did hearing your own voice help you understand the paragraph?
   b. Use your own words to explain what you read in this paragraph.

2. Read the following paragraph. Circle any words that are unfamiliar to you.

> The basic social unit of Paleolithic societies was probably the family, but the family bonds were no doubt stronger and more extensive than those of families in modern, urban, and industrialized societies. It is likely that the bonds of kinship were strong not just within the nuclear family of father, mother, and children but throughout the extended family of uncles, aunts, cousins, nephews, and nieces. People in nomadic societies typically depend on the extended family for cooperative work and mutual protection. The ties of kinship probably also extended beyond the family to the tribe. A *tribe* was a group of families, led by a *patriarch*, a dominant male who governed the group. Tribe members considered themselves descendants of a common ancestor. Most tribes probably consisted of thirty to fifty people.

   a. What specialized (course-specific) words did you circle?
   b. What general vocabulary words did you circle?
   c. How can you find the meanings of these words?

Find the Topic Sentence

The subject of a paragraph is called the topic. The topic is usually one, two, or three words. Begin by asking yourself: In one, two, or three words, what is this paragraph about? If you still do not know the topic, look for a word or phrase that appears a number of times in the paragraph. This word or phrase often is the topic.

Once you have determined the topic, you can now look for a broad sentence that contains that topic word. By definition, a paragraph is a series of sentences grouped together to develop one specific main idea. The main idea tells the important point the author wants to express in the paragraph; it is expressed in the topic sentence. In textbooks, the topic sentence is often the first sentence. To find the **topic sentence,** ask yourself these questions:

- Does this sentence have the topic word?
- Is this what the author is trying to get across?
- Does everything else in the paragraph relate to this one idea?

If, however, the first sentence does not seem to work as the most important sentence, examine the last sentence. Sometimes details are first presented and then summarized in the last sentence; then the final sentence serves as the topic sentence. The topic sentence can also be located within the body of the paragraph.

Some writers imply the topic sentence; they do not directly state it anywhere in the paragraph. If you cannot seem to find a topic sentence, ask yourself:

- What is the author saying in this paragraph? Answer the question in one sentence in your own words.
- Is there a sentence that says basically this same thing? If the answer is no, the topic sentence may be implied.

Look for Supporting Details   Once a topic sentence is stated, authors support, develop, or explain the topic sentence with supporting details. Supporting information may be

> facts
> statistics
> definitions
> examples
> expanded explanations
> reasons
> causes or effects (outcomes)

You now have the task of sorting through the details in the sentences to find the important **supporting details** and place them in your notes. (Chapter 7 gives you methods for identifying important supporting details.) If you do not identify the important supporting details, you may end up taking too many notes or studying the wrong information.

Exercise 6.5   Finding Topic Sentences and Supporting Details

Work with a partner to complete these questions.

1.   Underline the topic sentence in the following paragraphs:

> Paleolithic peoples also nourished themselves by gathering nuts, berries, and seeds. Just as they knew the habits of animals, so they had vast knowledge of the plant kingdom. Some Paleolithic peoples even knew how to plant wild seeds to supplement their food supply. Thus they relied on every part of the environment for survival.
>
> The basic social unit of Paleolithic societies was probably the family, but the family bonds were no doubt stronger and more extensive than those of families in modern, urban, and industrialized societies. It is likely that the bonds of kinship were strong not just within the nuclear family of father, mothers, and children but throughout the extended family of uncles, aunts, cousins, nephews, and nieces. People in nomadic societies typically depend on the extended family for cooperative work and mutual protection. The ties of kinship probably also extended beyond the family to the tribe. A *tribe* was a group of families, led by a *patriarch*, a dominant male who governed the group. Tribe members considered themselves descendants of a common ancestor. Most tribes probably consisted of thirty to fifty people.

2.   What methods did you use to find the topic sentences?

3. Tell which details in the paragraph provide support for the following topic sentence: "The basic social unit of Paleolithic societies was probably the family, but family bonds were no doubt stronger and more extensive than those of families in modern, urban, and industrialized societies."

Discover the Organizational Pattern   Some readers are able to identify supporting details, but they still have difficulty seeing how the details are related or why they belong in one paragraph under one topic sentence. Discovering the pattern used to organize the details in the paragraph so that they support the main idea can help with comprehension. Although there are many possible **organizational patterns** an author can use, the following patterns are the five most common patterns used in textbooks.

Chronological Pattern   If you look carefully at the details, you may notice that they are presented in a logical time sequence called chronological order. Chronological order is often used when a story is being told (a narrative) or when a procedure or process is being explained. The **chronological pattern** indicates that the details happen in a specific, fixed order to get to a conclusion or a result. The following clue words are used in this pattern: *when, then, before, next, after, first, second,* and *finally.*

Comparison or Contrast Pattern   When two or more objects or events are being discussed, a **comparison pattern** is being used. This pattern can include both likenesses and differences. However, if only differences between two or more objects are being discussed, a **contrast pattern** is used. After you are able to identify the comparison or the contrast pattern, you will more easily understand what is being said about each subject. Clue words that signal likenesses include *also, similarly,* and *likewise.* Clue words that signal differences include *but, in contrast, on the other hand, however, although,* and *while.*

Definition Pattern   Many textbook paragraphs simply explain the meanings of terms. If the term being used is a vital key to comprehending more complex information, an entire paragraph may be devoted to helping you grasp the meaning of the term. A **definition paragraph** often has the term to be defined in bold letters in the first sentence of the paragraph. Definition clue words are *means, is, can be considered,* and *is defined as.*

Examples Pattern   Once an important idea, term, or theory is presented, the author may feel it's important to expand your understanding by giving you clear examples before moving on to new information. In an **examples pattern,** you often see clue words such as *for example* or *another example,* or *an illustration of this.*

Cause/Effect Pattern   Often the relationship between two items shows that one item caused the other item to happen. Sometimes one cause can have more than one outcome or one effect. In other cases, several causes can produce a given effect or outcome. Whenever there is a relationship that shows that one item caused or made the other happen, a **cause/effect pattern** is being used. These clue words indicate a cause/effect pattern: *because, since, so, therefore, caused by,* and *result in.*

These five organizational patterns can help you follow the author's thinking and the purpose of each paragraph. It is important to realize, however, that one paragraph may use more than one organizational pattern. For example, a definition paragraph may use examples to help explain the definition; a cause/effect paragraph may also use chronological order. If you are able to identify more than one pattern working, you are reading carefully and thinking about the details as they are presented.

Review Your Notes   Remember that paragraphs are related to each other. Frequently, the last sentence of one paragraph is used as a transition to the new main idea of the next paragraph. Since you have already taken notes on preceding paragraphs, refer to your notes to see the flow of the ideas from one paragraph to another. With this information, try to predict what the next paragraph in the sequence will discuss. Relate this information to the paragraph you are trying to understand. How does this paragraph fit into the overall structure of all the paragraphs under this heading?

Exercise 6.6   Using Comprehension Strategies

Complete the following exercise with a partner.

1. Find the topic sentence. Underline it.

2. Circle any words you are not familiar with.

3. Find the important details. On the line, tell if you think the details are organized in

> **a.** a chronological pattern
> **b.** a comparison/contrast pattern
> **c.** a definition pattern
> **d.** an examples pattern
> **e.** a cause/effect pattern
> **f.** a combination of patterns

_____ Let the expert do most of the talking while you do the listening. Be alert for opportunities to follow up on responses by using probes, mirror questions, verifiers, or reinforcers. *Probes* are questions that ask the expert to elaborate on a response: "Could you tell me more about how you got the quality circles program started?" *Mirror questions* reflect back part of a response to encourage further discussion. . . . A *verifier* confirms the meaning of something that has been said, such as "If I understand you correctly, you're saying . . ." Finally, a *reinforcer* encourages the person to communicate further. A smile, a nod, or a comment such as "I see" are reinforcers that can keep the interview moving.

_____ *Individual branding* is the strategy in which a firm uses a different brand for each of its products. For example, Procter & Gamble uses individual branding for its line of bar soaps, which includes Ivory, Camay, Lava, Zest, Safeguard, and Coast. Individual branding offers two major advantages. A problem with one product will not affect the good name of the firm's other products. And the different brands can be directed toward different segments of the market. For example, Holiday Inns' Hampton Inns are directed toward budget-minded travelers, Residence Inns toward apartment dwellers, and Crown Plazas toward upscale customers.

_____ A striking idea emerged from observations of people with damage to language areas of the brain. It was noticed that damage to limited areas of the left hemisphere impaired the ability to see or comprehend language, while damage to the corresponding parts of the right hemisphere usually did not. Perhaps, then, the right and left halves of the brain serve different functions.

SUMMARY
- The goal of the SQ4R reading system is to comprehend information as you work through the chapter of a textbook so that you will not need to keep rereading these chapters to learn information.
- Careful, thorough, and accurate reading results when you use the six steps of the SQ4R reading system.

  1. Survey the nine features of the chapter.
  2. Write questions for each heading and subheading.
  3. Read paragraph by paragraph.
  4. Record notes after you read each paragraph.
  5. Recite important information.
  6. Review information frequently.

- Use one or more of the seven comprehension strategies as needed to understand difficult paragraphs.

PERSONALIZING WHAT YOU LEARNED
1. Score and record the score for your chapter profile.
2. On your own paper, expand this chapter's visual mapping.
3. Make your own vocabulary list of all the terms in this chapter that are printed in color.

"To the Student" (p. xv) provides you with more detailed directions for completing these activities.

Review Questions

True-False

To help keep your mind focused, underline the key words in the true-false questions before you answer them.

Write *T* if the statement is TRUE. Write *F* if it is FALSE.

_____ 1. Visual aids should be looked at during the survey step.

_____ 2. Writing study questions for headings and subheadings provides a purpose for reading and improves concentration.

_____ 3. A paragraph may use more than one organizational pattern for organizing the details.

_____ 4. Reciting is important because it includes the auditory channel and provides feedback for understanding.

_____ **5.** The topic sentence is always the first sentence of a paragraph.

_____ **6.** When you read, you should be able to define general vocabulary words and specialized vocabulary words.

_____ **7.** Details in a paragraph support the main idea found in the topic sentence.

_____ **8.** Reviewing notes from previous paragraphs can sometimes be used to help understand a difficult paragraph.

_____ **9.** The introduction and the objectives of a chapter should be skimmed quickly during the survey step of SQ4R.

_____ **10.** For textbook reading, you should usually stop reading after one paragraph so that you can take notes and recite.

Short Answer

1. List the nine parts of a chapter you should look at when you survey.

2. List the six steps of the SQ4R reading system in order. After each step, briefly explain the process to use during that step.

S_____ — _____

Q_____ — _____

R_____ — _____

R_____ — _____

R_____ — _____

R_____ — _____

3. Name at least three activities you can do during the review step of SQ4R.

4. Why is SQ4R an effective reading system?

5. What techniques can you use to find the topic sentence and the important details that support the topic sentence? List at least four.

Fill in the Blanks

The following sentences tell about the seven strategies for comprehending challenging paragraphs. Write a word in the blank to describe the strategy being used in the sentence.

1. I look for the _____ pattern when I try to determine if a paragraph uses chronological order, comparison/contrast or examples.

2. I try to find the _____ sentence, which expresses the author's main idea.

3. After _____ my reading skills, I decide to enroll in reading and vocabulary-building classes.

4. I decide that silent reading doesn't work well, so I _____ out loud.

5. Each time I encounter an unfamiliar word, I try to find its _____.

6. I look at _____ taken on previous paragraphs so I can get a sense of the flow of ideas.

7. After I have found the sentence with the main idea, I actively look for important supporting _____

    _____.

WRITING ASSIGNMENTS

1. Explain what you used in the past as your reading system. Then explain the changes you will make in reading a textbook as you use the SQ4R system.
2. Use the SQ4R system on the next chapter you are assigned to read in this class or in another class. Summarize the results by describing your reaction to using *each* step of the system.

Taking Notes in Textbooks

Contrary to what you may have been told most of your life, you *should* write in your books—especially in your textbooks. But even if you write in them, do you sometimes get confused about which information to mark? When you underline, do you find yourself underlining almost everything? Do you focus better on information highlighted in colors rather than underlined in pen? Are you puzzled about how to use your markings? This chapter shows you methods for selecting the important information to highlight, underline, or turn into notes in the margins of the book.

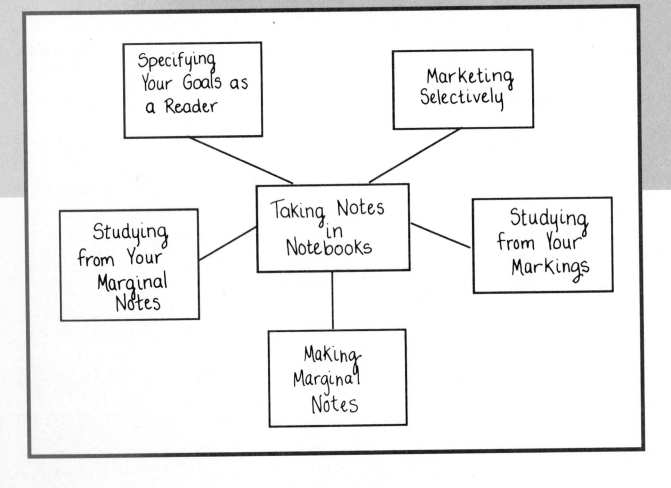

114

Notetaking Profile

Please answer honestly each of the following questions about your current attitudes and study habits. Your answers should reflect what you *do*, not what you *wish* you would do.

  After you read each statement, check YES if you do this *always* or *most of the time*. Check NO if you do this *seldom* or *never*.

		YES	**NO**
1.	I reread chapters at least three times when I am preparing for a test.	_____	_____
2.	When I read a chapter, I am usually able to pick out the important details to study.	_____	_____
3.	When I use highlighting or underlining, I mark most of the paragraph; maybe I underline too much.	_____	_____
4.	After I have read a paragraph, I can usually find the topic sentence with the main idea.	_____	_____
5.	I circle words I know I will have to define.	_____	_____
6.	I make brief notes in the margins of my books.	_____	_____
7.	I use introductions, special print (bold, italic, or colored), and numerals and number words to help me identify supporting details.	_____	_____
8.	When I study from my underlining or highlighting, I concentrate only on what I marked as important; I try to not read the information I didn't mark.	_____	_____
9.	I recite by trying to string the key ideas and supporting details into my own sentences.	_____	_____
10.	I try to recite exact words and phrases instead of paraphrasing.	_____	_____
11.	I know how to use a combination of highlighting and marginal notes.	_____	_____
12.	I allow sufficient time to use ongoing review and reciting of the information I have highlighted, underlined, or written in marginal notes.	_____	_____

Specifying Your Goals as a Reader

A good reader of textbooks and an effective college student must discover how to identify the information that she or he needs to learn. Once identified, this information can then be underlined, highlighted, or summarized in the margins of the book. The purpose of textbook notetaking is to reduce the amount of information to be studied. Underlining or making marginal notes on more than 30 percent of each paragraph is not being selective, whereas identifying just a few words may not lead to thorough understanding or learning.

A good reader of textbooks also reduces overall reading time so that he or she can devote more time to the process of learning. By reading the textbook thoroughly once, selecting the important information, and then focusing attention on that information in notes, a reader gains time to use many of the memory principles discussed in Chapter 4.

Marking Selectively

When you underline or highlight, you are marking the textbook. (Each time you see the term **marking** in this chapter, the term refers to both underlining and highlighting.) Underlining and highlighting use the same techniques but different writing tools. Underlining involves drawing lines under the print with a pen, a lead pencil, or a colored pencil. Highlighting involves covering the print by using light-colored felt markers or highlighting pens.

Experiment with both methods to find your preference. Some students find underlining distracting; the lines close to the print create a type of "double vision." If this is the case for you, experiment with different colors of highlighting pens. The goal is to have the information you select "stand out" and be separated from the non-essential words.

Marking can be done effectively in more than one way. Your marking will not be exactly like another person's, yet both of you can be correct.

Five Steps for Marking

1. Completely underline the topic sentence.

2. Underline key words or phrases that are supporting details.

3. Circle important terminology.

4. Use numbers to label steps or lists.

5. Use brackets or abbreviations in the margins.

Step One: Find the Topic Sentence

After you have read a paragraph, find the **topic sentence**—the main idea—and underline it completely. (For more on topic sentences, see ch. 6.) When you do your studying, a clearly marked topic sentence helps you keep your focus on the author's main point. This is the *only* sentence in a paragraph that should be completely underlined or highlighted. Notice in the following passage that each topic sentence is completely underlined.

> (Networking) In the job-getting process, networking refers to developing a group of acquaintances who might provide job leads and career guidance. The term has been used so much recently that it has perhaps become a buzzword, but it is still an important job-getting tool. Everyone—from the

most recent college graduate to the president of a Fortune 500 firm—has a network on which to draw in searching for a job.

Your initial network might include friends, family, professors, former employers, social acquaintances, college alumni, your dentist, family doctor, insurance agent, local business people, your minister or rabbi—in short, everyone you know who might be able to help. Ideally, your network will combine both personal and professional connections. That's one benefit of belonging to professional associations, and college isn't too early to start. Most professional organizations either have student chapters of their associations or provide reduced-rate student memberships in the parent organization.

Step Two: Find the Supporting Details

By finding the topic sentence, you know the main idea or main point of the paragraph. Now you need to identify the important details that support this topic sentence. If you were asked to explain the topic sentence or "prove" the point made in it, which key words, phrases, definitions, facts, statistics, or examples would you use in your explanation? Locate these **supporting details,** choose **key words** (often nouns, verbs, or adjectives for important details), and mark them. You can skip over words such as "to," "and," "with," "also," and "in addition" because they are not key words. If a key word is used several times, mark it only once. As you are looking for key words, take note of lists, **bullets** (dashes or dots), and marginal notes. All these may indicate important supporting details.

Notice which supporting details are underlined in the following example. Are these the same details you would choose to underline?

(Networking) In the job-getting process, networking refers to developing a group of acquaintances who might provide job leads and career guidance. The term has been used so much recently that it has perhaps become a buzzword, but it is still an important job-getting tool. Everyone—from the most recent college graduate to the president of a Fortune 500 firm—has a network on which to draw in searching for a job.

Your initial network might include friends, family, professors, former employers, social acquaintances, college alumni, your dentist, family doctor, insurance agent, local business people, your minister or rabbi—in short, everyone you know who might be able to help. Ideally, your network will combine both personal and professional connections. That's one benefit of belonging to professional associations, and college isn't too early to start. Most professional organizations either have student chapters of their associations or provide reduced-rate student memberships in the parent organization.

Most paragraphs that you read will have a topic sentence and supporting details. However, on occasion you may encounter a paragraph that does not seem to have any new information. This may be a **transition paragraph;** the information in it does not need to be marked. Transition paragraphs

1. Are designed to help ideas from one paragraph flow smoothly into the next paragraphs
2. Are usually short
3. Do not contain strong main ideas or new details

If the paragraph you are reading is more than a few sentences long and contains new terminology or new ideas, it is not a transition paragraph. Do not skip over it; read more carefully to find the important information to highlight.

Step Three: Find Important Terminology
More than 60 percent of most test questions are based directly on knowing and understanding specialized terminology. For this reason, it is important to identify and mark the terms you need to define. Words that are underlined or printed in bold, italic, or colored print are usually terms to know. Use these special print features to find such key terms. Circle key terms to make them stand out. Then mark the main points of the terms' definitions.

In the following example, notice how the main idea is underlined, key words and phrases are underlined, and terms to know are circled:

Leadership

(Leadership) has been broadly defined as the ability to influence others. A leader has power and can use it to affect the behavior of others. If the power is granted by an organization, the leader is said to have *authority* as well. Leadership is different from management in that a leader strives for voluntary cooperation, whereas a manager may depend on coercion to change behavior. A leader can be a manager, however, and an effective manager will probably display leadership skills. . . .

Styles of Leadership   For many years leadership was viewed as a combination of personality traits, such as self-confidence, intelligence, and dependability. A consensus on which traits were most important was difficult to achieve, however, and attention turned to styles of leadership behavior. In the last few decades several styles of leadership have been identified: authoritarian, laissez-faire, and democratic. The (authoritarian leader) holds all authority and responsibility, with communication usually moving from top to bottom. This leader assigns workers to specific tasks and expects orderly, precise results. At the other extreme is the (laissez-faire leader) who waives responsibility and allows subordinates to work as they choose with a minimum of interference. Communication flows horizontally among group members. The (democratic leader) holds final responsibility but also delegates authority to others, who participate in determining work assignments. In this leadership style, communication is active both upward and downward.

Step Four: Use Numbers
A topic sentence that uses words such as "kinds of," "reasons," "advantages," "causes," "effects," "ways," or "steps" often has a list of supporting details. **Ordinals,** or "number words," such as first, second, third, may point you in the direction of individual details. Use a pen to write the numerals (1, 2, 3) on top of the ordinals. Also watch for words such as "next," "another reason," and "finally," which are "place holders" used to replace ordinals. Read carefully and write a new numeral on these words as well.

Sometimes ordinals are not used. A clue may be given, however, as to the number of details you should find. For example, saying that there are "Five Reasons" for something lets you know that you should find five details. These details can be numbered clearly. With a pen, write "1" where the first item in the list is discussed, write "2" where the second item is discussed, and so on until each supporting detail is numbered. Your final number of details should match the original clue (five reasons).

In the following example, notice how the main idea (topic sentence) is completely underlined, only the key words of supporting details are underlined, and numbers are added to show a list of items:

Consumerism

Consumerism consists of all those activities that are undertaken to protect the rights of consumers in their dealings with business. Consumerism has been with us to some extent since the early nineteenth century, but the <u>movement came to life</u> only in the <u>1960s</u>. It was then that <u>President John F. Kennedy</u> declared that the <u>consumer</u> was entitled to a new "<u>bill of rights</u>."

The Four Basic Rights of Consumers   ①

<u>Kennedy's consumer bill of rights</u> asserted that consumers have a <u>right to safety</u>① <u>to be informed</u>② <u>to choose</u>③ and <u>to be heard</u>④. These four rights are the <u>basis of</u> much of the <u>consumer-oriented legislation</u> that has been passed during the last twenty-five years. These rights also provide an effective outline of the objectives and accomplishments of the consumer movement.

The Right to Safety   The right to safety means that <u>products purchased by consumers must</u>

①
②
③

- Be safe for their intended use
- Include thorough and explicit directions for proper use
- Have been tested by the manufacturer to ensure product quality and reliability

There are <u>several reasons why American business firms must be con</u>cerned about <u>product safety</u>① <u>Federal agencies</u> such as the Food and Drug Administration and the Consumer Product Safety Commission have the <u>power to force businesses</u> that <u>make or sell defective products</u> to <u>take corrective actions</u>. Such actions include offering <u>refunds, recalling</u> defective products, issuing <u>public warnings</u>, and <u>reimbursing</u> consumers—all of which can be expensive② Second, <u>consumers and the government</u> have been <u>winning</u> an increasing number of <u>product-liability lawsuits</u> against sellers of defective products. Moreover, the awards in these suits have been getting bigger and bigger. Producers of all-terrain vehicles, for example, have faced a number of personal injury lawsuits③ Another major reason for improving product safety is the <u>consumer's demand for safe products</u>. People will simply <u>stop buying</u> a product that they believe is unsafe or unreliable.

Step Five: Use Brackets and Abbreviations

After you have read a paragraph carefully, several sentences may seem extremely important because together they provide an important explanation or include many important terms. To avoid too much marking, draw a **bracket** next to the information instead of underlining or highlighting.

The following points are important to remember:

IMP.

1. The bracket reminds you to study the entire marked section.
2. You can use abbreviations in the margins to indicate the content inside the bracket.
3. Common abbreviations used include:

   EX. for example
   DEF. for definition
   IMP. for important
   ? for information you don't understand

4. Use brackets sparingly. Overuse reduces the effectiveness of marking your textbook.

Notice how in the following example, the topic sentence is completely underlined, key words in supporting details are underlined, words to define are circled, numbers are added to show a list, and a bracket is used to set off a large example:

Overcoming Listening Problems

The road to critical listening starts with acknowledging our listening problems. To become more effective listeners, we first need to become more aware of what causes our poor listening behavior. Listening problems are often a function of our personal reactions, our attitudes, and bad habits we have acquired. At best these problems pose a challenge to the careful listener; at worst they defeat communication. . . .

Reactions to Words.   As you listen to a message, you react to more than just the denotative meanings, or dictionary definitions, of words. You also respond to the connotative meanings, the emotional or attitudinal reactions that certain words arouse in you. You may react adversely, for example, to the use of the word *girls* in reference to adult females. The term *girls* acts as a trigger word that sets off a negative emotional response. Suppose a speaker is describing opportunities for advancement in the Crypton Corporation and makes reference to "one of the girls in the typing pool" who moved up into a personnel management position. His use of "girls" suggests to you that this is a sexist organization. As you sit there stewing over his semantic insensitivity, you miss his later statement that over the past three years two-thirds of all promotions into management have gone to women.

[handwritten: EX. "girls" (sexist)]

Exercise 7.1   Marking a Textbook Passage

Read the following passage. In each paragraph, underline the topic sentence and the supporting details. Circle any terms. Add numbers, brackets, and abbreviations as needed.

Body Movement

Because so much of your communication is accomplished face to face, you must understand the role of facial expressions, gestures, and body stance—both in terms of messages you send and in terms of those you receive. This is as true for business communication as it is for social communication.

By far, the most expressive part of your body is your face—especially your eyes. Research shows that receivers tend to be quite consistent in their reading of facial expressions; and many of these expressions, such as smiling, have the same meaning across different cultures. Eye contact and eye movements tell you a lot about a person, although maintaining eye contact with the person with whom you're communicating is not perceived as important (or even polite) in some cultures.

Gestures are hand and upper-body movements that add important information to face-to-face interactions. As the game of charades proves, you can communicate quite a bit without using oral or written signals. You've probably known people who "talk with their hands." Pointing, waving, clapping hands, placing your hands on your hips, and indicating how large something is are all gestures that help to illustrate and reinforce your verbal message.

Body stance (posture, placement of arms and legs, distribution of weight and the like) is another form of nonverbal communication. For example, leaning slightly toward the person you're communicating with would probably be taken as a sign of interest and involvement in the interaction. Leaning back, arms folded across the chest, on the other hand, might be taken as a sign of boredom or defiance.

Studying from Your Markings   The process of marking is only the beginning step in learning. You must now *use* these markings to help you learn important information.

How to Use Marking

1. Reread only the marked information.
2. String the marked information together to make sentences.
3. Recite and write the important information marked.

Reread   Read what you have marked. Do *not* let yourself reread the information that is not marked. Review these notes slowly to allow time for your mind to absorb, connect, and associate the information. You may want to read out loud to help your concentration and increase your comprehension.

String Ideas Together   Look at the marked information again. Instead of just reading, **string** the words, phrases, and sentences together by using some of your own words to connect the ideas together in full sentences. As you string the ideas together, include the main idea and the important supporting details. This is an ideal time to turn on a tape recorder if you would benefit from having a review tape to use for studying. In addition to verbalizing the ideas, you can practice picturing or visualizing the information in the paragraph.

The following example shows underlining and then one possible way to string the ideas together to make complete sentences:

> In her book *Writing the Natural Way*, Gabrielle Rico explains the method she devised to help her students get in touch with the creative, inventive part of themselves. Rico calls the part of ourselves that is always trying to be logical and put things in the right order the "Sign mind." The other creative part of ourselves that is longing to express our well-hidden imagination and artistic ability she calls the "Design mind." Rico's Sign mind . . . controls, judges, and supervises. To get out from under this watchdog, who tends to strangle our creative impulses in their early stages, Rico suggests the strategy she calls clustering as a way of giving your playful, curious Design mind free rein to generate ideas.
>
> IMP.   Begin with a nucleus word circled on an empty page. Then go with any connections that come into your head, writing each down in its own circle. Connect each new word or phrase with a line to the previous circle. "As you cluster," Rico warns, "you may experience a sense of randomness or, if you are somewhat skeptical, an uneasy sense that it isn't leading anywhere. . . . Trust this natural process, though. We all cluster mentally throughout our lives without knowing it; we have simply never made these clusterings visible on paper.

When you look only at the marked information, this is what you'll see:

- Gabrielle Rico explains the method she devised to help her students get in touch with the creative, inventive part of themselves.
- logical, right order—"Sign mind"

- other creative part, imagination and artistic ability—"Design mind"
- "Sign mind" controls, judges, and supervises
- strangle our creative impulses
- strategy, clustering
- playful, curious "Design mind," generate ideas
- Begin with a nucleus word circled on an empty page.
- natural process
- We all cluster mentally.

When you string the foregoing information together into your own sentences, you may end up with something like this:

Rico uses a method to get in touch with the creative, inventive part of people. The logical part of our minds that tries to put everything in a right order is called the "Sign mind." The other creative part of our minds has imagination and our artistic ability. This part is called the "Design mind." The Sign mind always tries to control, judge, and supervise our thinking. It strangles our creative impulses. Rico has a strategy called clustering that helps the playful, curious Design mind to generate ideas.

Clustering begins with a nucleus word circled on an empty page. New words that are related to the nucleus are written down and connected to the nucleus. This is a natural process. We all cluster mentally.

Exercise 7.2   Stringing Ideas Together

Select a partner. You and your partner will practice stringing ideas together in complete sentences. The following selections in this chapter can be used for this exercise. You and your partner should each choose a different selection.

Networking (pp. 116–117)
Leadership (p. 118)
Consumerism (pp. 118–119)
Overcoming Listening Problems (p. 120)
Body Movement (p. 120)
Writing the Natural Way (p. 121)

1. Take a few minutes to reread the chosen selection. Pay special attention to the marking. You may mark additional words or phrases to identify the main idea and the supporting details you feel are important.

2. Listen to each other string the underlined words, phrases, and sentences into meaingful, complete sentences.

3. Take turns looking away from your selection and reciting the information from memory. Your partner can tell you if you included the main idea and the supporting details in your reciting.

Recite and Write   You can now use reciting and writing to reinforce the information and plant it more firmly in your long-term memory. String ideas together again, except this time do *not* look at the marking to help you. *Recite from memory;* then look back to check your accuracy.

Writing is used to take notes either in the margins or on notebook paper (See Chapter 8). Writing can also be used to summarize the material. Writing a summary of the marked information is an excellent way to reinforce your learning and provide you with an overview of the material. A summary should include the *main idea* in a complete sentence and a brief statement of *major supporting details.*

Notice the use of underlining and summarizing in the following example about the art of narration:

The Art of Narrating

Whether it is written or told aloud, a narrative is simply a story that describes an event or a series of closely related actions. One of our great American writers, Flannery O'Connor, has written about telling stories. "There is a certain embarrassment about being a storyteller in these times when stories are considered not quite as satisfying as statements and statements not quite as satisfying as statistics; but in the long run, a people is known, not by its statements or its statistics, but by the stories it tells."

There are all kinds of stories, however, not just make-believe ones, that a writer can tell. In its simplest terms, narration gives a chronological account of what happened, such as when a newspaper reports on a forest fire or summarizes the events of a baseball game. To explain a theory, a physicist may narrate a hypothetical account of how our solar system was formed. Historians narrate their reconstructions of past events. . . .

Like all writing that tells a story, this paragraph uses blow-by-blow narration not simply for its own sake, but in the service of a main point. If you think about it, most stories you tell already have a point you want to get across—why you broke up with someone you were seeing and what happened afterward; why a certain relative is crazy and what he or she has done lately to prove it. These stories and others like them are narratives with a main point to illustrate.

A summary of the preceding information could read as follows:

A narrative is a form of writing that tells a story in chronological order. The narrative story tries to get across one specific main point. Narratives are used by many different kinds of writers, including newspaper reporters, physicists, and historians. Individuals who want to tell their own personal stories also use narratives.

Exercise 7.3   **Writing a Summary**

Read the following passage carefully. Mark the main idea and the important supporting details. Use your marking as a guide to write your own summary. Your summary should consist of at least one paragraph.

Metamemory

How people try to remember something, and consequently how well they perform, is shaped to a great extent by what they know about memory (Cavanaugh, 1988). **Metamemory** is the name for knowledge about how your own memory works. It consists of three types of knowledge (Flavell, 1985; Flavell & Wellman, 1977).

First, metamemory involves understanding the abilities and limitations of your own memory. Preschool children are notoriously weak in this kind of understanding. They know that the way people look does not affect their memory, that noise interferes with remembering, and that it is harder to remember many items than a few. But they deny that they ever forget anything and claim that they can remember quantities of information beyond their own (or someone else's) capacity (Flavell, Friedrichs, & Hoyt, 1970). Only in the school years do children learn the limits—and the strengths—of their memories.

Second, metamemory involves knowledge about different types of tasks. For example, children learn to use different strategies for memorization when they know they will face a short-answer test, which requires recall, rather than a multiple-choice test, which for the most part requires only recognition (Horowitz & Horowitz, 1975).

Third, metamemory involves knowledge of what types of strategies are most effective in remembering new information. This aspect of metamemory is the most likely to change dramatically with age and experience (Fabricius & Wellman, 1983). Consider the use of rehearsal. Children as young as five may rehearse items when they are asked to remember something (Flavell, Beach, & Chinsky, 1966; Istomina, 1975). But most five-years-olds do not use rehearsal to help them remember. They learn to rehearse in elementary school, and they refine their rehearsal strategies over the school years.

Making Marginal Notes

You can also write questions, lists, summaries, comments, or key words in the margins of the book. **Marginal notes** must remain brief so that the page is not cluttered or difficult to use.

You can make marginal notes after you have done your marking. When a textbook is relatively easy to read and does not contain large amounts of information, you may see no need to mark; notes in the margins are sufficient.

Note how marginal notes help clarify the following passage:

Sign Mind
-logical
-controls
-judges
- Strangles creativity

Design Mind
-creative
-imagination
-artistic
-curious

(Nucleus)

Clustering

IMP

In her book *Writing the Natural Way*, Gabrielle Rico explains the method she devised to help her students get in touch with the creative, inventive part of themselves. Rico calls the part of ourselves that is always trying to be logical and put things in the right order the "Sign mind." The other creative part of ourselves that is longing to express our well-hidden imagination and artistic ability she calls the "Design mind." Rico's Sign mind . . . controls, judges, and supervises. To get out from under this watchdog, who tends to strangle our creative impulses in their early stages, Rico suggests the strategy she calls clustering as a way of giving your playful, curious Design mind free rein to generate ideas.

Begin with a nucleus word circled on an empty page. Then go with any connections that come into your head, writing each down in its own circle. Connect each new word or phrase with a line to the previous circle. "As you cluster," Rico warns, "you may experience a sense of randomness or, if you are somewhat skeptical, an uneasy sense that it isn't leading anywhere. . . . Trust this natural process, though. We all cluster mentally throughout our lives without knowing it; we have simply never made these clusterings visible on paper.

In the following example, the student did not feel that marking was needed. Marginal notes were sufficient.

Using Context Clues

build rdg.
↓
guess unfamiliar word meanings

An important part of building your reading skills is learning how to guess what unfamiliar words mean. Very often a word that you have seen before will appear in a sentence. Perhaps it is a word that you have seen before,

Use
Context
Clues
first
<u>def.</u>
Context
Use
dictionary
last

but you do not remember its meaning. Maybe it is a word whose meaning you thought you knew, but the meaning does not make sense in the sentence that you're reading.

All readers, even the best and the most experienced, come across such words from time to time. You see a word, and it stumps you. You don't know its meaning quickly. But don't reach for a dictionary right away! (Use your dictionary when nothing else works.) Often you can figure out what a word means from clues in the sentence that it appears in or in surrounding sentences. Such clues are context clues; context here means surrounding words, phrases, sentences, and paragraphs that help you find out meanings.

Studying from Your Marginal Notes

Once you have taken marginal notes, your studying and reviewing should focus on these notes. When used properly, marginal notes provide you with excellent triggers to discuss and summarize what you have read. The following three techniques can be used.

How to Use Marginal Notes

1. Read and recite from your notes.
2. Explain the relationships between ideas and paragraphs.
3. Visualize the information.

Read and Recite   Read the lists of key words, words to define, or questions written in the margins. Discuss the information out loud, speaking in complete sentences. Look back at the paragraph only to check your accuracy.

Explain Relationships   Spend some of your studying time explaining how concepts relate to each other and how supporting details strengthen the main idea. Reflect on how the information in one paragraph relates to the information or the big picture of other paragraphs.

Visualize   As you recite and explain relationships, allow sufficient time to picture the information. Make a "movie in your mind" to help you comprehend and remember the information.

SUMMARY
- Review time should focus on working with your textbook markings and marginal notes, not on rereading chapters again and again.
- To use marking:
  1. Underline the main idea and the important details, circle important terminology, number steps and lists, and write brackets and abbreviations in the margins.
  2. Reread the marked information.
  3. String the marked information together into complete sentences.
  4. Recite and write the information.

- To use marginal notes:
    1. After you have completed marking the paragraphs, write questions, lists, summaries, comments, or key words in the margins of the book.
    2. Read and recite the marginal notes.
    3. Explain the relationships between ideas and paragraphs.
    4. Visualize the information.

PERSONALIZING WHAT YOU LEARNED
1. Score and record the score for your chapter profile.
2. On your own paper, expand this chapter's visual mapping.
3. Make your own vocabulary list of all the terms in this chapter that are printed in color.

"To the Student" (p. xv) provides you with more detailed directions for completing these activities.

Review Questions

Multiple Choice

Read each question carefully with all the options. Cross out the options that you know are incorrect. Select the best option that remains. Write the letter of the best option on the line.

_____ 1. Terms to be defined can be differentiated from other kinds of supporting details by

    a. underlining them.
    b. circling them.
    c. adding bullets.
    d. putting brackets by the definitions.

_____ 2. As you mark your textbook, you can use numbers when

    a. bullets are used to indicate details.
    b. ordinals are used in a paragraph.
    c. the topic sentence indicates a given number of items.
    d. all of the above.

_____ 3. Writing can reinforce learning each time you

    a. write summaries.
    b. take notes or write summaries.
    c. make notes in the margins.
    d. take separate notes on notebook paper.

_____ 4. A transition paragraph

    a. connects one paragraph smoothly to the next paragraph.
    b. introduces a new main idea.
    c. is always the shortest paragraph on the page.
    d. usually has the topic sentence as the first sentence.

_____ 5. Important supporting details can be marked by

    a. numbers.
    b. colored felt pens.
    c. brackets.
    d. all of the above.

_____ **6.** Studying from markings and marginal notes involves

    a. rereading entire paragraphs and reciting.
    b. rereading the chapter, reciting, and visualizing.
    c. reciting.
    d. reciting, visualizing, and writing summaries.

Short Answer

1. Explain how marking should be studied.

2. Explain how marginal notes should be studied.

Marking Textbooks

Read the following passage carefully. Mark _and_ make marginal notes.

Make Nervousness Work For You

As you give your first speech, it is only natural for you to have some **communication apprehension**. In fact, there would be something wrong with you if you didn't have such feelings. The absence of any nervousness could suggest that you do not care about the audience or your subject. Almost everyone who faces a public audience experiences some kind of concern. We once attended a banquet where an award was presented to the "Communicator of the Year." Before sitting down to eat, the recipient of this award confessed to us, "I really dread having to make this acceptance speech!" We were not at all surprised when he made a very effective speech.

There are many reasons why public speaking is somewhat frightening. The important thing is not to be too anxious about your apprehension. Accept it as natural and remind yourself that you can convert these feelings into positive energy. One of the biggest myths about public speaking classes is that they can or should rid you of any natural fears. Instead, they should teach you how to harness the energy generated by apprehension so that your speaking is more dynamic. No anxiety often means a flat, dull presentation. Transformed anxiety can make your speech come to life.

How can you put this energy to work for you? Begin by understanding how it can become a problem. Some people develop a negative dialogue with themselves and actually talk themselves into being less effective. For example, they might say to themselves, "Everybody will think I'm stupid," or "Nobody wants to listen to me." If you find yourself engaging in self-defeating behavior, consciously replace such statements with positive messages that focus on your ideas and your audience. For example, "I've done my research, so I know what I'm talking about" could substitute for "I'm going to sound stupid." This approach to controlling communication anxiety, called **cognitive restructuring**, is a habit you can acquire by deliberately replacing negative thoughts with positive, constructive statements.

WRITING ASSIGNMENTS

1. To be a successful student, you must learn how your own memory works. Write one paragraph for each aspect of memory as it relates specifically to you:

   a. The abilities and limitations you have noticed with your memory

   b. The different types of tasks that challenge your memory

   c. The kinds of strategies that enable you to learn new information

2. Write a summary of this chapter. Include the important categories of information that you have learned about marking and taking marginal notes.

Using Cornell for Textbook Notes

Strong notetaking skills are essential for college students, yet many students find it difficult to take good notes. Do you find it difficult to understand your notes after a short period of time? Do you end up with pages and pages of notes that you seldom study? Are your notes cluttered or difficult to read? This chapter introduces you to the five-step Cornell notetaking system, which enables you to take efficient and effective notes.

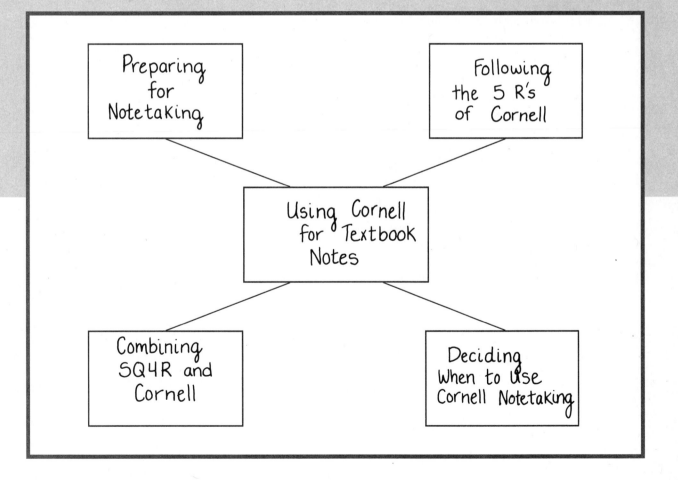

Preparing for Notetaking

Following the 5 R's of Cornell

Using Cornell for Textbook Notes

Combining SQ4R and Cornell

Deciding When to Use Cornell Notetaking

Cornell Notes Profile

Please answer honestly each of the following questions about your current attitudes and study habits. Your answers should reflect what you *do*, not what you *wish* you would do.

After you read each statement, check YES if you do this *always* or *most of the time*. Check NO if you do this *seldom* or *never*.

		YES	NO
1.	I take notes only on the front side of my notebook paper.	_____	_____
2.	I study more from my textbook than I do from the notes I take on textbook information.	_____	_____
3.	I am selective when I take notes; I write down only the important ideas and details.	_____	_____
4.	I use an organized, detailed outline when I take notes.	_____	_____
5.	I leave a double space in my notes before I begin a new heading.	_____	_____
6.	After I take notes on a paragraph, I recite what I wrote before moving on.	_____	_____
7.	My notes remind me about important charts, graphs, or pictures in the textbook.	_____	_____
8.	I practice reciting new information by using a special reduced column of notes.	_____	_____
9.	I take time to think about and reflect on the information in the chapter.	_____	_____
10.	I use the back side of my notebook paper to make lists of information or questions.	_____	_____
11.	I plan time each week to review information that I learned in previous weeks.	_____	_____
12.	I always use just one kind of notetaking when I am working with a textbook.	_____	_____

Preparing for Notetaking

This chapter introduces the powerful five-step Cornell notetaking system, which you can use for taking notes from textbooks and taking notes from lectures. The strength of the system is in its steps; if you choose to eliminate any one step, you weaken the system. This notetaking system was designed by Dr. Walter Pauk at Cornell University more than forty years ago when he recognized students' need to learn how to take more effective notes. Many college and university teachers consider this system to be the most effective notetaking system for college students.

Effective notetaking is important for several reasons:

1. You become an active learner when you seek out important information and write it down.
2. You focus on organizing the information logically.
3. You select the important information and reduce it to a form that is easy to study and review.
4. You have reduced notes to use for continual review throughout the term.

To begin, you need notebook paper with a *two-and-one-half-inch margin down the left side of the paper.* Many bookstores now carry Cornell notebook paper with this larger margin or a spiral "Law Notebook" with perforated Cornell-style pages. If you are not able to find the Cornell notebook paper for your three-ring notebook, draw a margin on the front side of regular notebook paper (see p. 132). All your notetaking is done on the front side only; the backs are for other purposes.

At the top of the first page, write the course name, chapter number, and date. For all the following pages, just write the chapter number and the page number of your notes. Later you may want to remove your notes from your notebook; having the pages numbered prevents disorganization.

Following the Five *R*'s of Cornell

The goal of notetaking is to take notes that are so accurate and that have such details that you *do not need to go back to the book to study.* Your studying, your learning, can take place by working with your notes as you use the **five *R*'s of the Cornell system:** record, reduce, recite, reflect, and review.

---

*T*he **R**'s of Cornell

1. *R*ecord your notes in the right-hand column.

2. *R*educe your notes into the recall column on the left.

3. *R*ecite out loud from the recall column.

4. *R*eflect on the information that you are studying.

5. *R*eview your notes immediately and regularly.

Step One: Record

The wider right-hand column is for your notes. In this first step, **record**, read each paragraph carefully, decide what information is important, and then record that information on your paper. Your notes should be *a reduced version* of the textbook. Be selective, or you will wind up wasting your notetaking time and your studying time.

The author of your textbook has helped you tremendously by providing you with a structured organization of the information through the use of headings and subheadings. Use these headings and the following suggestions for the first *R* of Cornell.

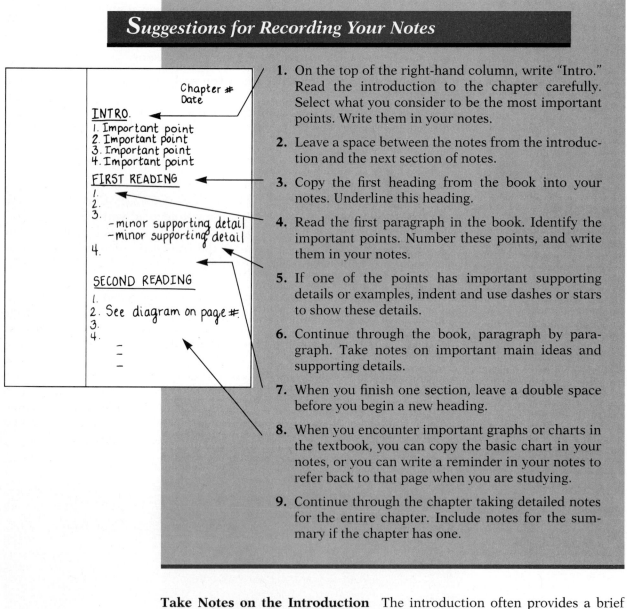

Suggestions for Recording Your Notes

1. On the top of the right-hand column, write "Intro." Read the introduction to the chapter carefully. Select what you consider to be the most important points. Write them in your notes.

2. Leave a space between the notes from the introduction and the next section of notes.

3. Copy the first heading from the book into your notes. Underline this heading.

4. Read the first paragraph in the book. Identify the important points. Number these points, and write them in your notes.

5. If one of the points has important supporting details or examples, indent and use dashes or stars to show these details.

6. Continue through the book, paragraph by paragraph. Take notes on important main ideas and supporting details.

7. When you finish one section, leave a double space before you begin a new heading.

8. When you encounter important graphs or charts in the textbook, you can copy the basic chart in your notes, or you can write a reminder in your notes to refer back to that page when you are studying.

9. Continue through the chapter taking detailed notes for the entire chapter. Include notes for the summary if the chapter has one.

Take Notes on the Introduction   The introduction often provides a brief overview of the content of the chapter. By listing the key ideas in your notes, you will be able to see later if you understood and captured all the key points.

Leave Spaces Between Sections   Notes that are crowded or cluttered are difficult to study. By leaving a double space between each new heading or section of your notes, you are visually grouping the information that belongs together. You are also **"chunking"** the information into smaller units, which will help your memory.

Use the Headings   The headings are the "skeleton," or outline, of the chapter. Take advantage of this structure by always starting a new section of notes with the heading. Underline the heading so that it stands out from the rest of your notes.

© 1994 by Houghton Mifflin Company

Record Important Points   Since you will use your notes for studying, *record enough information to be meaningful later:*

- Avoid using only individual words or short phrases that will lose their meaning when you return to them later.
- Use short sentences.
- Do not copy down information word for word. Shorten the information by rewording or summarizing it.
- If you find some sentences or short sections that are so clearly stated that you want to copy them, omit any of the words that are not essential for your understanding.
- If you have already marked the information, move the same information into your notes.
- Number the ideas as you place them into your notes. Numbering helps you remember how many important points are under each heading and breaks the information into smaller, more manageable units.

Record Important Minor Details   You will frequently encounter minor details that belong under an idea that you already numbered. Indicate these details by *indenting* and then using *dashes or stars* before writing the details.

Include Graphs and Charts   Graphs, charts, diagrams, and pictures contain valuable information. Do not overlook these visual materials when you are taking notes. You can include visual information in your notes by *copying the visual* into your notes or by *writing a reminder to review the page with that visual.*

The following example shows Cornell-style notes for Exercise 7.3:

<u>Metamemory</u>

1. How people try to remember and how well they perform are shaped by what they know about memory
2. Metamemory - DEF. - knowledge about how your own memory works
3. Metamemory = 3 types of knowledge:
   - understanding abilities and limitations of your memory
     - EX: Preschooler knows people's looks don't matter but noise interferes and it's harder to remember many items

   - involves knowledge about different types of tasks
     - EX: different strategies for memorizing for short-answer recall than multiple choice

   - involves knowledge of types of strategies most effective to learn new information
     - EX: this knowledge changes with age and experience
     - EX: refine rehearsal strategies as get older

Step Two: Reduce   After you have finished taking notes for the chapter, you are ready to close the book and begin **reducing.** Now for the first time, you will be writing in the left-hand column, the **recall column.** Remember, in step one you reduced the textbook information to the most important points and details. In step two, you are going to reduce your notes one step further. These reduced notes will provide you with a feedback system so that you will know what information you have learned well and what information needs more effort. You will also refer to this column frequently for review.

Suggestions for Reducing Your Notes

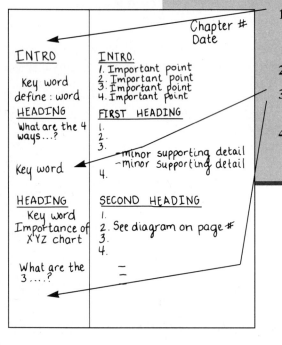

1. Copy the heading into the recall column directly across from the heading in your notes. Underline that heading.

2. Reread the notes that are under that heading.

3. Write a study question or a key word in the recall column directly across from the notes.

4. Be very brief so that you can challenge yourself and get immediate feedback.

Copy the Heading   In your notes, the heading provided organization. The same is true in the recall column. To avoid having rambling, unorganized reduced notes, place the heading directly across from the heading in your notes. Make it stand out by underlining it.

Reread the Notes   Learning the information continues as you reread your notes. If your notes seem vague, incomplete, or nonsensical, go back to the book and add any necessary details.

Write Study Questions and Key Words   Directly across from each important detail, write yourself a reminder about that detail. You can write it as a brief study question. You do not need to use complete sentences; abbreviated forms, such as the following, work: Why? How many kinds of . . . ? Name the 6 . . . Related to X how? Another option is to simply write key words. These may be words that you will need to define or relate to other ideas.

Be Brief   You will be using this recall column for the next step of studying. It is important that the column not be cluttered with too much information. If you give yourself all the answers, you will end up reading the information and not challenging your memory. Remember to be selective by focusing only on key words or study questions.

The following example shows the recall column for the notes on metamemory:

Metamemory	Metamemory
What shapes memory?	1. How people try to remember and how well they perform is shaped by what they know about memory
Metamemory – DEF.	2. Metamemory – DEF. – knowledge about how your own memory works.
3 types of knowledge in metamemory? 1. abilities + limitations	3. Metamemory = 3 types of knowledge: – understanding abilities + limitations of your memory EX: ✳ Preschooler knows people's looks don't matter but noise interferes and it's harder to remember many items
2. types of tasks	– involves knowledge about different types of tasks EX: ✳ different strategies for memorizing for short-answer recall than multiple choice
3. strategies	– involves knowledge of types of strategies most effective to learn new information EX: ✳ this knowledge changes with age and experience EX: ✳ refine rehearsal strategies as get older

Step Three: Recite   **Reciting** is a powerful tool for learning information and strengthening memory. If you are able to recite information accurately, you are learning. If you are not able to recite information accurately, you immediately know that more time and attention are needed. This **immediate feedback** is the strong benefit of this third step of Cornell.

Suggestions for Reciting

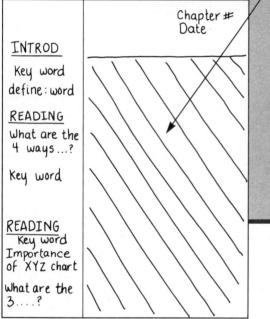

1. Cover up the notes on the right.

2. Start at the top of the recall column. Read the heading and the first key word or question.

3. Talk out loud in complete sentences. Explain the information.

4. If you don't remember the information, uncover the right-hand column. Reread the information. Cover it up and try reciting it again.

5. Move through your notes in this manner.

6. Adjust the recall column as needed.

Cover the Notes   Use a blank piece of paper to cover the notes on the right-hand side. Since you see only the recall column, you can now understand the importance of placing the headings in the recall column to help you remember the overall organization.

Read and Then Recite   Read the headings and the key words or questions. Without looking at your notes, answer the questions and tell what you remember about the key words. Pretend you are explaining the information to a friend. *Talk out loud in complete sentences*.

- If you can verbalize the information accurately, you probably understand it.
- If you "go blank," that is valuable feedback that you are not yet ready to move on. Simply pull the paper down, read the information, cover it up, and try again. Reciting after you reread enables your memory to begin processing the correct information.
- If you are not sure if you recited the correct information, also pull the paper down to check your accuracy. The positive feedback you receive for correct answers will strengthen your memory of them.

Continue Reciting   Move through your entire set of notes by reciting, checking accuracy, and reciting again. Remember to take full advantage of this system by using the feedback to look at your notes and recite again.

Adjust the Recall Column Sometimes it is difficult to know how much and what kind of information to put in the recall column.

- If you found that you did not give yourself enough cues to recite important points, add more key words or study questions to the recall column.
- If you found that you wrote all the important information in the recall column and you ended up reading what was there, you had nothing left to recite from memory. Cross out (or white out) some of the details before you recite again.
- Star the information you did not recall the first time. Pay extra attention to these areas the next time you recite.

Exercise 8.1   Using the First Three *R*'s

Read the following selection paragraph by paragraph. Mark the main ideas and important supporting details. Then do the first three steps in the Cornell system: Record, reduce, and recite.

Maslow's Hierarchy of Needs

The concept of a hierarchy of needs was advanced by Abraham Maslow, a psychologist. A **need** is a personal requirement. Maslow assumed that humans are "wanting" beings who seek to fulfill a variety of needs. He assumed that these needs can be arranged according to their importance in a sequence known as Maslow's **hierarchy of needs** (see p. 138).

At the most basic level are **physiological needs**, the things we require to survive. These needs include food and water, clothing, shelter, and sleep. In the employment context, these needs are usually satisfied through adequate wages.

At the next level are **safety needs**, the things we require for physical and emotional security. Safety needs may be satisfied through job security, health insurance, pension plans, and safe working conditions.

Next are the **social needs**, the human requirements for love and affection and a sense of belonging. To an extent, these needs can be satisfied through the work environment and the informal organization. But social relationships beyond the workplace—with family and friends, for example—are usually needed, too.

At the level of **esteem needs**, we require respect and recognition (the esteem of others), as well as a sense of our own accomplishment and worth (self-esteem). These needs may be satisfied through personal accomplishment, promotion to more responsible jobs, various honors and awards, and other forms of recognition.

At the uppermost level are **self-realization needs**, the needs to grow and develop as people and to become all that we are capable of being. These are the most difficult needs to satisfy, and the means of satisfying them tend to vary with the individual. For some people, learning a new skill, starting a new career after retirement, or becoming "the best there is" at some endeavor may be the way to satisfy the self-realization needs.

Maslow suggested that people work to satisfy their physiological needs first, then their safety needs, and so on up the "needs ladder." In general, they are motivated by the needs at the lowest (most important) level that remain unsatisfied. However, needs at one level do not have to be completely satisfied before needs at the next-higher level come into play. If the majority of a person's physiological and safety needs are satisfied, that person will be motivated primarily by social needs. But any physiological and safety needs that remain unsatisfied will also be important.

Maslow's hierarchy of needs provides a useful way of viewing employee motivation, as well as a guide for management. By and large, American business has been able to satisfy workers' basic needs, but the higher-order needs present more of a problem. They are not satisfied in a simple manner, and the means of satisfaction vary from one employee to another.

Self-realization needs

Esteem needs

Social needs

Safety needs

Physiological needs

Maslow's Hierarchy of Needs
Maslow believed that people seek to fulfill five categories of needs

Step Four: Reflect   To **reflect** means to "think or consider seriously." The reflect step can be individualized and can include a wide variety of activities and study tools. Several reflect activities are listed here. Chapters 11, 12, 13, and 14 cover many additional types of reflect activities, and Part III shows how flash cards, mappings, time lines, tapes, memory tricks (mnemonics), and more can be used in this step.

Suggestions for Reflecting

1. Take time to think about the information in your notes.

2. Line up your recall columns to see the overall structure of the chapter.

3. Relate the information to previous information and to your personal background.

4. Write your own summary at the bottom of your notes.

5. Use the back side of your note paper to make lists of information or questions.

Take Time to Think   Reflecting lets the information register and settle in your brain. It also allows you to look at the information from your own point of view and to think of ways to extend the information beyond its original context.

When you reflect, look away from the book and your notes. Spend time pondering the information. You may want to ask yourself some basic questions:

1. What were the major ideas in this chapter?
2. What did I find the most interesting?

3. How can I work with this information further?
4. How does the title reflect the content of the chapter?
5. Do I agree with everything I read? Why or why not?

Line Up the Recall Columns   To gain an overview of the entire chapter, remove your note paper from your notebook. Arrange your notes on a table so that you can see all the recall columns lined up in sequence from left to right. By looking at the headings and the details, you will see the entire outline for the chapter. If you enjoy studying from outlines, you could convert this information into outline form to use for review.

Find Relationships   Memory often gets triggered when you make associations between the information you are learning and the information you already know. Take the time to think about the relationships between ideas. Ask yourself a few basic questions:

1. How are ideas A and B alike? How are they different?
2. How do these ideas relate to those in the previous chapters?
3. Which ideas could be grouped together? Why?
4. How does this information relate to what I already know?
5. How does this information relate to my life?

Write a Summary   Without looking at your notes or textbook, write a summary that contains the important points in the chapter. Your summary should include the main ideas and brief statements of major supporting details. Compare your summary to the summary in your textbook (if there is one); if you find that you omitted some important ideas, add these to your written summary. Save this summary because it is a good review tool to use before tests.

Write on the Back Side of Your Note Paper   The back of your note paper is now available for you to make additional lists of information or summaries. You can also include diagrams or charts to show how different ideas are related. If you have questions that you would like to ask the instructor, jot them down on the back, too. The backs are convenient and available, so use them as needed.

Exercise 8.2   Reflecting on Maslow's Hierarchy

Work in groups of three or four students to discuss answers to the following reflect activities for Maslow's hierarchy (as presented in Exercise 8.1).

1. Do you agree that "humans are 'wanting' beings who seek to fulfill a variety of needs"? Why or why not?
2. Does Maslow say a person must completely meet the needs of one level before he or she can begin working on the next level? Do you agree or disagree? Why?
3. How do you think colleges and employers can help individuals fulfill these needs? Brainstorm your ideas and list them in the following chart for each level of needs.

Needs	Colleges Help Meet Individuals' Needs	Employers Help Meet Individuals' Needs
Physiological		
Safety		
Social		
Esteem		
Self-realization		

Step Five: Review   This last step of the Cornell system keeps the information active in your memory. Review provides the repetition you need to retrieve information quickly and accurately from your long-term memory.

Suggestions for Reviewing

1. Plan time for immediate review.
2. Plan time weekly for ongoing review.

Do an Immediate Review   Reviewing actually begins when you are working at the fourth step. In the reflect step, you take time to think about the information you have covered, and you take time to create additional study tools. However, **immediate review** goes one step further. Before you close your book and quit studying, take a few additional minutes to review your recall columns. This provides one final opportunity to strengthen your memory for the organization and content of the material.

Ongoing Review   **Ongoing review** means reviewing previous work so that you are continually practicing learned information. Ongoing review is necessary because you will be storing more and more information in your long-term memory as the term progresses and so you must make sure that "old" information is practiced. In addition, by including ongoing reviews in your weekly study schedule, you save time in the long run. When tests, midterm exams, or final exams approach, you won't need to cram for you will have kept the information active.

Several activities can take place during ongoing review:

1. Review the recall columns of your notes. The more frequently you review these, the faster you can move through the columns. Also, as the term progresses, you will find that information placed in your notes early in the term is now clear and easy to understand.
2. Review any reflect or review materials that you created earlier.
3. If you have a list of questions from the second step of SQ4R or your own written summary, review these.
4. Review chapter introductions, summaries, and lists of vocabulary terms for the chapter.

Deciding When to Use Cornell Notetaking

There are four main textbook notetaking options: marking, marginal notes, separate notes using the Cornell system, and visual mappings or hierarchies (see Chapter 12). You can select these options based on the course, the level of difficulty of the material, and your own preferences.

Choosing the Most Appropriate Notetaking System

1. Use *one* form of notetaking for easy textbooks.

2. Use *two* forms of notetaking for textbooks with larger amounts of information.

3. Use *three* and *four* forms of notetaking for textbooks that are difficult and challenging for you.

Use One Form of Notetaking

If the course and the textbook are relatively easy for you, *one form of notetaking* is sufficient. In other words, you can select marking important information, making notes in the margins, taking Cornell notes, *or* making visual mappings. Your choice of methods can be based on the following:

1. If I am going to use only one form of notetaking, which method will best help me clearly see the main ideas and important supporting details when I study?
2. If I decide to take only Cornell notes or visual mappings, is this choice made simply to avoid writing in my book? If the answer is yes, consider the benefits of being able to write directly in the book. The time saved and the benefits of choosing the method that works best for you may outweigh your reservations.

Use Two Forms of Notetaking

If the course and the textbook have large amounts of important ideas, facts, and supporting details that are new to you, using two forms of notetaking may bring better results. Consider several common combinations:

1. Mark main ideas and important details that support the main idea. Move this information into your Cornell notes.

2. Mark main ideas and supporting details. Make marginal notes.
3. Make Cornell notes for the chapter. Convert the Cornell notes into visual mappings to study and review.

Use Three or Four Forms of Notetaking

When you take a course that is very difficult or challenging, you may feel that you need "all the help you can get." Using three or four forms of notetaking allows you to work with the information in more than one way; this added variety and exposure often provide the practice, thinking, and memory work needed to learn thoroughly. Because of the time involved, you would not want to use this intensive approach for every course, but recognize that it is available.

There are several possible ways to sequence three or four forms of notetaking.

1. Marking, marginal notes, Cornell notes
2. Marking, Cornell notes, visual mappings
3. Marginal notes, Cornell notes, visual mappings
4. Marking, marginal notes, Cornell notes, visual mappings

Combining SQ4R and Cornell Notetaking

You have now learned two very powerful study methods for mastery learning. SQ4R (Chapter 6) is a six-step system for reading a textbook; Cornell is a notetaking system that can be used with textbooks. Consider how these two systems can be combined effectively.

Combining SQ4R and Cornell

Begin the SQ4R Steps

1. *Survey:* Do an overview for the chapter.

2. *Question:* Write questions for each heading.

3. *Read:* Read one paragraph.

4. *Record:* Take Cornell notes on separate paper.

5. *Recite:* Recite the important information in the paragraph.

6. Continue to read-recite-record to the end of the chapter.

Continue the Cornell Steps

7. *Reduce:* Make your recall column.

8. *Recite:* Cover your notes and recite from your recall column.

9. *Reflect:* Do one or more reflect activities.

10. *Review:* Review your notes, and complete the chapter and the questions you made in the second step of SQ4R.

Note that you begin with the first three steps of SQ4R: Survey, question, and read. The Cornell system then merges with the reading system for the record step. (Record is step four of SQ4R and step one of Cornell.)

Once you have completed the reading and taken the notes, put the book aside. Focus your attention on the Cornell notes you have taken and the remaining steps of Cornell: Reduce, recite, reflect, and review. Join the review step in SQ4R with the review step in Cornell. You have now successfully combined two powerful systems for learning.

Exercise 8.3   Taking Cornell Notes

Return to the selection "Make Nervousness Work for You," (Chapter 7, page 127). Use your marking as a guide for making a set of Cornell notes for this selection. Complete your notes by making the recall column.

Exercise 8.4   Taking Cornell Notes from Your Textbook

In any of your textbooks, select a heading that is followed by at least three paragraphs. Take Cornell notes on all the information given for that heading. Then prepare a recall column for your notes.

SUMMARY
- The Cornell system provides you with a five-step method for recording and learning information accurately and thoroughly.
- You will become an active learner when you use all five R's of Cornell:

1. Select the important information and record it in the right-hand column of your note paper.
2. Reduce the information to key terms or study questions; write this reduced information in the left-hand column.
3. Cover up the right-hand side of your notes while you recite information in complete sentences; use the left-hand column as a guide for reciting.
4. Reflect on the material, finding relationships and creating study tools.
5. Use immediate and ongoing review to rehearse information.

- The Cornell notetaking system can easily be incorporated into the SQ4R reading system; thus, two powerful study systems are combined to increase your learning potential.

PERSONALIZING WHAT YOU LEARNED
1. Score and record the score for your chapter profile.
2. On your own paper, expand this chapter's visual mapping.
3. Make your own vocabulary list of all the terms in this chapter that are printed in color.

"To the Student" (p. xv) provides you with more detailed directions for completing these activities.

Review Questions

True-False

To help keep your mind focused, underline the key words in the true-false questions before you answer them.

Write *T* if the statement is TRUE. Write *F* if it is FALSE.

_____   **1.** The majority of your review time should be spent working with your notes.

_____   **2.** Cornell notes are a reduced version of textbook information.

_____   **3.** It is best to read the whole chapter first and then go back to take notes.

_____   **4.** It is not necessary to take notes on graphs, charts, or pictures since they are always easy to remember.

_____   **5.** The best feedback occurs when you read the paragraph the first time.

_____   **6.** Too much information in the recall column causes you to read and not do much reciting.

_____   **7.** More questions or key words can be added to the recall column if there are too few cues to help you recite.

_____   **8.** If you are short on time, it is best to always skip the fourth step of Cornell.

_____   **9.** Ongoing review gets you in the habit of using repetition as a regular part of studying.

_____   **10.** If you mark your textbook and take Cornell notes, basically the same information will appear in both notes.

Short Answer

1. List the five *R*'s of Cornell in order.

2. List three activities you can do in the reflect step.

Notetaking
1. Read the following information about Howard Gardner's seven intelligences.
2. Take Cornell notes on this information.
3. Complete the recall column.
4. Practice reciting from your recall column.

5. Complete the reflect activity.
6. Review your work.

HOWARD GARDNER'S SEVEN INTELLIGENCES

Psychologist Howard Gardner challenges the traditional concept that IQ tests, which focus on verbal, visual-spatial, and logical mathematic skills, measure people's aptitudes or abilities. Gardner believes that these three categories do not cover the many other kinds of intelligence that people possess. In *Frames of Mind, The Theory of Multiple Intelligences*, Gardner presents a new approach to exploring intelligence. In it he identifies seven kinds of intelligence that recognize a wider range of human talents, abilities, and potentials.

Linguistic intelligence is composed of verbal and language abilities. People with high linguistic intelligence share several common characteristics. They have a definite curiosity about words, a fascination for meanings, and a love of language. They are sensitive to how words are used, how they sound, and the feelings that words convey. These individuals possess sharp, detailed, and vivid memories about written and spoken words and the emotions attached to them. They often express this ability through writing prose or poetry. People with well-developed linguistic intelligence often become writers, poets, or journalists.

Musical intelligence surfaces in people with an acute sensitivity to melody (pitch), rhythm, and tones. Strong auditory memory, imagination, and creativity enable these individuals to express feelings and images through music. Individuals with gifted musical intelligence often become composers, conductors, and performers.

Individuals with *logical mathematical intelligence* understand the properties of objects in the physical world as well as abstract numerical symbols, operations, and relationships. These individuals can use complex mathematical reasoning and think abstractly with great accuracy and speed. As a result, they often become mathematicians, computer programmers, or scientists.

Visual-spatial intelligence exists in people who can readily see sizes, shapes, textures, lines, curves, angles, and depths accurately and precisely. These people do not have difficulty distinguishing one form from another even when forms are rotated or portrayed in three-dimensional forms. They have a strong sense of direction and of spatial relationships between objects. Their ability to visualize is well developed. For example, a gifted chess player can play a challenging game of chess even if he or she is blindfolded. Individuals with developed visual-spatial intelligence may favor work in the areas of science, engineering, or visual arts.

A graceful dancer, a record-setting athlete, a talented actor, a sensational guitarist, and an inspiring mime artist all share the *bodily-kinesthetic intelligence*. They have developed fine and precise body rhythms, body movements, and motor coordination. Such individuals have an acute sense of timing and can judge how their bodies will respond in certain situations. This form of intelligence is evident in inventors, performers, instrumentalists (such as guitarists and pianists), and athletes.

Individuals with *intrapersonal intelligence* are genuinely concerned with their own personal growth, self-understanding, and achievement of greater personal potential. The prefix *intra* means "within" or "inside of." Individuals with this intelligence, therefore, strive to know their own feelings, sense of values, goals, and personal history. Such individuals often project a sense of pride, confidence, self-responsibility, control, and empowerment. They are able to select appropriate behaviors in public, monitor and control their emotions and reactions, and adapt to or cope with a wide variety of surroundings and circumstances. These talents by themselves can be used effectively in most kinds of work; however, they often are combined with interpersonal intelligence.

Interpersonal intelligence refers to effective communication, social skills, and leadership abilities. People with a high level of interpersonal intelligence are able to participate and work cooperatively in a group, create bonds with a variety of other people, and feel a sense of responsibility toward others. This intelligence enables individuals to accurately interpret the behavior, motivation, and intentions of others. Teachers, counselors, therapists, and people in healing arts often possess interpersonal intelligence or abilities. The skills involved in parenting also utilize this intelligence.

Howard Gardner encourages the academic world to broaden its thinking and approaches to teaching so that individuals with strong music, bodily-kinesthetic, intrapersonal, and interpersonal intelligence are also recognized for their talents. With this recognition, students will be able to experience greater successes in school and utilize the talents they possess.

Reflect on this article: How would your educational experiences have been different if all seven intelligences had been recognized?

WRITING ASSIGNMENTS

1. Write a short summary of each of the five steps of Cornell. Do not refer to your notes.
2. Compare your old notetaking system to the Cornell system. How are they alike? How are they different? What differences do you think you will see in your level of understanding and your grades when you begin using Cornell? Why?

Using Cornell for Lecture Notes

*C*apturing important information given during lectures is essential, yet without specific strategies, it can be difficult to do effectively. Do you have trouble writing fast enough to keep up with the speaker? Do part of your notes make no sense when you reread them? Do you ever decide to just listen because notetaking is too frustrating? Do some of your instructors seem to get off track and discuss information out of sequence? This chapter explores methods to help you reduce your notetaking frustrations and improve the quality of notes you take during lectures.

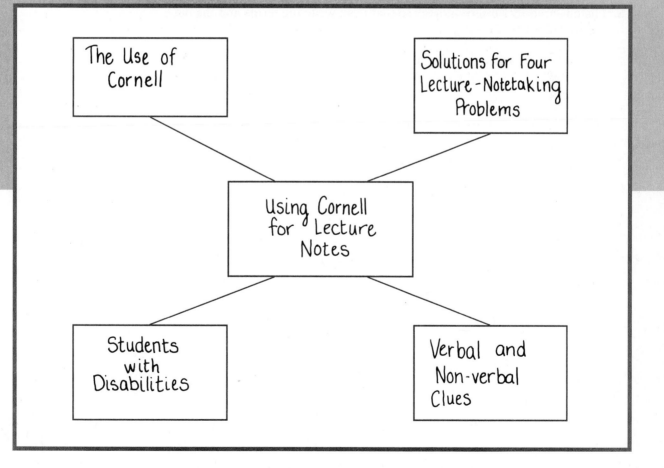

Lecture Notes Profile

Please answer honestly each of the following questions about your current attitudes and study habits. Your answers should reflect what you *do*, not what you *wish* you would do.

After you read each statement, check YES if you do this *always* or *most of the time*. Check NO if you do this *seldom* or *never*.

		YES	NO
1.	I have problems knowing what information to put into notes.	_____	_____
2.	My notes make little or no sense to me after the lecture.	_____	_____
3.	My notes are neat and easy to read.	_____	_____
4.	I spend time going over my notes and filling in missing information as soon after the lecture as possible.	_____	_____
5.	I use numbers to help identify the individual important points or supporting details.	_____	_____
6.	I listen carefully for terminology so that I can write the terms and the definitions in my notes.	_____	_____
7.	If I get behind and can't keep up, I stop writing and start listening more carefully.	_____	_____
8.	I know techniques for keeping my mind on the lecture if the speaker speaks slowly or is boring.	_____	_____
9.	I try to reword what is said so I don't write word for word.	_____	_____
10.	I practice reciting important information in my notes.	_____	_____
11.	I look for an instructor's verbal and nonverbal communication patterns to help me identify what information is important.	_____	_____
12.	I can usually take notes that are adequate and easy to use for studying.	_____	_____

The Use of Cornell

Capturing information from lectures is important for several reasons:

- Lectures help you understand the course content better.
- Lectures often clarify or expand textbook information.
- Lectures help identify and emphasize the important course information that you are expected to learn.
- Lectures provide additional information or points of view that are not included in the textbook.

The Cornell notetaking system presented in Chapter 8 showed you a five-step notetaking process to use with textbook information. You can use the same five steps to take notes from lectures. Review the five 5R's in the following box.

The Five R's of the Cornell System

1. *Record* information on the right-hand side of the page. Use headings. Number details.

2. *Reduce* the information into the recall column as soon after the lecture as possible.

3. *Recite* the information in the recall column. Use complete sentences. Check your accuracy.

4. *Reflect* on the information in your notes. Use a variety of reflect activities. Create new study tools.

5. *Review* your notes. Use immediate and ongoing review.

Exercise 9.1   Brainstorming About Lecture Notes

Brainstorming is a process of generating as many ideas as possible. Each group member contributes ideas, and all ideas are accepted by the group for the list. With a partner, or in a small group, brainstorm to make a list of problems you have encountered while trying to take good lecture notes. As you compile the list of notetaking difficulties, you will likely see that others have encountered the same problems. You will find solutions for these problems as you study this chapter.

Solutions for Four Lecture-Notetaking Problems

For many students, taking notes from a textbook is not too difficult because the information is printed and the pace for taking notes is controllable. Lectures, however, present new notetaking problems. In this section, you explore four common problems in taking notes from lectures and strategies for overcoming them.

Four Common Lecture-Notetaking Problems

1. Weak listening skills can result in notetaking difficulties.

2. The differences among *rate of speech, writing speed, and thinking speed* cause notetaking problems.

3. *Selecting and organizing appropriate information* to place in notes can be difficult.

4. *Spelling problems* can slow down notetaking.

Strengthen Your Listening Skills   Of the four verbal communication skills (listening, speaking, reading, and writing), listening skills are often the weakest. Unfortunately, many students have received limited or no training to strengthen listening skills, which are essential for understanding lectures. The following three solutions can strengthen your listening skills and thus have a positive effect on notetaking for lectures.

Use Concentrated Listening Strategies   Recall how you used the phrase **DATE IAN** to help you remember the seven methods for improved, concentrated listening. These seven methods are as follows:

- Use **concentration strategies** to eliminate internal and external *distractors* so that you are able to focus your attention on the speaker and his or her ideas.
- Pay *attention* to details as well as the large picture they form. This helps you follow the speaker's ideas better.
- Stay *tuned in*, even if information is difficult to follow. Continue to take notes. You can sort through the notes and try to increase your understanding after class.
- Monitor your *emotions*. Do not overreact to information that you disagree with or that stirs negative reactions. Your task is to listen and record, not debate the lecturer.
- Create an *interest* in the topic of the lecture. Look for its value and purpose.
- *Ask* questions at appropriate times. Asking questions creates an interest in the subject and can clarify information for your notes.
- Be *nonjudgmental* about the speaker's appearance, mannerisms, and speech patterns. You have plenty of work cut out for you during notetaking; keep your attention focused on content.

Practice, Practice, Practice   Make concentrated listening a habit by practicing it frequently during social get-togethers, business or organizational meetings, church, family conversations, and talks with friends.

Enroll in a Listening Course   Check your school catalog to see if your college offers a course designed to develop critical listening skills. If such a course is available, consider enrolling in it. The benefits of improved listening skills will be apparent in many areas of your life, including your skill at taking lecture notes.

Use Speaking,
Writing, and
Thinking Speeds
Wisely

The differences among the speaker's speaking speed, your writing speed, and your thinking speed create the largest obstacles to overcome in notetaking. When you take notes from a textbook, *you* control the pace. You have the liberty to reread, think through what you have read, and selectively decide what to place in your notes. These advantages do not exist during notetaking from a lecture; the control has shifted to the lecturer. Here are some strategies for using the differences in speed to your advantage.

Adjust to Speaking and Writing Speeds   Most instructors try to lecture at a rate that makes notetaking possible. The average **rate of speech** during a lecture is 100–125 words per minute. Instructors who speak rapidly may be speaking at the rate of about 150 words per minute. The problem is that the usual **rate of writing** is only about 30 words per minute. Obviously, it is not possible to write word for word what the instructor says. Yet getting every word written down is what some students try to do. Such notetakers get frustrated; they either quit taking notes completely, or they end up with fragmented notes that are meaningless.

The following solutions can help you deal with the difference between speaking rate and writing speed:

1. Ask other students in class if they are also having difficulties keeping up. If the problem exists for several students, *schedule an appointment* with the instructor. Many instructors are willing to slow down their rate of speech once they are aware that their rapid speech is creating notetaking problems.
2. Devise a system of *abbreviations*. For example:

BC. for because	PRES. for president
EX. for example	SOC. for social or sociology
IMP. for important	SOL. for solutions
POL. for politics	W/OUT for without

3. Develop a system of *symbols* to represented frequently used words.

ᕁ	and	→	leads to/causes
@	at	<	less than
↓	decreases	>	more than
≠	doesn't equal	#	number
≞	equals	+/–	positive/negative
↑	increases	∴	therefore

4. Practice writing *abbreviated sentences*. You can leave out small words such as "a, an, the," and unnecessary verbs. The general meaning of the sentence must, however, still be clear without these words.
5. *Leave a gap* in your notes when you get behind. Try to get on track again for as long as possible. After class, ask another student or the instructor to help you fill in the gaps.
6. *Practice taking notes* as often as possible. You can do this in every one of your classes; you can also practice at home. Practice taking notes as you watch an educational channel on television, attend a meeting, listen to a sermon, or talk on the phone.
7. If you have extreme difficulties keeping up, even after you have given serious effort to the preceding solutions, request permission from the instructor to

tape the lectures. Allow additional study time to listen to the tape or part of it again.

8. If you have documented disabilities and qualify for a notetaker, *arrange for these services* as soon as possible. (Accommodations are discussed at the end of this chapter and in Chapter 12.)

Adjust to Speaking and Thinking Speeds   Even though the average rate of speech during a lecture is 125 words per minute, the average **rate of thinking** is about 400 words per minute. A new form of notetaking problems occurs if you have an instructor who speaks too slowly or dwells too long on one example without saying anything new. In this case, you are listening, but you feel there is nothing new to write. Before long, your concentration decreases; your mind wanders, you begin to doodle, or you may simply stop taking notes.

The following four techniques are solutions that help you keep your mind focused on the lecture so that you can be an effective listener and notetaker:

1. *Keep writing.* Even if the details don't seem vital to your notes, write them anyway. This keeps you actively involved with the lecture.
2. *Mentally summarize.* Let the main ideas and supporting details that have already been discussed run through your mind. Try to mentally summarize them.
3. *Anticipate the next point.* Try to anticipate the speaker's next point. Then listen carefully to see if you were correct.
4. *Mentally question the information.* Do you agree with the information that has been presented? How does it relate to the information presented last week or the information in the textbook?

Select and Organize Appropriate Information   Most lectures are organized with headings that show main ideas and supporting details. You can learn to recognize when new headings or new main ideas are presented by listening for key words or clues that signal a shift from one idea to another. You can also learn to identify important details such as explanations, facts, statistics, steps, and reasons. When you do, you will be able to select important information and organize your notes more effectively. Try these strategies:

1. *Meet with your instructor* to discuss the problems you are having in organizing your notes. The instructor may be able to identify mistakes you are making or give you suggestions based on her or his style of lecturing.
2. Ask your instructor if you can *get an outline* of the lecture or if she or he can write an outline on the chalkboard or overhead at the beginning of class. Some instructors will provide this information once a student explains the value of being able to see the big picture before the lecture.
3. *Listen for key words* that often signal the beginning of a new heading. (These words also work to help you identify what information should be found in supporting details.) Some of these words include

advantages	effects	parts	stages
benefits	factors	principles	steps
causes	findings	purposes	techniques
characteristics	functions	reasons	types of
conclusions	kinds of	rules	uses
disadvantages	methods	solutions	ways

For example, if the instructor says, "According to Elisabeth Kübler-Ross, there are five stages a person goes through when he or she is faced with death," you know that this is the heading and that you will have five numbers or categories listed under that heading.

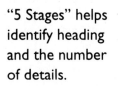

"5 Stages" helps identify heading and the number of details.

Sociology
October 14

KÜBLER ROSS'S THEORY OF DYING

5 Stages

1. Stage 1
   -supporting detail
   -supporting detail
2. Stage 2
   -supporting detail
3. Stage 3
   -supporting detail
4. Stage 4
   -supporting detail
5. Stage 5
   -supporting detail
   -supporting detail

4. *Number the ideas* under the heading. Indicate supporting details with dashes.

5. *Listen for ordinals* that signal individual points or details. When you hear "first," make that point number 1 under the heading. Remember to listen for other transition words that are place holders for ordinals. The following are common signals or indicators to help you number supporting details in a list:

first	next	in addition
second	also	last
third	another	finally

6. When you hear *words being defined,* get the information into your notes. Use the abbreviation *DEF.* in your notes. If you are not able to get complete definitions, refer to your textbook or glossary after class, and add additional information to your notes.

7. If the instructor talks too quickly for you to decide if a detail is a supporting detail to be numbered, or a minor detail that belongs under a supporting detail, instead of listing ideas, *change to a **paragraph style.*** By quickly rewording what you hear, you can **paraphrase** the information and then write it as a block of information. You can sort through the information later when you make the recall column.

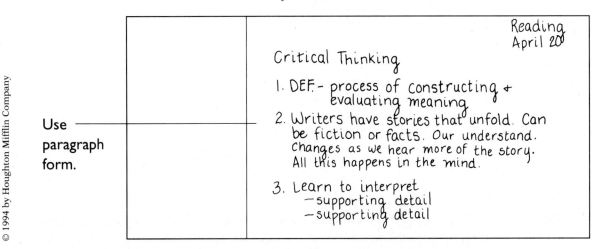

Use paragraph form.

Reading
April 20

Critical Thinking

1. DEF. - process of constructing + evaluating meaning
2. Writers have stories that unfold. Can be fiction or facts. Our understand. changes as we hear more of the story. All this happens in the mind.

3. Learn to interpret
   -supporting detail
   -supporting detail

8. Some organizational problems occur because the instructor discusses something that does not seem to fit the outline of the lecture. When you know this has happened, continue to *take notes on any of the "sidetracked" information* that may be important. Try to organize this information under headings with main ideas and important supporting details. Where should you place this information in your notes? There are two options that work well:

- Since you are taking notes on only one side of the paper, use the back side of the previous page of notes. Record your sidetracked notes here.
- Continue to take notes in the Cornell column. When you finish taking the sidetracked notes, draw a box around this information to set it off from your regular set of notes.

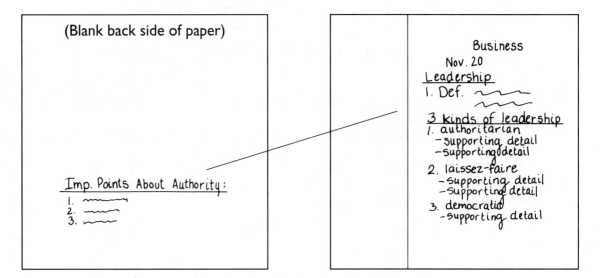

Sidetracked information

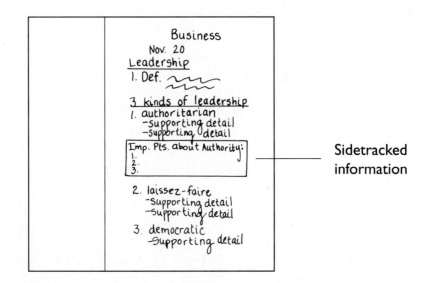

Sidetracked information

Overcome Spelling Problems Many students slow down their notetaking when they get stuck on the spelling of a word. In most cases only you will be seeing your notes, so spell the word the best you can. Later you can correct your spelling errors. Here are some other solutions for spelling problems:

1. If your instructor's lectures follow the textbook, plan to *read ahead* before the lecture. You will then be somewhat familiar with key words and their spellings. Even if you are not able to spell a word correctly, you may be closer to the correct spelling for having seen the word once or twice before.

2. *Sound the word out* by writing what you hear. As soon after class as possible, when you develop the recall column, correct the spelling. To correct spelling errors, you can:

   - Ask another student for the spelling.
   - Check with your textbook.
   - Use a reference book of common misspellings and correct spellings.
   - Use a portable spellchecker or a dictionary.

3. Enroll in a *spelling class.* Many strategies are available to help you learn how to spell more accurately. Approaches in teaching spelling have changed drastically over the years, so explore new strategies to improve your spelling skills.

Exercise 9.2   Taking Lecture Notes

Select any one of your classes. Use the Cornell system to take notes from one of the lectures. On your own paper, identify the class, the topic, and the instructor's name. Answer the following questions. Turn your answers in with your lecture notes.

1. What problems did you have taking notes from this lecture?

2. What are possible solutions for the problems you had?

3. How soon after the lecture did you work on the recall column? Did this seem effective? Why or why not?

4. Did the recall column work for you? Did it give you enough or too much information to help you with reciting? Explain.

Verbal and Nonverbal Clues

There are other verbal and nonverbal clues that can help you identify the important information to place in your notes. **Verbal clues** are words or directions given by the instructor. **Nonverbal clues** are directions given through body movements such as facial expressions, hand gestures, and body stance.

Notice Verbal Clues

Words such as "kinds of," "steps," "causes," and "advantages" are clues for main ideas or important supporting details that should be found in your notes. Following are additional verbal clues to listen for:

"This is important. You need to know and understand this."
"This will be on the next test."
"As I have already said (ideas are repeated)."
"Be sure you copy this information (from the overhead or chalkboard)."
"If you haven't already done so, be sure you read carefully the information on pages . . . "
"I can't emphasize enough the importance of . . . "

A person's intonation (pitch of the voice), volume of voice, and rate of speech can also be clues to important information. Listen to your instructor's patterns carefully. Does he or she speak louder, with more enthusiasm, with a higher pitch, or with a slower or faster pace when giving important information? Although these speech patterns vary from one person to another, once you have identified an instructor's pattern, you can use that to assist you in identifying important information that should be written in your notes.

Attend to Nonverbal Clues   Watch for nonverbal patterns used by your instructors. Perhaps eyebrows are raised, the head is tilted, hand gestures are used, or the body stance changes for important information. If the instructor pauses to look at her or his notes or simply pauses to allow enough time for you to write, this is a nonverbal clue that may signal important information. Because you are so busy listening and writing, nonverbal clues and patterns are sometimes difficult to learn, but they are usually present.

Nonverbal clues can include the writing of information on the board or a chart or graph shown on an overhead projector. Everything that is written on the board or placed on the overhead should be evaluated: Is it important, and should it be placed in notes? The answer is usually "yes."

Exercise 9.3   Observing Clues

Select one of your instructors this term. Indicate how well you have been learning the instructor's verbal and nonverbal patterns by answering the following questions on your own paper.

1. Does this instructor use key words such as "five kinds of," "three parts to know," "six rules to learn" to help you take notes? Give examples.

2. What other verbal clues have you noticed that assist you in taking better notes?

3. Does this instructor's voice change to emphasize important information (intonation, volume, rate of speech)? Explain.

4. Does this instructor use any facial expressions that are clues to important information? Explain.

5. Are there any hand gestures that help you know what is important? Explain.

6. Does this instructor's body stance change during a lecture? How does it help give you clues?

Students with Learning Disabilities   People with **learning disabilities**, by definition, have average or above-average IQs, but have a weakness in one or more of their information processing systems. Indeed, they have many areas of strength, but they process information differently and need to learn how to compensate for specific difficulties.

Notetaking from lectures is one skill that students with learning disabilities often have a difficulty mastering. Students who are having great difficulty taking notes from lectures may have an auditory processing deficit, processing speed deficit, or attention deficit disorder (ADD).

Students who have **auditory processing deficits** become very frustrated when faced with large amounts of oral information, as in the case of a lecture. The information can actually become scrambled or fragmented; they are not hearing or processing the information the way other students are able to do. These students can take much better notes from a textbook because then they are using visual processing skills.

People with **processing speed deficits** can process information if there is no time constraint involved. Given sufficient time, they can comprehend, organize, and work with new information. However, since lectures are based on the pace of the speaker, if the pace is too rapid, trying to process large amounts of information under pressure results in frustration, a feeling of being overwhelmed, and the loss of the overall organization of the lecture. Taking notes from a textbook is not as difficult because students establish the pace. Students with processing speed deficits can break tasks into smaller segments and process more slowly to avoid the feeling of becoming overloaded.

Students diagnosed with **attention deficit disorder** are unable to stay focused for longer periods of time, as is required with notetaking. External and internal distractors, many beyond their immediate control, interfere with their ability to follow lectures. Students with ADD should sit at the front of the classroom because closeness to the instructor helps maintain greater focus. They should continue to attempt notetaking and leave blanks in their notes when they lose concentration and are unable to keep up.

Students who have been tested and know that they have these disabilities should contact the instructor to make arrangements for **accommodations**. Accommodations include adjustments in a course or support services that provide a more equal opportunity to meet expectations. These students may be given permission to tape all the lectures. A special notetaker (either a trained notetaker or another student in class) may be assigned. Ideally, the notetaker should understand the Cornell system and take notes in this form. If the notetaker uses another system, the student should transfer the notetaker's notes into Cornell notes after class. Students with learning disabilities are still encouraged to continue applying as many of the notetaking strategies as possible and use the notetaker's notes as supplements.

Exercise 9.4   Evaluating Your Class Lecture Notes

You will be asked to take Cornell notes on a lecture in class. Turn your notes in with this evaluation sheet. When your work is returned to you, note the areas checked.

Record Column for Notes

_____ You identified and underlined the main headings. Well done!

_____ You need to listen for key words that indicate a new heading. Write the heading and underline it.

_____ Your notes are clear, well organized, and detailed.

_____ Your notes appear to be crowded or cluttered. Try spacing your notes apart more; leave spaces between new sections.

_____ Try using numbering to separate each new supporting detail.

_____ Your notes lack some important details. Try to write more.

_____ You are using too many short phrases that will lose meaning after time. Try to write more complete ideas or sentences.

_____ Your notes are very lengthy. Try to paraphrase and write shorter sentences. Be selective.

_____ Include information that was presented on the overhead or written on the chalkboard.

_____ Strive to improve legibility and neatness.

_____ Be sure you fill in the gaps after the lecture.

_____ Try to correct spelling errors after the lecture.

_____ See me so that we can discuss these notes together.

Recall Column

_____ The organization and content of your recall column are well done.

_____ Copy the heading from your notes into the recall column.

_____ Use a wider recall column so that you have more room to write.

_____ Try including more key words or questions so that you have clues for reciting.

_____ Put fewer key words and/or information in your recall column. With this much information, you will likely read, not recite.

_____ Align your recall column so that the key words or questions are directly across from the related information in the notes.

_____ Try using the recall column. Add or delete key words or questions to make it more effective.

SUMMARY

- The five *R*'s of Cornell (record, reduce, recite, reflect, review) can be used for taking notes during a lecture.
- You can use proven strategies for overcoming four common problems in taking notes during lectures:

  1. Strengthen your listening skills.
  2. Use the differences among the rates of thinking, speaking, and writing wisely.
  3. Learn to follow the organization or outline of the lecture—even if it is unpredictable.
  4. Strengthen your spelling skills.

- Attention to verbal and nonverbal clues helps increase your notetaking skills.

PERSONALIZING WHAT YOU LEARNED

1. Score and record the score for your chapter profile.
2. On your own paper, expand this chapter's visual mapping.
3. Make your own vocabulary list of all the terms in this chapter that are printed in color.

"To the Student" (p. xv) provides you with more detailed directions for completing these activities.

Review Questions

True-False

To help keep your mind focused, underline the key words in the true-false questions before you answer them.
    Write *T* if the statement is TRUE. Write *F* if it is FALSE.

_____   **1.** You should leave one or more blank lines before you begin to take notes on a new heading or main idea.

_____   **2.** People speak at a rate of 200–250 words per minute.

_____   **3.** Most people can write at a rate of 30 words per minute.

_____   **4.** Major ideas or headings should be underlined so that they stand out from the supporting details.

_____   **5.** Words such as "advantages," "purposes," "uses," "kinds of," and "steps" are signals that can help you organize your notes.

_____   **6.** You should copy most of the information written on the chalkboard into your lecture notes.

_____   **7.** A change in the teacher's voice can often help you identify important information to put in your notes.

_____   **8.** When you fall behind and miss information, stop writing and rely on your auditory memory skills.

_____   **9.** Tape recorders should not be used to replace notetaking during the lecture.

_____   **10.** When you use the recall column correctly, you are using the principle of reciting.

_____   **11.** You can increase your speed of writing by paraphrasing, using abbreviations, and writing sentences that are not grammatically correct.

_____   **12.** Take notes, summarize, anticipate, and question are strategies to use when you begin to lose concentration because the instructor is speaking too slowly.

_____   **13.** You should never write on the back side of your note paper.

_____   **14.** There are several reasons for working with your notes as soon as possible after the lecture.

_____   **15.** The Cornell steps for lectures notes are different from the steps for textbook notes.

Short Answer

1. Write the 5 R's of Cornell in order. After each step, briefly explain what to do during that step.

2. Give four suggestions on how to improve your notetaking speed when an instructor speaks rapidly and you have difficulty keeping up.

3. When should you move from listing ideas in your notes to writing notes in paragraph form?

WRITING ASSIGNMENTS

1. Return to the list of notetaking problems you created in Exercise 9.1. Next to each problem, write one possible solution by using information you have learned from this chapter.
2. Analyze yourself in terms of verbal and nonverbal clues you give when you talk with friends, with family members, or in class. Write a short summary of what you know about your own patterns.

PART

III

Rehearsing and Retrieving Information from Memory

*I*n Part I you learned to set the stage for effective learning. In Part II, you learned to select and process information from textbooks and lectures and to use reciting, reflecting, and reviewing. Part III provides an array of practical tools to use as you recite, reflect, and review.

Chapter 10 introduces study tools for vocabulary. Chapter 11 focuses on visual study tools, such as the mappings you have seen at the beginning of each chapter in this book. Chapter 12 focuses on multisensory strategies that use visual, auditory, and kinesthetic tools together. Chapter 13 shows you how to create original memory systems or devices. After you have become familiar with all the study tools in Part III, you will be able to personalize them by designing the combinations that work most effectively for your memory system.

Creating Study Tools for Vocabulary

A well-developed vocabulary enables you to explain your own ideas more precisely and comprehend more accurately when you read materials written on higher levels. Do you currently use a system for studying new terms or vocabulary? Do you find that words are "on the tip of your tongue" but that you just can't seem to say or write them when needed? When you read, can you find the meaning of most unfamiliar words without looking in the dictionary? The study tools and strategies in this chapter help you expand your vocabulary.

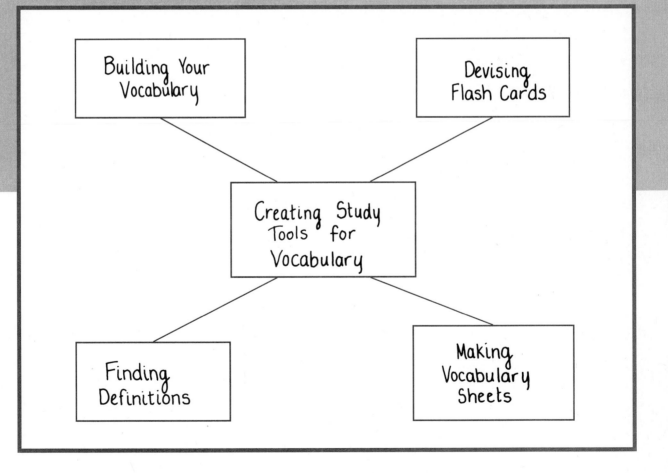

Vocabulary Profile

Please answer honestly each of the following questions about your current attitudes and study habits. Your answers should reflect what you *do*, not what you *wish* you would do.

After you read each statement, check YES if you do this *always* or *most of the time*. Check NO if you do this *seldom* or *never*.

		YES	NO
1.	I use a method to increase my vocabulary.	_____	_____
2.	I make flash cards that have general lists of related words and cards that give words and definitions.	_____	_____
3.	When I use flash cards, I read only from the front and try to recite what's on the back.	_____	_____
4.	I do well on test questions that ask me to write definitions for key words.	_____	_____
5.	I review vocabulary words and definitions when I have a few spare minutes during the day.	_____	_____
6.	I have problems finding the definitions of words in paragraphs.	_____	_____
7.	I know whether all my textbooks have glossaries in the back.	_____	_____
8.	I try to understand a new word by looking at its prefix, suffix, base, or root.	_____	_____
9.	I have problems writing clear, detailed definitions on tests.	_____	_____
10.	The only words I know I need to learn in a chapter are the words that are printed bold, italic, or underlined.	_____	_____
11.	I always have to use a dictionary to look up meanings of new words.	_____	_____
12.	I study vocabulary using techniques that give me immediate feedback.	_____	_____

Building Your Vocabulary

Understanding key terms and their definitions is essential for effective communication. **Receptive vocabulary** consists of words that you understand when you hear them or read them. With a well-developed receptive vocabulary, you are able to read and comprehend more material. **Expressive vocabulary** consists of words you understand well enough to use in your speaking and writing. With a well-developed expressive vocabulary, you are able to use more precise words to explain your ideas in conversation and in writing. The goal of most vocabulary programs is to first expand your receptive vocabulary and then transfer words from your receptive vocabulary into your expressive vocabulary. Developing both forms of vocabulary leads to more effective communication skills.

Since vocabulary or **terminology** is the foundation of understanding any course, you should learn key terms thoroughly. Two study tools are highly effective for developing your vocabulary skills: flash cards and vocabulary sheets.

Devising Flash Cards

Flash cards are valuable and effective study tools for several reasons. First, when used correctly, they provide you with immediate feedback when you are studying. Second, they are compact and easy to use when you sit down to study or when you have a few extra minutes to review. Third, your set of flash cards can easily be expanded to include information from the textbook as well as the lecture.

How to Use Vocabulary Flash Cards

1. Prepare the flash cards.
2. Make *general category* flash cards.
3. Make *definition* flash cards.
4. Study by reciting from the front and the back sides.
5. Use reflect activities by sorting, grouping, and summarizing.
6. Use ongoing review.

Prepare the Flash Cards

Use three-by-five-inch or five-by-seven-inch index cards to make flash cards (white, colored, lined, or unlined). If you use colored cards, different classes or chapters in the textbook can be assigned specific colors.

Flash cards accumulate quickly, so give some thought to storing them. Several options exist:

1. Use recipe boxes to store your cards and dividers to group cards by topics or chapters.
2. Punch holes in the cards; use a large metal ring to hold all the cards together.
3. Purchase "mini-notebooks" for holding flash cards from the college bookstores (dividers are included).
4. Label envelopes to store your different sets of flash cards.
5. Insert small sets of flash cards into "pencil pouches" in notebooks.

*Make General
Category Flash
Cards*

Vocabulary terms are often grouped under a larger category. Creating one general card that gives the category on the front and the related terms on the back helps you relate the individual terms to a larger concept (schema). If you know that several terms are related, begin with this **general category card.**

Assume you are studying five different theories of forgetting. Your instructor expects you to use the correct terms for these five theories when you speak and write. Before you create the definition cards, develop one general category card to help you remember the five theories. A list of related ideas appears on this card.

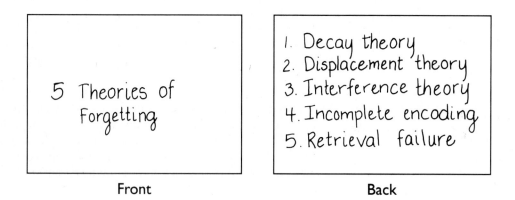

5 Theories of Forgetting	1. Decay theory 2. Displacement theory 3. Interference theory 4. Incomplete encoding 5. Retrieval failure
Front	**Back**

Notice that the *category is on the front* and the *list of related terms is on the back.* The terms are *not defined* on the back; you want to avoid cluttering the card with too much information. Once you've written the category card, proceed to the definition cards, one for each theory. Your complete set will consist of the number of vocabulary cards plus one general category card.

*Make Definition
Flash Cards*

Individual **definition cards** have the terms on the front and the definitions on the back. A definition card for one of the theories of forgetting may look like this:

Decay Theory	Forgetting theory – The stimulus that went into short-term memory was too weak, so it fades away.
Front	**Back**

Your goal is to learn about new words—what they mean and how to use them correctly. You may find that additional information on the back of the card gives you a better understanding of the word. You may want to include one or more of the following:

1. Examples showing how the word is used in sentences
2. The page number in the textbook where the word appears
3. The word broken into word parts (prefix, base, suffix)

4. The correct pronunciation and spelling of the word
5. The part of speech for the word
6. Other words that are related to this word but are different parts of speech (example: differential, different, differ)

The following card shows how you can include other kinds of information that may help you gain a more thorough understanding of the word:

Acrostic	(a mnemonic device) A sentence made by using the first letter of key words. Use the first letters to make your own memory sentence. (acros--Greek--a line of verse)
Front	Back

Exercise 10.1   **Making Flash Cards**

This chapter discussed expressive vocabulary and receptive vocabulary. On your own cards, make a general category card and two definition cards for these terms. Write whatever information you feel is valuable to help you learn these terms.

Exercise 10.2   **Making Flash Cards for a Class**

1. Select any one of your classes. Focus on the current chapter being discussed.

2. Make a set of at least five flash cards. If the words are related in some way, include a general category card. If the words are not related, develop only definition cards. Include whatever information you feel is important to help you learn the terms.

3. On your own paper, provide the following information and answers:

    Name of the class

    Instructor

    Have you used flash cards before in any of your college classes?

    What advantages do you see in using flash cards?

Study From Flash Cards

Once you've prepared flash cards, you must use them for studying, or they will have little impact on your learning. To study effectively from flash cards, plan to study from the front side and from the back side. The more practice you have working with these words, the more confident you will feel about using the words as you speak and write.

Study from the Front   When you study from the front of the cards, you place the words into your expressive vocabulary. On tests, this will be helpful with true-false, multiple-choice, short-answer, and essay questions. Work from the front of the cards as follows:

1. Begin by stacking the cards with the vocabulary words facing you. Say the word out loud.
2. Recite what you know about the word. Do *not* look at the back of the card.
3. After you have finished reciting, turn the card over for feedback. If you defined the term or gave the correct information for the general category, place the card in a "Yes, I know these" pile.
4. If your feedback indicated that you still don't know the information on the back of the card, read the back out loud slowly. Think about the information. Try to visualize it. Put the card in the "I need to study these more" pile.
5. Review the "I need to study these more" pile once again.
6. Use ongoing review for the complete set of flash cards.

Study from the Back   When you work from the back side of the flash cards, you are challenging your memory in new ways. This method also helps prepare you for fill-in-the-blank questions, which often require you to supply the missing vocabulary word, and for multiple-choice questions, which often give the definition and require you to identify the vocabulary term. To study from the back of the vocabulary cards, use these steps:

1. Read the definition or list of information on the back of the card.
2. Say the vocabulary term that you think is on the front of the card.
3. On a piece of paper, write the term.
4. Check the front of the card to see if you have the correct term and the correct spelling.
5. Once again, make two piles: one pile for cards that were correct and one pile for cards that need more work.
6. Review the cards that need more work.
7. Use ongoing review for the complete set of flash cards.

Reflect With Flash Cards

Many students enjoy working with vocabulary flash cards because they can be used in so many different ways. One obvious advantage is that you can make piles of cards that you know and piles of cards that you need to work with more. A second advantage is that you can use the cards for reflect activities such as the following:

1. Shuffle all your cards, and then sort them by categories. Be creative in devising your own categories.
2. Take one category of cards, and then lay all the cards out on a table. Try to summarize by using all the words on the cards in sentences to form a "speech." This type of summary rehearsal benefits you for essay writing.

Use Ongoing Review   Flash cards can easily be reviewed while you are waiting for or riding the bus or when you have a few minutes between classes. Ask friends, classmates, or family members to quiz you by showing you one side of the card and checking your reciting by looking at the other side of the card. Ongoing review gives you necessary practice rehearsing and retrieving vocabulary information from your long-term memory.

Making Vocabulary Sheets   A second option for creating vocabulary study tools is to use regular notebook paper instead of flash cards. The resulting vocabulary sheets contain the same kind of information found on the flash cards. Some students enjoy this option because they prefer having vocabulary work in their notebooks.

How to Use Vocabulary Sheets

1. Prepare a vocabulary sheet with Cornell columns.
2. Include words that describe general categories and words that need definitions.
3. Study by reciting from the left and the right columns.
4. Use ongoing review.

Prepare a Vocabulary Sheet   Begin by drawing a 2½" margin on the left side of the paper. Plan to write only on the front side of the paper. Title the top of each page by naming the course, the lecture, or the textbook chapter.

Include Categories and Specific Words   List the general category and the individual terms down the left side of the paper. Write items in the category and the definitions on the right side of the paper. So that your paper isn't cluttered, leave a blank line between each definition and term. (See p. 170 for a sample vocabulary sheet.)

Recite from Both Columns   To get the greatest benefit from your vocabulary sheets, recite and review them frequently. The more often you work with them, the faster the vocabulary words move into your receptive and then into your expressive vocabulary. When you work with your vocabulary sheets, use the following steps to study from both sides of your paper.

Study from the Left-Hand Column   Use a piece of paper to cover up the right-hand column. Proceed through these steps:

1. Read the term or category. Recite all the information you remember about the term. Use complete sentences.
2. Slide your paper down to get feedback. If you were correct, move on to the next term. If you were incorrect, read the definition again. Cover the definition and recite a second time.
3. Put stars by the terms you knew and little checks or symbols by the ones that need more work.

	Writing Lecture 11-10-92
Elements of a paragraph	1. Topic sentence with an attitude 2. Body with unity and coherence 3. Concluding sentence
Topic sentence	The main idea sentence that controls the information in the paragraph. Must have a specific subject and attitude.
Attitude	A specific feeling, emotion, or point of view (Ex., humorous, frightening, unforgettable)
Body	Body of a paragraph contains the supporting details to develop the controlling idea (main idea)
Unity	All ideas are related to the topic sentence; no getting off the subject
Coherence	A logical sequence to develop supporting details so the ideas flow together smoothly and reader follows easily
Concluding sentence	A final sentence that gives the conclusion; it echoes the topic sentence with the same subject and attitude

Study from the Right-Hand Column   Now reverse the order of studying, just as you did with the flash cards. Different mental operations take place when you reverse the process.

1. Cut or fold paper so that you have a strip of paper to cover up the left-hand column.
2. Read the definitions or the information on the right-hand side.
3. On the strip of paper, write the term being defined. Continue through the page.
4. Pull the strip of paper away. Compare your answers with the words in the left-hand column. Check your accuracy and your spelling.
5. After you get the feedback about the accuracy of your answers, use a symbol such as a star or highlight the words that need more practice.

Use Ongoing Review   To get the most benefit from your vocabulary sheets, review them frequently. Ongoing review should be a part of your studying strategies. When you first sit down to study, you can review vocabulary sheets as a warm-up activity. When you finish a study block, review the vocabulary sheets. The more you practice, the easier it will be for you to acquire new words for your receptive and expressive vocabularies.

Exercise 10.3	**Making a Vocabulary Sheet**

Select five key terms from a previous chapter in this book. Use your own notebook paper to create a vocabulary sheet that includes the five terms, their definitions, and one general category entry.

Practice reciting from both columns of your paper.

Finding Definitions   Most textbook authors want to be certain that you notice which words are important terms to know, so they use three methods to draw your attention to the specialized terminology:

1. *Special print.* Important terms may be underlined or printed in colored, bold, or italic type. Words in **special print** should be included on your flash cards or vocabulary sheets. These terms are also in the glossary of your book.
2. *Marginal notes.* Short definitions may be written in the page margins next to the paragraph that contains the important term. Pay close attention to the information given in margins.
3. *Chapter feature.* Your textbook may provide a list of key terms at the beginning or at the end of the chapter. You are expected to know all the terms on these lists; include these words on your vocabulary flash cards or study sheets.

Learning and understanding these specialized words and definitions become your responsibility. The following strategies provide you with additional ways to locate important definitions.

Strategies for Finding Definitions

1. Look for punctuation clues (commas, dashes, parentheses, colons).

2. Look for words that signal definitions ("is," "which is," "defined as," "means," "or," "also called," "referred to as").

3. Use context clues to gain greater understanding.

4. Use word structure clues (prefixes, word bases or roots, and suffixes) to determine general meaning.

5. Refer to the glossary of the textbook.

6. Refer to reference books: a dictionary for more detailed definitions or a thesaurus for synonyms.

Look for Punctuation Clues   The most common **punctuation clues** are commas, dashes, parentheses, and colons. A definition within a sentence is often set off from the rest of the sentence by **commas.** Notice how commas separate the definition from the rest of the following sentence:

> The use of a *quality circle*, a group of employees who meet on company time to solve problems of product quality, is one way that automakers are implementing this strategy at the operations level.

Dashes can replace commas. Notice how a dash leads into the definition in this example:

> Instead, Aristarchus propounded the *heliocentric theory*—that the earth and planets revolve around the sun.

Definitions are quite obvious when they are placed inside **parentheses.** The parentheses are usually placed right after the word being defined:

> Credibility problems can occur from improper or careless *enunciation* (the way you articulate and pronounce words in context).

The **colon** is a punctuation mark that means "as follows." Check the information following the colon to see if it provides you with a definition. Note how the colon is used in this example:

> An *empirical formula* is the simplest formula for a compound: the formula of a substance written with the smallest integer subscripts.

Look for Word Clues   A very common method for incorporating definitions into paragraphs is through the use of word clues that signal the presence of a definition. The following words are used frequently to link a vocabulary word to its definition:

also	defined as	referred to as
also known as	is	to describe
are	means	which is
called	or	

Notice how these **word clues** are used in the following sentences containing definitions:

> A *dialect* is a particular speech pattern associated with an area of the country or a cultural or ethnic background.
>
> Psychologists use the term *attribution* to describe the process people go through to explain the causes of behavior, including their own.
>
> The parts of the nervous system that provide input about the environment are known as senses, or *sensory systems*.
>
> When we talk about *culture*, we mean the customary traits, attitudes, and behaviors of a group of people.
>
> This newly discovered phenomenon of spontaneous radiation from certain unstable elements was called *radioactivity*.

The signal words in the preceding definitions are "is," "to describe," "or," "mean," and "was called," respectively. Since many words can be used to signal definitions, careful reading is essential.

As you watch for word clues that signal definitions, notice that punctuation clues are sometimes used with the word clues. You will see examples of both definition clues as you work through upcoming exercises.

| **Exercise 10.4** | **Finding Definitions** |

The following excerpts are taken from college textbooks. You are not expected to know many of the terms discussed in these passages. With a partner, find the definitions and underline them.

Psychology

1. "One method of studying intelligence, called the *psychometric approach*, analyzes test scores in order to describe the structure of intelligence."

2. "Between firings there is a brief rest, called a *refractory period*."

3. "In the case of the adrenal hormones, the result is a set of responses called the *fight-or-flight syndrome*, which prepares the animal or person for action in response to danger: the heart beats faster, the liver releases glucose into the bloodstream, fuels are mobilized from fat stores, and the organism is generally placed in a state of high arousal."

Chemistry

1. "A *physical property* is a characteristic that can be observed for a material without changing its chemical identity."

2. "It was Joseph Louis Proust, however, who, by his painstaking work, convinced the majority of chemists of the general validity of the *law of definite proportions* (also known as the *law of constant composition*): A pure compound, whatever its source, always contains definite or constant proportions of the elements by mass."

3. "Gaseous *diffusion* is the process whereby a gas spreads out through another gas to occupy the space with uniform partial pressure."

History

1. "A king (*lugal*) or local governor (*ensi*) exercised political power, and most of the city's land was the property of individual citizens."

2. "The term *Indo-European* refers to a large family of languages that includes English, most of the languages of modern Europe, Greek, Latin, Persian, and Sanskrit, the sacred tongue of ancient India."

3. "Perhaps the best way to describe the position of the free woman in Greek society is to use the anthropologist's term *liminal*, which means in this case that although women lacked official power, they nonetheless played a vital role in shaping the society in which they lived."

Use Context Clues   When punctuation clues and word clues are not provided, you will need to use the **context**—the surrounding words and sentences—to make assumptions about the definition. Because parts of the definition may be scattered throughout several sentences, careful reading is essential. To comprehend sentences and paragraphs, do not skip over words that are unfamiliar to you. Instead, take the opportunity to expand your vocabulary each time you encounter a new word. Use **context clues** to help you understand unfamiliar words even if they are not set off in special print, specified in the margins, or listed as terms to know. If context clues don't provide enough meaning, use a dictionary to find meanings.

Exercise 10.5	Using Context Clues

Read the following excerpts carefully. To comprehend the passages, it is essential that you understand all the words in the passages. Since punctuation or word clues are not given, you'll need to use context clues to determine some word meanings. Answer the questions that follow each excerpt.

> The *leati*, refugees or prisoners of war, were settled with their families in the areas of Gaul and Italy under supervision of Roman prefects and landowners.

1. Did you already know the meaning of the word *prefects*?

2. Using context clues, what do you think it means?

3. Did you already know the meaning of the word *Gaul*?

4. Based on context clues, what would you guess it means?

> Instead, Aristarchus propounded the *heliocentric theory*—that the earth and planets revolve around the sun.

1. Do you know who Aristarchus was?

2. Why does it seem important to know who he was?

3. Did you already know the meaning of *propounded*?

4. Using context clues, what do you think it means?

> Communal living, moreover, provided training for the aspirant in the virtues of charity, poverty, and freedom from self-deception. Those seeking personal growth and self-fulfillment of such ambitions attuned with this environment.

1. Did you already know the term *aspirant*?

2. Using context clues, what do you think it means?

3. Did you already know the term *virtues*?

4. Using context clues, what would you guess it means?

Use Word Structure Clues

Words can consist of several structural parts: prefixes, base words, roots, and suffixes. **Prefixes**, often from Greek or Latin, are units of meaning placed before the base word. For example, the prefix *re* means "again." The same is true for **suffixes**, the units of meaning placed after the base word to help indicate the part of speech of a word (noun, verb, adjective, or adverb). For example, the suffix *ness* means "a state, quality, or condition," and it forms a noun. **Base words** are words in English that can stand by themselves. **Roots** are units of meaning, also often from Greek or Latin, that do not form English words until other roots, prefixes, or suffixes are attached to them. For example, *ject* means "to throw"; however, we don't use it as a word until we add another word part (inject, reject, project).

By knowing the meanings of frequently used prefixes, suffixes, and roots, you can figure out the basic definition of many unfamiliar words. For example, the word *electroencephalogram* can be broken into its word parts. "Electro" refers to electrical. "Enceph" refers to the brain, and "gram" refers to a graph. The glossary definition in a psychology textbook is "a recording of the electrical signals produced by the nerve cells of the brain, obtained through electrodes attached to the surface of the skull."

You can learn hundreds of common word parts to help you determine meanings. Your comprehension of words can be greatly increased by learning the meanings of common prefixes, suffixes, and roots. Check if your college offers vocabulary skill-building courses and if there is a source on campus to obtain lists of structural word parts that you could study and keep in your notebook for quick reference.

Refer to the Glossary

The **glossary** is a condensed dictionary that gives definitions of key terms in the textbook. It usually defines only the terms that were identified by underlining or by colored, bold, or italic print.

When you work with a glossary, keep these three important points in mind:

1. Words that are not key terms for the course, even if they are new words for you, are not in the glossary.
2. The definitions given in the glossary are limited ones. The words may also have other meanings.
3. If the glossary definition is not clear to you, return to the textbook page to read the word in context or learn more about the word by using a dictionary.

You can also use the glossary as you study. When making flash cards or vocabulary sheets, compare the glossary definition to the one derived from the chapter. Include any additional information or wording that may help you learn the word more accurately. At the end of the term, use the glossary as a review tool: read through the glossary of terms and then recite the definitions. If the glossary gives page numbers where the terms were used, refer back to those pages for more information as needed. If page numbers are not given, you can use the index in the back of the book to locate page numbers.

If your textbook has no glossary, plan to develop your own glossary or system for listing key terms and definitions.

Refer to Reference Books

A **dictionary** is an excellent reference book for learning more about word meanings, definitions, structure, pronunciation, parts of speech, and **etymology** (the origin and development of words). Every college student should have a dictionary on his or her desk or in the study area. Although paperback dictionaries are adequate, in the long run a hardbound dictionary is a much sounder investment. Once you have access to a dictionary, use it frequently to explore the English language.

A **thesaurus** is a reference book that provides lists of **synonyms**, (words with the same or similar meanings). When you use a thesaurus, do not, however, automatically substitute a synonym for the word you have looked up. Words may have several connotations or subtle differences in meanings. One synonym may not have the correct meaning to fit the context used. When in doubt about the meaning of a synonym, check it in a dictionary.

Many hand-held spellcheckers also have built-in dictionaries and thesauruses. These can be used for quick reference. The word bank in some spellcheckers, however, is limited. Their dictionary or thesaurus may not contain as many entries as reference books would.

Learn to use each reference efficiently. Directions for using references are included in their front sections.

SUMMARY

- Developing a strong vocabulary helps you comprehend what you read in textbooks and what you hear in lectures. It also enables you to express your ideas clearly when you speak or write.
- Vocabulary flash cards and vocabulary study sheets should include

1. Words in special print (bold, italic, color)
2. Words defined in marginal notes
3. Words included in chapter lists of terms to know
4. Unfamiliar words you encounter as you read or listen
5. General categories of words as well as individual words

- The meanings of unfamiliar words can often be learned through punctuation clues, word clues, context clues, word structure clues, glossaries, and reference books (dictionaries or thesauruses).

PERSONALIZING WHAT YOU LEARNED

1. Score and record the score for your chapter profile.
2. On your own paper, expand this chapter's visual mapping.
3. Make your own vocabulary list of all the terms in this chapter that are printed in color.

"To the Student" (p. xv) provides you with more detailed directions for completing these activities.

Review Questions

Identifying Definitions

Underline the definitions for the words in italics. Indicate on the line the type or types of clues that you used to find the definition by writing *p* (punctuation clue), *w* (word clue), or *c* (context clue).

_____ 1. "A *brand mark*, on the other hand, is the part of a brand that is a symbol or distinctive design, like Planters' 'Mr. Peanut'."

_____ 2. "Hence, money serves as a *store of value*, or a means for retaining and accumulating wealth."

_____ 3. "A *generic product* (sometimes called a generic brand) is a product with no brand at all."

_____ 4. "This gave rise to the *piece-rate system*, under which employees are paid a certain amount for each unit of output they produce."

_____ 5. "It eventually led to *scientific management*, the application of scientific principles to management of work and workers."

_____ 6. "Any false and malicious statement that is communicated to others and that injures a person's good name or reputation may constitute *defamation*. Defamation in a temporary form such as in oral communication is called slander."

_____ 7. "The second type of note is a *direct quotation*—the exact words of another."

_____ 8. "Whereas the mean, median, and mode tell how the scores tend to be similar (and are called measures of central tendency), the *range* is a measure of variability and tells how the scores tend to be different."

_____ 9. "The plague took two forms—bubonic and pneumonic. In the *bubonic* form, the rat was the vector, or transmitter, of the disease."

_____ 10. "The word *Machiavellian* entered the language as a synonym for the politically devious, corrupt, and crafty, indicating actions in which the end justifies the means."

Multiple Choice

Read each question carefully with all the options. Cross out the options that you know are incorrect. Select the best option that remains. Write the letter of the best option on the line.

_____ 1. Provides immediate feedback, is compact to use, and is easy to expand with more words are three reasons

    a. flash cards are effective study tools.
    b. general vocabulary cards should be developed.
    c. definitions should be learned.
    d. vocabulary sheets must have specific definitions.

_____ 2. When you use vocabulary cards or vocabulary sheets, you should get feedback

    a. by looking at the front side of the cards or the left column of the vocabulary sheets.
    b. by reciting what is on the back of the cards or what is in the right column.
    c. by reciting from both sides of the cards or the vocabulary sheets.
    d. by writing down all your answers and checking.

_____ 3. As you read, you can identify important terms by

    a. paying attention to specialized print.
    b. reading notes written in the margins.
    c. using lists of terms provided in the chapter.
    d. doing all of the above.

_____ 4. You can locate definitions of important terms by

    a. using punctuation clues.
    b. recognizing signal words ("is," "means," "defined as").
    c. using context clues surrounding the key term.
    d. using punctuation, word structure, and context clues.

_____ **5.** A definition is not directly stated when you have to use

    a. context clues.
    b. punctuation clues.
    c. signal words.
    d. all of the above.

Short Answer

1. Name at least three reflect activities that can be done with flash cards.

2. Name at least four ways authors try to help readers identify important terminology and definitions.

WRITING ASSIGNMENTS

1. Choose any five words from this chapter that are unfamiliar to you. Do not use key vocabulary words presented in special print. Use the dictionary to explore the meanings of the words. Create flash cards or vocabulary sheets. (You may continue this method throughout the term to explore unfamiliar words.)
2. Write an honest discussion about your current vocabulary. How would you rate it? Do you want to make changes? Why? How do you plan to expand your vocabulary?

11 Creating Visual Study Tools

Visual study tools offer you an opportunity to use originality, creativity, pictures, drawings, and colors to help you learn and retrieve information from memory. Do you find it is easier to remember information presented in pictures, graphs, or diagrams? Can you clearly picture something seen on a chalkboard several days ago? Can you visualize colors? Do you often draw or sketch information on paper that was originally written in paragraph form? In this chapter you learn to organize and utilize visual tools to process new information for memory.

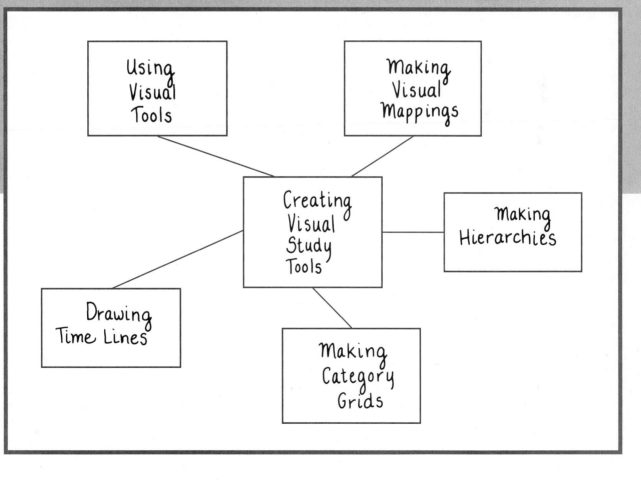

Visual Tools Profile

Please answer honestly each of the following questions about your current attitudes and study habits. Your answers should reflect what you *do*, not what you *wish* you would do.

After you read each statement, check YES if you do this *always* or *most of the time*. Check NO if you do this *seldom* or *never*.

		YES	NO
1.	I am comfortable reorganizing or rearranging information rather than studying it in the same order it was presented.	_____	_____
2.	I use reciting frequently when I study.	_____	_____
3.	I draw various kinds of pictures to help me remember what I've read.	_____	_____
4.	I understand the concept of different levels of information.	_____	_____
5.	I learn main ideas well but I often overlook important details.	_____	_____
6.	I use these two principles of memory frequently when I study: Recite and review.	_____	_____
7.	I close my eyes or look up in the air to visualize or picture charts.	_____	_____
8.	When I recite, reflect, and review, I stop to get feedback so that I know if I am remembering information correctly.	_____	_____
9.	I know how to make mappings and hierarchies.	_____	_____
10.	I know how to organize information into subjects and categories so that I can make a chart.	_____	_____
11.	I know how to create and study from a time line.	_____	_____
12.	When I make drawings, I experiment with layout and use of colors.	_____	_____

Using Visual Tools

In Chapter 1 you explored your learning styles or learning preferences. If you have strong visual skills, visual study tools such as visual mappings, hierarchies, category grids, and time lines may become your preferred methods for learning new information.

Although visual study tools are generally used to create reflect activities, some students become so proficient with visual tools that visual forms of notetaking can replace the Cornell notetaking system. The goal of this book is to help you find the methods that work best for you. Use visual study tools as your main system of notetaking if they help you learn and remember new information more easily.

Visual study tools offer you an opportunity to organize and record information in creative ways. Because they draw on your originality, there is more than one way to correctly present information. You do not need to be artistically talented to use visual study tools; stick figures or basic sketches are sufficient as long as you understand the pictures you create. Because visual methods involve a relatively new form of study tools, you may at first feel uncomfortable with these methods. Give yourself time and practice to learn these tools; they just may be your key to a stronger memory and system for recalling information quickly.

Students with weak visual skills, especially students with learning disabilities related to visual processing, may want to adapt some of the steps used to study from visual study tools. If picturing or visualizing information is a struggle, the following suggestions are recommended; they help transfer the visual aspects of the study tools in this chapter to an auditory approach.

1. Complete the visual study tools as discussed in this chapter.
2. Turn on a tape recorder. Look at the visual study tool you created.
3. Follow the recommended steps for studying the information. Instead of visualizing, verbalize. Discuss the information out loud and speak in complete sentences.

Making Visual Mappings

You have already had some experience with **visual mappings** if you have completed the Personalizing What You Learned exercise at the end of each chapter. The chapter mappings provide you with a visual picture of key ideas covered in the chapter.

Mappings can be used in a variety of ways. You can make a visual mapping of

1. A paragraph or a group of paragraphs under one heading
2. A topic or a subject presented in several chapters and lectures
3. Your lecture notes (in addition to Cornell or as an alternative notetaking method)
4. Information to review for a test
5. Each chapter you have covered
6. Ideas brainstormed for a paper or a speech

How to Create Mappings

Four basic steps are involved in creating visual mappings. Your choice of borders, shapes, pictures, and colors in each step gives you the opportunity to be creative.

*H*ow to Create Mappings

1. Write the topic in the center of your paper.

2. Write the main ideas or the main headings; use lines to connect them to the topic.

3. Add major details to support the main ideas.

4. Add any necessary minor details.

Write the Topic   In the center of your paper, write the topic. The topic can be the title of a chapter, the name of a lecture, or the subject you wish to map. For example, SQ4R is a subject, not the name of a chapter or a lecture.

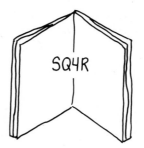

Border   The border can be a box, a circle, or even a picture. If you are making a mapping on types of real estate investments, you may want the center picture to be a house or a building. If you are making a mapping on memory, you may want the center picture to be a person's head.

Paper Size   If you know that your mapping will include many details, you may want to work on legal-sized paper (eight and a half by eleven inches) or drawing paper that is even larger. If your mapping is on a smaller topic, notebook-sized paper is sufficient.

Write Main Ideas   Next add the second level of information, the main ideas of the topic. For a visual mapping of a chapter, use the main headings found in the chapter. For a visual mapping of a subject, show the main categories of information related to the subject. (See sample mapping on next page.)

Borders, Shapes, or Pictures   To make the main ideas or categories stand out, place a border or shape around each item on level two. You may want to use a different shape than that used for the topic. Pictures can be used instead of geometric shapes or pictures can be placed inside shapes.

Colors   Some people's memories are strengthened with the use of color. Experiment with colors by shading in the main ideas. Use different colors for each level of information.

Spacing   Visually appealing and uncluttered mappings are easier to visualize or memorize. Before you begin adding the level two information, count the number of main ideas to decide how to space them evenly around the page. Place them relatively close to the topic so that you'll have room to add details later.

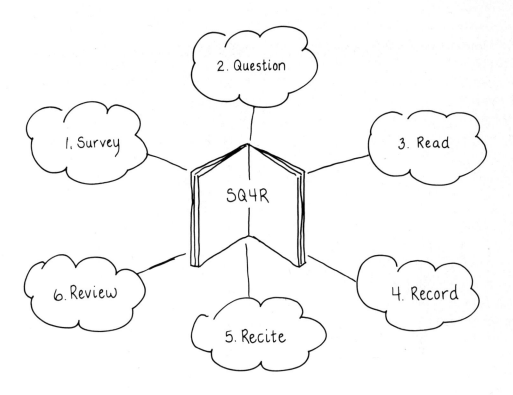

Organization   The most common organization is clockwise, beginning at the eleven o'clock position. If there is a definite sequence to the information, such as steps that must be learned in order, you may want to add numbers to the lines that extend from the topic or inside the borders.

Connections   Draw a line from each main idea to the topic. This gives a visual representation of their relationship. Each main idea is thus represented as a subtopic of the topic in the center of the paper.

Add Major Details   Now add the major supporting details for each main idea. This is level three information. Write only key words that serve as "triggers" for you to recite in full sentences. Avoid the tendency to write long phrases or full sentences; your mapping will become too cluttered. Draw lines from these key words to the main ideas they support.

Quantity of Details   Be selective. Include only as many major details as you need to help you remember the important information. You do not need to have the same number of details for each main idea. It is up to you to determine how many details will help your memory.

Horizontal Writing   To make your mapping easy to read, keep all your writing horizontal. Avoid writing at a slant, or sideways or turning the paper as you write, resulting in words written upside down.

Borders   If the major details stand out clearly without borders (as shown in the SQ4R mapping), don't include any. If you are color-coding levels of information, you may want to enclose these major details with a border so color-coding can be used.

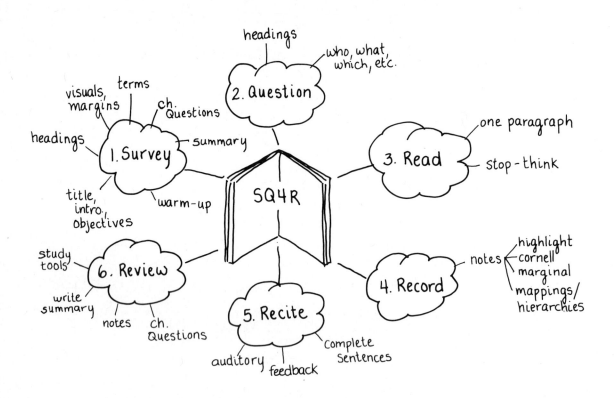

Add Minor Details   If you need some minor details, use the same guidelines as for major details. (Note the minor details for the record step in the preceding example.) If you find that you need one or more levels of information beyond the minor details, such as may be the case with a long chapter, consider reorganizing the information into several different topics and creating several mappings. You may find that narrowing or limiting the topic of a mapping will be more beneficial for visualizing and studying. By reorganizing, you chunk information into more meaningful groups. Your big picture is not so big that it is difficult to memorize, visualize, or comprehend.

Exercise 11.1	Mapping for Review Work

Break into groups of three or four people. Each group will be assigned one of the following topics to use to create a mapping. You may be asked to work on large-sized chart paper, legal-sized paper, or regular paper. One person in the group should do the drawing. The other members of the group can give suggestions on ways to arrange the mapping and the kinds of options to use (pictures, color, shapes, layout, levels of information).

You will have the opportunity to see the results from each group. If the mappings are on large chart paper, each mapping can be displayed. If the work is on notebook or legal-sized paper, your teacher may photocopy the results for you to use for review.

Mapping 1:   Create a mapping to show the kinds of resources you should know how to use. (Refer to Chapter 1.)

Mapping 2:   Create a mapping that shows the strategies for finding definitions in your textbook. (Refer to Chapter 10.)

Mapping 3:   Make a mapping of the nine concentration techniques for dealing with internal and external distractions. (Refer to Chapter 3.)

Mapping 4:   Make a mapping to show the 5 *R*'s of Cornell. (Refer to Chapters 8 and 9.)

Mapping 5:   Make a mapping to show the parts of a book you should examine when you survey. (Refer to chapter 5.)

Mapping 6:   Make a mapping to show the parts of a chapter you should examine when you survey. (Refer to Chapter 6.)

How to Study from Visual Mappings   Visual mappings are powerful and work effectively because they are based on memory principles that boost your ability to learn new information. The information in mappings is organized logically, shows relationships, and helps you associate one idea to another. Concentration and interest increase as you work to present information creatively. As you recite, review, receive feedback, and visualize, the process of learning is enhanced.

How to Study from Mappings

1. Visualize and recite the topic in the center of your paper.

2. Visualize and recite the main ideas.

3. Check your accuracy by looking at your mapping.

4. Return to the first main idea. Without looking at your paper, recite the major and minor details associated to that main idea.

5. Check your accuracy by looking at your mapping.

6. Continue until you have recited all the main ideas, major details, and minor details.

7. Use reflect activities.

8. Use ongoing review.

Visualize and Recite the Topic   Begin visualizing by picturing the mapping in your mind. Many people find it helpful to close their eyes and see the mapping on the back of their eyelids. Or you may want to look up to the left and toward the ceiling. Try to picture the topic written on your paper.

Visualize and Recite the Main Ideas   Strengthen the visual image of the skeleton of the mapping by picturing only the topic and the number of main ideas or categories directly connected to the topic. Now recite by naming the topic and each of the main ideas.

Your visualizing SQ4R may *look* like this:

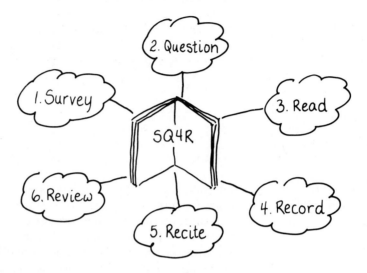

Your reciting may *sound* like this: "In SQ4R there are six main ideas branching off the topic SQ4R. They are survey, question, read, record, recite, and review."

Check Your Accuracy Refer back to your mapping to verify that you recited correctly. If you were correct, move on to the next step. If you were not correct, study the skeleton with the topic and the main ideas. Look away to visualize and recite again. Get more feedback.

Recite Main Ideas and Details Now that you can clearly picture the skeleton, return to the first main idea. Without looking, try to tell all that you remember about this main idea. Your goal is to include all the key words (major and minor details) that were shown on your mapping. Talk to yourself in complete sentences.

It is not necessary to visualize all major and minor details written on your paper. It is important, however, that you include these details in your reciting.

Check Your Accuracy Refer to your mapping to see if you included all the major and minor details for the main idea you just recited. Did you forget to include some information? If yes, try reciting and including the information as you look at your mapping. The major and minor details can be visual clues for you. Then look away and recite. Get feedback again to be sure that this time you incorporated the details in your reciting.

Continue Through Each Main Idea Continue this process for each of the main ideas. Don't rush the process; work through each category in a careful, thoughtful way. When you are finished with the entire mapping, move on to a reflect activity.

Use Reflect Activities   You can reflect in several ways:

1. Draw the skeleton of your mapping on paper. Then without referring to the mapping, fill in the words for the topic and the main ideas.
2. Try to redraw the mapping with as many major and minor details as possible without looking and without first giving yourself the skeleton.
3. Repeat the process of visualizing and reciting the entire mapping. Turn on a tape recorder as you recite. The tape can become an auditory study tool for review.

Use Ongoing Review   Since visualizing does not require you to have materials such as notebooks, paper, or pencil available, you can review any time you have a few available minutes. As you wait in between classes, ride a bus, take a shower, or wash dishes, try to reconstruct the mapping in your mind.

You may want to make a smaller version of your mapping to place on flash cards for review. These cards can also be placed around your house where they are easy to see and quick to review.

As you remember, the final step of the information processing model is retrieval. To access this mapping from your long-term memory, practicing retrieval is essential. With more practice, you'll see the picture more sharply more readily.

Exercise 11.2	**Creating Mappings from a Textbook**

Select a chapter from one of the textbooks you are using this term. Write the name of the chapter in the center of your page. Use the headings in the chapter as the main ideas. Identify and add the major details for each heading. Add any necessary minor details. Your visual mapping should have four levels of information.

If the textbook chapter has more than six major headings, make a mapping of only a section of the chapter so that you are not covering more than six major headings.

As you create your visual mapping, use these reminders:

1. Use only key words so that the mapping is not cluttered.
2. Write horizontally.
3. Use borders or shapes to help each level of information stand out clearly.
4. Use color-coding if you wish.

Making Hierarchies

Hierarchies are a form of visual mapping in which information is arranged in levels of importance from top down. If visualizing mappings with lines extending in all directions was difficult for you, you may prefer the organized structure of hierarchies. A hierarchy for **SQ4R** could look like these:

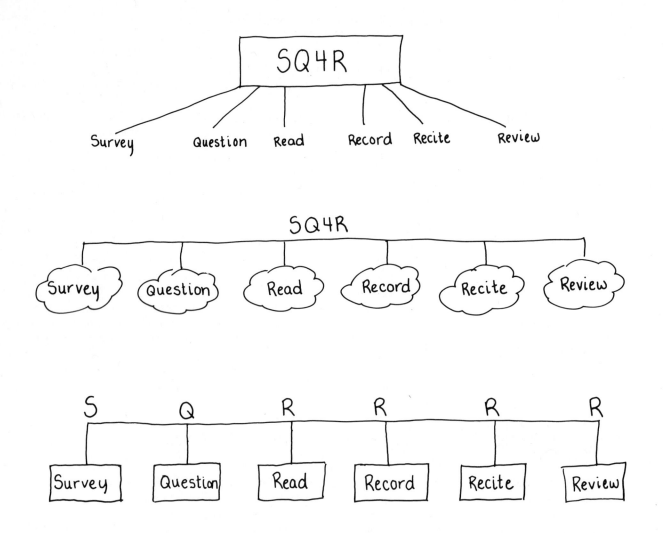

How to Create Hierarchies   The steps for creating hierarchies are similar to the steps for mappings. The same levels of information are used: topic, main idea, major details, and minor details.

How to Create Hierarchies

1. Write level one information (the topic) on the top line of the hierarchy.

2. Draw lines downward from the topic to show level two information (the main ideas).

3. Under each main idea, branch downward again for level three information (major details).

4. Add level four information (minor details) under the major details if needed.

Write Level One Information   Place the topic or the subject on the top line. You do not need to put a box or border around the topic, but you can if you wish.

Show Level Two Information   When hierarchies are created for textbook chapters, the headings in the book become level two information. When you create a hierarchy for a general topic such as SQ4R, level two information represents general categories.

Determine the number of main ideas to be placed under the topic. Branch *downward* to level two to write the main ideas. Consider using legal-sized paper for more extensive hierarchies. Space the main ideas evenly on the paper to avoid a cluttered or crowded look. Always write horizontally. Try adding color-coding and various shapes or pictures to strengthen the visual image.

Many textbooks provide informative introductions; these can be included in your hierarchies under a category labeled "Intro." Key words, concepts, or objectives can now be added to the hierarchy. Another category can also be included, if needed, to show graphs, visual aids, lists of terminology, or any other information you want to remember.

Add Level Three Information   Because level three often has numerous supporting details, you need to consider how you will place the details on the paper. To avoid a cluttered or crowded look, the details can be staggered or arranged in a variety of layouts as shown in the illustrations.

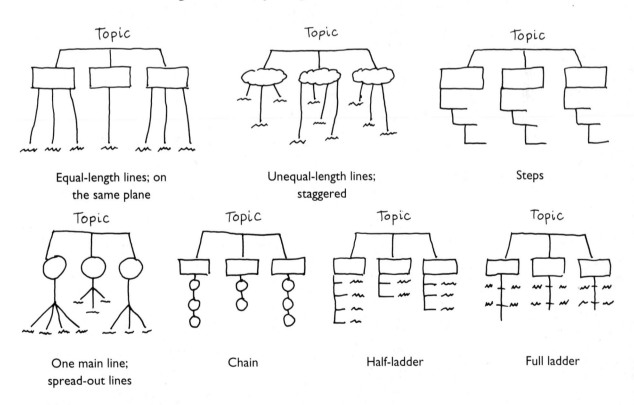

Equal-length lines; on the same plane

Unequal-length lines; staggered

Steps

One main line; spread-out lines

Chain

Half-ladder

Full ladder

Provide Level Four Information   Minor details can be added by branching *downward* from level three. Be selective. Include only essential key words that you feel you need to help you remember the information. Again, select a layout that will organize the details clearly. Borders, pictures, and color-coding can also be used.

How to Study from Hierarchies   As with mappings, hierarchies need to be visualized, recited, and reviewed to work as effective study tools. Since the study techniques are the same as those used with visual mappings, they are summarized, rather than detailed, here.

---

*H*ow to Study from Hierarchies

1. Visualize and recite the topic written on the top line.

2. Visualize and recite the main ideas on level two.

3. Get feedback by looking at your hierarchy to check your accuracy.

4. Return to the first main idea on level two. Recite the level three and level four major and minor details.

5. Get feedback by looking at your hierarchy to check your accuracy.

6. Continue until all the main ideas have been recited.

7. Use reflect activities.

8. Use ongoing review.

Reciting, reflecting, and reviewing are essential. In Chapter 4, you learned that short-term memory can handle only a limited amount of information at one time. If your hierarchy has more than seven main ideas on level two, you are wise to divide your reciting, reflecting, and reviewing into smaller sections.

For example, if you are studying a mapping or a hierarchy for the twelve principles of memory, find ways to divide the information into smaller parts. Visualize and recite the first section; then continue to work with additional sections. Your reciting may sound like this: "There are twelve principles of memory. The first four are selectivity, association, visualization, effort; they spell the word *SAVE*. The second four spell the word *CRIB*: concentration, recitation, interest, and big picture–little pictures. The last four (*FOTO*) are feedback, organization, time, and ongoing review. Selectivity means . . .

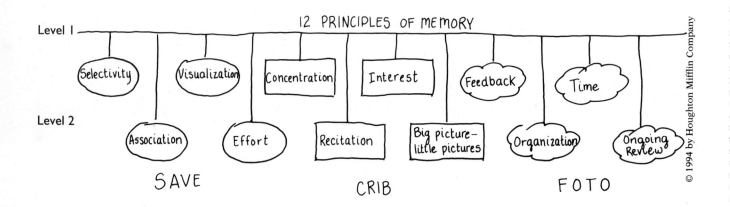

| Exercise 11.3 | Turning Mappings into Hierarchies |

Take the visual mapping from Chapter 10 (p. 163). Use the same topic and the same information for level two. Convert the mapping into a hierarchy. Add level three details.

Making Category Grids

Category grids are charts with columns and rows used to compare or contrast two or more subjects. Whenever you are working with several related subjects, whose various characteristics you must learn, take the time to develop a category grid. A sample grid may look like this:

	Column 1	**Column 2**	**Column 3**
Row 1			
Row 2			
Row 3			
Row 4			
Row 5			

How to Create Category Grids

In a grid, *columns* run up and down, and *rows* run across the page. Important information about each subject is written inside the boxes. The number of columns and rows is determined by the amount of information being covered. The following steps show how to organize information for grids.

How to Create Category Grids

1. Identify the number of subjects to be compared or contrasted. Write one subject on each row.

2. Identify the categories of information to be discussed. Write one category at the top of each column.

3. Complete the grid by writing key words in each box where columns and rows intersect.

Identify Subjects and Label Rows   Since category grids are designed to compare or contrast information for two or more subjects, begin by identifying the number of subjects. Sometimes the subjects are grouped together in the information you have read. For example, the reading in Chapter 7 on styles of leadership conveniently grouped these styles together for you: authoritarian leader, laissez-faire leader, and democratic leader. Other times you may need to think through the information you have read to identify subjects for comparison or contrast.

Once you have identified the number of subjects, you can begin to make the rows for your grid. If you have two subjects, you will need two rows. Write the name of one subject on each row.

Identify Categories and Label Columns   Identifying categories requires you to think carefully about the information you have read. What categories of information were discussed for all or most of the subjects? You can almost always use a general category titled "Characteristics," but more specific categories are more useful. For example, the styles of leadership reading specifies three aspects of style: attitude toward responsibility, nature of tasks, and flow of communication.

The number of categories you select determines the number of columns in your grid. Label the top of each column. The styles of leadership grid would appear as follows:

	Responsibility	Tasks	Communication Flow
Authoritarian Leader			
Laissez-faire Leader			
Democratic Leader			

If you have difficulties finding appropriate labels for the columns, try using this approach to help you organize important information for the grid:

1. List each of the subjects across the top of a piece of paper.
2. Under each subject, list important details associated with that subject.
3. Look at your list of details. Can the details be grouped into larger categories?
4. If you see a logical category of information under one subject, is that same kind of information also given for the other subjects? If so, you have discovered an appropriate title for a category.

Complete the Grid   There are two ways to complete the boxes in the grid: Complete one column at a time, or complete one row at a time.

In the preceding example, you would complete column one first by writing key ideas that show how each type of leader handles responsibility. The next step would be to describe the kinds of tasks given by each kind of leader. Continue until every column is filled.

The second way to complete the grid would be to complete all the boxes in row one; all the key words for the first style of leadership would be placed within the row one boxes. Then you would move on to the next row and the next style of leadership.

How to Study from Category Grids   Reciting and visualizing from a category grid can be more demanding than reciting and visualizing from mappings or hierarchies because you are telling about more than one subject or main idea. You are also comparing or contrasting it to other subjects or main ideas. You can use the following steps to study from category grids.

How to Study from Category Grids

1. Name and visualize the topic, the subjects in the rows, and the categories across the top of the grid.

2. Recite information by moving across the rows or down the columns. Get feedback.

3. Use reflect activities.

4. Use ongoing review.

Name and Visualize the Rows and Columns   The skeleton of the grid includes the title, the subjects written down the side of the grid (labels of the rows), and the categories written across the top of the grid (labels of the columns). Take time to create a strong visual image of this grid before reciting information inside the boxes. Explain the grid to yourself as you try to restructure it visually without looking.

Recite and Get Feedback   Recite in a logical order. Decide if you want to recite row by row, telling everything about one subject at a time, or column by column, telling how one specific category is used for each of the subjects. After you recite either a row or a column, refer back to the grid to check your accuracy. Immediate feedback is important; recite again if you found that you made mistakes. Continue until you can recite the entire grid.

Use Reflect Activities   If adding pictures to visual study tools helps you remember information, add pictures inside each box. If color helps you remember visual information more easily, add color. You can use colored pencils to shade each subject (each row) in a different color (or to complete the boxes of the grid so that the key words appear in different colors).

There are three basic reflect activities that are effective for grids. The first two can be done by looking at the grid.

1. Read through the grid row by row. Turn the key words in the boxes into complete sentences. Speak so that the information is clear and organized. Use a tape recorder to record your presentation. Listen to the recorder several times for review. Visualize each part as you hear it on the recorder. Use the same process reading and speaking in full sentences as you explain each column.

2. With the grid in front of you, write a summary that includes all the key points. First write a summary that explains all the categories one row at a time. Then write a summary that explains one category at a time as it relates to each subject. This activity is basically the same as the activity in (1), except that it is a written, rather than a verbal, exercise.

3. Try to redraw the entire grid without looking at your original. First label your rows and then your columns. Go back to each box and fill in the key words.

Use Ongoing Review As with any study tool, category grids need to be reviewed often so that they stay fresh and accessible in your mind. Because a grid contains so much information, practice retrieving it frequently.

| **Exercise 11.4** | **Categorizing the Kinds of Leadership** |

1. Work with a partner. Refer back to Styles of Leadership in Chapter 7 (p. 118).

2. Add key words to the boxes in the grid on p. 192.

3. Check to be sure that the boxes are not cluttered with too much information. Use only key words, not full sentences.

Drawing Time Lines

The last visual study tool is the time line. A **time line** is a visual representation of a series of events in chronological order (time sequence). Time lines are used most frequently in history courses because the events within a chapter are often written in a time sequence. Events in later chapters may cover the history of another part of the world during the same time period. A time line can help you get a clear picture of the years specific events happened and what events occurred in the same time period.

How to Create Time Lines

Time lines vary in length. They can be made for sections of a chapter, a full chapter, a lecture, or an entire course. Use the following steps to create time lines that show the chronological sequence of important events.

How to Create Time Lines

1. Select appropriately sized paper for your time line.

2. Draw a horizontal line and label it with dates.

3. Write events above their dates.

Select Paper   For shorter sections of a chapter or for one lecture, regular notebook paper can be used. If you plan to make an ongoing time line for a full chapter or a course, expect to create a lengthy study tool. For example, you may want to begin a time line for an entire history course. You will add information to the time line after each lecture and as you work through each chapter. Because of the length of this time line, you may want to use the following options:

- Tape pieces of blank paper together, or use computer paper that has not been separated.
- Use a roll of adding machine tape.
- Tape a long piece of butcher paper to a wall.

Draw and Label a Horizontal Line   Draw a solid line across the middle of your paper. Divide the line into equally sized segments. Below the line, label each segment with dates. You may want to label year by year, five years at a time, or even longer, depending on the length of the time period you are covering.

Add Events   Each time a new event is introduced in the book or in the lecture, add it to the time line. Locate the correct date on the horizontal line; draw a line upward and name the event. You can also use the following options for adding events to your time line:

- Add pictures for greater visual impact.
- When you have more than one event for a time period, write the events in a column above the date or "branch them upward."
- Color-code or draw boxes around events to separate them.

The two following time lines for information from a Western history textbook show possible ways to arrange information about the Old Stone Age:

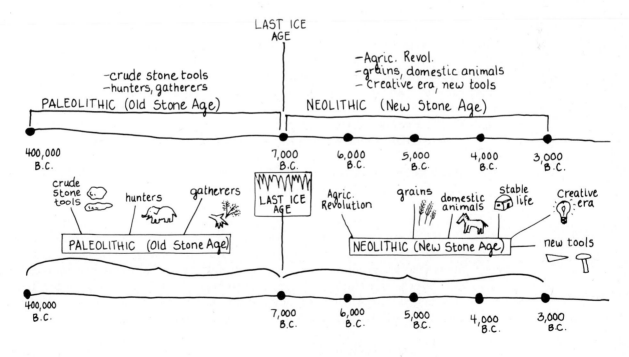

How to Study from Time Lines   Time lines give you constant visual input if they are taped or tacked to the wall where you study. The more you look at them and think about the different events, the stronger the image will be in your memory. Several other techniques are also available.

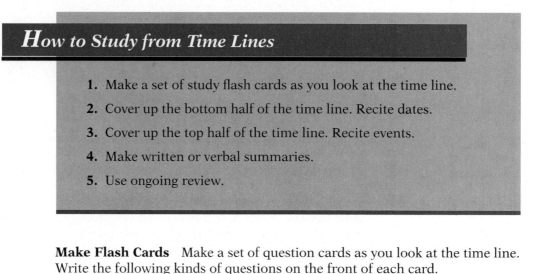

How to Study from Time Lines

1. Make a set of study flash cards as you look at the time line.
2. Cover up the bottom half of the time line. Recite dates.
3. Cover up the top half of the time line. Recite events.
4. Make written or verbal summaries.
5. Use ongoing review.

Make Flash Cards   Make a set of question cards as you look at the time line. Write the following kinds of questions on the front of each card.

1. What happened in the year _____?
2. What important event happened right before _____?
3. What event took place right after _____?
4. What effect did _____ have on _____?
5. When did _____ take place?

Write the answers on the back of the cards. Use the cards the same way you use vocabulary flash cards. Sometimes you can study by looking at the questions and referring to the time line for answers. Other times you can refer to the back of the cards for feedback.

Recite Dates   Use your hand, arm, or paper to cover the bottom half of the time line. All you will see are events. Recite the dates for each event.

Recite Events   Reverse the process. Cover up the top of the page. All you will see are dates. Recite what events occurred on each date.

Write Summaries   Look at the beginning section of your time line. Use complete sentences to write a summary that includes the main events and their dates. As you complete one section of the time line, continue to the next section until you have a summary of all the dates and events on your time line.

If you prefer to give a verbal summary, turn on a tape recorder. Clearly discuss the dates and the events on the time line; speak in full sentences. Students who are auditory learners may prefer this verbal summary approach or may choose to write a summary and then read it into a tape recorder. If you choose to record the information, be sure to pause between dates to give yourself time for the information to "register" in your memory.

Use Ongoing Review   Ongoing review is always necessary. Recite from your flash cards, your time lines, and your summaries throughout the term. Each time you add new information to your time line, spend some time reviewing the information that is already there.

| **Exercise 11.5** | **Drawing Your Time Line** |

Make a time line that shows significant events in your life. Be as creative as you like. Reveal only the information that you are comfortable sharing.

SUMMARY
- Visual mappings, hierarchies, category grids, and time lines are all visual representations of information.
- Use visual mappings and hierarchies to show the relationships between main ideas and supporting details.
- Use category grids to compare or contrast two or more subjects.
- Use time lines to present chronological information.
- Visual study tools must be studied thoroughly after they have been created. Steps for studying include:

  1. Visualize the image you drew without looking at it.
  2. Recite the topic and the main ideas. Then recite the details for each main idea.
  3. Get feedback to check your accuracy.
  4. Reflect by reproducing the visual study tool on paper, by writing summaries, or by working with the information in other ways.
  5. Review the image frequently to keep it active in your memory.

PERSONALIZING WHAT YOU LEARNED
1. Score and record the score for your chapter profile.
2. On your own paper, expand this chapter's visual mapping.
3. Make your own vocabulary list of all the terms in this chapter that are printed in color.

"To the Student" (p. xv) provides you with more detailed directions for completing these activities.

Review Questions

Multiple Choice

Read each question carefully with all the options. Cross out the options that you know are incorrect. Select the best option that remains. Write the letter of the best option on the line.

_____ **1.** Mapping can be used to

  a. take lecture notes.
  b. take textbook notes.
  c. make reflect activities.
  d. do all of the above.

_____ **2.** Hierarchies

    a. contain the same information found on visual mappings.
    b. show main ideas of what you read or heard.
    c. use rows and columns.
    d. always arrange information chronologically.

_____ **3.** Visual study tools require the use of

    a. visualization.
    b. creativity.
    c. recitation.
    d. all of the above.

_____ **4.** If you have large amounts of information for a mapping,

    a. use complete sentences.
    b. use larger paper.
    c. omit some ideas.
    d. do all of the above.

_____ **5.** If a mapping shows specific steps or a specific order of information,

    a. remember the order.
    b. don't use mappings.
    c. add numbers to the lines.
    d. do none of the above.

_____ **6.** It is acceptable to

    a. write full sentences in each cell of a category grid.
    b. write sideways if needed.
    c. put more than one event on a time line date.
    d. do none of the above.

_____ **7.** When you visualize your study tools, you should

    a. try to see the skeleton first.
    b. be creative and make changes as you go.
    c. stare at the paper for five minutes.
    d. add new information that you forgot to put in the original mapping.

_____ **8.** Feedback

    a. is nonessential when you work with visual tools.
    b. lets you know how well you are learning.
    c. comes only in auditory form.
    d. is characterized by none of the above.

_____ **9.** Reflect activities often include

    a. making tapes as you recite in full sentences.
    b. reproducing the visual tool from memory.
    c. summarizing the information in new ways.
    d. doing all of the above.

_____ **10.** Students with weak visual processing skills

    a. shouldn't try visual study tools because they're too frustrating.
    b. can develop visual study tools and then incorporate auditory systems for reviewing.
    c. should use mappings and hierarchies for class notes.
    d. should ask a notetaker to make the visual tools.

_____ **11.** To avoid having cluttered hierarchies,

    a. stagger the information on lower levels.
    b. write more complete sentences.
    c. eliminate some main ideas.
    d. eliminate some key words.

_____ **12.** If your mapping or hierarchy has more than seven main ideas,

    a. chunk the ideas so that you study sections at a time.
    b. consider making two visual study tools.
    c. use boxes and/or color to separate each part.
    d. do all of the above.

_____ **13.** On a time line

    a. the earliest date is on the right.
    b. the earliest date is on the left.
    c. the number of years is hard to see immediately.
    d. the dates are written above the line.

_____ **14.** The columns on category grids

    a. show the different topics or subjects.
    b. show the categories, characteristics, or traits that will be compared and contrasted.
    c. cannot contain more than five cells.
    d. label the rows to be studied.

_____ **15.** When reciting is done with visual study tools,

    a. it should begin from the bottom up.
    b. it should move counterclockwise.
    c. it should go from details, to main ideas, to topic.
    d. it should go from topic, to main ideas, to details.

Visual Study Tools

1. Read the following information carefully.
2. Create a visual study tool for this information. You can create a visual mapping, a hierarchy, a category grid, or a time line.

Recent Technological Developments

Today's electronic computers are the result of five stages (sometimes called generations) of research and development. The first generation of computers (1946 to 1958) relied on glass vacuum tubes to control the internal operations of the computer. The vacuum tubes were quite large and generated a great deal of heat. As a result, the overall computer was huge and required special air conditioning. . . .

The second generation (1959 to 1964) began when tiny, electronic transistors replaced vacuum tubes. Transistors greatly reduced the size of the computer. They helped solve the heat problem that plagued computers in the first generation. In addition, transistors were more reliable, required less maintenance, and processed data much faster. . . . Finally, the second generation computers were programmed with high-level languages such as FORTRAN and COBOL.

The third generation (1965 to 1971) began when computer manufacturers started using integrated circuits (ICs), small silicon chips containing a network of transistors. Integrated circuits were quite a bit faster and more reliable than the single transitors used in the second generation. . . . Third-generation computers had more storage capacity and greater compatibility of computer components. The concept of remote terminals that communicate with a central computer became a reality at this time.

The fourth generation (1971 to the present) began when computer manufacturers began using large-scale integrated (LSI) circuits. LSI circuits are silicon superchips that contain thousands of small transistors. As a result of LSI circuits, fourth-generation computers are smaller. . . . Both Apple and the IBM personal computers were developed during this generation.

To date, we have experienced four generations of computer development. Now, many experts believe we are entering the fifth generation— computers that can simulate human decision making. . . . We stress that computers must be programmed or given step-by-step instructions to complete a specific task. Programming is necessary because the computer doesn't have the common sense or the ability to think on its own. This may change in the near future. Today, researchers are studying the human brain in an attempt to learn how people reason and think. Scientists have known for years that the human brain is more efficient than any computer when comparing storage capacity, data retrieval, and information processing. The researchers' goal is to duplicate the same process with a computer and thus create a form of artificial intelligence.

WRITING ASSIGNMENTS

1. Write an explanation for a friend that tells how to create a visual mapping, a hierarchy, a category grid, or a time line.
2. Write your reaction to visual study tools. Express your likes, dislikes, concerns, and problems regarding this method of studying.

Creating Multisensory Study Tools

*T*o be an effective learner, you must be familiar with how your memory works and with what strategies support your unique style of learning. Do you remember information presented in pictures better than information that you hear? Can you learn by using rhymes or tunes? Do you remember better when you are involved in hands-on experiences? This chapter introduces you to multisensory study tools that incorporate your learning style preferences and boost your ability to remember new information.

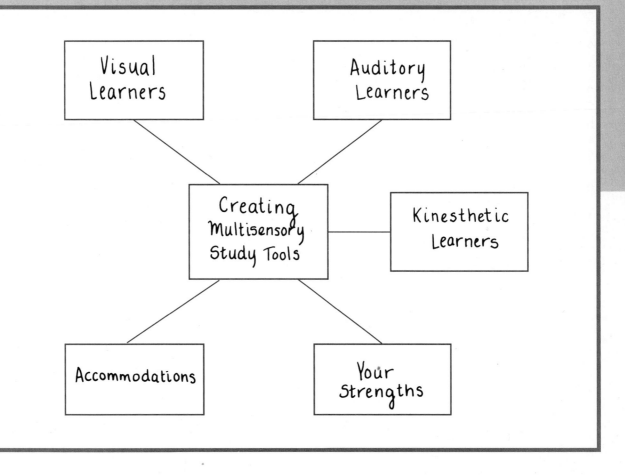

Multisensory Profile

Please answer honestly each of the following questions about your current attitudes and study habits. Your answers should reflect what you *do*, not what you *wish* you would do.

After you read each statement, check YES if you do this *always* or *most of the time*. Check NO if you do this *seldom* or *never*.

		YES	NO
1.	I am fairly familiar with the way my memory works.	_____	_____
2.	I need to learn how to use a greater variety of study skill techniques appropriate for the way I learn.	_____	_____
3.	I know at least four study skill strategies that are recommended for kinesthetic learners.	_____	_____
4.	I know at least four study skill strategies that are recommended for auditory learners.	_____	_____
5.	I know at least four study skill strategies that are recommended for visual learners.	_____	_____
6.	I try to use some study tools from each of the three modalities (visual, auditory, and kinesthetic).	_____	_____
7.	I am willing to try new study tools to see if they work for me.	_____	_____
8.	I understand how tape recorders can be used to prepare for tests.	_____	_____
9.	I understand how color-coding can be used on visual study tools.	_____	_____
10.	I understand how exaggerated movements and drama or dance can be used to help the learning process.	_____	_____
11.	I use at least two different study tools each time I study.	_____	_____
12.	I create multisensory study tools that match my learning style or preference.	_____	_____

Visual Learners   A wide variety of learning strategies capitalize on a preference or an ability to learn visually. Chapter 1 introduced you to several basic strategies for visual learners, and Chapter 11 discussed visual study tools in depth. If you are a **visual learner,** incorporate as many of the following strategies as possible each time you study. To be multisensory, recite frequently as well.

Strategies for Visual Learners

1. Visualize pictures or movies in your mind as you read and study new information.

2. Convert information into visual mappings, hierarchies, category grids, and time lines.

3. Include pictures (sketches, cartoon, or stick figures) in as many study tools as possible. Use pictures in mnemonics (see Chapter 13) when possible.

4. Create a strong visual image by using different colors as you mark textbooks, take notes, or create study tools.

5. Copy and write information in your own words by taking notes, making flash cards or vocabulary sheets, and using any other study tools that require information to be on paper.

6. Observe nonverbal clues of instructors during lectures; these visual effects can alert you to important information for notes and can be used to associate and recall the information from memory when needed.

7. Record directions and important information on paper; do not rely on your auditory memory for details.

Strategies for Nonvisual Learners   If you have weak visual skills, a different set of strategies may be needed. However, remember that learning styles are often preferences; the goal is to learn to work effectively in all modalities. If you make a serious effort to use visual study tools, but they continue to be ineffective, consider the following:

1. *Have you given yourself enough time to learn how to use these new visual strategies?* If you have not been in school for many years or if you have never been introduced to visual study tools before, your difficulties may be related to lack of experience with these methods. Practice, experience, and willingness to continue working with these strategies may be part of the solution.

2. *When was the last time you had a thorough vision test?* Visual learning requires your eyes to take in and process information accurately. Optometrists are now able to test for much more than nearsightedness and farsightedness. Perhaps you would benefit from thorough screening for visual acuity, light and color sensitivities, depth perception, astigmatism, spatial perception, and other visual abilities. Many vision problems can be corrected through specialized lens or vision therapy.

3. *Have you ever been diagnosed with learning disabilities involving visual processing?* Some visual processing difficulties may arise because your neurological structure does not enable you to process visual information accurately. If you have been tested and diagnosed with visual processing deficits, your task is to convert visual information into auditory information. Refer to the strategies for auditory learners and to possible accommodations at the end of this chapter.

| Exercise 12.1 | **Assessing Your Visual Skills** |

This exercise helps you explore your visual strengths. Complete each item in as much detail as possible.

1. Most people have a daily routine that they use when they get up in the morning. Close your eyes and try to make a movie in your mind that shows you going through your daily routine. Answer the following questions after you have viewed your movie.

   Was the picture clear?_____

   What colors did you see?_____

   Name several details other than yourself that were in your movie._____

   _____

2. Recall the last time your instructor wrote information on the chalkboard.

   Can you actually picture your instructor writing the information?_____

   What was written on the chalkboard?_____

   Name a specific detail you remember about this situation other than the information written on the board.

   _____

3. Without looking back in your notebook, draw any visual mapping that has been used this term in this class. Include as many details as possible.

Auditory Learners

Auditory learners have strong auditory memories and have a "good ear" for language and, oftentimes, music. Strong language skills may include well-developed vocabularies, an interest in words and languages, appreciation of poetry, and the ability to be articulate (to express ideas clearly). These learners often have a good sense of rhythm, enjoy rhymes, and can easily pick out tones and notes in music. If your auditory skills are average, through effort and training you can strengthen and use them more effectively.

Study Tools for Auditory Learners

The goal for auditory learners is to utilize as many study tools based on auditory skills as possible. You can use the following strategies with the material in all your courses.

Strategies for Auditory Learners

1. *Talk out loud and recite regularly.*
2. *Tape* information.
3. Add *rhythms* or *tunes* to your learning.
4. Learn to use *computerized technology*.

Talk Out Loud and Recite Regularly Every opportunity you get, talk out loud. You are much more likely to remember information after you hear yourself say it. Memory is also strengthened when you link the visual and the auditory information together as you practice rehearsing or retrieving information during your review. Auditory learners should use these four techniques when possible:

1. Repeat directions out loud to yourself or to the instructor to check for accuracy. Directions can be paraphrased by asking, "Do you mean we should . . . ?" or "Are you saying that we must . . . ?"
2. As you study, always practice putting information in your own words until you can express it clearly.
3. Increase your reading comprehension by reading out loud. Use this strategy for reading textbooks, directions on assignments, test questions, and test answers. The myth that "all good readers read silently" simply is not true. The benefits of oral reading far outweigh the drawbacks. As a courtesy to others who may be within hearing range, try to read out loud in an isolated place so as not to distract them.
4. Seek opportunities to discuss information with others. There are many ways to take advantage of your auditory and language skills. Participate in class discussions; ask questions about information presented. Form a study group or find a study partner with whom to discuss assignments and course information. Ask about classes that use **cooperative learning,** which emphasizes working in groups within the classroom.

Tape Information A small, portable tape recorder (preferably with a built-in microphone) is an essential piece of equipment for auditory learners. The auditory channel to memory can be used effectively by taping information as it is presented during a lecture or as it is recited during the reflect or review steps of studying. Tape recording can be used effectively in four ways:

1. Actively take Cornell notes during a lecture, but also use a tape recorder to record the lecture. At home, use the lecture tape to add missing details to your class notes; do not, however, tape lectures intending to listen to them again and again without taking any notes. Too many hours of listening would be required.
2. Once you have made Cornell notes, marginal notes, markings, or visual study tools, practice reading and reciting the information into a tape recorder. The tape you create now is effective and efficient because it contains selective information to rehearse.
3. A week or two before a test, make review tapes that contain only the information that you need to study further. Your tape may include words and definitions from flash cards, a main idea or subject and lists of supporting

details, names, dates, events, or any other reminders you predict will be needed for the test. Review the tape frequently; you may want to explore the effects of reviewing the tape right before you sleep.

4. If you have a learning disability that makes reading difficult and auditory learning is your strength, ask about getting your textbooks on tape from the Library for the Blind or from your student services office on campus.

Add Rhymes or Tunes   Many auditory learners have a strong sense of rhythm, rhyme, and melody. These strengths can be used in a variety of ways. Chapter 13 discusses specific mnemonics (memory tricks) based on rhymes and rhythms. The following strategies can also be used:

1. Put the information you are learning to music. Use a familiar tune to sing what you are trying to remember. If you are wondering if this really works, do you still sing when you are asked to recite the alphabet?
2. Rap music is based on rhythm and rhymes. If you are a fan of rap music, you are familiar with its creative use of language. Identify the important information you are learning, and set it to original rap tunes.
3. As you recite information, use an exaggerated voice with more pronounced intonation (rise and fall of the voice) and volume. Dramatically emphasizing information you are learning can be effective as well as fun!

Use Computerized Technology   Portable calculators and portable dictionary spellcheckers or language masters are now available with voice to assist auditory learners. These computerized learning aids are sold at most electronic stores, or they may be available for use on your campus.

Speech synthesizers are also available for computers. The information on a computer is read by a computerized voice. The voice quality varies, but most voices are easy to understand. Speech synthesizers are valuable for auditory learners in two ways:

1. They can assist auditory learners with proofreading. These learners can do an assignment on the computer and then activate the voice synthesizer to hear what they have written. Students who have difficulties proofreading visually can often quickly detect errors when they hear the information read.
2. Voice synthesizers can read any printed information once it has been scanned into the computer. The information can then be read to the auditory learner. Check with your library or counseling department to see if your school has this technology.

Strategies for Nonauditory Learners   Auditory learning may not be the preferred modality for many students, but they can operate in this modality when necessary. Often that entails hearing the information and immediately transferring it to a visual form, such as notes.

However, if you are not able to function well when information is presented auditorally, try exploring the following four areas:

1. *Do you have poor listening skills?* Review the listening skills required for concentrated listening in Chapter 3.
2. *Do you have limited experience using auditory strategies?* If you have worked hard for many years to do all your memory work "in your head," you may not be comfortable talking out loud, learning from tapes, and interacting with others through discussion. Be willing to experiment and practice auditory techniques. Continue to use these strategies more effectively by incorporating them into your study methods whenever possible.
3. *When was the last time you had your hearing checked?* Hearing problems definitely affect your ability to use auditory learning strategies. An audiolo-

gist can check your hearing acuity and ability to hear different pitches, tones, frequencies, and volumes. If you find yourself straining to hear what is being said or if words sound muffled or disorganized, schedule a check-up with your doctor or with student health services.

4. *Have you been tested and diagnosed with a learning disability related to auditory processing?* Students with auditory processing disabilities often have difficulties mastering language skills, following directions or lectures, and blocking out external distractions when trying to listen. Accommodations for these learning disabilities are discussed at the end of the chapter.

Exercise 12.2   Assessing Your Auditory Skills

You will need two pieces of notebook paper. Your teacher will read two sets of directions for you to follow. Listen carefully to the directions that will tell you what to draw on your paper. Do the best you can.

Kinesthetic Learners

Kinesthetic learners are doers. They learn best through hands-on experiences, and they concentrate better when there is movement involved. They may prefer to pace as they recite or tap a foot or use a lot of hand gestures as they study. Kinesthetic learners are often talented in painting, drawing, sculpturing, playing an instrument, acting, inventing, or engaging in sports.

Study Tools for Kinesthetic Learners

Individuals who have a preference for kinesthetic learning find that their preference must be supplemented with visual or auditory strategies since many concepts to be learned in the classroom and through textbooks do not lend themselves as easily to movement or kinesthetically oriented strategies. The following strategies, however, should be used by kinesthetic learners whenever possible.

Strategies for Kinesthetic Learners

1. Learn by using your hands.
2. Learn by using larger body muscles.

Use Your Hands   Kinesthetic learning involves touching, feeling, and using fine muscles and fine motor skills. The following strategies all offer the opportunity to learn by using your hands:

1. *Handle Objects.* Clearer understanding is often possible if there are solid objects involved in the learning. For example, if you are in a science class and there isn't lab time, schedule time after class to get closer to examine, touch, pick up, and move objects around. The objects may be instruments for measuring, plants, or rocks. If you are learning about parts of a computer,

sit at a computer so that you can see, touch, and use the parts being described. If you are in a vocational class, pick up, hold, and examine the different parts of the engines, the tools used, and the supplies required.

2. *Create manipulatives.* Create manipulatives, objects that can be moved around as you study. The following examples demonstrate the use of manipulatives.

   ■ Take squares of paper or blank index cards. Write one key word or concept on each card. Move the cards around on a table to create a mapping, a hierarchy, a category grid, or a time line. Use string or yarn to connect the different levels of information, or tape or glue cards to large chart paper and then draw the lines.
   ■ Create a visual study tool on paper; then cut the pieces apart. Shuffle them and reassemble them to form the visual study tool.
   ■ Write each vocabulary word on one card and its definition on another card. Leave all the backs of the cards blank. Shuffle the cards. Work on a large desk or countertop. Match the words and the definitions.
   ■ Place all the vocabulary cards you've just created face down. Turn two cards up at one time. If they match, remove them from the table. If they don't match, turn them face down and continue with two more cards. (Visual memory skills are also required for this type of concentration game.)

3. *Use exaggerated movements.* Exaggerate your hand gestures to help learn and remember important points. Add a sense of drama to the process of studying. For example, if there are ten parts to a piece of machinery, thrust your arms forward and in a loud, exaggerated voice state; "There are TEN PARTS to learn." Spread your ten fingers in an exaggerated motion. Proceed to name the parts and move each finger as you name the part. Muscle memory can assist long-term memory.

4. *Type or use a word processor.* Use your kinesthetic skills by typing review information to study. You can type summary notes from lectures or from the textbook, answers to your chapter questions, vocabulary study sheets, and homework assignments.

Use Larger Body Muscles   Students who learn best kinesthetically are often able to remember more when their whole body is actively involved in the learning process. The following strategies, which utilize large muscle movement, can be incorporated as often as possible in studying:

1. *Pace as you study.* Pacing (walking the floor in a steady pattern) is one option when you start to feel restless while sitting down. Try pacing as you hold the book and read out loud. If you are using taped materials, walk, listen, and repeat the important information back. Reflecting is easy while you pace. Ask yourself questions. Talk out loud. Explain how the information can be used in other ways or how it is related to previously learned information. When you feel ready to sit, continue studying at your desk.

2. *Use a chalkboard.* As you review information, stand and write it on a chalkboard. You can easily draw visual study tools, words and definitions, and graphs on a chalkboard. Experiment using colored chalk.

3. *Make wall charts.* Make visual study tools on large chart paper, which you then tape or hang on your walls. Use wide-tipped felt pens as you make visual mappings, hierarchies, time lines, category grids, or vocabulary sheets.

4. *Learn by doing.* When a process is described, actually complete the steps of the process. In a culinary class, reading the steps to create a gourmet dish is much less effective than actually performing the steps. In math, if you are to use a formula to calculate the perimeter of an area, get a large tape

measure and actually measure the perimeter. The formula becomes real once you have actually applied it in the physical world.

5. *Use drama or dance.* Incorporating body movement into learning often makes the task of learning easier and more enjoyable. If you are taking a literature class, dramatize/role-play the characters you are studying. Stand up, change voices, read, and act out some of the different characters' significant experiences. If you have a study partner who also prefers this learning modality, try pantomiming some of the information you are studying.

You may want to make a tape of information that you are learning; dance to the tape and repeat the information as you move. Many colleges now have programs called **integrated studies.** Courses from several disciplines are taught together; for example, a literature course may be linked with an acting course. Since integrated studies often include teaching approaches well suited to the kinesthetic learner, ask if your college has courses taught through integrated studies.

Kinesthetic learners constantly need to devise creative ways to use their kinesthetic abilities because the standard approaches used in schools are not usually kinesthetically oriented. However, kinesthetic learners need to recognize the power of this learning modality and be willing to experiment with new learning techniques that involve movement.

Exercise 12.3   Assessing Your Sensory Skills

Work with a partner to solve the following problem. As you search for the solution, pay attention to the strategy you are using to come up with your answer.

> A parent and a child are standing together on the sidewalk. They both start walking at the same time. Each person begins the first step with the right foot. The child must take three steps for every two steps the parent takes. How many steps must the child take until they both land again on the same foot (either the right or the left foot)?_____

Did they finish on the left foot or the right foot?_____
Explain how you figured this out.
Did you use visual, auditory, or kinesthetic skills to solve the problem?_____

Exercise 12.4   Using Multisensory Skills

Work with a partner. Read each description of a study tool or a study strategy used by a student. Decide if the item uses mostly visual, auditory, or kinesthetic skills. Write *v* for visual, *a* for auditory, and *k* for kinesthetic. You may use more than one letter for each example.

_____ **1.** Find a "study buddy"—someone who wants to discuss what you are studying in class.

_____ **2.** Use a scanner and a speech synthesizer to put a test on the computer so that the test and the answers can be read with a voice.

_____   **3.** In geometry class, you use your finger or hand to trace different angles on the surface of the desk.

_____   **4.** Because you always get numbers confused or reversed, you use a talking calculator, which is based on your greatest processing strength.

_____   **5.** Spend time studying your Cornell recall column so that you can clearly picture the columns when you need to retrieve information.

_____   **6.** Tape the lecture. It's the only way you will be able to take notes on the lecture by yourself.

_____   **7.** After you have marked your textbook, read the information you marked. String the ideas together into complete sentences; have a tape recorder turned on.

_____   **8.** Make movies in your head to visualize the story that you just read.

_____   **9.** Writing is important, so create your own flash cards.

_____   **10.** Make time lines with clever cartoon pictures to show the different events.

_____   **11.** Pretend you are on a stage. Walk across the stage reciting with exaggerated expression the information you need to learn.

_____   **12.** Someone showed you a trick for remembering the spelling of difficult words. You trace it again and again on the chalkboard and then you close your eyes and "see yourself" tracing the letters in order.

Now create five examples of study tools or study strategies that are based on the modality or modalities shown on the following lines. Do not use any of the activities just described. Your answers can be based on personal experiences or on information in this chapter.

_v, a_   **1.** _____

_____

_____

_____

_k, a_   **2.** _____

_____

_____

_____

_v_   **3.** _____

_____

_____

_____

k, v   **4.** _____

_____

_____

_____

a   **5.** _____

_____

_____

_____

Your Strengths

A student once expressed his frustration that textbooks do not incorporate enough multisensory approaches. Nevertheless, if you compare today's textbooks to the textbooks published fifty years ago, you will find more multisensory materials today. There is greater use of visual study tools such as graphs, diagrams, pictures, and visual mappings; notes in the margins; and colored print. Many courses include supplementary computer programs or interactive videos. Teachers are also incorporating a wider variety of methods in the classroom. Greater attention and focus are being given to the three basic learning modalities.

However, textbooks and teachers cannot incorporate all the available multisensory study tools because textbooks would be too lengthy and too expensive and classes would be much too long. In addition, multisensory study tools are very individualized. The value of the study tool begins in the process of creating it specifically to match your own individual style of learning. Your personal touch is essential.

Therefore, the responsibility for creating multisensory study tools is yours. You are the most qualified individual to develop a multisensory study tool that meets your needs and your style of learning. You have had many opportunities to explore a wide variety of visual, auditory, and kinesthetic approaches to learning. Your task now is to take the time and effort to apply what you have learned and to create the types of study tools that will bring you desired results.

Exercise 12.5   **Working in Threes**

Work in groups of three to complete this group project. The following three areas must be included in your project: visual study tools, auditory study tools, and kinesthetic study tools. Each person must select a different area so that all three areas are covered.

1. Each person selects one of the three areas to cover. The group will be making a study tool to show the range of possible multisensory tools.

2. Before you begin working, discuss with your partners different ways to arrange the information. Also discuss if you want to use colors or pictures, a tape recording, or any other tool.

3. On large chart or poster paper, begin creating a visual mapping or hierarchy to show multisensory study tools, with each group member working on the particular area she or he has selected.

4. Use your own ideas and ideas from this textbook to make your section of the mapping. Try to show as many different kinds of study tools or strategies that can be used in this kind of learning.

Accommodations   Students with documented learning disabilities are eligible to receive services that enable them to have an equal opportunity to succeed in college. Learning disabilities have been discussed for processing speed, visual or auditory processing, and attention deficit. Specialized testing can also reveal learning disabilities in the following areas:

- Short-term memory processing
- Comprehension-knowledge (the amount of background information stored in long-term memory)
- Long-term memory retrieval
- Fluid reasoning (integrating information, problem solving)
- Quantitative processing (math abilities)

If you have difficulties in these areas, testing can identify specific disabilities, and eligibility for accommodations can be established. Check with your counseling department or special student services office for testing, eligibility requirements, and available services. The following accommodations are possible for students with learning disabilities:

1. A tutor to help explain or discuss lecture and textbook information, vocabulary, and study tools
2. A notetaker if large amounts of information are given in a lecture class
3. Taped textbooks and four-track tape recorders with varied speeds; compact tape recorders for classroom use
4. Access to computers and adaptive hardware and software (spellcheckers, grammar-checkers, voice synthesizers, scanners)
5. Talking calculators, portable spellcheckers, language masters, or laptop computers
6. Testing alternatives: oral tests, dictated answers, separate testing sites, extended time to complete tests (or assignments), modified tests or assignments
7. Special classroom requests: assignments given in written form, desired seating, lecture outlines
8. Reduced courseloads or modified degree requirements

SUMMARY
- The most effective study tools are those that are compatible with your visual, auditory, or kinesthetic strengths.
- Visual learners benefit by using visualizations, pictures, color-coding, copying, and nonverbal clues.
- Auditory learners benefit by taping material, reciting, reading out loud, discussing material, creating rhymes or tunes, and using voice synthesizers.

- Kinesthetic learners benefit from activities that involve manipulatives, keyboarding, and large muscle movements.
- Multisensory study tools use a combination of modalities that strengthen the process of moving information into your memory and retrieving it when needed.
- Students with learning disabilities are eligible to receive accommodations to increase their opportunity to succeed.

PERSONALIZING WHAT YOU LEARNED
1. Score and record the score for your chapter profile.
2. On your own paper, expand this chapter's visual mapping.
3. Make your own vocabulary list of all the terms in this chapter that are printed in color.

"To the Student" (p. xv) provides you with more detailed directions for completing these activities.

Review Questions

True-False

To help keep your mind focused, underline the key words in the true-false questions before you answer them.
Write *T* if the statement is TRUE. Write *F* if it is FALSE.

_____ **1.** An effective learner knows how his or her memory works and has a choice of strategies to assist in learning.

_____ **2.** Once you understand your learning preferences, you should always try to select strategies that work on your areas of weakness.

_____ **3.** Weak listening skills can affect auditory processing skills.

_____ **4.** Vision and hearing problems should be ruled out as a reason for poor performance in the visual and auditory modalities.

_____ **5.** A kinesthetic learning strategy involves some form of movement.

_____ **6.** Taped lectures should be listened to at least four times.

_____ **7.** Questioning, paraphrasing, and participating in discussions are effective strategies for auditory learners.

_____ **8.** Taped information is most beneficial when it is based on selected study and review information.

_____ **9.** Large motor skills are used when you write on a chalkboard, dance, and pace as you study.

_____ **10.** The most effective multisensory study tools are those created by an individual and designed to use the individual's personal strengths.

Short Answer

1. List the three basic modalities.

2. Name your preferred modality and name three study tools you can create that use this modality strength.

Identifying Modalities

Read each item below. Decide if the study tool or strategy would be most effective for an auditory, a visual, or a kinesthetic learner. Write *a* for auditory, *v* for visual, and *k* for kinesthetic. You may use more than one letter per line.

_____   **1.** Make up a creative story that uses all your new vocabulary words. Practice reciting the story, and then tell it to a friend.

_____   **2.** Enroll in a section of a course that you know uses cooperative learning methods.

_____   **3.** Put a large piece of poster board on your door. Use felt pens to make a list of the important terms you need to learn.

_____   **4.** Stand by the chart with a tape recorder turned on. Recite the definitions of the words on the chart. Check your accuracy.

_____   **5.** Use pieces of paper or index cards to make a concentration-style game to match dates with historical events.

_____   **6.** Read a chapter and then take time to convert the information into a color-coded mapping or hierarchy.

_____   **7.** You have to remember a list of ten items. You decide to learn these by singing them to the melody of your favorite song.

_____   **8.** Use a typewriter or computer to type summary notes to prepare for the next test.

_____   **9.** You get a little silly and start reading a poem with extra loud volume and exaggerated intonation. You know this works to help you remember the poem.

_____   **10.** You tape chart paper to the wall so that you have lots of room to draw a color-coded mapping with pictures to show the contents of a textbook chapter.

WRITING ASSIGNMENTS

1. Write a summary, make a mapping, or draw a hierarchy titled "Strategies That Work Best for Me." Include both your own multisensory study strategies and the best classroom teaching methods.
2. Discuss the kinds of study tools that are difficult for you to use effectively. Which ones are they? Why do you think they are not effective for you?

13 *Creating Mnemonics*

Mnemonics, a Greek term meaning "to remember" or "to be mindful," are tricks that help trigger associations in your mind. Do you find that some information is difficult to remember even after you have used a variety of study strategies? Do you sometimes find you can remember only part of the information given in lists or series of items? Is information easier to retrieve when you can associate it to other information, to a rhythm, a rhyme, or a short saying? This chapter teaches you nine mnemonics for learning and retrieving information that is otherwise difficult to remember.

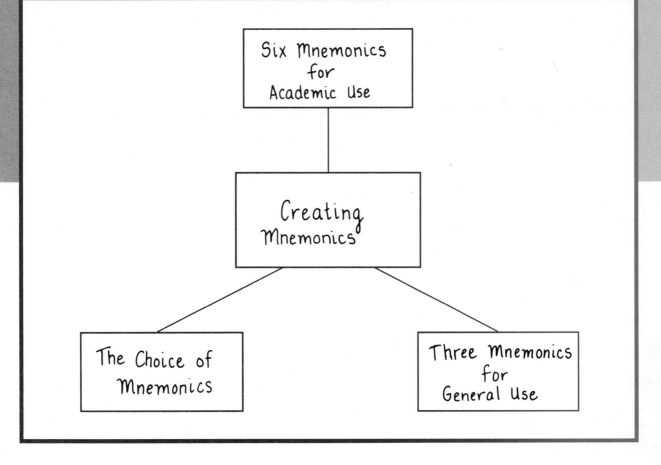

Mnemonics Profile

Please answer honestly each of the following questions about your current attitudes and study habits. Your answers should reflect what you *do*, not what you *wish* you would do.

After you read each statement, check YES if you do this *always* or *most of the time*. Check NO if you do this *seldom* or *never*.

	YES	NO
1. I understand the term *mnemonics*.	_____	_____
2. I know how to use the first letter of words to create a memory tool to remember words in a list.	_____	_____
3. I remember what SAVE CRIB FOTO means.	_____	_____
4. I can give an example of a rhythm, rhyme, or jingle used as a mnemonic.	_____	_____
5. I should use a mnemonic for everything I need to learn.	_____	_____
6. I have used a memory system to help me remember items in a list.	_____	_____
7. I can use the memory principle of association to remember someone's name.	_____	_____
8. I should avoid using cartoons or pictures when I study because they are childish.	_____	_____
9. I know how to use mental imagery to help me learn.	_____	_____
10. When I use mnemonics, I rehearse so that they are 100 percent accurate.	_____	_____
11. I make sure that I can translate each part of the mnemonic to show that I know what it represents.	_____	_____
12. I know how to use a story line as a mnemonic device.	_____	_____

Six Mnemonics for Academic Use

Learning to use mnemonics serves three important purposes:

1. Mnemonics can help you remember information that is otherwise difficult to remember.
2. Mnemonics provide you with extra clues to help trigger your memory to recall information.
3. Mnemonics add an element of interest to studying.

The mnemonics presented in this chapter can be used effectively if they are used selectively, studied thoroughly, and recited with accuracy.

Many types of mnemonics are available. The six mnemonics listed here can be used effectively with academic material.

Six Mnemonics for Academic Use

1. Acronyms—words made from the initial letters of key words

2. Acrostics—sentences made from the initial letters of key words

3. Rhythms, rhymes, and jingles—sayings for auditory learners

4. Association—two ideas linked together

5. Cartoons/pictures—pictures for visual learners

6. Story lines—creative stories for auditory learners

Acronyms

An **acronym** is a word or a group of words made by taking *the first letter* of a *key word* in a list of items you wish to remember. Here are the steps used to make an acronym.

1. Make a list of the items you need to remember—for example, the five Great Lakes in the northern United States:

   Lake *Superior*
   Lake *Huron*
   Lake *Erie*
   Lake *Ontario*
   Lake *Michigan*

2. If each item in your list consists of more than one word, underline *one* key word that would help you remember the item. Do not choose two key words for an item, or you will end up trying to remember more items than are actually there.
3. Write the *first letter of each key word* on the side or the bottom of your paper. For the Great Lakes, the letters would be *S H E O M*.
4. Rearrange the letters until you can form a word or a group of words—in this case, HOMES. Usually the letters in their original order do not spell out a meaningful word. If the list must be remembered in order and a word is not formed by the letters in order, a different kind of mnemonic is needed.
5. Practice memorizing the mnemonic. Then practice translating it accurately by reciting what each letter represents.

The following examples show how the letters of key words were rearranged to form an acronym:

- When a child has a stomach flu, what should he or she be fed? My doctor told me the foods to give: *b*anana, *r*ice, *a*pplesauce, *t*oast. The acronym is BRAT.
- How should you treat sudden muscle injuries? The answer is to *c*ompress, use *i*ce, *e*levate, and *r*est. The acronym is RICE.
- A quartet consists of four voices: *s*oprano, *a*lto, *t*enor, and *b*ass. An acronym can be STAB.

As you create acronyms, remember, first, to select only *one* key word for each item. For example, in the second example just cited, you must select only one key word for "use ice." If you use both words, you may think that each letter represents two treatments. Second, sometimes two or more words can be used for an item. Try one letter first; if you can't create an acronym, try using the other letter. Since words need vowels, if you have a choice, try working first with a vowel.

Exercise 13.1   Creating Acronyms

1. In Chapter 3 you learned an acronym for effective listening. The acronym is shown here. What does each letter represent?

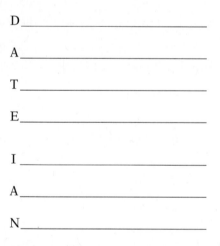

D_____

A_____

T_____

E_____

I_____

A_____

N_____

2. In Chapter 6, you were offered seven strategies for comprehending paragraphs more effectively. They are summarized here. Note how a key word is underlined in each.

   a. Assess your <u>reading</u> skills.
   b. Read the paragraph <u>out loud</u>.
   c. Find <u>definitions</u> of unknown words.
   d. Find the <u>topic</u> sentence.
   e. Look for the supporting <u>details</u>.
   f. Discover the <u>organizational</u> pattern.
   g. Review the <u>notes</u> from the preceding paragraph.

Use the first letter of the key words to create an acronym. Hint: The first word is a contraction. The second word is a name.

_____ _____ _____ _____ , _____ , _____ _____ _____

Acrostics   **Acrostics** are sentences made from the initial letters of key words. If you must learn a list of items in a given order and the letters of the key words don't form an acronym, try forming a sentence. Here are the steps to make an acrostic:

1. Make a list of the items you need to remember. For example, you need to remember the order of operations in a math problem. They are:

   parentheses
   exponents
   multiplication
   division
   addition
   subtraction

2. If there is more than one word per item, underline *one* key word that would help you remember the item.

3. Write the *first letter of each key word* on the bottom of your paper. Leave space after each letter.

   P_____   E_____   M_____   D_____   A_____   S_____

4. Make a sentence using the letters in order. Sometimes it is easier to remember a sentence if it is *silly, bizarre,* or *significant to you*. An acrostic for the order of mathematical operations is as follows:

   Please excuse my dear Aunt Sally.

5. Memorize the sentence. Then practice translating the mnemonic by reciting what each word represents.

   After you have underlined key words, sometimes you may have more than one word that begins with the same letter. To avoid confusion, try using words that begin with the *first two letters of the key words*. For example, in the twelve memory principles, there are two principles that begin with *O*—organization and ongoing review. If *organization* and *ongoing* review are the key words you selected for the acrostic, try words that begin with *OR* and *ON*.

| **Exercise 13.2** | **Brainstorming Acronyms and Acrostics** |

Work with a partner to brainstorm ways to make an acronym or an acrostic for the following items. The items do not need to be learned in order unless specifically stated.

1. The five theories of forgetting: decay, displacement, interference, incomplete encoding, retrieval failure

   mnemonic:_____

2. Four communication skills: reading, writing, spelling, listening

   mnemonic:_____

3. The planets in the order that they orbit the sun: Mercury, Venus, Earth, Mars, Jupiter, Saturn, Uranus, Neptune, Pluto

   mnemonic:_____

4. The five steps for planning a long-range assignment. The steps must be in order.

> a. Break the task into individual steps.
> b. Estimate the time needed for each step.
> c. Double the estimated time.
> d. Use the calendar to map due dates.
> e. Begin right away.

mnemonic:_____

Rhythms, Rhymes, and Jingles

Auditory learners and those with strong language skills enjoy learning through rhythms, rhymes, and jingles. When you find yourself singing commercials, the advertisers have found a way into your memory through mnemonics. If you know the spelling rule *"I* before *E* except after *C,"* you already use one rhyme.

Rhythms, rhymes, and jingles often show special creativity. They are formed by listening for words that rhyme or by attaching a catchy tune to your sayings. Notice the originality in the following examples.

- Who invented dynamite? *Alfred Nobel had quite a fright, when he discovered dynamite.*
- Which way should you turn to open a jar or tighten a bolt? *Righty Tighty . . . Lefty Loosy.*
- Stalactites are icicle-shaped deposits that hang down from the roof of a cave. Stalagmites are deposits in a cave that build up from the floor. *When the mites go up, the tights come down.*

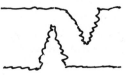

Association

Oftentimes an item can be remembered when it is associated to something that is familiar or has a similar characteristic. For example, if you want to remember someone's name and the person has the same name as your aunt, connect the person to your aunt. When you see the person again, you think about your aunt and remember this person's name. You can also connect the person to an object. If the person's last name is Carpenter, picture the person wearing a carpenter's apron and holding a hammer in one hand.

The following examples show other kinds of **associations** that have been created to remember specific information:

- How high is Mount Fuji in Japan? You can remember the height by stringing the number of months in a year to the number of days in a year and then adding 24 hours: 12, 365 + 24 = 12,389 feet.
- Do you enjoy a nice "dessert" or a nice "desert" after dinner? After dinner, you want dessert, the word with two *S*'s. Just remember this mnemonic that has two *S*'s: *so sweet.*
- You must remember to get your gym clothes out of the dryer tomorrow before you go to school. Since you always start coffee in the morning, go to bed with a clear mental picture of your gym clothes stuffed inside the coffee pot. The association occurs in the morning when you see the coffee pot.

■ If you are talking about the administrator at school, are you referring to the principal or the principle? If you are studying geometry, are you learning principles or principals? This mnemonic, which uses association, will help: The princi*pal* is your *pal*. He or she is the *main* person. (The principal role in a play is the *main* role.) Any time you are referring to some type of standard or ru*le*, you need to use the spelling princip*le*.

Cartoons and Pictures   Students with artistic talents as well as visual learners often use pictures to add visual cues for memory. You have learned that pictures can effectively be added to mappings, hierarchies, time lines, flash cards, or any other study tools. A picture, however, can be created as a starting point. Key words and details can then be written next to or within the picture.

Whether you can draw detailed pictures, whimsical cartoons, or basic stick figures, you can use them to strengthen your visual imagery and boost your memory. The following examples show a few possible ways to convey ideas through pictures:

■ Five *R*'s of Cornell

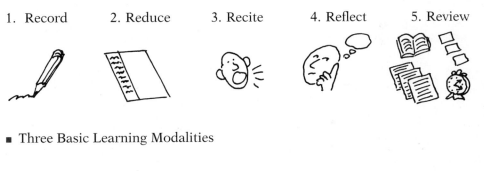

1. Record   2. Reduce   3. Recite   4. Reflect   5. Review

■ Three Basic Learning Modalities

■ Seven intelligences

Visual-spatial
Linguistic
Music
Logical math
Body-Kinesthetic
Intrapersonal
Interpersonal

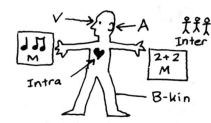

■ Do you sometimes forget which direction is *latitude* and which direction is *longitude* on a map or globe? Say each word and exaggerate your mouth as shown in the pictures. Notice when your mouth is *long*? Say "latitude" with your mouth smiling (going *around* the globe).

- Is the Tropic of Cancer north or south of the equator? Which is the Tropic of Capricorn? Well, when you have *corns* on your feet, are they on the northern or the southern half? The picture helps with the visual image.

Exercise 13.3	**Drawing Cartoons and Pictures**

Do one of the following on your own paper.

1. Write the steps of SQ4R. Next to each step, add a picture that serves as a visual cue for you.

2. Draw a large triangle with five levels inside. Label the five stages of Maslow's hierarchy. Add a picture for each level.

Story Lines   **Story lines** are a form of short, creative writing. This technique works for students who have strong auditory skills, can memorize lines well, and possess good language abilities. Story lines are not difficult to write, but they can be difficult to memorize quickly and accurately.

The following steps can be used to create story lines:

1. Make a list of the key ideas or words that must be remembered.
2. Begin to tell (tape-record) or write a story that includes the first word. If the story can include the definition or proper use of the word, the story will be even more useful.
3. Continue until you have developed a story that includes all the words.
4. Visualize the story happening. Make a movie in your mind.
5. Review the story until you can recite it from memory. As you recite, write down the key words. These words should match the original list of words.

The following story line reviews the techniques for dealing with external and internal distractions. The key words are underlined.

There's <u>no need</u> to <u>take charge</u> of the <u>red bow</u>. <u>Break down</u> and <u>keep score</u> on your <u>to do list</u>. <u>Check the doc</u> for <u>tunnel vision</u> and <u>active learning</u>.

Exercise 13.4	**Creating Mnemonics**

1. Six helpful hints were given in Chapter 2 to help you reach goals. The mnemonic was EVA BAT. What were the six hints?

E_____   B_____

V_____   A_____

A_____   T_____

2. Make any kind of mnemonic for the four suggestions for making effective use of the difference between speaking and listening speeds explained in Chapter 9: Take Notes, Summarize, Anticipate, and Question.

_____

_____

3. Make any kind of mnemonic for the eight parts of speech: nouns, pronouns, verbs, adverbs, adjectives, prepositions, conjunctions, and interjections.

_____

_____

4. Make any kind of mnemonic for the skeletal structure (bones) of the arm: humerus, ulna, radius, carpals, and phalanges.

_____

_____

5. Make an acronym for the four defense mechanisms people use: repression, denial, identification, and projection.

_____

_____

6. Make an acronym for the three angles in geometry: right, acute, and obtuse.

_____

_____

Three Mnemonics for General Use   The following three mnemonics are excellent for using in your daily life and for strengthening your visualization skills. They do not always lend themselves well as memory tools for academic information, but they do provide you with effective mental exercises.

*T*hree Mnemonics for General Use

1. Stacking—visualizations stacked one on top of another

2. Peg system—twelve consistent pegs to hang objects on

3. Loci—visualizations of objects in a familiar place

Stacking   If you have a list of ten items that you have to buy when you go shopping, you can make a visual **stack** of these items instead of writing them down. Each time you add an item, make a strong visual image in your mind. To review the list, begin naming items from the bottom up. Each time you can name all the items in order, you are ready to add one more item.

cereal

film

apples

toilet paper

watermelon

mayonnaise

milk

shampoo

cabbage

hot dogs

Peg System   The **peg system** is similar to the stacking system except that you begin with a set of twelve pegs, which never change. (Larger peg systems do exist.) You must begin by memorizing these pegs. Each peg is an object that resembles the shape of the number.

Close your eyes. Name the twelve pegs. Picture them clearly in order. Then practice picturing each peg randomly. What is number seven? What is number three? What is number five? What is number ten? What is number two? What is number nine?

Once you have the pegs memorized, you are ready to "hang objects" on them. Let's say you need to remember eight chores over the weekend. You can use the pegs to make a mental memory system. Take the first task and associate a mental picture to the pencil. In the following example, your first task is to start the laundry. You could picture a washing machine with an enlarged shirt with a pencil in the pocket as it is about to enter the machine. The funnier your picture is, the easier it will be to remember. After you see the picture clearly, work with the second item. Review items one and two mentally. Proceed to add one item at a time. With practice, you can hang items quickly on the pegs. The following example demonstrates visualizing eight different tasks on the first eight pegs.

Loci   **Loci** is a mnemonic that dates back to the time of great Greek orators (speakers), who could deliver lengthy speeches without ever writing notes on paper. Instead of writing notes, orators made notes in their minds by associating parts of their speeches to familiar rooms or places in a building. (Loci means place or location.) As they walked into each room of the building, they visualized items in the room that were associated to the topic to be remembered.

For example, picture your school (you can, however, use any building). Walk in the front doors and see a long hallway. On the right side of the hallway are lockers. Halfway down the hallway is the cafeteria. When you walk through the cafeteria, you reach another hallway. The first room on the right is the science room. The second room is the foreign language room. Proceed throughout the school.

Once you have clearly memorized and visualized the floor plan, add the items you want to remember, in order, to the rooms on the floor plan. You can exaggerate or hang items in awkward positions so that your attention is attracted to them. Continue walking through the floor plan, attaching an item that represents a part of your speech until there is one item in each room. Practice walking through the building and reciting the items in each room.

Exercise 13.5	Using Loci

On your own paper, draw a basic floor plan of your house or apartment. Then follow these directions.

1. Plan a discussion or an important conversation you want to have with a friend. List the separate topics on your paper.

2. Draw a picture or symbol in each room of your house to show the important topics you'll cover in your conversation. Your "walk" through the rooms should show the order of your topics.

The Choice of Mnemonics

After trying the different mnemonics and studying strategies, only you can decide which ones work for you. Notice if you learn best by using visual, auditory, or kinesthetic strategies. The following questions may help you identify which mnemonics are best for you:

1. How does your memory system work?
2. Did these mnemonics help you remember information, or did they confuse you?
3. If your preference is for visual strategies, were you able to visualize some mnemonics more effectively than others?
4. If your preference is for auditory strategies, did rhymes, rhythms, jingles, or story lines work well for you?
5. If you prefer kinesthetic strategies, did creating and writing specific kinds of mnemonics seem effective?
6. Are there particular situations where mnemonics seem to make a positive difference?
7. How could you use mnemonics selectively?
8. Do you enjoy the creativity involved in designing your own mnemonics?

Exercise 13.6	Checking Your Memory

How much do you remember from the mnemonics used in this chapter? Answer as many questions as you can without looking back.

1. What does each letter of HOMES mean? _____

_____

2. What should you feed a child with flu symptoms? _____

_____

3. What does DATE IAN represent? _____

_____

4. What does each word in the mnemonic *Please excuse my dear Aunt Sally* mean?_____

_____

5. If you want to loosen a lid on a jar, which way should you turn the lid?_____

6. Do stalagmites point up or down?_____

7. How high is Mount Fuji?_____

8. Check the sentences that are correct.

_____ I had chocolate cake for dessert.

_____ I had chocolate cake for desert.

_____ The principle called me about my son.

_____ The principal called me about my son.

_____ I did not receive it.

_____ I did not recieve it.

_____ The principles of accounting are complex.

_____ The principals of accounting are complex.

9. Is the Tropic of Cancer north or south of the equator?_____

10. What were the first four stacked items needed at the store?_____

_____

11. What was the second job that needed to be done on the weekend in the peg system?_____

_____

SUMMARY
- Mnemonics—when used selectively—are helpful for remembering information that is otherwise difficult to retrieve from memory.
- To be effective, mnemonics must be rehearsed and recited with 100 percent accuracy.
- Six mnemonics can be used with academic material.

  1. Acronyms are made by creating real words.
  2. Acrostics are made by creating sentences.
  3. Rhythms, rhymes, and jingles are effective for auditory learners.
  4. Association links two items together so that thinking of one item leads to remembering the other.

5. Cartoons and pictures are effective for visual learners.
6. Story lines, a form of creative writing, link key words into an original story.

■ Three additional mnemonics (stacking, the peg system, and loci) strengthen your visual memory and sequencing skills.

PERSONALIZING WHAT YOU LEARNED

1. Score and record the score for your chapter profile.
2. On your own paper, expand this chapter's visual mapping.
3. Make your own vocabulary list of all the terms in this chapter that are printed in color.

"To the Student" (p. xv) provides you with more detailed directions for completing these activities.

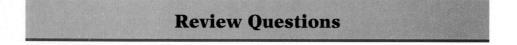

Review Questions

Short Answer

1. Write a definition for each of the following terms:
    mnemonics

    acrostics

    acronyms

    loci

    stacking

2. What are the advantages of using mnemonics?

3. What are the steps for making an acrostic?

4. Name or draw the twelve pegs in the peg system.

5. Can acronyms be used for all material? Why or why not?

6. Create an association to remember each of the following names. You can explain your association in writing, or you can draw a picture.

Charleston

Hatfield

Mandle

Seymour

Vineberg

7. Write a story line to remember these four steps (STSR) for writing effective goals.

1. Be *specific,* clear, and realistic.
2. Set a specific *time line* or target date.
3. Identify the *steps* involved.
4. Plan a *reward* for reaching the goal.

Translating Mnemonics

1. Each of the following pictures represents one kind of mnemonic. Write the name of the mnemonic on the line below the picture.

_____   _____   _____

C. A. T.

_____   _____

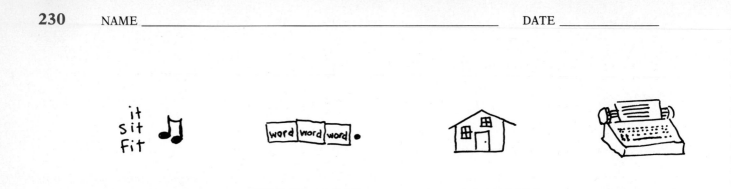

_____   _____   _____   _____

2. The acrostic "Pass Car, Al" can be used to remember the nine kinds of mnemonics. Translate each word into the name of the mnemonic.

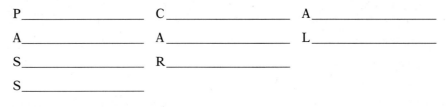

P_____   C_____   A_____

A_____   A_____   L_____

S_____   R_____

S_____

WRITING ASSIGNMENTS

1. Write a short summary of your reaction to mnemonics. Explain what you like or don't like about them. Explain how you will use them in your studying.
2. Write a letter to one of your teachers explaining how mnemonics help you learn. Suggest how valuable it would be if your teacher included mnemonics in class for some of the information being studied.

IV

Testing Your Skills and Your Memory

*T*he first three parts of this textbook provided you with essential study tools designed to help you learn and remember more effectively. In Part IV you learn ways to improve your testing skills.

Chapter 14 provides you with techniques for taking tests with less anxiety and stress. Chapter 15 is devoted to strategies for objective tests. Chapter 16 presents educated guessing strategies that can be used as a last resort for objective questions. Chapter 17 focuses on test-taking strategies for recall or recall-plus test questions. After you learn to use the essential test-taking skills in Part IV, you will be able to perform better on tests and demonstrate how much information you have learned and stored in your memory system.

Taking Tests with Less Stress

*M*any students experience strong physical, emotional, and behavioral reactions or anxieties when they are faced with taking tests. Do you get headaches, stomachaches, anxiety, or short-temperedness in testing situations? Does your mind go blank in the middle of a test? Do you often feel underprepared for tests? Does your performance on tests reflect the amount of studying and learning you have accomplished? In this chapter, you learn test-taking techniques that diminish or eliminate test anxiety and help you perform more effectively each time you are required to complete a test.

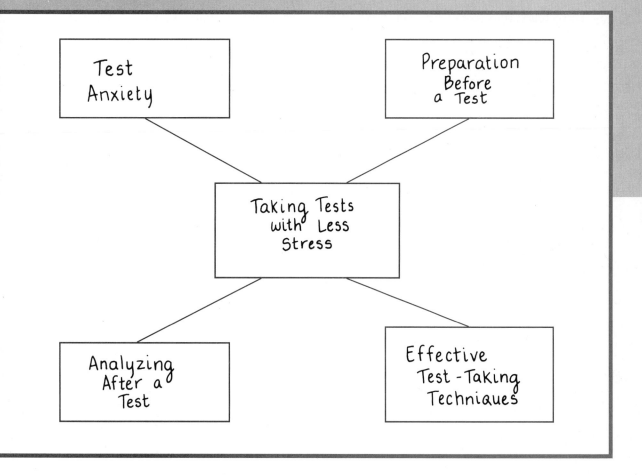

Test Strategies Profile

Please answer honestly each of the following questions about your current attitudes and study habits. Your answers should reflect what you *do*, not what you *wish* you would do.

After you read each statement, check YES if you do this *always* or *most of the time*. Check NO if you do this *seldom* or *never*.

		YES	NO
1.	Even though I know the material, my mind goes blank when I take tests.	_____	_____
2.	I usually feel prepared for tests.	_____	_____
3.	I am often nervous, feel sick, or have physical problems (headache, stomachache, clammy hands) right before a test.	_____	_____
4.	I am able to go into tests with an attitude of confidence.	_____	_____
5.	I often remember my past failures in school and fear the same experiences will happen in college.	_____	_____
6.	I use relaxation techniques, self-talk, affirmations, and/or visualizations to get ready for a test.	_____	_____
7.	During a test I get concerned about other students—how well they are doing or how much further they are on the test.	_____	_____
8.	I am so relieved when I finish a test that I leave as soon as I answer the last question.	_____	_____
9.	If I run out of time, I just leave blanks for the questions I don't have time to answer.	_____	_____
10.	I work straight through the test and answer every question in the order it is given.	_____	_____
11.	I try to find out as much information as possible about a test before it is given.	_____	_____
12.	I spend time analyzing my answers and study techniques after the test is graded.	_____	_____

Test Anxiety   Understanding anxiety first begins with understanding stress. **Stress** is your reaction or response to events or situations that threaten to disrupt your normal pattern or routine. You may have physical, emotional, or behavioral reactions because of a job interview, financial problems, an argument with a friend, relationship problems, or a test. Stress is a natural reaction to situations in which you must perform or make decisions. Stress in each of these situations has the potential to work for you or against you. Stress can work for you when

1. You are able to recognize that a specific event is creating stress.
2. You are able to maintain control of your reaction to the stress.
3. The stress motivates you to search for solutions to the situation.

Some students claim to suffer from test anxiety, yet what they experience may be **normal stress.** Effective study skills for preparing for and taking tests can reduce stress about such tests. However, when stress becomes excessive, anxiety occurs. **Anxiety** robs you of the ability to recognize the source of your stress, gain control of the situation, and begin the search for solutions. The strategies in this chapter are designed to help you handle stress and prevent anxiety attacks.

Understanding Test Anxiety

1. Indicators of test anxiety can be easily recognized.

2. Being underprepared and/or replaying past experiences are two common sources of test anxiety.

Indicators of Test   **Test anxiety** is usually focused *inward*. It often begins with negative emo-
Anxiety   tional thinking or reactions that trigger physical symptoms or behavioral reactions. Negative thinking must be dealt with as soon as it surfaces. Signs of anxiety may include:

- Panicky or depressed feelings
- Increased desire to **procrastinate** (put things off for later)
- Short temper or frequent tendency to blame others for your situation rather than take personal responsibility and control
- Negative self-talk that reflects feelings of low self-esteem and a low level of confidence.

> *They are all smart and I'm not.*
> *I can't do this even if I try.*
> *I never should have taken this class. I know I'll fail.*
> *I've never done well on tests.*
> *The teacher doesn't like me.*

Negative thinking patterns often lead to other physical or behavioral responses, which can include rapid heartbeat or increased blood pressure, tightened muscles or headaches, sweaty or clammy hands, nausea or upset stomach, shakiness or nervousness, wandering mind, poor concentration, a blank mind, confusion, or disorientation.

Exercise 14.1   Recognizing Anxiety

Work in groups of three or four. Brainstorm all the indicators you have ever experienced during an anxiety attack, and make a list of them. Then list the methods you have tried to get the anxiety under control.

Sources of Anxiety   Test anxiety often stems from one of two sources: (1) feeling underprepared or (2) replaying past "tapes" of previous experiences. Strategies are available to combat both sources of text anxiety, but first you must recognize which source is the more likely cause of your feelings of test anxiety.

Underpreparedness   Students whose anxiety stems from not being prepared don't just think they are not prepared; they *know* they are not ready for a test. They know what has taken place (or has not taken place), and they are being honest with themselves. The following possible situations are grounds for being concerned, creating anxiety, and having feelings of **underpreparedness.**

- Reading and/or homework assignments have not been done on time and may not even be finished by the day of the test.
- Topics in the course were discussed, but the student did not understand. Information is still confusing.
- Work, family, or personal problems have disrupted the study schedule, and the student simply did not put in the time necessary to recite, reflect, and review for the test.
- The student knew what *could* be done to study, and knew what *should* be done to review, but did not follow through.
- The student studied from the book but missed many classes and did not get class notes for the lectures missed.
- Sickness slowed down the student's normal pace and affected his or her regular study habits.

Feeling underprepared for a test can trigger panic attacks before the student is even close to the classroom. Some students start to get concerned the day or the night before a test. They try to handle their feelings of underpreparedness by **cramming**. Cramming is an attempt to learn large amounts of information in a short period of time. Since the brain needs time to process large amounts of information, cramming may put some information into memory, but it will not lead to thorough understanding or confidence. This "survival technique" can itself cause anxiety as students become aware of how much they *don't* know.

Past Experiences   Some anxiety attacks stem from past experiences that affected one's belief system, self-esteem, and confidence. It becomes difficult to see a similar situation, such as a test, from a new perspective. There's the belief that what happened in the past will occur again in the present. For some people who suffer true test anxiety, their experiences may have occurred ten, twenty, or thirty years ago. Many belief systems are strong and firmly planted in one's personality or behaviors; for cases that are tied back to years of childhood experiences, traumas, abuse, or extreme emotional distress, the help of a certified counselor or therapist is highly recommended.

The following situations are examples of beliefs based on past experiences that may trigger test anxiety (strategies are available to combat these):

- The last time you took a test in this class you did not do well, even though you thought you had studied, thought you knew the material, and thought you were ready. *The same thing will happen this time; I just know it.*
- You have experienced many test-taking problems in the past.
- You have been influenced by negative comments that parents, teachers, and friends made about you when you were in elementary, junior high, or high school. *I'm just not trying hard enough. Why can't I do better? I'm just lazy. All I need is to get motivated. What's wrong with me?*
- You have transferred feelings of failure, low self-worth, or low confidence from one situation, such as work or relationships, to the testing situation. *I was no good at work. I'm not going to be any good in school. My whole life is a failure. I'm not capable of being good at anything.*
- You suffer from perfectionism. A perfectionist *has* studied and is ready to perform well on a test but can never find enough time to study so thoroughly that there's no doubt that he or she will get the highest grade in the course. *I only want a 100 percent—96 percent is not good enough—and I'll do any extra credit that is available.*
- You fear what will happen academically or financially if you don't do well on the test. Scholarships, team eligibility, financial aid, or agency benefits may be at stake. Parents or partners may have agreements with you based on your level of performance. Fear of failure becomes the dominant emotion that triggers excessive stress. *I'll lose my grant if I don't pass this course. I won't be eligible to play ball if I fail this test.*

Test anxiety that stems from underpreparedness can be reduced or eliminated by learning *and* using effective study strategies. Test anxiety that stems from past experiences can be more difficult to diminish because of the complexity and the dynamics of belief systems, established behaviors, and emotions. The strategies presented here can reduce test anxieties in most cases; however, severe test anxiety cases that are not reduced or eliminated by these strategies should be discussed individually with a counselor, therapist, or psychologist.

Preparation Before a Test

As you prepare for a test, you are challenged to meet your emotional, physical, and mental needs. Test anxiety can be reduced and your performance can be increased by proper preparation.

Emotional Preparation

Before a test, especially a larger test such as a midterm or final exam, your emotions may be more pronounced. The following techniques will help you become emotionally prepared:

1. *Seek support and cooperation.* Notify your roommates, family, or friends about an upcoming test, and share with them how important doing well on the test is to you. Ask for their support.
2. *Use affirmations, self-talk, and visualizations.* Focus on what you have done well, the efforts you have made, and the strategies you have applied. Talk to yourself in a positive manner. Write yourself affirmations that remind you of the positive approach you choose to take. Picture yourself being successful, handling the test without excessive stress, and being able to show what you have learned. Here are a few examples of affirmations:

   I have studied. I am ready. I know this information.
   I have used feedback that proves I have learned this.

I now know and use effective study techniques.
I have been to every class and have done all the work.
I have understood everything in class.
I used enough time and effort to review well.

3. *Use relaxation techniques.* Chapter 3 discussed several relaxation techniques that can be used before you begin studying, as you study, right before the test begins, and during the test if needed. The soothing mask, the relaxation blanket, breathing by threes, deep breathing, and perfect place require little time to use, but the effects are immediate. Heart rate, blood pressure, and breathing rate can all be reduced through the use of relaxation techniques. Select one or two of these methods to use consistently throughout your study-review-testing cycle.
4. *Give and receive praise and encouragement.* If you have a study partner or work in a study group, realize the power of praise and encouragement. Recognize that others in the group may be feeling the pressure. Acknowledge their right answers, and make an effort to give words of encouragement. Their self-confidence and self-esteem can be boosted. Accept their acknowledgment and praise for you and your contributions to the group.

Physical Preparation

Before a test, getting ready physically is also of primary importance. You can physically get ready for a test in several ways:

1. Get a good night's sleep the night before a test. Do not stay up too late studying; if you have used effective study techniques, you won't need to cram. You want to have minimal fatigue and an alert mind, both of which can come through a restful sleep.
2. Allow time for a healthy breakfast. A nutritious breakfast begins your day with a high energy level that is maintained for several hours. Avoid sugary foods such as doughnuts—they may give you an "energy boost" but will wear off quickly and leave your energy level lower than before you ate.
3. Check that you have all the necessary supplies, such as paper, pencils, pens, calculator, spell-checker, and review notes.
4. Allow extra time to get to school the day of the test. Take care of basic needs (restroom, drink of water) before you go into the classroom.

Mental Preparation

Your mental preparation for a test should have started from the first day of class and continued throughout the term. Have all homework and reading assignments completed on time and well before you begin reviewing for a test. Focus on understanding information and linking or associating information by using visual and auditory strategies. Use studying strategies based on your modality preference, and then use alternative strategies if you need more rehearsal. Ongoing review is essential to practice retrieval. Effective study habits are going to incorporate the twelve principles of memory, and use of these principles must occur over time.

In addition to using the basic study skills, there are a few other suggestions for preparing for a test:

1. Organize your materials for studying. Gather important handouts, homework assignments, notes, old tests, or flash cards you have created.
2. Take time to make a special study schedule for test preparation. Prior to final exam week, create a new weekly schedule to reflect the demands for study time.
3. Make a special set of notes that contain summaries or information that requires more of your attention. Focus most of your study time on these special notes.

4. Use study methods that give ample feedback. To help you identify areas that need more review, have a friend, study partner, or family member quiz you.

5. Anticipate test questions. Use information from your notes, lectures, and textbook to predict test questions. If you have a study partner, anticipate and ask each other test questions. Practice answering the questions.

6. Attend any review sessions that might be offered. If your teacher doesn't offer any, perhaps several interested students can form their own.

7. Find out as much as you can about the upcoming test. Some teachers give you access to old tests; some students who have already completed the class may give you some suggestions about how to study for this teacher's test, the topics to cover, and the kinds of test to expect.

| Exercise 14.2 | **Getting Ready** |

On your own paper, make three categories with lists of things you do to get emotionally, physically, and mentally ready. You may use the ideas in this chapter plus any other techniques that you know to get ready for a test.

| Exercise 14.3 | **Finding Out About a Test** |

If you have a test scheduled for the next few days, try finding answers to the following questions. If you don't have a test within the next few days, answer the questions based on what you knew *before* the last test was given. Write your answers on your own paper.

1. What kinds of questions are there (true-false, multiple choice, matching, fill in the blank, short answer, essays)?

2. How many questions are there?

3. Do all the questions have the same point value?

4. How much time is allotted for the test?

5. Can I have more test time if I need it?

6. What chapters or part of the course does the test cover?

7. Do I need to know theorems, definitions, names, dates?

8. Are points taken off for spelling or grammar errors?

9. Can I use a dictionary, spell-checker, calculator?

10. Are there any sample tests available to review?

11. Is there a review session, study guide, or study sheets?

12. What percentage of my grade comes from this test score?

13. When do I get the test back? Is it discussed in class?

14. Is any extra credit available?

Effective Test-taking Techniques   After days of anticipation, the day of the test arrives. The following techniques for getting a good start, reading carefully, answering questions, and finishing a test will help you perform well on all your tests. Use each technique every time you face a test-taking situation.

Getting a Good Start   Make the following five suggestions a part of your test-taking habits. These suggestions help you shift your focus from other thoughts to the test.

Getting a Good Start

1. Arrive early and ready to begin.
2. Jot down important information to remember.
3. Listen carefully to all the directions.
4. Survey the test before you begin.
5. Budget your time.

Arrive Early and Ready   Allow extra time to get to school early so that you don't feel the need for last-minute rushing. Sit in your usual place unless you get too distracted by friends sitting near you. Use your time right before class productively:

1. Get your necessary supplies ready on your desk.
2. Take a few minutes to focus on the subject. Mentally rehearse some of the information you have reviewed.
3. Use a familiar relaxation method, or visualize yourself successfully completing the test.

Jot Down Important Information   As soon as you get the test, on the side or back of the test jot down any information you want to be sure to remember. This may include formulas, mnemonics, lists, or facts. If you are not allowed to write on the tests, ask if you can have blank paper available for organizing ideas.

Listen to Directions   As the teacher begins to talk, pay close attention to the directions. There may be changes on the test, corrections, or suggestions.

Survey the Test   Take a quick look through the test to find out:

1. The types of questions
2. If questions are printed on the back of the pages
3. Where to place your answers
4. The point value of questions
5. The length of the test

Budget Your Time   Once you have surveyed, make a quick plan to budget your time. This is especially important if you have essay questions. Next to each major section of the test, estimate and jot down how much time to spend on each section so that you have time to complete the entire test. Be sure to leave enough time to write and proofread essay answers.

Working Through the Test   When the test begins, every minute is valuable. Your primary goal is to answer each question the best that you can so the test results accurately reflect your level of knowledge.

The following suggestions can help you work through the test efficiently and can lead to test-taking with less stress.

Suggestions for Working Through the Test

1. Read directions and questions carefully.

2. Direct your thoughts and actions outward.

3. Go through the four stages of answering questions.

4. Ignore other students.

Read Carefully   Read all the directions carefully. Before you begin answering questions, get a clear picture of what is being asked. Use the same techniques as you read the questions. Pay close attention to modifiers and signal words (Chapter 15).

Direct Your Thoughts Outward   Remember that anxiety keeps your focus inward. The following techniques focus your eyes, your mind, and your behavior outward to the test itself:

1. If you start to panic, become a more active learner. Circle direction words and underline key terms in directions and in questions. These markings help keep your eyes and your mind focused on the task at hand.
2. Mouth the questions or even read them in a whisper. This activates your auditory channel and asks one more of your senses to help you out.
3. Use a blank paper or your arm to block off the rest of the test. Since anxiety often results in the eyes jumping around or moving randomly, this method helps keep your eyes focused on one question at a time and produces a calming effect.

Go Through the Four Stages of Answering Questions   As you strive to answer questions, use the following four stages for each question.

Four Stages of Answering Questions

1. Immediate response
2. Delayed response
3. Assisted response
4. Educated guess

Immediate response is what you hope happens for each question. This is the payoff for effective studying. After carefully reading the question, you are immediately able to provide the correct answer. The question automatically triggers associations, and the information from long-term memory is available. Immediate response boosts your confidence and moves you through the test more quickly.

Delayed response occurs when you read the question but are not sure of the answer. Read the question *twice*. Try to recall the information by linking or associating the key words in the question to clusters of information in your memory. For example, if the true-false question reads, "Metacognition involves knowing a wide variety of strategies and being able to choose the correct strategy for the learning task involved," try recalling the definition you learned for metacognition. Do the learned definition and this statement mean the same thing? Or try to visualize the notes that you made on metacognition or hear the teacher discussing metacognition. If you are still not sure of the answer, delay your response. *Skip the question for now.* Return to it after you have answered as many questions as you can using immediate response. *Make a small check next to the question or on your answer sheet.* This serves as a reminder to return to the question later. Move to the next question.

Assisted response occurs when you return to the unanswered questions. Now you use the rest of the test to help you find a possible answer. Look at the key words in the question. In the preceding example, the key words would be "metacognition" and "strategies." Skim through the test looking for these words. The information used in other questions may assist you in finding the correct answer. It may be that as you worked through the test, you found information that triggered your memory and enabled you to answer a question that you had left unanswered. During assisted response, utilize whatever you can to produce an answer.

When all else fails, guess. Chapter 16 provides you with some strategies for **educated guessing.** These strategies improve your odds at guessing correctly, but they are not foolproof. Educated guessing strategies are *never* more effective than knowing the answers.

Ignore Other Students   Sometimes a relaxed attitude can be altered or influenced by other students or friends. Do not watch others to see if they are farther ahead than you or working more easily than you. The first students to leave do not necessarily know the information the best; they may in fact not know the information so that is why they left early. Try very hard not to compare yourself or your performance to others. Work at your pace, always doing the best you can with your answers. Keep your mind and your eyes on your test. Avoid looking at someone else's desk; your glances may be interpreted as attempts to cheat or get answers from someone else. Every minute during a test is valuable time; don't waste it by getting sidetracked worrying about others.

Using Test Time Wisely   Students with effective test-taking skills do not finish a test and then rush out of the room; instead, they use the extra time to review all the answers on the test, proofread for mistakes, and strengthen short-answer or essay questions by adding more information.

The following questions about using test time wisely are frequently asked by students:

1. *Should I change answers while I'm reviewing the test?* Do not change answers if you are panicking and feel time running out. Change answers only if you can justify the change; perhaps other questions on the test gave you clues or helped you recall information necessary to answer the question.
2. *Are there any other reasons to stay longer?* Yes. Some students feel more comfortable asking questions about the test when fewer students are present. The teacher's response to a question may trigger your memory or give you a needed clue.
3. *What if I don't have time to finish the test?* If you run out of time, guess at answers rather than leaving them blank. A blank space can only be wrong; an educated guess can add a few more points if it is correct. For essay questions, take a few minutes to list the points you would have included in your essay if you had had more time. Listing your main points usually leads to some test points.

If you often have problems finishing tests on time, *before* the day of the test ask if more time will be allowed if it is needed. Some teachers will make arrangements for extended time on tests if the request is made prior to the day of the test.

Analyzing After a Test

Tests are valuable learning tools. Right after a test, make a list of the questions that confused you. Write down topics that you did not study thoroughly enough; return to your notes or your book to look up answers or information that is still on your mind.

When the test is returned, analyze it.

1. What kinds of questions did you miss the most? Do you see a pattern? For example, if you missed the most points on fill-in-the-blank questions—that's a signal that you need to learn better strategies for that kind of question. (See Chapters 15 and 17.)
2. Did you make any careless mistakes? Which ones and how?
3. What was the source of the information you missed? Was it discussed in a lecture, was it from the textbook, or was it on a handout or overhead?
4. Which parts of the test had the best scores? Why?

Learn the information that was incorrect on the test. You don't want the incorrect answers to stay in your memory. Make notes or flash cards with the correct answers. Discuss any of the questions you missed with your teacher if you still don't understand the information. On your final exam you will likely see these questions again, so learn from your mistakes right away.

Also look at the study skills you used to prepare for the test. Be honest with yourself as you answer these questions:

1. Did you spend enough time getting ready for the test?
2. What strategies worked to help you remember information? Which strategies did not seem to be effective? How will you adjust your study techniques?
3. Which twelve memory principles did you ignore? How can you incorporate them more effectively in your study techniques?

If you did not score as well as you had hoped, don't be too hard on yourself. This is just one test. Use it as motivation to improve your studying and test-taking techniques. Give yourself credit for the parts that you did well. Discuss your progress with your teacher. Find out if there are options to retake the test or if any extra credit can be undertaken to improve the grade. Be willing to ask for help and listen to suggestions. Learning is a lifelong process; you won't master it all at once. You can, however, continue searching for new keys to success and new strategies that are right for you.

Exercise 14.4   Reflecting After a Test

After you have completed a test, answer the following questions on your own paper.

1. What grade did you get?

2. Were you pleased with the results? Why or why not?

3. Were all your assignments done on time before the test?

4. How much time did you spend preparing for this test?

5. Did you make any kind of review sheets to help you study?

6. Did you review your notes, textbook objectives, summary and review questions, and handouts from class?

7. Did you recite while you studied?

8. Did you study alone or with a partner?

9. Which memory principles did you use when you studied?

10. Did you have more errors on any one specific kind of question?

11. Did you have any indicators of test anxiety? If yes, explain the indicators and suggest ways to control them on the next test.

SUMMARY
- Test anxiety, a state of excessive stress, results from being underprepared or from being ruled by past negative experiences.
- Emotional, physical, and behavioral reactions shown during a state of anxiety reduce your ability to concentrate, retrieve information, and perform well.

- There are strategies that you can use to prepare emotionally, physically, and mentally for tests.
- Get a good start, which includes listening to directions and surveying the test.
- As you work through the test, follow these four steps for answering questions:

1. Use immediate response for answers you definitely know.
2. Use delayed response for those answers that you do not know right away.
3. Use assisted response after you have answered all the questions you know; use other parts of the test to help locate correct answers.
4. Use educated guessing strategies when you've exhausted other options.

- Analyzing your test when it is returned enables you to adjust your study techniques and learn from your tests.

PERSONALIZING WHAT YOU LEARNED

1. Score and record the score for your chapter profile.
2. On your own paper, expand this chapter's visual mapping.
3. Make your own vocabulary list of all the terms in this chapter that are printed in color.

"To the Student" (p. xv) provides you with more detailed directions for completing these activities.

Review Questions

Multiple Choice

Read each question carefully with all the options. Cross out the options that you know are incorrect. Select the best option that remains. Write the letter of the best option on the line.

_____   **1.** Test anxiety can stem from

    a. underpreparedness.
    b. underpreparedness and past experiences.
    c. past problems taking tests.
    d. lack of sufficient study time.

_____   **2.** Being underprepared can create

    a. panic and concern.
    b. the need to cram.
    c. test anxiety.
    d. all of the above.

_____   **3.** Cramming

    a. is a survival technique used for underpreparedness.
    b. uses most of the memory principles.
    c. processes large amounts of information efficiently.
    d. can be effective when done correctly.

_____   **4.** Test anxiety can be reduced by

    a. ignoring other students in class.
    b. focusing on outward thoughts and actions.
    c. recognizing your strengths and accomplishments.
    d. doing all of the above.

_____   **5.** Before a test, it is important to get ready

       a. physically by having a good night's sleep and an energy-producing breakfast.
       b. mentally by reciting, reflecting, and reviewing.
       c. physically, emotionally, and mentally.
       d. emotionally by thinking positively and securing support from others.

_____   **6.** To prepare mentally for a test, a person should

       a. spend time cramming.
       b. study as late as possible.
       c. use strategies based on modality preferences.
       d. relax by going to a movie the night before.

_____   **7.** A student who uses a wide variety of study techniques to learn thoroughly should be able to answer most questions on a test by using

       a. educated guessing.
       b. delayed response.
       c. assisted response.
       d. immediate response.

_____   **8.** When you skim through the test looking for clues to questions, you are using

       a. educated guessing.
       b. delayed response.
       c. assisted response.
       d. immediate response.

_____   **9.** On tests, you should keep your original answer

       a. always.
       b. unless you find a valid reason for changing it.
       c. because your first "hunch" is always the best.
       d. unless you get a sudden impulse to change it.

_____   **10.** If you run out of time on a test, you should

       a. use educated guessing.
       b. use immediate response.
       c. leave the answer space blank.
       d. cry.

Short Answer

1. Define each of the following terms:

   ▪ anxiety

   ▪ assisted response

   ▪ cramming

   ▪ immediate response

   ▪ natural stress

2. List three ways that you can anticipate what questions may be on a test.

3. List at least four things that you should look at when you survey a test.

4. Name at least three questions you should ask yourself when analyzing a test after it has been returned to you.

5. Name at least three strategies that you can use if you have an anxiety attack while you are taking a timed test.

WRITING ASSIGNMENTS

1. Write one paragraph about your test-taking strengths. Write a second paragraph about your test-taking weaknesses. In a third paragraph, explain what test-taking strategies might strengthen your weaknesses.
2. Teachers often watch students for signs of true test anxiety. Imagine that you are a teacher. Write a description of a student who is suffering from test anxiety during a test. Then describe the actions that you would take to help the student reduce her or his anxiety.

Developing Strategies for Objective Tests

*L*earning to read and answer objective test questions (true-false, multiple choice, and matching) is essential for college students. Do you have difficulties understanding exactly what is being asked on tests? Do you treat each part of a multiple-choice question as a true-false question? Do you often miss points on matching questions because you get confused about which answers you already used? The strategies in this chapter provide you with step-by-step methods for answering objective questions and improving your test scores.

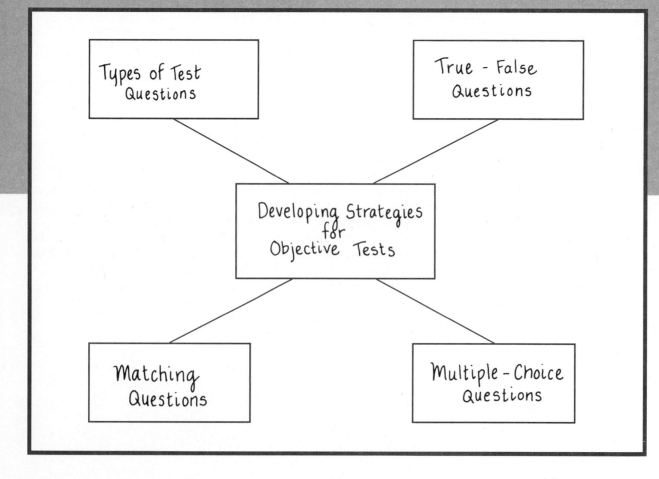

Objective Test Profile

Please answer honestly each of the following questions about your current attitudes and study habits. Your answers should reflect what you *do*, not what you *wish* you would do.

    After you read each statement, check YES if you do this *always* or *most of the time*. Check NO if you do this *seldom* or *never*.

YES   **NO**

1. I am able to answer true-false questions without making many mistakes.   _____   _____

2. True-false questions are confusing for me because I don't understand what they are asking.   _____   _____

3. I have problems selecting the right answer on multiple-choice questions.   _____   _____

4. I use a system for answering matching questions so that I don't use an answer twice.   _____   _____

5. I watch for modifiers in questions because they can affect the meaning of the question. (Modifiers include words such as: "no," "never," "some," "few," "always," "often.")   _____   _____

6. I can tell when a question is testing a definition or a cause/effect relationship.   _____   _____

7. I make too many careless mistakes on tests.   _____   _____

8. I turn each part of a multiple-choice question into a true-false question before I answer.   _____   _____

9. The first time I work through a test, I leave answers that I don't know blank and then return to them when I have time.   _____   _____

10. I use other parts of the test to help me find answers I don't immediately know.   _____   _____

11. I read both columns of items on a matching test before I even begin answering.   _____   _____

12. I write the letters for answers in a sneaky manner so that they could be interpreted in more than one way.   _____   _____

Types of Test Questions

Test writers generally use three types of test questions. **Recognition questions,** also known as **objective questions,** are the easiest form of question to answer. Information is presented in a true-false, multiple-choice, or matching format. In the most basic form of questioning, information is presented in a straightforward manner; you read the information and recognize if it is accurate. On a more challenging level, objective questions require you to apply information to a given situation. Both forms of questioning require that you have the information in your long-term memory.

The second type of test questions, **recall questions,** and the third type of test questions, **recall-plus questions,** are also known as **subjective questions.** Fill-in-the-blank questions and those that require you to list information are recall questions that challenge you to recall or retrieve information from your long-term memory. Recall-plus questions, which include short answer, definition, and essay, require you to retrieve information from your long-term memory and organize it in a meaningful way. Both recall and recall-plus questions are discussed in Chapter 17.

---

*T*ypes of Test Questions

1. Recognition questions: true-false, multiple choice, matching (Chapter 15)

2. Recall questions: fill in the blank, listing (Chapter 17)

3. Recall-plus questions: short answer, definition, essay (Chapter 17)

True-False Questions

For a statement to be true, all parts of the statement must be true and accurate. If a series of items is included in the statement, every item must be true before the question can be marked true. In the following examples, notice how commas are used to separate each item in the series.

_____ 1. Acrostics, loci, acronyms, and rhymes are all mnemonics.

The statement is true.

_____ 2. The peg system, red flag words, stacking, and cartoon pictures are all mnemonics.

The statement is false. The peg system, stacking, and cartoon pictures are mnemonics. However, red flag words, as you will learn, are not mnemonics.

Careful reading of the true-false statement is essential. As you read, to help maintain a focus on the question, underline the key words. Key words are important main ideas or supporting details such as facts, definitions, or vocabulary words. Careless reading may result in omitting important words or misinterpreting the question.

| **Exercise 15.1** | **Answering True-False Questions** |

Read the following true-false questions, which test on information taken from previous chapters. Mark each statement true or false. Pay close attention to the items listed in the series.

_____   **1.** The school calendar gives important dates for changing grades, holidays, class tests, and final exams.

_____   **2.** The three areas of life that need to be balanced are school, leisure, and studying.

_____   **3.** You can increase your speed in notetaking by paraphrasing, using abbreviations, and writing sentences that are not grammatically correct.

_____   **4.** The recall column in the Cornell system should have the headings, key words, study questions, and all the answers.

_____   **5.** Questioning, paraphrasing, and participating in discussions are effective strategies for auditory learners.

_____   **6.** Taking notes, summarizing, anticipating, and questioning are strategies to use when there's a tendency to lose concentration during a lecture.

_____   **7.** Engineers, inventors, musicians, and philosophers are often kinesthetic learners.

_____   **8.** An organized desk, a supportive chair, and two sources of lighting help concentration.

Red Flag Words   **Red flag words** are significant words that may alter the meaning of a question or affect your answer. The four kinds of red flag words should alert you to read carefully: definition clues, negatives, modifiers, and relationship clues. These words contribute significantly to the meaning of a true-false question. Circle these words when you see them in a true-false question. Your reading accuracy can improve greatly if you are aware of these words and consider their usage before you answer a true-false question.

*R*ed Flag Words

1. Definition clues—"is," "are," "means," "refers to"
2. Negatives—"no," "not," and certain prefixes (*dis, in, im, non*)
3. One hundred percent and in-between modifiers ("always," "never," "some")
4. Relationship clues—"reasons," "because," "since," "cause"

Definition Clues   The following words can signal that a question is evaluating your understanding of a term's definition:

also	defined as	or
also known as	involves	referred to as
are	is	states that
called	means	which is

Read the statement carefully. Circle the red flag word, and underline the key term and the key words in the definition. Does the definition given match the definition that you learned? If the answer is "yes," mark true. If the definition is quite different from the one you learned and is incorrect, mark false.

In the following examples, the **definition clue** is circled. The key term and the definition being tested are underlined.

_____   1. Information processing speed (is) the rate that information can be processed through the sections of the information processing model.

This statement is true. The definition matches the one given in Chapter 10.

_____   2. Information processing speed (is) the difference between listening and thinking speeds.

This statement is false. The definition given is not the definition for processing speed.

Exercise 15.2   Using Definition Clues

Underline the key words. Circle the red flag words that indicate a vocabulary term and the definition being tested. Decide if the question is true or false.

_____   1. The increasing-decreasing method in time management states that every time you increase your sleep, you decrease productivity.

_____   2. Concentration is defined as the ability to focus on two or more things at one time without being distracted.

_____   3. RAVES is a formula for solving external distractors.

_____   4. Knowledge of results, also referred to as feedback, is important to include in study techniques.

_____   5. Schemas is another term for the feedback loop.

_____   6. Reflect is the third step of the Cornell notetaking system.

_____   **7.** Metamemory involves knowledge about how your own memory works.

_____   **8.** Acrostics refers to a type of mnemonic in which visual pictures are stacked in chronological order.

_____   **9.** Bibliographies in textbooks are also called references.

_____   **10.** Time lines are visual study tools used to organize information chronologically.

Negatives   **Negatives** are words that carry the meaning of "no" or "not." Negatives appear in three basic forms:

The words *no* or *not*
The words *but* or *except*
Words with *prefixes* that mean no or not, such as:

dis- (disorganized)	ir- (irresponsible)
il- (illogical)	non- (nonproductive)
im- (imbalanced)	un- (unimportant)
in- (incomplete)	

As you read true-false questions, pay close attention to any of the red flags that indicate negatives. *Negatives do not mean that the sentence is going to be false.* Rather, negatives affect the meaning of the sentence and require you to read carefully and think about the significance of the negative in the sentence. If you overlook these negatives, your answer will often be the opposite of what is correct. In the following examples, notice how the red flag negatives are circled and the key words in the sentence are underlined.

_____   **1.** A (dis)organized desk is an external distractor.

   The statement is true. A desk that is not organized can distract.

_____   **2.** An organized desk is (not) an external distractor.

   This statement is also true. An organized desk helps concentration; it is not a distractor.

_____   **3.** A (dis)organized desk is (not) an external distractor.

   This statement is false. A disorganized desk is an external distractor.

_____   **4.** All of the following (except) the last item are external distractors: noise, lighting, people, and a disorganized desk.

   This is false. Noise, lighting, and people are external distractors. The word except *means that the last item is* not an external *distractor. However, a cluttered desk is an external distractor. Because each item in a series must be correct, this statement has to be false.*

Exercise 15.3   **Finding Negatives**

Work in a group of three or four people or with a partner. Circle the red flag words that are negatives. Underline other key words in the question. Answer true or false.

_____   **1.** Studying on the floor or on a bed is not recommended.

_____   **2.** Tape recorders should not be used to avoid notetaking during a lecture.

_____   **3.** The use of music, rhymes, and tunes is unacceptable as a learning strategy.

_____   **4.** Ongoing review is essential in the Cornell system but is optional in the SQ4R system.

_____   **5.** The goal of time management is to use effective strategies to lead an imbalanced life.

_____   **6.** Copying the same notes again and again is a nonproductive use of study time.

_____   **7.** Anxiety is not based on irrational fears and old belief systems.

_____   **8.** An unprepared student may resort to cramming the night before an exam.

_____   **9.** Irregular study hours can lead to misuse of the 2:1 ratio.

_____   **10.** There is no survey step in the Cornell notetaking system.

Modifiers   **Modifiers,** or words that tell to what degree or frequency something occurs, are red flag words of great importance. There is a huge difference between saying that something *always* happens and saying that something *sometimes* or *often* happens. You must learn to pay close attention to these words to determine how often or how frequently something actually occurs. As you notice in the following list, there are other kinds of modifiers, too. Words such as "best" or "worst" show the extremes and indicate that there is *nothing* that is greater or better.

Modifiers can be shown on a scale. The **100 percent modifiers** are on the extreme ends of the scale. They are the absolutes with nothing beyond them. The **in-between modifiers** are in the middle of the scale. They allow for more flexibility or variety because they indicate that a middle ground exists where situations or conditions do not occur as absolutes (100 percent of the time).

Modifiers as Red Flag Words

100 Percent	In Between	100 Percent
all, every, only	some, most, a few	none
always, absolutely	sometimes, often, usually, may, seldom, frequently	never
everyone everybody	some people, few people, most people	no one nobody
best	average, better	worst
Any adjective that ends in *est*, which means "the most" (largest)	Any adjective that ends in *er*, which means "more" (larger)	least fewest

In the following examples, the modifiers are circled and the key words are underlined. Notice if the modifier is a 100 percent modifier or an in-between Modifier.

_____ **1.** (All) teachers will accept late assignments.

This statement is false. Every single teacher in every single school will not accept late assignments.

_____ **2.** (Some) teachers will accept late assignments.

This statement is true. It doesn't tell how many teachers will accept late assignments; it simply indicates that some teachers do.

Exercise 15.4   Finding Modifiers

Underline key words. Circle the red flag words that are 100 percent or in-between modifiers. Try answering each question.

_____ **1.** Your GPA is only important for self-esteem.

_____ **2.** Some students have learning preferences, whereas other students work well in all learning modalities.

_____ **3.** A course syllabus often states expectations and consequences.

_____ **4.** Attendance in college is required in every class.

_____ **5.** The amount of time spent on social or leisure activities should always be more than the total hours for work.

_____   **6.** Everyone should always try to divide her or his "life's pie" into three equal parts.

_____   **7.** All college courses require you to use the 2:1 ratio for studying.

_____   **8.** It is always best and most productive to study late at night when there's no one around to bother you.

_____   **9.** Always begin by studying your favorite subject first so that you can get motivated.

_____   **10.** Reviewing notes from a previous paragraph can sometimes help you understand a difficult paragraph.

Relationship Clues   Some true-false questions test if a certain relationship exists. Relationships often show cause/effect—one item causes another item to occur. Become familiar with the following red flag words for relationships. When you see these **relationship clues** in true-false sentences, think carefully about the relationship being discussed before you decide if the statement is true or false.

affects	creates	increases	result
because	decreases	produce	since
causes	effect	reason	so, so that

The relationship clue is circled in the following examples. The two or more items that form the relationship are underlined.

_____   **1.** Accurate and thorough reciting, reflecting, and reviewing (result in) efficient long-term retrieval of information.

The answer is true. Reciting, reflecting, and reviewing, when used correctly, enable you to retrieve information from your long-term memory.

_____   **2.** In terms of memory, decay occurs (because) only part of the information was rehearsed correctly to move into long-term memory.

The answer is false. Decay occurs because the stimulus was too weak to be processed.

Exercise 15.5   Using Relationship Clues

Circle the red flag words for relationships. Underline key words. Answer each question as true or false.

_____   **1.** Procrastination increases when you use time management.

_____   **2.** Reciting is important because it utilizes the auditory channel and provides feedback for understanding.

_____ **3.** Massed practice is preferred so that the student can learn masses of information quickly.

_____ **4.** Too much information in the recall column of your Cornell causes you to read instead of recite.

_____ **5.** It is not necessary to take notes on graphs, charts, or pictures since they are always easy to remember.

_____ **6.** The principle of selectivity is important because we have to select the important information to put into memory.

_____ **7.** Major ideas or headings should be underlined so that they stand out from supporting details.

_____ **8.** Because terminology is so obvious, you don't need to write terms or definitions in your notes.

Multiple-Choice Questions

Careful reading is also essential for answering multiple-choice questions correctly. Begin by reading the directions carefully. *Usually* the directions say to select only *one* answer; however, do not assume this is always the case. Read the directions to find out. The directions often say to select the *best* answer. One or more of the answers may be correct, but the answer that is the most inclusive (includes the most information) is the best answer. Notice how careful reading is essential in the following example:

_____ **1.** In true-false questions, you should

    a. watch for negatives because they can change the meaning of a sentence.
    b. recognize when a definition is being tested.
    c. consider the importance of a 100 percent modifier.
    d. use red flag words to help you read more carefully.

Answers (a), (b), (c) are correct; however, (d) includes all the answers in (a), (b), and (c). Red flag words are definition clues, negatives, modifiers, and relationship clues.

Stems and Distractors

Multiple-choice questions have two parts: the *stem*, which begins the question, and the **options.** Only one option is correct. The other options are called **distractors.**

(Stem)   _____ **1.** The index in a book

(Distractor)   **a.** provides you with a list of titles for units and chapters.

(Distractor)   **b.** can be organized only by subjects.

(Distractor)

    c. is an alphabetical listing of special-ized words and their definitions.

(Correct option)

    d. is an alphabetized list of subjects or authors discussed in the book.

Too many students make the mistake of reading the stem, seeing one possible option, and then making that option the answer. A better option may exist further down the list. Using a system to think through and answer multiple-choice questions can improve your performance on this type of objective questions.

A Six-Step Strategy for Multiple-Choice Questions

Careful reading of the stem and all the options is essential for multiple-choice questions. Once you have identified distractors, you can work through the four stages of answering questions presented in Chapter 14.

A Six-Step Strategy for Multiple-Choice Questions

1. Read the stem and each option as a true-false question.
2. Eliminate as many distractors as possible.
3. Use immediate response if you know the answer.
4. Use delayed response if you don't know the answer.
5. Use assisted response when you return to unanswered questions.
6. Use educated guessing if necessary.

Step One: Make True-False Statements Read the stem with option (a). Underline key words and circle red flag words if you need help focusing on the question. Then decide if the statement by itself is true or false:

1. If the statement is false, you have discovered a distractor. Cross it out; it will not be the correct answer.
2. If the statement is true, this *may* be the correct answer. Do not select it yet.
3. Continue making true-false statements with the stem and *each* of the options so that you will be able to select the *best* answer.

The following example shows how to think through this process:

_____   **1.** The principle of big picture–little pictures

      a. encourages you to memorize individual facts and details.
      b. is based completely on rote memory.
      c. recommends that you process information only in clusters.
      d. recommends that you strive to "see the trees" *and* "see the forest" when you study.

By adding each option to the stem, these are the true-false statements that result. Decide if each statement is true or false.

_____ **a.** The principle of big picture–little pictures encourages you to memorize individual facts and details.

_____ **b.** The principle of big picture–little pictures is based completely on rote memory.

_____ **c.** The principle of big picture–little pictures recommends that you process information only in clusters.

_____ **d.** The principle of big picture–little pictures recommends that you strive to "see the trees" *and* "see the forest" when you study.

(A) is true, but you don't know yet if it is the best *answer. (B) is false. (C) is false because of the red flag word only. (D) is true. You have identified two distractors. The choice is now between (A) and (D). Which answer is the best? Why?*

Step Two: Eliminate Distractors   Eliminate as many distractors as possible. The more distractors you can definitely eliminate, the closer you are to the correct answer.

Step Three: Use Immediate Response   If you know the correct answer, write it on the line. Be sure your writing is easy to read. If the letter is not clear, it will be marked wrong.

Step Four: Use Delayed Response   If you don't know the correct answer even after you have eliminated a distractor, read the possible options a second time. If you don't know the answer, put a check next to the question. Return to this question after you have gone through all the other questions on the test.

Step Five: Use Assisted Response   When you return to an unanswered question, use an assisted response. Skim back through the test to search for other parts of the test that are related and may be able to help you decide which option is best. If you underlined key words to help you stay focused on the question, skim the test to find those words. You may find information to help you select an answer, or the process of skimming may trigger some association in your memory to help you with the answer.

Step Six: Use Educated Guessing   If none of the foregoing strategies helps you find the correct answer, guess. If you were not able to eliminate any of the answers, you have a 25 percent chance of guessing correctly. If you were able to identify one or more distractors, you have increased your odds at guessing correctly. Chapter 16 discusses educated guessing strategies. However, until then, if you must guess, guess "c."

<table>
<tr><td>Exercise 15.6</td><td>**Answering Multiple-Choice Questions**</td></tr>
</table>

Read the stem and *each* option. Watch for key words and red flag words to help you focus on the question. Eliminate as many distractors as possible (eliminate "false" statements). Cross out the distractors. Write the letter of the *best* answer on the line. (Most of these questions are adapted from previous chapter reviews.)

_____ 1. Visual mapping is also called

    a. hierarchy restructuring.
    b. clustering.
    c. mind makers.
    d. none of the above.

_____ 2. Mapping can be used to

    a. take lecture notes.
    b. take textbook notes.
    c. make review study tools.
    d. do all of the above.

_____ 3. It is acceptable to

    a. put many key words in each cell of a category grid.
    b. write sideways on visual mappings if needed.
    c. put more than one event on a time line date.
    d. do none of the above.

_____ 4. When you visualize a mapping, you should

    a. try to see the skeleton first.
    b. always be creative and make changes as you go.
    c. never stare at the paper for as long as five minutes.
    d. add new information that you forgot to put in the original mapping.

_____ 5. When making a hierarchy on information from a chapter, level two information

    a. should reflect only the chapter headings.
    b. should show all important terminology.
    c. should always include pictures.
    d. may include your own categories and chapter headings.

_____ 6. Cramming

    a. is one of the most effective short-term memory processing strategies available.
    b. uses all the memory principles.
    c. processes large amounts of information efficiently.
    d. is not a technique used by prepared students.

_____ 7. Anxiety refers to

    a. controlled stress.
    b. uncontrolled stress.
    c. a natural form of stress.
    d. motivational stress used to be productive.

_____ 8. Test anxiety can be reduced by focusing on

    a. test-taking tasks and ignoring others.
    b. outward thoughts and actions.

    c. your strengths and accomplishments.
    d. all of the above.

_____ **9.** The process of surveying can be used to

    a. become familiar with new books.
    b. get a sense of what is in a chapter.
    c. quickly see what is on a test.
    d. get an overview of unfamiliar printed materials.

_____ **10.** If a person's goal is not based on self-motivation,

    a. success is likely.
    b. it may be difficult to visualize obtaining the goal.
    c. creating minigoals would be impossible.
    d. it is always created by parents' expectations.

Matching Questions

Matching questions are based on **paired associations.** Paired associations are items that were linked together when you learned the information. For example, a word is linked or paired to its definition. When you think of the word, you associate it to the definition. When you think of the definition, you pair it with the word. Paired associations for matching may include:

- Words and their definitions
- People and what they did
- Dates and events
- Terms and their function or purpose

A Seven-Step Strategy for Matching Questions

When you are faced with matching questions on tests, you will see a list of words on the left and their paired associations on the right. The key to answering these questions is to work through them in a systematic way. The following steps begin with directions for reading through the two columns and then applying the four stages of answering questions.

A Seven-Step Strategy for Matching Questions

1. Read the directions carefully.

2. Find out if each list has the same number of items.

3. Read through the list with the shortest entries first.

4. Use immediate response for definite right answers by working from the list with the longest entries.

5. Use delayed response and helper words.

6. Use assisted response.

7. Fill in the remaining spaces with leftover answers.

Step One: Read the Directions   Begin by reading the directions carefully. Usually each item on the right can be used only once; if an item can be used more than once, the directions will probably say so.

Step Two: Count the Items   Count the number of items in the left column and then the number of items in the right column. If both lists contain an equal number of items, each item will be used once. Sometimes the list on the right is longer, indicating that some of the items will not be used. Extra items make matching questions a little more difficult to do because you cannot automatically match up what is left over.

Step Three: Read the Shortest List   Usually the column on the left will have the shortest entries. These may be words (terminology), names, dates, or events. Read these so that you are aware of the choices that are available. Also notice what types of pairing will be used. Are these people, events, dates, or vocabulary terms? Notice the difference in length in the following entry:

_____	**1.** intrinsic reward	**a.**	a technique used to switch the time blocks of specific activities
_____	**2.** trading time	**b.**	material items or activities used when goals are met
_____	**3.** motivation	**c.**	a feeling, emotion, or desire that moves a person to take action
_____	**4.** extrinsic reward	**d.**	feeling proud, relieved, or satisfied

The terms on the left are shorter and take less time to read than the entries on the right. Therefore, read the list on the left first.

Step Four: Use Immediate Response   Now that you are familiar with the items on the left, begin reading the first item on the right. Read the item carefully, and quickly scan your memory for an association to that item. Look on the left to see if the associated word is on the list. For example, if the item on the right is a definition, scan your memory for the vocabulary term. Look for that term in the column on the left.

   If you see the definite association or match, write the letter of the answer next to the item on the left. If answers cannot be used more than once, *cross out the letter that you used in the right column.* If you do not know the correct answer, do *not* do any guessing at this point. If you guess incorrectly, you will miss this answer and at least one more since you cannot use an item as the answer in more than one place. Continue reading through the list on the right, matching only those that can be answered with immediate response.

Step Five: Use Delayed Response   Read the statement on the right one more time. Add a helper word, such as any of the following, to connect the two items. **Helper words** are words or phrases that can link an item from each column into a complete sentence.

happened when	is	means
happens with	is called a	tells about
involves a	is related to	

Assume that you were not certain of an answer or an immediate response. Notice how you can use delayed response with helper words.

_____	**1.** intrinsic reward	**a.**	a technique used to switch the time blocks of specific activities
_____	**2.** trading time	**b.**	material items or activities used when goals are met
_____	**3.** motivation	**c.**	a feeling, emotion, or desire that moves a person to take action
_____	**4.** extrinsic reward	**d.**	feeling proud, relieved, or satisfied

Begin with answer (a). Try to make a complete sentence: "A technique used to switch the time blocks of specific activities is called_____? Glance down the list on the left to find a term to complete this sentence. The sentence can be completed with number 2, trading time.

Continue this process for each item. If you are not able to find a definitely correct answer, do *not* write an answer yet. Skip the item; you can return to it later. Work through the list making all the matches you can with immediate and delayed response.

Step Six: Use Assisted Response   Look at all the items that remain. These will be items on the right that have not been crossed out and items on the left that have no letter answer on the line. Skim back through the test to look for clues. Look for the key words on the left to appear other places in the test. Oftentimes other questions can assist you with the answer or can trigger the associations for you. Match up as many of the remaining pairs as possible.

Step Seven: Fill in the Remaining Spaces   If you have not matched items at this point, there are few clues left to use. Grammatical clues can sometimes help you match up the remaining answers. Information from the same category or subject can be a clue. If you have no clues, simply write the remaining answers on the remaining blanks so that every blank has an answer.

Matching questions themselves are not usually too difficult because they require only recognition and because all the information you need to generate answers is printed on the paper in front of you. The greatest difficulty with matching occurs when a student begins without a definite system. One answer may get used too many times; used answers are not systematically crossed out, so they get used again. Jumping all around the lists can cause some people great confusion; to avoid this, work systematically. Begin at the top and work your way down.

Exercise 15.7	**Answering Matching Questions**

Use the systematic steps just discussed. Match the items on the left to the items on the right. Write the letter answer on the line. Each answer can be used only once.

_____   **1.** Red flag words

_____   **2.** 100 percent modifiers

_____   **3.** In-between modifiers

_____   **4.** Relationship clues

_____   **5.** Prefixes with negative meanings

_____   **6.** Recognition questions

_____   **7.** Recall questions

_____   **8.** Recall-plus questions

_____   **9.** Stem

_____   **10.** Distractors

a. words such as "sometimes," "often," "some," "perhaps"

b. units of meaning that are attached to the beginning of words and have the meaning of "no" or "not"

c. questions that require you to retrieve information from long-term memory

d. significant words that may alter meaning if they are not read carefully

e. the beginning part of a multiple-choice question

f. answers that are known immediately

g. options that are incorrect answers

h. questions that require you to retrieve information from memory and organize it in a meaningful way

i. words that are absolutes

j. objective questions

k. a response given after you skim the test for clues

l. words that often show cause/effect

SUMMARY
- Recognition questions, also called objective questions, include true-false, multiple choice, and matching.
- Red flag words, which must be read carefully in objective questions, include:

  1. Definition clues
  2. Negatives
  3. 100 percent and in-between modifiers
  4. Relationship clues

- Both the stem and all the options in a multiple-choice question should be read as true-false statements before they are answered.
- A six-step strategy can enable you to answer multiple-choice questions.
- Objective questions utilize the steps of immediate response, delayed response, assisted response, and educated guessing.
- A seven-step approach is recommended when you are answering matching questions.

PERSONALIZING WHAT YOU LEARNED
1. Score and record the score for your chapter profile.
2. On your own paper, expand this chapter's visual mapping.
3. Make your own vocabulary list of all the terms in this chapter that are printed in color.

"To the Student" (p. xv) provides you with more detailed directions for completing these activities.

Review Questions

True-False

To help keep your mind focused, underline the key words in the true-false questions before you answer them.

Write *T* if the statement is TRUE. Write *F* if it is FALSE.

_____ 1. The easiest level of questions is the recognition level.

_____ 2. The words "reason," "because," and "since" are often relationship clues.

_____ 3. All items listed in a series must be false before you can use a false answer.

_____ 4. True-false statements that use negatives are always false.

_____ 5. The most inclusive option in a multiple-choice question is the best answer.

_____ 6. A distractor in a multiple-choice question is the correct answer.

_____ 7. If a multiple-choice question has four options, the question should be read as four true-false statements.

_____ 8. Paired associations are two ideas or items that should be linked together in your memory.

_____ 9. In matching questions, the column that contains the definitions usually has fewer words than the other column.

_____ 10. Answers that were used on a matching test should be crossed off so that they don't get used again.

Short Answer

1. What two strategies can you use to help focus clearly on what is being asked in a question?

2. List three 100 percent modifiers and three in-between modifiers.

3. List four red flag words that signal you to look at a relationship between two items.

4. List four red flag words that signal you to look at a definition being tested.

5. What are the four different kinds of red flag words?

6. What is paired association?

Application of Skills in True-False Questions

In the following questions, circle the red flag words. On the line tell the type of red flag word used. You may use more than one code for a question. Use the following codes:

> D = definition clue
> N = negative
> M = modifier (100 percent and in-between)
> R = relationship clue

_____   **1.** A sole proprietorship is a business that is owned by one person.

_____   **2.** In a sole proprietorship, the person who owns the business is usually the one who also operates it.

_____   **3.** Sole proprietorships are popular because of the simplicity and personal control of the business.

_____   **4.** A sole proprietorship does not need contracts, and there are no legal documents required.

_____   **5.** All profits earned by a sole proprietorship become the personal earnings of its owner.

_____   **6.** The use of alcohol and other psychoactive drugs lead to major political, economic, social, and health problems worldwide.

_____   **7.** All people become psychologically dependent on psychoactive substances without becoming addicted to them.

_____   **8.** Prolonged overuse of alcohol can result in life-threatening liver damage, vitamin deficiencies that can lead to an irreversible brain disorder, and a host of other ailments.

_____   **9.** The behavioral theory suggests that people learn to use alcohol because they want to become more sensitive to others.

_____   **10.** Alcoholic parents, hyperactivity, and antisocial behavior in childhood are reasonably good predictors of alcoholism in adults.

Application of Skills in Multiple-Choice Questions

Read each question carefully with all the options. Circle any red flag words and underline key words. Cross out the options that you know are incorrect. Select the best option that remains. Write the letter of the best option on the line.

_____   **1.** The reflect step

 a. is an unnecessary step of Cornell.
 b. promotes critical thinking.
 c. seldom shows relationships of ideas.
 d. never uses the recall column.

What four true-false sentences could you make from this multiple-choice question?

_____   **2.** Reciting

 a. activates the auditory channel.
 b. is never done alone.
 c. works because it is kinesthetic.
 d. activates the auditory channel and gives feedback.

Explain how you determined which options were the distractors.

Application of Skills in Matching Questions

1. Use your test-taking strategies to match the terms in column A to the definitions in column B.

_____ **1.** Five *R*'s of Cornell	**a.**	helpful hints to use to achieve goals
_____ **2.** STSR	**b.**	steps in a notetaking system
_____ **3.** EVA, BAT	**c.**	an acronym used to remember the techniques for mentally preparing to study
_____ **4.** SAVE CRIB FOTO	**d.**	four steps for writing effective goals
_____ **5.** SQ4R	**e.**	the six steps used in textbook reading
_____ **6.** DATE IAN	**f.**	an acronym used to learn techniques for concentrated listening skills
_____ **7.** RAVES	**g.**	the principles used to learn information and strengthen your memory

2. Did you *first* read column A or column B? Explain why.

3. Which questions were you able to answer using immediate response?

4. Explain the thinking you used to match the items that you could not match using immediate response.

―――――――――

WRITING ASSIGNMENTS

1. Explain in your own words what you learned from this chapter that will be valuable to you when you take tests in the future.
2. Analyze one or more tests that have been graded. Discuss the kinds of mistakes you made. Explain how you can reduce these kinds of mistakes on future tests.

Using Educated Guessing

*E*ducated guessing is a method for selecting an answer for a true-false or multiple-choice question when all other methods for finding the correct answer have failed. Do you ever lose test points because you leave spaces blank? Do you look for important key words to help you guess at an answer? Do you eliminate some of the multiple-choice options before you guess? The educated guessing strategies in this chapter enable you to increase your odds at guessing. Be aware, however, that there are no guarantees for correct answers, so use educated guessing only as a last resort.

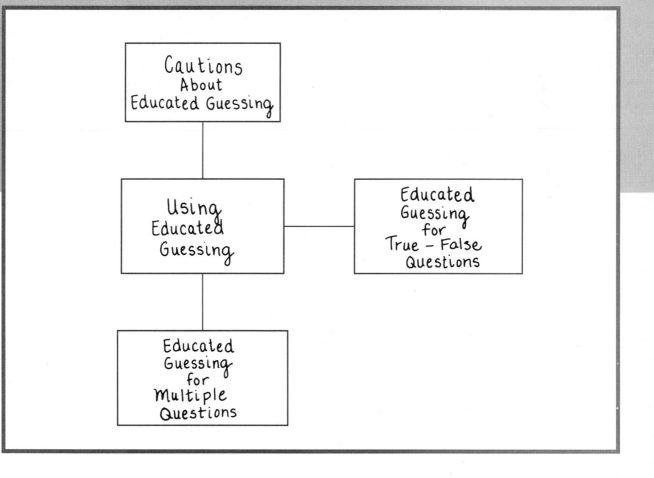

NAME _____ DATE _____

Educated Guessing Profile

Please answer honestly each of the following questions about your current attitudes and study habits. Your answer should reflect what you *do*, not what you *wish* you would do.

   After you read each statement, check YES if you do this *always* or *most of the time*. Check NO if you do this *seldom* or *never*.

	YES	NO
1. I feel that I am guessing most of the time when I take tests.	_____	_____
2. I would prefer to find answers by immediate response, delayed response, and assisted response.	_____	_____
3. When I guess at true-false, I alternate my answers by putting T-F-T-F-T-F.	_____	_____
4. I feel that guessing on tests is dishonest and a form of cheating.	_____	_____
5. When I see a 100 percent qualifier in a true-false question, I usually guess true.	_____	_____
6. I always guess false when I see a negative word or negative prefix in a question.	_____	_____
7. If I see an unfamiliar term in a multiple-choice option, I usually choose that option because I feel I must have overlooked that term when I studied.	_____	_____
8. If the options in a multiple-choice question are numbers, I usually guess the lowest number.	_____	_____
9. If I see the option "all of the above" in a multiple-choice question, I choose that option without reading the other ones.	_____	_____
10. I often choose an answer quickly without really thinking it through.	_____	_____
11. I turn multiple-choice options into true-false questions before I choose an answer.	_____	_____
12. I form questions to myself about possible multiple-choice options to think through to the correct answer.	_____	_____

Cautions About Educated Guessing

A few words of caution are needed before we explore the game of "playing the odds" called **educated guessing.**

1. Educated guessing is a *last resort effort* to be used only after you have tried the immediate response, the delayed response, and the assisted response. This is the least favorable way to get a right answer. Knowing the answer, having learned the information, is *always* the best method and the one used by successful college students.

2. Do not get a *false sense of security* because you know educated guessing strategies. There are still no guarantees that these strategies will always result in correct answers. Teachers who are aware of these strategies may intentionally write their tests so that educated guessing backfires.

Some students feel that educated guessing is not an honest way to take tests. However, if you are not able to come up with an answer, your choice is to leave the space blank, which is a guarantee of a wrong answer, or use this remaining strategy to guess. If you choose the latter, do so sparingly. Then immediately after the test, review your notes and textbook to find the correct answers so that the next time you see the same information on a test, you will not have to guess. (Review Chapter 14 on how to learn from your tests.)

Educated Guessing for True-False Questions

On a true-false question, you have a one in two chance of getting the right answer by guessing. Since there are only two possibilities, you could just toss a coin to decide on your answer. However, there are four strategies at your command for increasing your odds at guessing correctly. Two of these strategies assume you understand the **red flag words** that are modifiers. One strategy assumes that you can recognize red flag words for relationships. The last strategy is the wild shot guess.

Educated Guessing for True-False Questions

1. If there is a 100 percent modifier, guess false.

2. If there is an in-between modifier, guess true.

3. If there is a relationship word, guess false.

4. If you take a wild shot guess, guess true.

Look for 100 Percent Modifiers

Common 100 percent modifiers are "all," "every," "only," "always," "everyone," "best," "none," "never," "no one," "worst," "least," and "fewest." (Review Chapter 15 if needed). These words are *absolutes*, meaning that they are the extremes with no exceptions allowed. When you see a 100 percent modifier (and you have tried all other methods), *guess false.* Few things happen or exist without exceptions. The odds are in your favor that there are exceptions, so the 100 percent modifier makes the question false.

The following examples have 100 percent modifiers. Notice how these modifiers make statements that have no exceptions to them. Each of these statements is false.

Attendance in college is required in <u>every</u> class.
<u>Always</u> begin by studying your favorite subject first.
<u>Never</u> use a tape recorder in class.

The foregoing examples are false because exceptions to each statement exist. There are some courses where attendance is not required. You should begin by studying your hardest or least-liked subjects first. There are times when a tape recorder can be used effectively in class.

When you see a 100 percent modifier, ask yourself, "Could there be exceptions to this?" Realize, however, that sometimes there are no exceptions and that statements with 100 percent modifiers can be true. For example, the statement "*All* human beings require oxygen" is true even though it has a 100 percent modifier.

Be Aware of In-between Modifiers

In-between modifiers are words such as "some," "few," "often," "usually," "seldom," and "most." (Review Chapter 15 if needed.) These modifiers are not absolutes; there's room for exceptions or for the statement to sometimes apply and sometimes not apply. When you see an in-between modifier (and you have already tried immediate, delayed, and assisted response), *guess true.* Odds are in your favor that the answer is correct.

Notice the in-between modifiers in the following examples:

Reviewing notes from a previous paragraph can <u>sometimes</u> be used to help understand a difficult paragraph.
In a sole proprietorship, the person who owns the business is <u>usually</u> the one who also operates it.

In the preceding examples, the in-between modifiers allow for exceptions, so the statements are true. For example, there are times when reviewing notes from a previous paragraph does not help you understand a difficult paragraph. There are cases where a person who owns a business does not actually operate it.

Because these are guessing strategies, they will not always lead you to the correct answer. As you can see in the following examples, there are statements with in-between modifiers that are false:

Banks <u>seldom</u> approve loans for cars.
Rivers <u>usually</u> begin in the middle of cities.

Notice Relationship Clues

True-false questions often test you on knowledge of specific facts. However, true-false questions can be written on a higher level of difficulty to test your understanding of relationships. The kinds of relationships you will often see are *cause/effect* or *explanation through reasons.*

Identifying the red flag words for relationships is essential. The most common ones are "since," "so," "because," "cause," "effect," and "reason." (Review Chapter 15 if needed.) When you see these red flag words, ask yourself if the two parts of the sentence are truly related in the way stated. After you have tried immediate, delayed, and assisted responses, guess *false.*

The red flag relationship word is underlined in each of the following statements. Notice how the two items or parts of the questions do not show the true relationship. The following examples are false:

Massed practice is discouraged <u>because</u> information is presented in series of details, not masses.
Procrastination is the <u>reason</u> unsuccessful students avoid using time management.

Is massed practice discouraged for the reason given? Massed practice is discouraged because our memory systems are usually not capable of learning large amounts of information in a small amount of time. Massed practice can also lead to poor concentration, physical fatigue, or cramming. There are many reasons why massed practice is discouraged, but the reason given is not one of them. Why do unsuccessful students avoid using time management? Is the reason the given answer or can you think of a variety of answers to the question?

Since you are guessing and there are no guarantees, remember that sometimes red flag relationship words can also be used in statements that are true. Here are two examples of true statements with relationship words:

> Sole proprietorships are popular <u>because</u> of the simplicity and personal control of the business.
>
> The difference in thinking and speaking speeds <u>creates</u> concentration problems for some students.

Take Wild Shot Guesses   If there are no modifiers to use and there is no relationship shown, you will need to take a **wild shot guess.** Recall that Chapter 15 stated that if you run out of time on a test and simply must guess, *guess true.* There is a logical reason for this. When teachers write tests, they usually prefer to leave the correct, accurate information in your mind. They know that you are likely to remember what you read. Therefore, they tend to write more true statements than false statements.

Know When You Can't Guess   In Chapter 15, you learned that it is important to pay close attention to negatives ("no," "not," "but," "except") and words with prefixes that have negative meanings. When you see negatives, read carefully and realize that no guessing strategies exist for negatives. *A statement with a negative red flag word can be true or false.*

Words such as "means," "are," and "called" are clues that you are being tested on a definition. These clues assist you in being a careful reader. However, there are no guessing strategies for definition questions. *A statement with a definition can be true or false.*

Exercise 16.1   Guessing at True or False

This exercise has test questions on topics that may not be familiar to you. However, if you apply the four educated guessing strategies to answer these questions, you will be correct. Work with a partner and discuss your answers.

_____   **1.** A sole proprietorship does not need contracts, and there are no legal documents required.

_____   **2.** All matter exists in only one of three physical forms: solid, liquid, or gas.

_____   **3.** The liquid form of a given material is always less dense than the solid form.

_____   **4.** Prolonged overuse of alcohol can result in life-threatening liver damage, vitamin deficiencies that can lead to an irreversible brain disorder, and a host of other ailments.

_____   **5.** Rome's early wars often gave plebeians the power to demand that their rights be recognized, but their demands were seldom met.

_____   **6.** Because monasteries believed in isolation, they never conducted schools for local people.

_____   **7.** In 1013 the Danish ruler Swen Forkbeard invaded England.

_____   **8.** The only objective of medieval agriculture was to produce more cattle for meat and dairy products.

_____   **9.** Historians have determined for certain that the bubonic plague originated in southern Russia and was carried to Europe by traveling soldiers.

_____   **10.** Economic growth was rapid during the Italian Renaissance.

List all the modifiers you found in the preceding statements:

_____

_____

Educated Guessing for Multiple-Choice Questions

In the case of multiple-choice questions, you have eight strategies to draw on. Recognize, however, that in some situations more than one strategy can apply. Hope that luck is with you when you choose. Again, it is always better to *know* the information rather than counting on luck or on any educated guessing.

If a question has four options, you have a one in four chance of guessing the right answer. Your goal is to eliminate as many options as possible to increase your odds of guessing correctly. If you can eliminate one option so that you are choosing from three, your odds of being correct increase to one in three. If you can eliminate two options, you have a one in two chance of guessing correctly since only two options are left.

Begin this process by reading the stem with each option so that you can form a true-false statement. All false statements are distractors and can be eliminated (see Chapter 15). Use the following strategies then for the remaining choices.

Educated Guessing for Multiple-Choice Questions

1. Eliminate any options with 100 percent modifiers.

2. Eliminate any foolish or insulting options.

3. Eliminate any options with unfamiliar terms.

4. Eliminate the highest and lowest numbers in number options.

5. If there are look-alike options, choose one of them.

6. If one option is longer or most inclusive, choose it.

7. If "all of the above" is given, choose it.

8. If a wild shot guess is needed, choose (c).

Eliminate 100 Percent Modifier Options

When an option with a 100 percent modifier is added to the stem, a true-false question is created. The true-false guessing strategy for 100 percent modifiers is to guess false. Notice how this same strategy is used in the following example:

_____ 1. The prefix intra-

    a. is never used in English words.
    b. always means "between."
    c. means "within" or "inside of."
    d. means none of the above.

__F__   **a.** The prefix *intra-* is never used in English words.

__F__   **b.** The prefix *intra-* always means "between."

__T__   **c.** The prefix *intra-* means "within" or "inside of."

Eliminate Foolish or Insulting Options

If you see answers that are meant to be humorous, ridiculous, or unreasonable, treat them as distractors. If answers are insulting or demeaning, treat them as distractors. (An example is included in the next section.)

Eliminate Options with Unfamiliar Terms

If you have thoroughly studied your textbook and your lecture notes, you will be familiar with all the key terms covered in the course. If you see options that are totally unfamiliar, treat them as distractors. In the following example, the stem and the options are turned into true-false statements. Notice the option that contains a foolish answer and the option that contains an unfamiliar term.

_____ **1.** Interpersonal intelligence

    a. is a form of type B behavior.
    b. is shown by those who party instead of study.
    c. is not a useful quality in school.
    d. belongs to those with social and leadership skills.

__F__   **a.** Interpersonal intelligence is a form of type B behavior. *(This term has not been discussed in this course.)*

__F__   **b.** Interpersonal intelligence is shown by those who party instead of study. *(This is ridiculous!)*

__F__   **c.** Interpersonal intelligence is not a useful quality in school. *(Having strong communication, social, and leadership skills is useful in school.)*

__T__   **d.** Interpersonal intelligence belongs to those with social and leadership skills. *(This is true. It matches the definition of interpersonal intelligence.)*

Eliminate the Highest and Lowest Numbers

When the options are numbers, chances are better that the correct answer is one of the numbers in the middle range. Therefore, treat the highest and the lowest numbers as distractors. That leaves you with two options. Try to reason through to make the better choice. If any one of the other guessing strategies apply (such as choose [c]), incorporate that strategy as well to choose your answer. Notice how this strategy is used in the following example:

_____ **1.** The average rate of thinking is

   a. 100 words per minute.
   b. 200 words per minute.
   c. 400 words per minute.
   d. 650 words per minute.

Eliminate 100 and 650. Think back to the material on the rate of thinking. Which one sounds familiar? If you have to guess, take a wild shot guess and choose (c)—which is correct.

Choose One of the Look-alike Options   Some questions have two options that look almost the same. Perhaps only one or two words are different. Chances are good that the correct answer is one of these two. Eliminate the other options and focus on these two look-alikes. Carefully think through and associate the information to what you have learned. If you can't decide, choose either one.

_____ **1.** Compared to the left hemisphere of the brain, the right hemisphere of the brain

   a. understands spoken language better.
   b. has better logical abilities.
   c. perceives words better.
   d. perceives emotions better.

Focus on (c) and (d) because they are look-alikes. Now try to reason your way through this. You have already eliminated (a), which deals with language. Because (c) also relates to language, it, too, must be incorrect. This leaves you with (d) as the correct answer, which it is. (Notice in this case how the guessing strategy to use [c] does not work—there are no guarantees!)

Choose the Longest or Most Inclusive Option   This guessing strategy is based on two premises. First, sometimes more words are needed to give complete enough information to make a correct answer. Second, an answer that covers a wider range of possibilities is more likely correct.

You can begin by looking at the *length* of the answer. If one option is much longer than the others, choose it. Also look at the content of the answers. Sometimes two or three answers may be correct to some degree, but one answer contains more information or a broader idea. This answer is the most inclusive. Notice how the **most inclusive answer** in the following is the best answer.

_____ **1.** Test anxiety can be reduced by focusing

   a. on yourself and ignoring others.
   b. on outward thoughts and actions.
   c. on your strengths and accomplishments.
   d. on the five strategies to reduce test anxiety.

All of the answers are correct to some degree. However, (d) is the longest and includes a wider range of information. The answers (a), (b), and (c) fit under the category given in (d).

Choose "All of the Above" If you know for sure that two options are correct, but you are not sure about the third option, and the fourth option is "all of the above," choose it. This is a safe guess since you can choose only one answer and you know that two are correct. If you do not know for certain that two are correct, and you have tried each option in a true-false form and don't know the answer, go ahead and choose "all of the above." This strategy is not a very reliable one, so be sure to check out all other possibilities before you decide to use this strategy.

_____ **1.** Cramming is

    a. the result of being underprepared.
    b. a frantic attempt to learn a lot of information in a short amount of time.
    c. a method that does not use very many memory principles.
    d. characterized by all of the above.

Your first reaction might be to choose (b) because it is the longest answer. However, if you know that at least two of these are correct, your only choice then is to choose (d), which is correct.

Choose (C) as a Wild Shot Guess Many teachers favor the (c) answer for the correct answer. If you try writing some of your own multiple-choice questions, you may find that you too tend to put more correct answers in the (c) position than in any other position. Here are a few explanations for why (c) is the most common answer:

- (A) is not used as often because many students would stop reading the question and stop thinking about the answer if the correct answer was given first.
- (B) is not used as often for the same reason as (a) is not.
- (C) seems to hide the answer best and force the reader to read through more of the options.
- (D) seems to be too visible because it is on the last line.

Which Strategy is Best? Because there are eight strategies for guessing multiple-choice answers, it should not surprise you that some of these strategies will clash with each other. For example, should you choose (c) or another option that has the longest, most inclusive answer? Sorry, there is no answer to this dilemma. You will simply need to reason through your choices the best you can. Always remember that you are playing with odds here and that you will not always be right. The only way to be right is to know the information.

Exercise 16.2   Guessing at Multiple Choice

Work with a partner. Use the educated guessing strategies to answer these questions about information that probably is not familiar to you. After you answer the question, tell which strategy you used to guess at your answer.

_____ **1.** The triarchical theory of intelligence deals with

    a. internal components.
    b. the relations of internal components to experience.
    c. external effects.
    d. all of the above.
    Strategy: _____

_____ **2.** Divergent thinking is the

    a. ability to create many solutions for one problem.
    b. ability to lose your train of thought.
    c. same as rote memory.
    d. thinking process of rats and mice.
    Strategy: _____

_____ **3.** Signs of post-traumatic stress disorder are

    a. never being able to sleep.
    b. shown in a frequency histogram.
    c. poor concentration, anxiety, and nervousness.
    d. apparent at the time of the trauma.
    Strategy: _____

_____ **4.** The domestication of plants and animals began around

    a. 7000 B.C.
    b. 4000 B.C.
    c. A.D. 1200
    d. 9000 B.C.
    Strategy: _____

_____ **5.** Egypt is called the "gift of the Nile" because

    a. death always results from the flooding river.
    b. the Nile River gives gifts to children.
    c. the Nile conquers the land and declares it a country.
    d. the Nile River treats the country well by being tame and not flooding the land.
    Strategy: _____

Exercise 16.3   Using the Eight Strategies

Use educated guessing strategies to select the best answer.

_____ **1.** In a restaurant, the recommended tip for a waiter or waitress is

    a. nothing.
    b. 10 percent of the food portion of the bill.
    c. 15 percent of the total bill.
    d. 40 percent of the total bill.

_____ **2.** The Atlantic Ocean touches the shores of

    a. Maine.
    b. Brazil.
    c. North America and Africa.
    d. North and South America, Europe, and Africa.

_____ **3.** Cumulus clouds

    a. are never higher than five hundred feet above the ground.
    b. are usually dark at the bottom and billowy white at the top.
    c. look like fluffy rabbits' tails.
    d. are always associated with heavy rain showers.

_____ **4.** The thirty-fifth president of the United States was

- **a.** Harry S Truman.
- **b.** Dwight D. Eisenhower.
- **c.** John F. Kennedy.
- **d.** Lyndon B. Johnson.

_____ **5.** Coordinating conjunctions are the words

- **a.** *for, and, nor, but, or, yet, so.*
- **b.** *for, and, but, too.*
- **c.** found by the verb.
- **d.** *small, kind, old.*

_____ **6.** Summary writing involves

- **a.** listing all the supporting details.
- **b.** briefly discussing the main features or points.
- **c.** briefly discussing the vocabulary.
- **d.** creating a complete, detailed description.

_____ **7.** the word *etymology* means

- **a.** "learning what animals eat."
- **b.** "to always study."
- **c.** "the study of moles."
- **d.** "the study of the history of words."

_____ **8.** Reinforcement theory is

- **a.** based on giving rewards for behavior you want repeated.
- **b.** based on forcing issues.
- **c.** never to be used by effective managers.
- **d.** the very best training to use for infants.

_____ **9.** In business, the agency shop

- **a.** never charges dues.
- **b.** charges annual fees of $10 or less.
- **c.** requires employees to pay dues even if they don't join.
- **d.** requires employees to always be union members.

_____ **10.** Volcanic mountains are formed from

- **a.** cinder piles and ash.
- **b.** cinder piles, lava rock, ash, and shields of magma.
- **c.** erosion.
- **d.** sandstone and shale.

SUMMARY
- Educated guessing is a set of thinking and analyzing strategies that can be used to increase your odds of getting a correct answer when you don't actually know the answer.
- Do not become falsely confident because you know these strategies; the best approach is to be prepared and learn as much information as possible so that you do not need educated guessing on a regular basis.
- Four strategies are available for educated guessing on true-false questions:

1. Choose false when you see a 100 percent modifier.
2. Choose true when you see an in-between modifier.
3. Choose false when you see a red flag relationship word.
4. Choose true when you are taking a wild shot guess.

- Negative words and definition clues in questions must be read carefully. There are not, however, any guessing strategies for these clues.
- For multiple-choice questions, eight strategies can help you make a correct educated guess:

1. Eliminate options with 100 percent modifiers.
2. Eliminate silly options.
3. Eliminate options with terms you don't know.
4. Eliminate lowest and highest numbers.
5. Choose a look-alike option.
6. Choose the most inclusive option.
7. Choose the option that says, "All of the above."
8. Choose (c) for a wild shot guess.

PERSONALIZING
WHAT YOU
LEARNED

1. Score and record the score for your chapter profile.
2. On your own paper, expand this chapter's visual mapping.
3. Make your own vocabulary list of all the terms in this chapter that are printed in color.

"To the Student" (p. xv) provides you with more detailed directions for completing these activities.

Review Questions

Fill in the Blanks

A key word is missing in each sentence. Write the term that will correctly complete each sentence.

1. Guess false if a true-false question has a _____ modifier.

2. Eliminate any options in a multiple-choice question that have a _____ modifier.

3. Choosing (c) for a multiple-choice question is called a _____ _____ _____.

4. The _____ numbers should be considered as possible right answers in a multiple-choice question.

5. Two kinds of red flag words, _____ and _____ clues, appear in true statements and in false statements; there are no educated guessing strategies for these clues.

6. Guess true if you see an _____ modifier in a true-false question.

7. Guess _____ if you see a relationship word such as "because" or "reason."

8. The wild shot guess in a true-false question is _____.

9. If you see a word such as "some," "often," or "seldom" in a true-false question, guess _____.

10. Treat the _____ and the _____ numbers as distractors in a multiple-choice question.

Short Answer

1. Explain when you should use educated guessing.

2. Give three reasons why you should not rely heavily on educated guessing for tests.

3. What are four strategies to help you eliminate distractions and select correct options on a multiple-choice test?

4. Discuss four educated guessing strategies for true-false questions.

5. Explain how to use the wild shot guess in multiple-choice and true-false questions.

WRITING ASSIGNMENTS

1. Some people are very uncomfortable about the idea of guessing on a test; they believe that the test should show only what they really know. Other people use guessing frequently and don't feel there's anything wrong with guessing. Explain your feelings about this issue.
2. Explain the steps you will go through before you try educated guessing on a test.

CHAPTER 17

Developing Strategies for Recall and Recall-Plus Tests

Recall and recall-plus questions require students to retrieve information from memory, apply it, and express the answer in well-written sentences, paragraphs, or essays. Do you sometimes feel that you know the information but that you just can't seem to get it written on paper? Does your written response not really answer the question? Do you have difficulties organizing your ideas clearly? Do you run out of time and leave essay questions unfinished? This chapter provides you with valuable strategies for answering fill-in-the blank, listings, definition, short-answer, and essay questions.

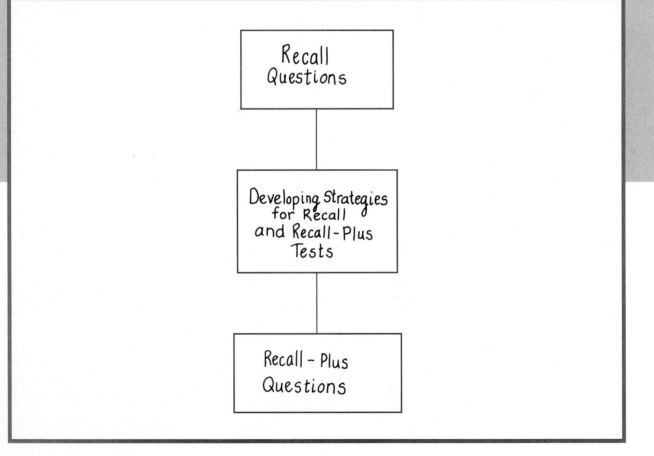

Recall and Recall-Plus Profile

Please answer honestly each of the following questions about your current attitudes and study habits. Your answers should reflect what you *do*, not what you *wish* you would do.

    After you read each statement, check YES if you do this *always* or *most of the time*. Check NO if you do this *seldom* or *never*.

		YES	NO
1.	I go blank when I have to come up with exact words to fill in the blanks of sentences.	_____	_____
2.	When I don't know an answer for a recall question, I do a memory search to find the information stored in long-term memory.	_____	_____
3.	Open-ended recall questions that have many possible answers are more difficult for me than the ones that need specific answers in order.	_____	_____
4.	If I don't know the exact answer for a recall question, I substitute another word or phrase.	_____	_____
5.	When I am asked to define a word, my definition is usually one sentence long.	_____	_____
6.	I make a quick outline, mapping, or plan before I begin writing an essay answer.	_____	_____
7.	I understand the different answers needed for questions that require me to define, explain, discuss, or compare.	_____	_____
8.	I often lose points on essays because I don't include enough details.	_____	_____
9.	I often get off track and don't answer the question that is being asked.	_____	_____
10.	If I have to list specific details, I usually am not able to remember all the items in the list.	_____	_____
11.	I often try to "bluff" my way through essays because I don't know how to write them or because I don't know the information.	_____	_____
12.	When there is time during a test, I proofread my answers.	_____	_____

Recall Questions

The two most common types of **recall questions** are fill-in-the-blank questions and listing questions. Thorough learning and efficient long-term memory retrieval techniques are essential for answering such questions. No educated guessing strategies are available for these questions; however, you can learn to answer recall questions more effectively by using the following strategies.

Fill-in-the-Blank Questions

A **fill-in-the-blank question** is a sentence with one or more words missing. You must read the sentence carefully and decide what key words will complete the sentence correctly. The following points are important to remember:

■ Unless the directions say otherwise, place only one word on each blank line.
■ The length of the line is not an automatic clue to the length of the word that will fit on the line.
■ The completed sentence should make sense and be grammatically correct.
■ Blanks that are separated with commas indicate a series of items.
■ Several blank lines without commas between them indicate that you will be completing a phrase with a specific number of words.

Notice how these points are shown in the following examples:

1. _____ is another term for overviewing.

2. An _____ _____ is something occurring "inside you" that breaks your focus or concentration.

3. No specific guessing strategies in true-false questions exist for _____,

    _____ clues, or items in a _____.

In example 1, there is only one line, so only one word is expected for the answer. In example 2, there are two lines, so a two-word answer or phrase is needed. In example 3, the commas indicate that the answer is a series of three separate words.

How to Study for Fill-in-the-Blank Questions   Many fill-in-the-blank questions are based on key vocabulary terms. Spend extra time studying from the *back* of your flash cards so that you can readily recall the terms on the front. If you are studying from vocabulary sheets, cover up the left column. Read the definitions and practice reciting and spelling the terms in the left column. Your flash cards or vocabulary sheets should include all the key terms in the chapter and other terms given in lectures.

Steps for Answering Fill-in-the-Blank Questions   Each time you are faced with fill-in-the-blank questions, you can use four steps for answering. The first three steps (immediate, delayed, and assisted response) are familiar to you from other chapters. The last step is specifically related to this form of questioning.

Steps for Answering Fill-in-the-Blank Questions

1. Try immediate response.

2. Use delayed response. Do a memory search and pose a question to trigger your memory.

3. Use assisted response. Look for key vocabulary terms.

4. Try a synonym or related phrase.

Try Immediate Response   If you created, recited, and reviewed vocabulary cards or vocabulary sheets using the method just described, you can often give an immediate response. When you read the sentence, you recall the exact word needed to complete the sentence.

Use Delayed Response   If an immediate response isn't available, use the following strategy:

■ Search your memory for the general category, or topic related to the information in the sentence.

■ Once you identify the category, search your memory for specific details. Try to recall the specific chapter in the book or the study aid or mnemonic you rehearsed for the category.

■ Turn the sentence into a question by using any of the following words or phrases:

What is _____?
What do we call _____?
Where is _____?
Who _____?
When _____?

Notice how this strategy is used to find the answers to the following questions:

1. _____ is another term for overviewing.

Overviewing is related to reading a book.
What is another word for overviewing?

2. An _____ _____ is something occurring "inside you" that breaks your focus or concentration.

This comes from the section on concentration.
What occurs inside me to break my focus and concentration?

3. No specific guessing strategies in true-false questions exist for _____,

_____ clues, or items in a _____.

This is from the section on educated guessing.
When don't guessing strategies exist in true-false questions?

This **memory search** or process of thinking back and associating to information learned, needs to be done quickly. If you have difficulties identifying the category, recalling the study tool you used to learn the information, or answering the question you have formulated, delay your response. Do not spend too much test time on one question. You can come back to the question after you have answered all the questions you know on the test. *If you need to leave the question blank, place a checkmark next to the question so that you remember to come back to it later*. Move on to the next question.

Use Assisted Response   After you have answered all the questions you can on the test, return to the unanswered ones. Since fill-in-the-blank questions are usually key vocabulary terms, use the rest of the test to look for the terms or their categories. For example, if you know the term belongs to the category "concentration," skim through the test looking for other questions about concentration. Sometimes you will find the word or an item on the test that will trigger an association to the missing word.

Try a Synonym or Related Phrase   You may be able to pick up partial points by writing something in the blank even though you know it is not the correct term. Try one of the following possibilities:

- Use a **synonym** (a word with a similar meaning) or a substitute word. You may not get full points for your answer, but you may be given partial credit.
- If necessary, write a short phrase. Some teachers (not all) will recognize your effort.

In the following examples, sentence A has the correct response. Sentence B uses a synonym, a substituted word, or a phrase.

A. Surveying is another term for overviewing.
B. Previewing is another term for overviewing.

A. An internal distractor is something occurring "inside you" that breaks your focus or concentration.
B. An inner distractor is something occurring "inside you" that breaks your focus or concentration.

A. No specific guessing strategies in true-false questions exist for negatives, definition clues, or items in a series.
B. No specific guessing strategies in true-false questions exist for no/not, vocabulary clues, or items in a listing.

Filling in the blank using synonyms, substitutions, or phrases does show an effort on your part. Realize, however, that you may put effort into using this approach but that your answer will still be marked wrong because the *exact* answer was needed. Make a mental note to find the correct answers after the test.

Exercise 17.1   Filling in the Blanks

Work with a partner. Read the following questions carefully. They are all review questions based on key terms from previous chapters. First try an immediate response; then try a delayed response by doing a memory search and posing a question.

1. The _____ _____ technique is a concentration technique for letting other people know that you do not want to be disturbed.

2. The beginning part of a multiple-choice question is called the _____.

3. _____ questions require you to retrieve specific information from your long-term memory.

4. After you schedule all your study blocks on a weekly time management schedule, add a few hours of _____ time in case you need more study time.

5. _____ practice is the process of breaking your study blocks into several different periods spread out over several days of the week.

6. The _____ page in a book tells when the book was published and gives the Library of Congress catalog number.

7. _____ _____ is the mnemonic for learning the strategies for effective listening.

8. _____ are units of meaning added to the end of words.

Listing Questions   **Listing questions** require you to recall a specific number of ideas, steps, or vocabulary words. The answers are usually key words; full sentences are not usually required. There are two kinds of listing questions.

1. **Closed questions** require very specific answers; sometimes the answers must be in order. For example, if you are asked to list the steps of the Cornell notetaking system in order, there is only one answer—record, reduce, recite, reflect, and review.
2. **Open-ended questions** can have many possible correct answers. For example, if you are asked to list five study tools you can *make* for use during the reflect step of Cornell, there are more than five possible answers: mappings, cartoons/pictures, mnemonics (all kinds), time lines, study tapes, summaries, and your own test questions.

How to Study for Listing Questions   As you read, take notes, and create study tools, you encounter many opportunities to recognize or anticipate possible items for questions that involve listing:

- On your vocabulary cards or study sheets, the general category card or entry contains a list of items related to the topic. These items often appear as listing questions.
- When you review the recall column in your Cornell notes, you may often see study questions that ask for lists of information. Anticipate that these may appear as questions requiring listings.
- Use the information in chapter objectives, headings, and introductions under headings. Ordinals or numbers can help you identify items that belong in a list for a specific category.
- Each level two part of your visual mapping for the chapter could be turned into a listing question.

Steps for Answering Listing Questions   You can use the following steps to help you retrieve lists of information from your long-term memory.

*S*teps for Answering Listing Questions

1. Underline the key words in the directions.

2. Try immediate response.

3. Use delayed response. Do a memory search and pose a question to help trigger your memory.

4. Use assisted response.

5. Use synonyms or short phrases.

Underline Key Words   By underlining the key words in the question, you will be able to focus specifically on the information being asked:

> Lining up the Cornell columns is one reflect activity you can do. In the reflect step, you can make study tools to help you learn. List five study tools that you can make for use during the reflect step.

Try Immediate Response   After you have underlined the key words in the directions, you may be ready with the answer. Being able to give an immediate response is the reward for effective studying. Immediate response indicates that you organized and rehearsed information effectively, which enabled you to quickly retrieve from long-term memory what was needed.

Use Delayed Response   If immediate response wasn't available, move to delayed response. Association triggers are needed to help you connect the key words in the directions to the information you want to find in your memory bank. Use the following technique:

- Focus on the key words you underlined in the directions. These will help you identify the category.
- Search your memory for study tools that you created to rehearse the information. Try to picture the flash cards, the Cornell recall column, or the introductions in the chapter headings.
- Turn the information into a new question. In the preceding example, you might pose the question "What study tools help me reflect on information that I am learning?"

Because you probably have many other questions to deal with on the test, memory searching and questioning must be done relatively quickly. If you are able to retrieve an answer, or part of an answer, write it down. If you are not able to complete the listing, *place a checkmark next to the question.* You can come back to it later after you have completed as many questions as possible.

Use Assisted Response   When you return to the unanswered or partially answered questions, skim through the rest of the test for possible clues. Many times important information appears in the test in more than one place, but in a different questioning format. Focus on the key words that you underlined in the directions. When you find a possible answer, check it against the question that you posed earlier.

Use Synonyms or Short Phrases   If you were not able to locate the exact terms for the listing, use synonyms or short phrases. These answers are not as accurate, yet they show your effort and general understanding. An empty space can bring only one result: no points. You may receive full points or partial points for using synonyms or short phrases.

Notice how synonyms or short phrases complete the following answer in a listing question.

1. List the five theories of forgetting.
   a. Decay theory
   b. Displacement theory
   c. Retrieval failure theory
   d. Encoding—only part recorded in memory
   e. Old and new information get confused

This student remembered the first three theories of forgetting but could remember only the general ideas for the last two theories. If you were the teacher, would you give the student points for calling the incomplete encoding theory "encoding—only part recorded in memory" and the interference theory "old and new information get confused"?

Exercise 17.2   **Making Lists**

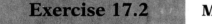

Work with a partner. Underline the key words in the following directions. Use immediate and delayed response to write your answers on your own paper. Since there is no test here to refer to for assisted response, try synonyms or short phrases to complete answers if needed.

1. SQ4R is a system for effectively reading and learning information in textbooks. List the steps of SQ4R in order.

2. If you read a paragraph and don't understand what it means, do not move on. Use one or more of the seven strategies we learned to understand the paragraphs you read. List any four of the strategies recommended to improve comprehension.

3. The acronym *PASS CAR, AL* represents the nine different kinds of mnemonics. List these nine types of mnemonics.

4. Many verbal and nonverbal clues are given to help students recognize what information is important. List any three non-verbal clues your instructors may use to help you identify important ideas.

Recall-Plus Questions

Definitions, short answers, and essays are **recall-plus questions.** Each of these kinds of questions requires you to recall specific information from memory *and* organize the information into well-developed sentences, paragraphs, or essays. Strong writing skills will enable you to communicate your ideas clearly and effectively. To explain information clearly, you will need to use

- Well-developed vocabulary
- Accurate sentence and grammar structure
- Correct spelling and punctuation
- Logical organization of details

Definition Questions   Any question that directs you to "define" a specific term is a **definition question.** You can use the following steps when you are faced with questions that ask you to define terminology.

Steps for Writing Definitions

1. Begin your sentence by naming the term.
2. Identify the general category of the term.
3. Give the specific definition.
4. Expand your definition by giving further information or examples.

Name the Term   Read the directions carefully. Underline the term that you are asked to define. Begin your opening sentence by naming and focusing your reader's attention on the term. Notice how the term is underlined in the following example:

> Successful students learn to use many kinds of reference books. Dictionaries and thesauruses are two references that are valuable for expanding vocabulary skills. Define a <u>thesaurus</u>.

Your answer can begin this way: A thesaurus is . . .

Identify the General Category   The general category is the larger picture or concept that the term is related to in your memory. The category can be identified by asking yourself these questions:

- What is this term related to?
- What was the larger topic we studied when we learned this?
- What would be the topic of a mapping or hierarchy with this term on it?
- What chapter is this from?

In the preceding example, the category was given in the question itself. The word *thesaurus* belongs in the larger category "reference books." Many times, however, you will have to identify the category through your own efforts and retrieval skills.

In the following definition, notice how the word being defined is followed by the general category: A thesaurus is a reference book . . .

Give the Specific Definition   Complete the opening sentence by using paired association to give the definition. When you used vocabulary cards or vocabulary study sheets, your reciting, reflecting, and reviewing activities should have focused on pairing the word to the definition. Pause to "hear" or "see" what is on the back side of your flash card or the right column of your vocabulary sheet. Use that information to complete the first sentence.

In the preceding example, your opening definition sentence can now be completed: *A thesaurus is a reference book that provides lists of synonyms.*

Expand Your Definition   To receive full points for your definition answer, *add one or two more sentences* (or more if indicated in the directions) to show that you understand the term. Expand the definition with further information or examples. Show how the term can be used, why it is important, and where it should be used, or give specific examples. Sometimes the question will suggest ideas for inclusion in your expanded information. For example, the thesaurus question mentions vocabulary skills. You can use this as a possible avenue for expansion. The way a definition is expanded varies from person to person, so in many ways this last part of the answer is open-ended.

If a student defines a thesaurus simply as "a book of words," the answer is too vague and insufficient. However, if a student clearly defines and expands the word *thesaurus*, full point value is awarded. Both of the following examples are well-developed ones:

> A thesaurus is a reference book that provides lists of synonyms (words with the same or similar meanings). The thesaurus can be used to help you find more precise words for writing. It can also be used to quickly look up known synonyms of the unfamiliar words that you encounter as you read.

> A thesaurus is a reference book that provide lists of synonyms. A thesaurus can help you expand your vocabulary by listing words that have the same or similar meanings. When you see an unfamiliar word in a thesaurus, you should look it up in a dictionary so that you can learn the subtle differences that occur because of connotations or context.

Exercise 17.3   Writing Definitions

Work in groups of two, three, or four people. On your own paper, write a good definition answer for each of the following terms. Use Term + Category + Definition + Expansion.

1. Sensory input

2. Visualization

3. Paired association

4. Mnemonics

5. Anxiety

Short-Answer Questions
Questions that require short answers can often be completed in three to five well-planned and well-written sentences. Even though the content of your sentences is very important, teachers tend to grade higher when you use correct grammar, punctuation, and spelling.

There are two kinds of **short-answer questions:**

1. *Closed questions* require specific facts or details, which may even have to be in a specific order.
2. *Open-ended questions* have many possible correct answers. These questions may require you to connect or relate ideas from more than one chapter or source, or they may require you to apply your knowledge to new situations.

If you know the information adequately, you then have to organize your answer to include details. The following four steps can help you write an effective answer on a test.

Steps for Answering Short-Answer Questions

1. Identify the direction word and know what is expected.
2. Make a mental plan of your answer with the key ideas.
3. Write a strong, focused opening sentence.
4. Add three or four more sentences with specific details.

Identify the Direction Word   The first step is to pay attention to the direction word in each question. Each type of direction word requires a specific kind of answer. To get full points for your work, your answer must match the question. The following direction words are common for short-answer questions.

Direction Word	What Is Required
Discuss/Tell/Name	Tell about a particular topic.
Identify/What are?	Identify specific points. (This is similar to a listing except that you are required to answer in full sentences.)
Describe	Give more specific details or descriptions than are required by "discuss."
Explain/Why?	Give reasons. Answer the question "Why?"
Explain how/How?	Describe a process or a set of steps. Give the steps in chronological (time sequence) order.
When?	Describe a time or a specific condition needed for something to happen, occur, or be used.

Circle the key direction word when you first read the question. Review in your mind what is required by this direction word. Because you want to respond quickly, become very familiar with the preceding descriptions of direction words.

Each of the following test questions has the same subject: visual mappings. However, because of the different direction words, each answer will be slightly different.

(Name) the different parts of a visual mapping.
(Why) are visual mappings effective study tools?
(Explain how) to create a visual mapping.
(How) should you study from a visual mapping?
(When) should visual mappings be used?

Make a Mental Plan   Before you begin writing an answer, underline any key words that are important and should be included in your answer. Pause and think through your answer. Do a quick memory search for appropriate information. What are the main points you want to make in a few sentences? Plan to do only what is expected; do not include unnecessary or unrelated information in an attempt to impress the instructor.

In the following example, notice the underlining; then notice the possible thinking process used to generate a mental plan.

Example: (Name) the different parts of a visual mapping.
Think: "To answer this question, I need to name the parts of a mapping. OK. There's level one for the subject, level two for the main ideas, level three for important detail, etc.

Write a Strong Opening Sentence   Since you will not have much space to write a long answer, begin your answer with a sentence that is direct and to the point. Your first sentence should include the key words of the question and show that you are heading in the direction required by the direction word. Do not beat around the bush or save your best information for last. The first sentence, when well written, lets the teacher know right away that you are familiar with the subject.

Notice the difference in quality in the following opening sentences. The first one does not get to the point. The second and third examples are direct and show confidence.

Q: (Name) the different parts of a visual mapping.
A: Visual mappings are easy to make.
A: There are at least three parts or levels to a visual mapping.
A: The parts of visual mappings show a subject, main ideas or categories, and at least one level of details.

Add Sentences with Details   After you write your opening sentence, expand your answer with more information. Give appropriate details to support your opening sentence; try to use course-related terminology in your answers.

In the following example, all three answers are very underdeveloped and inadequate. What do you think is wrong with each answer?
Q: (Name) the different parts of a visual mapping.
A: Level one, level two, and level three are the parts.
A: The parts of a mapping are in the center; then branches tell what you want it to.
A: The parts of the mapping are drawn to spread all over the page to make a visual study tool.

Compare the preceding answers to the well-developed ones that follow. These answers have strong opening sentences and additional sentences to expand with details.

Most visual mappings have at least three parts or three levels to show a subject, main ideas or categories, and details. The subject is on level one; it is usually placed in the middle of the paper. The main ideas or category words, which branch off the subject, are considered level two. Level three details, which branch off each of the main ideas, are supporting details. More levels (parts) can be added if there are minor details.

The parts of a mapping are the topic, the main ideas, and the details. The topic tells the subject. The main ideas branch off the subject. The details branch off each main idea. More parts can be added if there are more details to branch off the main details.

Exercise 17.4   Writing Opening Sentences

With a partner, choose one of the following questions. Circle the direction word. Underline key words that should be a part of the answer. On paper, together write a strong, focused opening sentence. Then by yourself, expand the answer by adding one or more sentences with relevant details.

1. Discuss two strategies for dealing with an anxiety attack while you are taking a test.

2. Name three important reasons notetaking from lectures is more difficult than notetaking from a textbook.

3. Discuss at least three different ways that you can use surveying.

4. Explain how you use the principle of feedback when you study from flash cards.

Essay Questions   **Essay questions** are a larger version of short-answer questions. The questions are broader in scope and cover more information or require more details in the answer. Because of the increased content, greater organizational skills are required so that the ideas can be understood clearly and the relationships can be readily shown. Essay questions carry higher point values. The following steps can help you receive higher points in your answers.

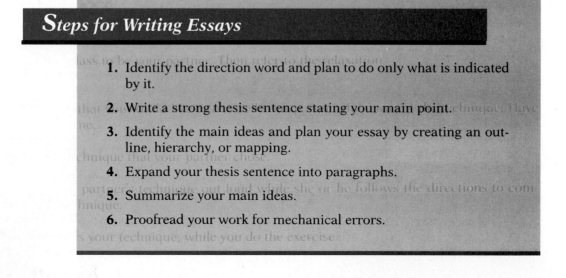

Steps for Writing Essays

1. Identify the direction word and plan to do only what is indicated by it.

2. Write a strong thesis sentence stating your main point.

3. Identify the main ideas and plan your essay by creating an outline, hierarchy, or mapping.

4. Expand your thesis sentence into paragraphs.

5. Summarize your main ideas.

6. Proofread your work for mechanical errors.

Identify the Direction Word   The direction words used in short-answer questions also appear in essay questions. (Review the boxed direction words on p. 292.) The following direction words also appear in essay questions. Study these direction words so that you will know the kind of information that is expected in your answer.

Direction Word	*What Is Required*
Compare	Show the similarities and differences between two or more items.
Contrast	Present only the differences between two or more items.
Define	Expand the definition with more examples and greater details.
Trace	Discuss the sequence of events in chronological order.
Summarize	Identify and discuss the main points or the highlights of a subject. In-depth details are not expected.
Evaluate/Critique	Offer your opinion or judgment, and then back it up with specific facts, details, or reasons.
Analyze	Identify the different parts of something. Discuss each part individually.

Exercise 17.5   **Understanding Direction Words**

Read each of the following essay questions. Circle the direction word. On the line, describe the type of information that is expected in your answer.

Example: (Discuss) the steps of SQ4R.
I should <u>tell all about SQ4R.</u>

1. Explain why the use of effective time management skills can reduce stress.

I should _____

2. Summarize any six of the twelve principles of memory.

I should _____

3. Compare the organizational structures of hierarchies and mappings.

I should _____

4. Contrast the capabilities and functions of short-term memory and long-term memory.

I should _____

5. Analyze the information processing model in terms of the principles of memory used in each part of the model.

I should _____

Write a Strong Thesis Sentence   A **thesis sentence** directly states the main point you want to make in the entire essay. A thesis sentence for an essay on a test

- Clearly states the topic of the essay
- Can include key words that are a part of the question
- May indicate a given number of main ideas you'll discuss
- Should show that you understand the direction word

The following examples have the direction words circled, the key words underlined, and the expectations in parentheses. Notice how the thesis sentence is developed to show the direction that the essay will take and the general topics or main ideas that will be included.

(Why) is metacognition beneficial to the college student?
(Reasons will be given for why metacognition is beneficial.)

Thesis sentence: Metacognition, the ability to understand, select, and use different study strategies, is valuable to college students for three main reasons.

(Discuss) the characteristics of each of Howard Gardner's multiple intelligences.
(Tell all about the characteristics of each of Gardner's multiple intelligences.)

Thesis sentence: Each of Howard Gardner's seven intelligences has clearly recognizable characteristics.

Identify the Main Points and Plan Your Essay   The essay question itself sometimes leads you to the logical main points to be discussed; other times it will be up to you to identify the main points you wish to develop. Note how question 1 below clearly states the topics you are to discuss in your essay and what kind of explanation is required. Question 2 indicates the *number* of topics to discuss, but it is up to you to identify the topics. Question 3 is the most general example; the topics and the number of them to be discussed in your essay are not specified.

1. *Time management, concentration, notetaking, and textbook reading skills are all necessary study skills for college students. (Explain why) each of these study skills is essential for success in college.*

   In this essay question, you are asked to *explain* or give reasons why four different study skills are essential for college success. The four areas have been identified for you. Your essay will be limited to these four topics.

2. *Many study skills that help you become a more effective, successful student were discussed this term. Select the four study skills that you feel are most important for your personal success. (Discuss) the key strategies for each of the four study skills that you selected.*

   In this essay question, the key direction word is *discuss*. The main points will be *four study skills* and the *strategies valuable* for you. The number of study skills is identified for you; it is up to you to decide which four study skills and which strategies to discuss in your essay.

3. *(Discuss) the study skill strategies that will lead you to greater personal success in school.*

   In this essay question, you will need to identify the *strategies* you feel are important for *your success*. No set number of strategies is required. The direction word is to *discuss* or "tell all about." Your topic sentence should give the sense that you know which strategies lead to your personal success.

   After you have analyzed the essay question in terms of the direction word and the main points that are required, and you have written a strong opening thesis sentence, take a few minutes to plan your essay before you begin writing. Your plan may be written in the form of a mapping, a hierarchy, a time line, or a basic outline. Select the format that works best for showing how your ideas will be developed and connected.

Basic Outline Format

Thesis Sentence: _____

A. First Main Idea
   1. Details
   2. Details

B. Second Main Idea
   1. Detail
   2. Detail

Etc.

Your plan is valuable for three reasons. First, it helps you organize the order in which you will discuss different ideas. Second, you can use it as a guide as you write so that your ideas stay on track. Third, if you run out of time to write the entire essay, your plan can be turned in for possible points.

Some instructors give the essay question in advance. This allows you time outside class to develop your thesis statement and to identify and plan the main points. Practice writing and reciting your essay before the test.

Expand Your Thesis Sentence   Develop each of your main ideas. If you are using an outline, develop the topic listed in "A" with supporting details to form the first paragraph of your essay. If you are using a mapping or a hierarchy, include the first level two category and the details connected to it in your initial paragraph.

As you expand your thesis statement into paragraphs, *avoid wordiness*. Make each sentence contribute a valuable detail in support of your main idea. Also, try to incorporate as many *key vocabulary terms* as possible in your paragraph. Using well-developed expressive vocabulary and important terms related to the subject will result in a much more impressive essay than if you use only basic, nontechnical language.

Once you have finished developing the first main idea, indent and begin a new paragraph. Continue this process until you have developed each of your main points or supported it with sufficient details.

Summarize Your Main Points   Finish your essay with a short summary sentence or paragraph. Summarizing leaves a clear picture of your main points in the reader's mind and signals that you have finished with your thoughts. Your summary should reflect the same information you used in your thesis sentence. If your summary and your thesis sentences do not focus on the same subject, check to see where you got sidetracked when you developed the body of your essay.

In the following examples, notice how the concluding sentences or concluding paragraphs "echo" the thesis sentences:

Thesis sentence: Metacognition, the ability to understand, select, and use different study strategies, is valuable to college students for three main reasons.

Summary paragraph: In summary, metacognition is valuable for three reasons. It encourages students to learn different strategies that use different modalities. It allows students to select from many different strategies so that the best strategy for the situation can be used. It also enables students to analyze the approaches they have used to get specific results and then to adjust their strategies based on their goals.

Thesis sentence: Each of Howard Gardner's seven intelligences has clearly recognizable characteristics.

Summary sentence: Linguistic, musical, logical math, visual-spatial, bodily kinesthetic, intrapersonal, and interpersonal intelligences each have unique characteristics based on the abilities that can be demonstrated.

Proofread Your Work   After you have completed your essay, take a few minutes to **proofread** for mechanical errors such as spelling, grammar, word usage, or sentence structure. Many teachers try to grade mainly on the content, but mechanical errors are distracting, and maintaining a focus on the ideas is therefore more difficult.

If your writing skills are still weak for college-level writing, consider enrolling in writing skill-building courses to improve your spelling, grammar, punctuation, and organizational skills. Also ask your instructor if you can use a dictionary, thesaurus, spell-checker, or laptop computer when you write essays.

Additional Suggestions for Recall-Plus Questions   The following general suggestions are important for all recall-plus questions, but they are especially important for essays:

1. Use ink and write on only one side of the paper. There is less eye strain for the reader, and you avoid the possibility of ink bleeding through to the other side of the paper and blotting out what you've written.

2. Double space when you write so that you have room to add information or make changes when you proofread.
3. Write legibly. Illegible writing makes it difficult for the teacher to read and to follow the development of your ideas.
4. If you run out of time, jot down ideas in phrases or include your organizational plan (outline, mapping, hierarchy, or time line). Add a comment that you ran out of time but would have developed the information listed if you had had more time.

Exercise 17.6   Writing an Essay

Select any one of the essay questions used as examples in this chapter. Develop a plan for organizing the information. Write an essay answer. Proofread your essay.

SUMMARY
- Recall questions in the form of fill in the blanks or listings require single words or short phrases for answers. The strategies used to answer both types of questions are similar.
- Recall-plus questions require you to retrieve information from memory and organize it into sentences, paragraphs, or essays. These questions may require you to write

  1. definitions.
  2. a short paragraph.
  3. a longer essay.

- The answers to recall-plus questions often begin with a strong opening sentence, which is followed with additional sentences that expand the first sentence.
- Understanding the direction words and the key words in the questions enables you to write focused, to-the-point answers.

PERSONALIZING WHAT YOU LEARNED
1. Score and record the score for your chapter profile.
2. On your own paper, expand this chapter's visual mapping.
3. Make your own vocabulary list of all the terms in this chapter that are printed in color.

"To the Student" (p. xv) provides you with more detailed directions for completing these activities.

WRITING ASSIGNMENTS
1. Write an essay that discusses the value of taking a study skills course in college. What are the benefits? Why are these skills essential?
2. Discuss specific strategies you have learned in this chapter that will help you combat problems you have had in the past responding to definition, short-answer, or essay questions.

APPENDIX

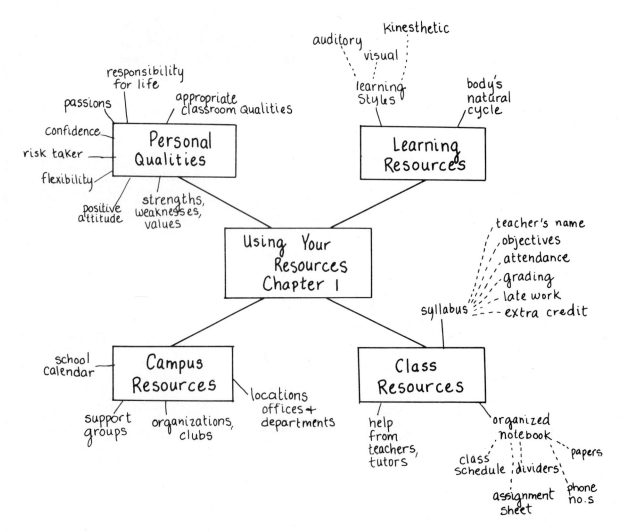

MASTER ASSIGNMENT SHEET

For the week of _____

Class	Monday	Tuesday	Wednesday	Thursday	Friday

WEEKLY TIME MANAGEMENT SCHEDULE

For the week of _____

Time	Monday	Tuesday	Wednesday	Thursday	Friday	Saturday	Sunday
12–6A.M.							
6–7:00							
7–8:00							
8–9:00							
9–10:00							
10–11:00							
11–12:00							
12–1:00							
1–2:00							
2–3:00							
3–4:00							
4–5:00							
5–6:00							
6–7:00							
7–8:00							
8–9:00							
9–10:00							
10–11:00							
11–12:00							

MASTER ASSIGNMENT SHEET

For the week of _____

Class	Monday	Tuesday	Wednesday	Thursday	Friday

WEEKLY TIME MANAGEMENT SCHEDULE

For the week of _____

Time	Monday	Tuesday	Wednesday	Thursday	Friday	Saturday	Sunday
12–6 A.M.							
6–7:00							
7–8:00							
8–9:00							
9–10:00							
10–11:00							
11–12:00							
12–1:00							
1–2:00							
2–3:00							
3–4:00							
4–5:00							
5–6:00							
6–7:00							
7–8:00							
8–9:00							
9–10:00							
10–11:00							
11–12:00							

Name _____   Date beginning-of-the-term profile _____

                                            Date end-of-the-term profile _____

Master Profile Chart

Resources	Goals and Time	Concentration	Learning Model	Textbook Surveying	Reading System	Notes in Textbooks	Cornell for Texts	Cornell for Lectures	Vocabulary	Visual Tools	Multisensory Tools	Mnemonics	Taking Tests	Objective Tests	Educated Guessing	Recall and Recall Plus
1	2	3	4	5	6	7	8	9	10	11	12	13	14	15	16	17
12	12	12	12	12	12	12	12	12	12	12	12	12	12	12	12	12
11	11	11	11	11	11	11	11	11	11	11	11	11	11	11	11	11
10	10	10	10	10	10	10	10	10	10	10	10	10	10	10	10	10
9	9	9	9	9	9	9	9	9	9	9	9	9	9	9	9	9
8	8	8	8	8	8	8	8	8	8	8	8	8	8	8	8	8
7	7	7	7	7	7	7	7	7	7	7	7	7	7	7	7	7
6	6	6	6	6	6	6	6	6	6	6	6	6	6	6	6	6
5	5	5	5	5	5	5	5	5	5	5	5	5	5	5	5	5
4	4	4	4	4	4	4	4	4	4	4	4	4	4	4	4	4
3	3	3	3	3	3	3	3	3	3	3	3	3	3	3	3	3
2	2	2	2	2	2	2	2	2	2	2	2	2	2	2	2	2
1	1	1	1	1	1	1	1	1	1	1	1	1	1	1	1	1
0	0	0	0	0	0	0	0	0	0	0	0	0	0	0	0	0

Beginning-of-the-Term Profile
1. As you begin a new chapter, complete the chapter profile chart.
2. Score your profile. (See "To the Student.") Find the chapter number above. Circle your score to show the number correct.
3. Connect the circles with lines to create a graph.

End-of-the-Term Profile
1. Return to the orginal profile in each chapter.
2. Cover the YES/NO column so that you cannot see your original answers.
3. Read the question. Answer yes or no honestly. Circle the *Y* or the *N* under the column shown below for the chapter.

4. After you have completed all profiles, use the answer key to score them. Count the number of correct responses, as you have done throughout the course.
5. Chart your new scores Master Profile. Use a different color of ink so you can compare these scores with your orginal scores.

1: Resources	2: Goals and Time	3: Concentration	4: Learning
1. Y N	1. Y N	1. Y N	1. Y N
2. Y N	2. Y N	2. Y N	2. Y N
3. Y N	3. Y N	3. Y N	3. Y N
4. Y N	4. Y N	4. Y N	4. Y N
5. Y N	5. Y N	5. Y N	5. Y N
6. Y N	6. Y N	6. Y N	6. Y N
7. Y N	7. Y N	7. Y N	7. Y N
8. Y N	8. Y N	8. Y N	8. Y N
9. Y N	9. Y N	9. Y N	9. Y N
10. Y N	10. Y N	10. Y N	10. Y N
11. Y N	11. Y N	11. Y N	11. Y N
12. Y N	12. Y N	12. Y N	12. Y N

5: Text Survey	6: Reading System	7: Text Notes	8: Cornell for Texts
1. Y N	1. Y N	1. Y N	1. Y N
2. Y N	2. Y N	2. Y N	2. Y N
3. Y N	3. Y N	3. Y N	3. Y N
4. Y N	4. Y N	4. Y N	4. Y N
5. Y N	5. Y N	5. Y N	5. Y N
6. Y N	6. Y N	6. Y N	6. Y N
7. Y N	7. Y N	7. Y N	7. Y N
8. Y N	8. Y N	8. Y N	8. Y N
9. Y N	9. Y N	9. Y N	9. Y N
10. Y N	10. Y N	10. Y N	10. Y N
11. Y N	11. Y N	11. Y N	11. Y N
12. Y N	12. Y N	12. Y N	12. Y N

9: Cornell for Lectures	10: Vocabulary	11: Visual Tools	12: Multisensory Tools
1. Y N	1. Y N	1. Y N	1. Y N
2. Y N	2. Y N	2. Y N	2. Y N
3. Y N	3. Y N	3. Y N	3. Y N
4. Y N	4. Y N	4. Y N	4. Y N
5. Y N	5. Y N	5. Y N	5. Y N
6. Y N	6. Y N	6. Y N	6. Y N
7. Y N	7. Y N	7. Y N	7. Y N
8. Y N	8. Y N	8. Y N	8. Y N
9. Y N	9. Y N	9. Y N	9. Y N
10. Y N	10. Y N	10. Y N	10. Y N
11. Y N	11. Y N	11. Y N	11. Y N
12. Y N	12. Y N	12. Y N	12. Y N

13: Mnemonics	14: Taking Tests	15: Objective Tests
1. Y N	1. Y N	1. Y N
2. Y N	2. Y N	2. Y N
3. Y N	3. Y N	3. Y N
4. Y N	4. Y N	4. Y N
5. Y N	5. Y N	5. Y N
6. Y N	6. Y N	6. Y N
7. Y N	7. Y N	7. Y N
8. Y N	8. Y N	8. Y N
9. Y N	9. Y N	9. Y N
10. Y N	10. Y N	10. Y N
11. Y N	11. Y N	11. Y N
12. Y N	12. Y N	12. Y N

16: Educated Guessing	17: Recall and Recall Plus
1. Y N	1. Y N
2. Y N	2. Y N
3. Y N	3. Y N
4. Y N	4. Y N
5. Y N	5. Y N
6. Y N	6. Y N
7. Y N	7. Y N
8. Y N	8. Y N
9. Y N	9. Y N
10. Y N	10. Y N
11. Y N	11. Y N
12. Y N	12. Y N

Profile Answer Key

1: Resources
1. (Y) N
2. (Y) N
3. Y (N)
4. Y (N)
5. (Y) N
6. (Y) N
7. (Y) N
8. (Y) N
9. Y (N)
10. Y (N)
11. (Y) N
12. (Y) N

2: Goals and Time
1. (Y) N
2. Y (N)
3. (Y) N
4. Y (N)
5. (Y) N
6. Y (N)
7. Y (N)
8. (Y) N
9. Y (N)
10. (Y) N
11. Y (N)
12. (Y) N

3: Concentration
1. Y (N)
2. Y (N)
3. Y (N)
4. (Y) N
5. (Y) N
6. (Y) N
7. (Y) N
8. Y (N)
9. (Y) N
10. Y (N)
11. (Y) N
12. Y (N)

4: Learning
1. (Y) N
2. Y (N)
3. (Y) N
4. Y (N)
5. (Y) N
6. Y (N)
7. (Y) N
8. Y (N)
9. Y (N)
10. (Y) N
11. (Y) N
12. (Y) N

5: Text Survey
1. (Y) N
2. (Y) N
3. (Y) N
4. Y (N)
5. Y (N)
6. (Y) N
7. (Y) N
8. (Y) N
9. (Y) N
10. (Y) N
11. Y (N)
12. Y (N)

6: Reading System
1. Y (N)
2. (Y) N
3. (Y) N
4. Y (N)
5. Y (N)
6. (Y) N
7. Y (N)
8. Y (N)
9. Y (N)
10. (Y) N
11. (Y) N
12. (Y) N

7: Text Notes
1. Y (N)
2. (Y) N
3. Y (N)
4. (Y) N
5. (Y) N
6. (Y) N
7. (Y) N
8. (Y) N
9. (Y) N
10. Y (N)
11. (Y) N
12. (Y) N

8: Cornell for Texts
1. (Y) N
2. Y (N)
3. (Y) N
4. Y (N)
5. (Y) N
6. (Y) N
7. (Y) N
8. (Y) N
9. (Y) N
10. (Y) N
11. (Y) N
12. Y (N)

9: Cornell for Lectures
1. Y (N)
2. Y (N)
3. (Y) N
4. (Y) N
5. (Y) N
6. (Y) N
7. Y (N)
8. (Y) N
9. (Y) N
10. (Y) N
11. (Y) N
12. (Y) N

10: Vocabulary
1. (Y) N
2. (Y) N
3. Y (N)
4. (Y) N
5. (Y) N
6. Y (N)
7. (Y) N
8. (Y) N
9. Y (N)
10. Y (N)
11. Y (N)
12. (Y) N

11: Visual Tools
1. (Y) N
2. (Y) N
3. (Y) N
4. (Y) N
5. Y (N)
6. (Y) N
7. (Y) N
8. (Y) N
9. (Y) N
10. (Y) N
11. (Y) N
12. (Y) N

12: Multisensory Tools
1. (Y) N
2. Y (N)
3. (Y) N
4. (Y) N
5. (Y) N
6. (Y) N
7. (Y) N
8. (Y) N
9. (Y) N
10. (Y) N
11. (Y) N
12. (Y) N

13: Mnemonics
1. Ⓨ N
2. Ⓨ N
3. Ⓨ N
4. Ⓨ N
5. Y Ⓝ
6. Ⓨ N
7. Ⓨ N
8. Y Ⓝ
9. Ⓨ N
10. Ⓨ N
11. Ⓨ N
12. Ⓨ N

14: Taking Tests
1. Y Ⓝ
2. Ⓨ N
3. Y Ⓝ
4. Ⓨ N
5. Y Ⓝ
6. Ⓨ N
7. Y Ⓝ
8. Y Ⓝ
9. Y Ⓝ
10. Y Ⓝ
11. Ⓨ N
12. Ⓨ N

15: Objective Tests
1. Ⓨ N
2. Y Ⓝ
3. Y Ⓝ
4. Ⓨ N
5. Ⓨ N
6. Ⓨ N
7. Y Ⓝ
8. Ⓨ N
9. Ⓨ N
10. Ⓨ N
11. Y Ⓝ
12. Y Ⓝ

16: Educated Guessing
1. Y Ⓝ
2. Ⓨ N
3. Y Ⓝ
4. Y Ⓝ
5. Y Ⓝ
6. Y Ⓝ
7. Y Ⓝ
8. Y Ⓝ
9. Y Ⓝ
10. Y Ⓝ
11. Ⓨ N
12. Ⓨ N

17: Recall and Recall Plus
1. Y Ⓝ
2. Ⓨ N
3. Y Ⓝ
4. Ⓨ N
5. Y Ⓝ
6. Ⓨ N
7. Ⓨ N
8. Y Ⓝ
9. Y Ⓝ
10. Y Ⓝ
11. Y Ⓝ
12. Ⓨ N

QUICK REFERENCE LIST

Learning Styles
(Chapter1)
1. Visual
2. Auditory
3. Kinesthetic

STST—How to Write Goals
(Chapter 2)
1. Specific
2. Target Dates
3. Steps Involved
4. Rewards

EVA, BAT—How to Reach Goals
(Chapter 2)
1. Evaluate Goals
2. Visualize
3. Affirmations
4. Break into Smaller Goals
5. Ask for help
6. Tell Goals

RAVES—How to Prepare for Learning
(Chapter 3)
1. Relaxation
2. Arrange Goals
3. Visualize
4. Emotional E Words
5. Self-Talk

DATE IAN—Concentrated Listening Skills
(Chapter 3)
1. End Distractors
2. Pay Attention
3. Stay Tuned-In
4. Monitor Emotions
5. Create Interest
6. Ask Questions
7. Be Non-Judgmental

Information Processing Model
(Chapter 4)
1. Sensory Input
2. Short-Term Memory
3. Rehearsal
4. Feedback Loop
5. Long-Term Memory
6 Long-Term Memory Retrieval

SAVE CRIB FOTO— 12 Memory Principles
(Chapter 4)
1. Selectivity
2. Association
3. Visualization
4. Effort
5. Concentration
6. Recitation
7. Interest
8. Big Picture/Little Pictures
9. Feedback
10. Organization
11. Time
12. Ongoing Review

SQ4R—Reading System
(Chapter 6)
1. Survey
2. Question
3. Read
4. Record
5. Recite
6. Review

Five R's of Cornell— Notetaking System
(Chapter 8)
1. Record
2. Reduce
3. Recite
4. Reflect
5. Review

Kinds of Mnemonics
(Chapter 13)
1. Acronyms
2. Acrostics
3. Rhythm, Rhymes, Jingles
4. Associations
5. Cartoons, Pictures
6. Story Lines
7. Stacking
8. Peg System
9. Loci

Stages of Answering Questions
(Chapter 14)
1. Immediate Response
2. Delayed Response
3. Assisted Response
4. Educated Guess

How to Find Definitions
(Chapter 10)
1. Punctuation Clues
2. Word Clues
3. Context Clues
4. Word Structure Clues
5. Glossary
6. Reference Books

Red Flag Words on Tests
(Chapter 15)
1. Definition Clues
2. Negatives
3. Modifiers
4. Relationship Clues

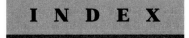

INDEX

Instructor's Resource Manual

Essential Study Skills

Linda Wong
Lane Community College

HOUGHTON MIFFLIN COMPANY　　BOSTON　　TORONTO
GENEVA, ILLINOIS　　PALO ALTO　　PRINCETON, NEW JERSEY

As part of Houghton Mifflin's ongoing commitment to the environment, this text
has been printed on recycled paper.

ACKNOWLEDGMENTS

The author is grateful to the following for granting permission to reprint excerpts from their works:

Bernstein, et al., PSYCHOLOGY, Second Edition. Copyright © 1991 by Houghton Mifflin Company. Used
with permission.

McKay, John P., Bennett D. Hill, and John Buckler, A HISTORY OF WESTERN SOCIETY, Fourth
Edition. Copyright © 1991 by Houghton Mifflin Company. Adapted with permission.

Osborn/Osborn, PUBLIC SPEAKING, Second Edition. Copyright © 1991 by Houghton Mifflin Company.
Used with permission.

Pride, et al., BUSINESS, Third Edition. Copyright © 1991 by Houghton Mifflin Company. Used with
permission.

Sponsoring Editor: Mary Jo Southern
Senior Development Editor: Barbara Roth
Associate Project Editor: Nicole Ng
Production/Design Coordinator: Jill Haber
Senior Manufacturing Coordinator: Priscilla Bailey
Marketing Manager: George Kane

Printed in the U.S.A.

ISBN: 0-395-69108-7

123456789-B-97 96 95 94 93

Contents

Teaching *Essential Study Skills*

Essential Study Skills allows you to present skills in the manner and order best suited to your teaching style. If you are an experienced study skills teacher, you will find a wealth of materials in the text and in the Instructor's Resource Manual to incorporate into your classroom. If you are new at teaching study skills, you will find that the text and the IRM guide you comfortably and successfully through the teaching of sequential skills. In either case, you can adapt suggestions in this IRM to meet your students' needs and your preferences.

Part I of the IRM provides complete answer keys and teaching tips. Part II contains twenty-two additional exercises and eight transparency masters. Part III provides part tests (with answer keys) that assess students' retention and integration of material across the chapters in each of the book's four parts.

For more on understanding and teaching study skills, see the following sources:

Bell, Nanci. *Visualizing and Verbalizing for Language Comprehension and Thinking.* Academy of Reading Publications, 1720 Filbert Street, Paso Robles, CA 93446. 1991.

Gardner, Howard. *Frames of Mind: The Theory of Multiple Intelligences.* Basic Books, 10 E. 53rd St., New York, NY 10022. 1985.

Mather, Nancy. *An Instructional Guide to the Woodcock Johnson Psycho-Educational Battery—Revised.* CPPC, 4 Conant Square, Brandon, VT 05733. 1991.

Postsecondary LD Network News. Quarterly newsletter, University of Connecticut, Pappanikou Center, U-64, 249 Glenbrook Rd., Storrs, CT 06269.

Smith, Sally L. *Succeeding Against the Odds: Strategies and Insights from the Learning Disabled.* Jeremy P. Tarcher, Inc., 5858 Wilshire Blvd., Suite 200, Los Angeles, CA 90036. 1991.

Their Word. Publication of the National Center for Learning Disabilities, 99 Park Ave., New York, NY 10016.

Teaching the Chapters

1. Begin by having students complete the self-assessment profile on the second page of the chapter. In Personalizing What You Learned at the end of the chapter, students are asked to score their profiles. You can direct them to do so in either of the following ways:

   - Have students use the Profile Answer Key in the Appendix to score their profiles either in class or outside class.
   - Make an overhead transparency of the profile. Discuss each correct answer in class as students score their profiles.

2. Make an overhead transparency of the chapter mapping as a preview of the chapter. Ask students to anticipate the kind of information that will be discussed in each part of the mapping.

3. Call students' attention to the boxed information throughout. Here are two ways to do so:

- Assign students to read the chapter. In the next class meeting, show overhead transparencies of all the boxed information. As you display each transparency, either summarize each point, or ask students questions about each point in the box. This is a more independent approach to use for higher level classes.
- Show overhead transparencies of the boxed information in the chapter. As you display the main points, discuss the details related to each point. Then ask students to read the complete information in their textbooks as a review of the class lecture. This is a more guided approach to use for slower-paced classes or students with lower reading levels.

4. Read through the IRM material for the chapter to identify any additional teaching tips, activities, enrichment exercises, or transparency masters you wish to use.

5. Assign the exercises. Note that the exercises can be done in class individually, with partners, in a group, or as a class. Spend class time discussing the skills and concepts presented in the chapter.

6. Assign the Personalizing What You Learned activities. These assignments can be graded or simply checked for completion.

7. Use the Review Questions as an in-class test or as homework. Spend time in class reviewing the correct answers and providing students with test-taking tips for each question or kind of question format.

8. Assign the Writing Assignments as regular homework or as extra credit.

Grading Assignments

1. Homework assignments can be graded by percentage scores or points. Calculate percentages by dividing the number of correct points by the total number of possible points. To use the point system, give each assignment a certain number of points (such as ten) if completed correctly. Vocabulary sheets or flash cards and extended visual mappings can also be graded by either of these systems.

2. Written assignments can be graded on a point system. When you give the assignment, make your expectations clear. Let students know whether you will grade solely on content (the correctness and completeness of the answers) or on writing skills as well (punctuation, grammar, spelling).

3. Review tests are best graded by percentage scores.

4. If you grade the unit tests (in Part III of this IRM), you should weigh these scores more heavily toward the term grade than the scores from the review tests or the homework assignments.

Your Attitude

Always try to maintain a positive, encouraging attitude. Help students learn from their mistakes. Focus on the fact that many scores will contribute to their final grades. If a student genuinely tries to do an assignment but has a great deal of difficulty with it, you might want to meet with the student to help him or her complete it correctly.

Skills Integration

As often as possible, relate new skills and strategies to previously learned information. When you use examples in class, include some that refer to information from earlier chapters.

Most of all, *enjoy* the process! Be creative and enthusiastic!

PART I
Answer Keys and Teaching Tips

1 Using Your Resources

PART II includes:	Enrichment A (p. 63)
	Enrichment B (p. 64)

Resources Profile

1. Y 2. Y 3. N 4. N 5. Y 6. Y 7. Y 8. Y 9. N 10. N 11. Y 12. Y

Your Personal Qualities: Discussion Questions

1. Which personal qualities or attitudes toward life do you draw on quite regularly? Can you give some examples?
2. Which personal qualities would you like to use more effectively?
3. What counseling classes on campus would help you develop some of the personal qualities you wish to have?
4. Explain the difference between labeling something a "challenge" and labeling it a "problem."
5. How do you define the word *passions*? What are your passions?

1.1 Recognizing Your Personal Qualities

Answers will vary. This exercise is designed to build self-esteem and help students focus on their positive traits. Ask students to select a partner. Each partner reads the list of his or her positive traits to the other person. Allow time for students to explore any words they circled for themselves.

1.2 Clarifying Classroom Behaviors

Discuss the Guidelines for Group Work before beginning this exercise. (You may want to make an overhead of these guidelines to use as needed throughout the course.)

Once groups are formed, allow ten minutes for each group to generate its answers. Divide the chalkboard in half. On the left write "Positive Qualities," and on the right write "Problem Qualities." List the ideas of groups one and two on the left and groups three and four on the right. Taking time at the beginning of the term to clearly identify appropriate classroom behavior and expectations can set the tone for the class and reduce/eliminate inappropriate classroom behaviors throughout the rest of the term.

The following ideas are only a few of the possibilities students may generate. Add your own ideas to their lists.

Positive Qualities:
- Arriving on time
- Coming prepared with materials.
- Sitting near the front of the room
- Being ready before class starts
- Sitting with good posture
- Making direct eye contact
- Keeping your mind on the task
- Getting notes if you are absent
- Asking for further directions
- Being willing to share ideas
- Being honest when you answer
- Offering to help others
- Showing interest in the topic
- Listening when someone speaks
- Taking notes
- Writing down homework
- Participating in discussions
- Asking questions
- Smiling; being friendly
- Showing confidence and enthusiasm

Problem Qualities:
- Talking instead of listening
- Showing a poor attitude
- Doodling, doing other homework
- Dominating discussions
- Being disorganized
- Eating or chewing gum loudly
- Arriving late
- Challenging everyone
- Using inappropriate language
- Passing notes to others
- Reading instead of listening
- Criticizing others
- Making excessive noise
- Being unprepared
- Using lots of excuses
- Making inappropriate jokes
- Slouching or stretching out

Extra activity: Ask students to do the following: Identify a student in one of your classes who possesses many positive qualities for success. Describe those qualities that you admire and would like to have. Brainstorm ways you could begin to acquire some of these qualities.

1.3   Discovering Your Learning Style

Students are identifying learning-style preferences. Answers will vary. The questions that emphasize visual skills are listed in the *V* box (*A* for auditory and *K* for kinesthetic). Seldom will any student have *all* the numbers in any one of the boxes circled since most people use different preferences for different situations.

Strong preference: more circles in one of the three areas
Weakness: significantly fewer circles in one of the three areas
No significant preference or weakness: ability to function in all three modes

Learning Style: Discussion Questions

1. What did Exercise 1.3 indicate about your learning style? Do you agree with it?

2. If you are a visual learner, what are some of the study methods you already use to tap into your visual skills? (Repeat the same question for auditory and kinesthetic learners.)

Enrichment A: This small group auditory activity can be used to identify students who have learned to use auditory skills as a means of learning new information.

1.4   Discovering Your Peaks and Slumps

Answers will vary. Discuss the following questions.

1. What are your peak energy times? Do you currently use those times for studying?
2. What do you currently do during the times when you have low energy? What kinds of problems does this response create?

1.5   Recording Your Classes This Term

Answers will vary. If the work is being graded or given points, full credit would be given as long as the questions are answered.

After students complete this exercise, you may want to photocopy the charts students completed in questions 1 and 2 for future reference. Specific classes, feelings about classes and schedules, and concerns or fears given in students' answers can often be incorporated into future lectures and classroom discussions.

1.6   Examining a Course Syllabus

Answers will vary. (This form could be duplicated for use with more than one course.)

Ask students to write "not given" for particular information not available on a syllabus. (A blank space may mean a student simply skipped the question.) Remind students that they should ask about any of the information on this form that is not clearly stated on the syllabus. It is the student's responsibility to find out.

Organizing Your Notebook

Give suggestions for ways students may want to organize their notebooks for your class, such as using dividers to show chapters, topics, or weeks of the term. If you identified topics/chapters by the week when the course was introduced, refer students to that list.

Master Assignment Sheet

Students often need several weeks to create new habits. Consider asking students to make three copies of the master assignment sheet (in the Appendix), or provide them with copies. Require them to place the sheet in the front of their notebooks and use it to record assignments for every class for three weeks.

Note: The weekly time management schedule (Chapter 2) can be printed on the back of the master assignment sheet. Both schedules can be required for three weeks.

1.7   Increasing Your Campus Awareness

Answers will vary. Refer to your campus catalog, directory, term schedule, and newspaper. Contact the counseling department if there are questions you need to answer.

After students have completed the exercise in groups, discuss the answers. Add additional information pertinent to your campus. Encourage students who have utilized any of the services to share their experiences or additional knowledge with the class.

Enrichment B: This enrichment can be used to analyze or summarize the group process any time throughout the term.

Review Questions

True-False

1. F   Some recognition needs to be given to weaknesses.
2. T
3. F   A flexible person sees change as a positive process.
4. T
5. F   He or she does need to make choices; not all choices will bring positive results.
6. F   This describes a visual learner.
7. T   "Most" is a key word. Students with learning disabilities or physical impairments may be unable to use all modalities.
8. F   The best way is to identify the problem area more specifically.
9. T
10. F
11. T
12. F   Support groups are designed to meet a variety of needs.
13. F   It does not give dates for class tests.
14. T
15. T

Definitions

1. A *learning style* is that pattern or method that a person uses to learn and remember information. There are three general learning styles (also called modalities): visual, auditory, and kinesthetic.

2. A *kinesthetic learner* is a person who learns best by working with her or his hands, working with objects, using large body movements, and engaging in hands-on experiences. Such learners are sometimes called "doers."

3. An *auditory learner* is a person who learns best by hearing information rather than seeing it. An auditory learner is able to remember spoken details given in conversations or lectures.

4. A *syllabus* is a printed handout that provides the student with information about the teacher, office hours, the objectives for the course, and attendance and grading policies. It may also state other policies related to late work, late tests, or extra credit.

Use What You Learned: Culminating Activities

1. Get names and phone numbers of at least two students in each class. Place this information in the front of your notebook for quick reference if you need to discuss assignments or ask questions.

2. Locate a campus map. Color-code areas of special importance to you.

2 Setting Goals and Managing Your Time

PART II includes: Enrichment C (p. 65)   Enrichment D (p. 66)   Enrichment E (p. 67)   Enrichment F (p. 69)

Goal Setting and Time Management Profile

1. Y   2. N   3. Y   4. N   5. Y   6. N   7. N   8. Y   9. N   10. Y   11. N   12. Y

2.1 Dividing Your Life's Pie

Answers will vary. Use them to gain insight into students and to generate class discussion. Use the information from the increase-decrease method to discuss ways to change the pie.

Enrichment C: This enrichment is a checklist that students can use to find ways to balance the main areas of their lives. Answers will vary. The answers they check could later be applied to goal setting; students can write specific goals for the changes they desire.

Using Goal Setting: Discussion Questions

1. What are some short-term goals that you would like to accomplish within the next two weeks?
2. Long-term goals often need to be broken into a series of short-term goals. What do you think the series of short-term goals would be to: finish a one-year math sequence; sew a wedding dress; build new kitchen cabinets?
3. Name a goal that you set and were able to reach. How did you feel about the accomplishment? What were your rewards?
4. Name a goal that you set but were not able to reach. What happened to prevent you from doing so?
5. How do you motivate yourself to work on and reach goals?

Following Helpful Hints for Reaching Goals

Down the side of the blackboard write EVA, BAT. Ask students to use the memory words to identify each of the helpful hints (evaluate, visualize, affirmation, break, ask, tell). Discuss each of these hints. Refer to the text when applicable.

Enrichment D: This enrichment provides you with a class activity for working with goals and affirmations. The first two sections of this exercise can be done individually, with partners, in a group, or as a class. Answers will vary on the last two questions.

1. a. Y   b. N   c. N   d. Y   e. Y
2. a. Y   b. N   c. N   d. Y   e. Y

2.2   Planning Study Time

This form can be turned in with the first weekly time management schedule. The information on this form can be used to identify the student's classes and to check if sufficient study blocks are scheduled for each class. If some students estimate what seems to be "too few" or "too many" study hours, discuss their answers with them individually.

Creating a Weekly Time Management Schedule

Make an overhead for Exercise 2.3. Model for students how to create a weekly schedule. First, write in fixed activities. Second, add fixed study times. Whenever possible, use the principles in the text to place study blocks in effective time slots. Third, add flex study times (two or three for the week). Fourth, add specific goals. Fifth, add in time for other responsibilities. Sixth, add social, leisure, and family time.

Enrichment E: Make an overhead or print copies of this enrichment for students. Use this sample time management schedule to answer the questions in the enrichment. Additional sample schedules can be created if you would like to analyze more than one schedule. (You may want to copy a few students' schedules to have as examples for future terms.)

2.3   Creating Your First Weekly Schedule

Have students follow the steps for creating a schedule. Ideally, assign this exercise toward the end of the week so that students can use Sunday to plan a schedule for a week. Have students *keep* the schedule so that they can follow it for the week. After the week is over, they can turn the schedule in for grading. The entire assignment for grading may include:

1. Exercise 2.2 so that you can see all the student's classes

2. The weekly schedule

3. A short written report that answers the following questions:

   - Were you able to follow your schedule? Which parts were difficult to follow? Which parts worked well?
   - What did you like about using a schedule?
   - What did you not like about using a schedule?
   - What changes will you make on next week's schedule?

Evaluating Time Management Schedules

Since the students are the ones who must follow their schedules, it is not appropriate to tell them what they must do or how they must live their lives. However, by evaluating weekly schedules, you can identify potential problem areas or suggest ways the schedules can be more efficient or realistic. Students then have the choice to take your suggestions into consideration.

Enrichment F: This enrichment is a form you can duplicate to help you analyze students' schedules. Checking the appropriate spaces is much easier to do than writing extensive individual comments on weekly schedules.

Additional Suggestions

1. As mentioned in Chapter 1, printing weekly schedules on the back side of weekly assignment sheets is convenient for students. Consider printing on colored paper.
2. Require students to keep weekly time management schedules for three weeks. At the end of three weeks, all three schedules can be turned in. You can create a short writing assignment to accompany these schedules. Questions may include:
   - What changes did you notice over the last three weeks in terms of feeling more organized, being more productive, and so on?
   - Will you continue using a weekly schedule for the rest of the term? Why or why not?

Review Questions

True-False

1. F   The three areas are school, work, and leisure.
2. F   Procrastination decreases.
3. F   The method refers to increasing and decreasing the three areas of life.
4. F
5. T
6. T
7. F   You can name some courses on your campus where the 2:1 ratio is too much and other courses where it is too little.
8. T
9. T
10. F   Use trading time after you have already developed enough self-discipline to follow your schedule.
11. F   Begin with the hardest or least-liked subject.
12. F   Use the study blocks to really learn information; review the information, put it into memory, practice it.

Short Answer

1. The steps should be (a) fixed activities, (b) fixed study times, (c) flex study times, (d) time for goals, (e) time for other responsibilities/chores, and (f) leisure, social, and family time.
2. The steps should be (a) be specific, clear, and realistic; (b) set a target date; (c) identify the individual steps involved; and (d) plan an intrinsic or extrinsic reward.

Use What You Learned: Culminating Activities

1. Explain goal setting to a friend who is not in this class. Discuss important aspects such as how to set goals, how to keep working on goals, and how to achieve success.
2. Write an affirmation that is appropriate for you. Put the affirmation on cards around your house and in your notebook. Practice repeating the affirmation several times a day for a week.
3. Make a time management schedule for every week of this term. Keep all your completed schedules for the term so that you can turn them in.
4. Outline a plan for a long-term assignment you have been given this term. Include the target dates, the individual steps, and the reward.

---

3 Improving Your Concentration

PART II includes: Overhead 1 (p. 89)

Concentration Profile

1. N   2. N   3. N   4. Y   5. Y   6. Y   7. Y   8. N   9. Y   10. N   11. Y   12. N

Setting the Physical Stage: Discussion Questions

1. Refer to the necessary supplies checklist. Does your study place at home have all these supplies? If not, which ones are missing? Would it be helpful to have them added to your area?
2. What other supplies do you have in your area?
3. How do you organize your supplies? (Students often have excellent suggestions and solutions.)

3.1   Analyzing Your Study Area

Answers will vary. Some students must have total silence; others find silence distracting. Some students can tune out only some noises; some can block out almost anything. Many students may insist that they can study with the television or stereo turned on; this often demonstrates a habit they are not willing to give up. Strongly encourage students to turn off the television or stereo; if they need some noise, urge them to try classical (particularly baroque) music, which does not seem to interfere as easily with thought patterns.

You may find some students insisting that they can study around clutter or while sitting on the couch or lying on the bed. Encourage them to try another approach for three weeks. Change requires flexibility; trying other methods may open up new awareness.

Setting the Mental Stage: Discussion Questions

1. Do you currently use any type of relaxation technique? Which one?
2. Have you ever been taught techniques for visualizing? What are they?
3. What do you already know about the term *self-talk*?

3.2   Learning to Relax

Give students three important pointers before they try this activity: (1) If you feel funny about closing your eyes, realize that many people in the room may be feeling the same way. If you can't seem to relax enough to close your eyes, stare down at the floor. (2) The person reading the relaxation technique should use a slow, calming voice. Do not rush through the reading. (3) Pausing between directions or at the end of sentences adds one last calming effect.

3.3   Writing a RAVES Review

Answers may vary, but the following are likely:

1. Use Relaxation Techniques
    a. Use the soothing mask.
    b. Use the relaxation blanket.
    c. Use breathing by threes.
    d. Use deep breathing.
    e. Use perfect place.

2. Arrange your goals and priorities
    a. Use the say no technique.
    b. Set goals for studying.
    c. Use warm-up activities such as review and preview.

3. Visualize Yourself Concentrating
    a. Use framing to put a border around visualizations.
    b. See success.

4. Remember the Emotional E Words
    a. Use *E* words related to success and motivation.
    b. Some *E* words are effort, excitement, enthusiasm, energy, and eagerness.

5. Use Positive Self-Talk
    a. Turn negative self-talk into positive self-talk.
    b. Positive self-talk can be made into affirmations.

3.4   Identifying External and Internal Distractors

Answers will vary. After each group has completed its lists, compile the lists on the blackboard or overhead. Have students add ideas that are different from those generated by their group.

3.5   Choosing Your Techniques

Answers will vary. The internal and external distractors selected can come from the distractors listed in Exercise 3.4.

Setting the Stage for Concentrated Listening: Discussion Questions

1. What are some distractions that you have experienced while trying to listen to a lecture or a speech?

2. What distractions have you experienced in class that were related to your different senses (sight, sound, smell, taste, touch/texture)?

3. In which of your classes is it most difficult for you to concentrate while listening? Why do you think this occurs?

4. Have you ever tuned out a speaker because he or she was talking over your head or discussing information unfamiliar to you? Describe the situation and the feelings you experienced.

Setting the Stage for Concentrated Listening

Write the mnemonic DATE IAN down the side of the blackboard. Ask students to use the first letter to name the concentrated listening technique. Ask students to explain the technique in their own words.

Suggest that students use these techniques as a checklist each time they have problems concentrating while listening. Once they are able to identify the reasons for not concentrating, they can activate the appropriate techniques.

3.6   Practicing Concentrated Listening

This exercise can be used for a variety of listening situations. Encourage students to share their choice of listening settings for the assignment. The questions move through the seven techniques for concentrated listening. Through this activity, students will be able to identify both their listening strengths and listening weaknesses for the given setting.

Review Questions

True-False

1. F   Concentration is the ability to focus on one thing.
2. T
3. T
4. T
5. F   RAVES is the formula for mentally preparing to study.
6. T
7. T
8. T
9. F
10. F   Selected techniques are used to deal with the situation.

Multiple Choice

1. a   This is the best of the choices. The other choices definitely promote concentrated listening. Asking questions during a lecture *could* reduce concentrated listening.
2. b
3. d
4. d
5. b

Matching

1. f   2. a   3. h   4. k   5. b   6. j   7. c   8. e   9. 1   10. d   11. g   12. i

Use What You Learned: Culminating Activities

1. The concentration techniques in this chapter focused on increasing your attention span while you study. These same techniques can be used in areas other than studying. Choose any five techniques. Discuss other areas or situations in which these techniques could be useful.

2. For one week, rate your concentrated listening skills in each of your classes. Use the scale one to ten. One indicates "poor" and ten indicates "excellent." Record your daily ratings; at the end of the week, look for patterns. Are your listening skills higher in some classes? If so, why? What can you do to improve the lower ratings?

---

4 Understanding How You Process and Learn Information

PART II includes: Enrichment G (p. 70)
Enrichment H (p. 71)
Enrichment I (p. 72)
Overhead 1 (p. 89)

Information Processing Profile

1. Y   2. N   3. Y   4. N   5. Y   6. N   7. Y   8. N   9. N   10. Y   11. Y   12. Y

The Information Processing Model

Make an overhead transparency of the model. Summarize each part of the model, or ask individual students to read the section in the text that describes the first part and then summarize it for the class. The students' summaries can be expanded by discussing the examples in the text and/or adding additional examples.

4.1 Understanding the Information Processing Model

The model should look similar to the one presented in the book.

1. long-term retrieval
2. rehearsal
3. rehearsal, retrieval
4. short-term memory
5. long-term retrieval
6. long-term memory
7. feedback loop
8. rehearsal, retrieval
9. short-term memory
10. sensory input

4.2 Understanding What's Happening

More than one answer can be justified.

1. Manuel is not using rehearsal, the feedback loop, or long-term retrieval.

2. Teresa did not use long-term retrieval.

3. Leon did not use a variety of rehearsal techniques or the feedback loop. He focused on rote memory without meaning.

4. Cindy did not use effective rehearsal to include all the needed information; she studied only part of the information needed.

5. Kim failed to use the feedback loop.

Enrichment G: This enrichment helps students understand the concept of schemas (clusters of information already learned). As students work in groups, they will become familiar with the variety of information they have in their long-term memories as well as the schemas that are not well-developed in their memory systems. Additional topics can be added to this exercise.

Twelve Memory Principles

SAVE CRIB FOTO is the mnemonic to help students remember the twelve principles of memory. These principles are presented in groups of four; following each group is an exercise that focuses on only those four principles. Familiarity with these principles enables students to identify where they are having trouble learning information and why. Having such insight enables students to adjust their methods of study to include the principles that had been neglected. Stronger memory will result.

4.3   Using the SAVE Principles

Answers will vary. If time is available, students can learn from each other by sharing their answers in class.

4.4   Using the CRIB Principles

1. Concentration, Recitation, Interest, Big Picture-Little Pictures
2. Answers will vary.
3. The center of the circle should say "Forgetting," "Types of Forgetting," or "Forgetting Theories." Since five theories were discussed, these five details should surround the circle: Decay, Displacement, Interference, Incomplete Encoding, and Retrieval Failure. Students could also add minor details around these five theories.

4.5   Using FOTO Principles

1. Feedback, Organize, Time, Ongoing Review
2a. Feedback occurs as information is being processed along the rehearsal path.
2b. You can get feedback by reciting. You can also get feedback by using any study methods in which you are quizzing yourself.
2c. The states are the categories; the cities are the related details.

California	*Oregon*	*Louisiana*
Los Angeles	Portland	Baton Rouge
San Francisco	Salem	New Orleans

Texas	*Florida*
Houston	Orlando
San Antonio	Miami
Austin	

2d. Answers will vary.
2e. Answers will vary.

4.6   Reviewing the Memory Principles

1. The twelve principles should be listed. The principles in order are: (SAVE) = Selectivity—Associate—Visualize—Effort; (CRIB) = Concentrate—Recite—Interest—Big Picture-Little Picture; (FOTO) = Feedback—Organize—Time-Ongoing Review

2. The drawings will vary.

3. Students can practice on their own. In class, ask for volunteers to name the twelve principles (any order).

Memory Principles: Discussion Questions

1. How could you use the principle of association in one of your other classes? What information could be paired?

2. What objects, sentences, or paragraphs from other classes could you create a movie about? Describe your movie.

3. Why would the twelve principles of memory be useful if they were written as a checklist and placed in your area of study?

Enrichment H: This enrichment provides students with the opportunity to recite what they understand about the twelve memory principles and gives students the necessary feedback to show their depth of understanding.

Enrichment I: This enrichment is a checklist for students to place in their study areas. They should refer to this checklist each time they study.

Review Questions

True-False

1. F   Some stimuli are not given attention and do not make it to long-term memory.
2. F
3. T
4. T
5. T
6. T   Effort is used in rehearsal, feedback loop, and retrieval.
7. F
8. T
9. T
10. T

Short Answer

1. Answers will vary. Examine the explanations.

   a. Marsha used association, visualization, and effort
   b. Damon used recitation, interest, and effort
   c. Elena used feedback, time, and ongoing review

2. The model should appear as it is in the book. The short descriptions should reflect key ideas about each part of the model.

Use What You Learned: Culminating Activities

1. Identify a topic you are currently studying in another class. Practice associating the new information to a cluster of information you already have stored in long-term memory. Describe the process you used to associate the information.

2. Select a textbook from one of your other classes. First practice visualizing an object from one of the chapters. Then read one sentence at a time, and practice visualizing the sentence. Then make a movie in your head by visualizing all the information in a paragraph. Finally, visualize all the information under one heading.

3. Use the checklist of the twelve principles of memory. After each study block, rate yourself on a scale of one to ten to show how effectively you are using all these principles.

---

5 Surveying a Textbook

Textbook Surveying Profile

1. Y   2. Y   3. Y   4. N   5. N   6. Y   7. Y   8. Y   9. Y   10. Y   11. N   12. N

Surveying: Discussion Questions

1. How many of you spent time looking through the different parts of your books at the beginning of the term?

2. How many parts of a book (besides the chapters) can you name?

3. What could you gain by spending time examining your textbooks at the beginning of the term?

5.1   Surveying Introductory Material

1. The introductory material is found at the beginning of the book in the section "To the Student." The purpose of the book is discussed in the first and the last paragraphs:

    —provide you with skills to unlock your learning potential as a student
    —result in more thorough learning and more powerful memory of information learned
    —provide valuable skills that become a part of your approach to learning in any situation so you can achieve success

2. The special features are:

    —Boxed information
    —Chapter summary
    —"Personalizing What you Learned" that includes chapter profiles, visual mappings and key terms printed in color
    —Review questions
    —Writing assignments

3. Answers will vary.

5.2　Surveying Tables of Contents

Psychology

1. From Cell to Society: The Scope
   The Goals of Research
   Methods of Research

2. Page 29

3. Description, prediction, correlation, control, explanation

History

1. Yes. They begin with the first human beings and then move forward in a time sequence.

2. 1650 to 338 B.C.

3. 500 B.C. to 338 B.C.

The Front Four: Discussion Questions

Take out any other textbooks you have with you besides the textbook for this course. If you don't have any other books with you, look at another student's books. (Ask the following questions.)

1. Who is the author of this book?

2. What is the copyright date?

3. Look at the introduction. Have you read it? Begin reading it. Stop and raise your hand as soon as you have learned something valuable from the introduction. (Ask individual students what information they learned.)

4. Look at the beginning of the table of contents through to the end of the table of contents. What can you tell us about the organization of the book or the scope of the topics it will cover?

The Back Four: Discussion Questions

Again ask students to take out textbooks other than books for this course. Ask the following questions:

1. Is there an appendix? Tell the class the kinds of information found in the appendix.

2. Is there a glossary? How are the terms in the glossary marked within the chapters?

3. Is there a references section or a bibliography? Where is it located?

4. Is there more than one kind of index? If so, name them.

5. Select any word from the glossary, or randomly open the text and find a key term. Use the index to find the pages where the word is explained.

6. For additional practice, copy one part of any textbook (table of contents, glossary, index, appendix). Write your own questions to match the material you copied.

5.3　Surveying a Textbook

Answers will vary.

Review Questions

1. 5   2. 3, 4   3. 8   4. 2   5. 3, 4   6. 6   7. 3, 8   8. 4   9. 7   10. 1

Short Answer

1. Answers will vary.
2. Answers will vary.
3. Refer to the index of the textbook for the answers.

Use What You Learned: Culminating Activities

1. Take time to survey all the textbooks you are using this term.
2. As you survey a variety of textbooks, make a list of parts of a textbook that you encountered that were not listed in the "front four" and the "back four" as discussed in this chapter.

---

6 Using a Reading System   PART II includes: Enrichment J (p. 73)

Textbook Reading Profile

1. N   2. Y   3. Y   4. N   5. N   6. Y   7. N   8. N   9. N   10. Y   11. Y   12. Y

Learning SQ4R: Discussion Questions

1. What procedure do you currently use to start a new chapter?
2. Do you often need to reread chapters to learn the information in them?
3. What parts of a chapter could you look at before reading so as to gain some insight into the contents of the chapter?

6.1   Surveying a Chapter

1. Producing the answer should take ten to fifteen minutes.
2. Glanced: title
   Read: introduction
   Read: objectives
   Glanced: headings/subheadings
   Glanced: visual aids
   Read: marginal notes/inserted boxes
   Glanced: terms
   Read: chapter study questions
   Read: summary

3. Ideally, students' response will be "all the parts." However, accept any answers that students are able to explain or justify.

6.2 Writing Questions

Refer to the chapter for the headings and subheadings to be used.

6.3 Knowing the Six Steps

Review the information generated with partners. Ask different students to read what they wrote.

Extra activity: Have students list on paper the questions they wrote in the Q step. Have them either write short answers for their questions or exchange papers with a partner and write answers to the partner's questions.

Enrichment J: Three separate activities are listed in this enrichment. Each activity could be done individually, with partners, in a group, or as a class. Use one, two, or all three activities.

6.4 Reading Out Loud to Find Definitions

1a. In most cases, the answer will be yes.
 b. Answers will vary.

2a. The words *tribe* and *patriarch* should be circled.
 b. General vocabulary words will vary but may include paleolithic, kinship, nuclear family, extended family, nomadic societies, mutual, dominant, and descendants.
 c. You can use context clues or a dictionary.

6.5 Finding Topic Sentences and Supporting Details

1. First paragraph: last sentence; second paragraph: first sentence

2. Answers will vary.

3. The supporting details are (a) strong bonds within the nuclear family and in the extended family and tribe, (b) the dependence on the extended family for cooperative work and protection, and (c) the belief among the tribe's members that they all descended from a common ancestor.

6.6 Using Comprehension Strategies

Paragraph 1
- Topic sentence: first sentence
- Circled words: probes, mirror questions, verifiers, reinforcers
- Details are organized by (c) a definition pattern.

Paragraph 2
- Topic sentence: first sentence
- Circled words: individual branding (possibly: segments, dwellers, upscale)
- Details are organized by (d) an examples pattern.

Paragraph 3
- Topic sentence: last sentence

- Circled words: possibly: emerged, left/right hemispheres, impaired, comprehend
- Details are organized by (e) a cause-effect or (b) a comparison-contrast pattern.

Extra activity: An excellent way to build your resource file of example paragraphs is to ask each student to photocopy one page from any textbook and then place a box around one paragraph that could be used to look for the topic sentence, vocabulary words, and organizational patterns. Use the directions from Exercise 6.6 for these paragraphs.

Review Questions

True-False

1. T
2. T
3. T
4. T
5. F   It can be found any place in the paragraph, or it can be implied.
6. T
7. T
8. T
9. F   They should be read, not skimmed.
10. T

Short Answer

1. The nine parts of a chapter to survey are:
    - Title
    - Introduction
    - Objectives
    - Headings, subheadings
    - Visual aids
    - Marginal notes, inserted boxes
    - Terms in special print
    - Chapter questions
    - Summary

2. The six steps are survey, question, read, record, recite, and review. Brief descriptions will vary.

3. Answers will vary, but they may include:
    - Answer chapter questions.
    - Answer the questions written in the Q step.
    - Study and recite from notes.
    - Ask personalized questions about the information.
    - Create additional study tools.

4. Answers will vary. A basic answer may include: It is a consistent method to use for all books. The steps build stronger paths to your memory. It helps improve comprehension.

5. Find the topic (one, two, or three words). Look for a broad sentence that contains the topic. Ask what the author is saying in the paragraph. Find the details that support or explain the topic sentence. They can be facts, statistics, definitions, examples, expanded explanations, reasons, causes, or effects.

Fill in the Blanks

1. organizational
2. topic
3. assessing/evaluating
4. read

5. meaning/definition
6. notes
7. details

Use What You Learned: Culminating Activities

1. Use the SQ4R process for the next chapter you are assigned to read in this class or any other class. Use all the steps. Record your reactions to each step of the process.

2. In the next chapter, use the SQ4R system. For the Q step, make a list of questions based on the headings; write this list on your own paper. The questions will be used as review questions in class.

---

7 Taking Notes in Textbooks

PART II includes: Enrichment K (p. 74)

Notetaking Profile

1. N 2. Y 3. N 4. Y 5. Y 6. Y 7. Y 8. Y 9. Y 10. N 11. Y 12. Y

Specifying Your Goals as a Reader: Discussion Questions

1. Do you use a method to help you decide what to underline? If yes, what is the method?
2. How do you mark important words and definitions?
3. On the average, what percentage of a page do you underline or highlight?
4. After you have marked your textbook, how do you study what you have marked? Do you have a system that seems to work? If yes, describe what you do.

7.1 Marking a Textbook Passage

Answers for details may vary.

Paragraph 1
*   Topic sentence completely underlined (or because it is long, it may be in a bracket): first sentence
*   Details underlined: business, social

Paragraph 2
*   Topic sentence completely underlined: first sentence
*   Details underlined: consistent in reading of facial expressions . . . smiling . . . same meaning . . . cultures, eye contact . . . movements tell . . . a lot

Paragraph 3
*   Topic sentence completely underlined: first sentence

- Details underlined: communicate ... without ... oral or written signals, talk with ... hands, reinforce ... verbal message
- Terms circled: gestures

Paragraph 4
- Topic sentence completely underlined: first sentence
- Details underlined: leaning ... toward ... sign of interest, leaning back, arms folded ... boredom
- Terms circled: body stance

7.2   Stringing Ideas Together

It's a good idea to demonstrate this exercise in class with one or more students before students work with partners. You may want to use the underlining from Exercise 7.1 to demonstrate.

7.3   Writing a Summary

Possible underlining could include the following (this same information should be stated in the summary):

Paragraph 1
- Topic sentence: first sentence
- Circled vocabulary: metamemory
- Details underlined: knowledge, how ... memory works, three types

Paragraph 2
- Topic sentence: first sentence
- Place a 1 on the word *first*.
- Details underlined: preschool children ... weak, school years ... learn limits ... strengths ... memory

Paragraph 3
- Topic sentence: first sentence
- Place a 2 on the word *second*.
- Details underlined: different strategies for memorization ... short-answer test ... multiple-choice

Paragraph 4
- Topic sentence: first sentence
- Place a 3 on the word *third*.
- Details underlined: change ... with age ... experience

Making Marginal Notes

Extra activity: Have students return to any of the example paragraphs in this chapter. Have them make marginal notes. Discuss the kinds of information, lists, or summaries they felt would be helpful. (Leadership, Overcoming Listening Problems, Body Movement, and Metamemory are especially good examples to use.)

After the marginal notes are made, have students read, recite, explain relationships, and visualize the information covered in the marginal notes.

Enrichment K: This enrichment is another passage that can be used for practice in marking text, making marginal notes, stringing ideas together, and summarizing.

Review Questions

Multiple Choice

1. a   2. d   3. c   4. a   5. d   6. d

Marking Textbooks

Answers will vary. However, the topic sentences should be underlined. The important details may vary, but details frequently selected are given below. Marginal notes can be in the form of lists, terms and definitions or questions.

Paragraph 1
- Topic sentence: first sentence
- Details: absence of nervousness could suggest . . . not care . . . faces a public audience . . . some kind of concern

Paragraph 2
- Topic sentence: second sentence
- Details: accept . . . as natural . . . convert . . . feelings into positive energy . . . public speaking classes . . . teach . . . how to harness the energy . . . speaking more dynamic . . . no anxiety . . . dull presentation . . . transformed anxiety . . . speech come to life

Paragraph 3
- Topic sentence: last sentence
- Details: negative dialogue . . . talk themselves into being less effective . . . self-defeating behavior . . . replace . . . with positive messages

Short Answer

1. Reread only the information marked. String the ideas together to make your own sentences. Look away. Recite and write.

2. Reread and recite from your marginal notes. Explain how different ideas are related. Visualize the information.

Use What You Learned: Culminating Activities

1. Photocopy one section from one of your other textbooks. Use marking and marginal notes to show important main ideas and details. With a partner, practice studying from your marking. (String ideas together; then recite.)

2. Use marking and marginal notes for the next chapter you are assigned to read.

8 Using Cornell for Textbook Notes

PART II includes:	Overhead 2 (pp. 90–91)
	Overhead 3 (p. 92)
	Enrichment L (p. 75)

Cornell Notes Profile

1. Y   2. N   3. Y   4. N   5. Y   6. Y   7. Y   8. Y   9. Y   10. Y   11. Y   12. N

Following the Five *R*'s of Cornell: Discussion Questions

1. What system have you previously used to take notes on textbook information? Which Cornell steps did your system have?

2. How is the Cornell system different from any system you have previously used?

8.1   Using the First Three *R*'s

Students should underline main idea sentences and key words. The information underlined should then be transferred into Cornell notes. Since the recall column can have questions or key words, the recall columns will vary from the overhead. (See Part III for Overhead 2.)

Show students the sample notes on Overhead 2. Then cover up the notes so only the recall column shows. Ask different students to recite the information. If they are not able to, emphasize that this is okay. They have received feedback. Pull the paper down, review the information, and let them recite again.

(Caution: Students should not write too much information in the recall column. If they tell themselves all the facts or information, they will *read* instead of *recite* the information.)

8.2   Reflecting on Maslow's Hierarchy

1. Answers will vary. Listen to explanations.

2. Answers will vary. Listen to explanations.

3. Answers will vary. Possible answers follow.

Needs	Colleges	Employers
Physiological	financial aid clothing exchange bus passes temporary housing emergency funds	adequate wages employee discounts cost-of-living increases
Safety	campus security campus rules health services smoke alarms heat, air conditioning counseling	job security seniority health insurance pension plans savings plans safe conditions safety rules heat, air conditioning
Social	clubs, groups classroom groups special events support services intramurals	sports teams potlucks, picnics gatherings working teams newsletters

Esteem	recognition for work or
	   accomplishment
	dean's list
	praise
	good grades
	displays, exhibits
	respect, manners
	channels to discuss complaints,
	   petitions
		awards, honors
		promotions
		more responsibility
		announcements
		letters of praise
		verbal praise
		verbal thanks
		recognition for work

Self-realization	help in planning new goals new positions encouragement of new areas	chance for new career/role challenge of new skills/technology encouragement of growth

Extra activity: Use your own words to write a summary of Maslow's theory of the hierarchy of needs. Write the summary without looking back at your notes.

Cornell 5 *R*'s: Discussion Questions

1. If your recall column doesn't provide you with enough cues for reciting, how can you change the recall column?
2. What will happen if you put too much information in the recall column?
3. How can reciting help you learn information?
4. Why is the feedback you get from reciting important for learning?
5. What is the value of reflect activities?
6. Why is reviewing necessary?

Extra activity:

1. Return to Exercise 7.3. Have students use the marking that they already did as guides to the important information to put in Cornell notes. Have them make their own Cornell notes and compare them to the Cornell notes in this chapter. Then have students practice reciting the recall columns with partners.

2. Write a five-paragraph summary. In the first paragraph, describe what happens in the first step of Cornell. Use one paragraph for each of the remaining steps. Remember that a summary highlights the most important ideas.

Deciding When to Use Cornell Notetaking: Discussion Questions

1. Which form of notetaking do you prefer? Why?
2. Which combination(s) of notetaking do you think would work best for each of your courses? Why would you not necessarily use the same method for every class?

Once students know how to use all four notetaking systems, it is their responsibility to choose the system that works most effectively for them and for the material.

Some students are shocked to hear that in some cases they may want to use two, three, or four forms of notetaking. Emphasize that the goal is to learn the information. If the information is complex or very detailed, they need to be willing to do whatever is necessary to get the information clearly imprinted in their memories.

Combining SQ4R and Cornell Notetaking

Discuss the combination of these two powerful study systems by using Overhead 3.

8.3   Taking Cornell Notes

Notes will vary; however, the main ideas and most important supporting details which were marked in the selection in Chapter 7 should appear in the students' notes. Enrichment L is an evaluation form that can be used to grade students' Cornell notes.

8.4   Taking Cornell Notes from Your Textbooks

This exercise provides students with notetaking practice for other courses. Rather than repeatedly writing the same kinds of comments on many different papers, the Enrichment L worksheet can be used as an evaluation form.

If you are not familiar with the students' textbooks, you may want to request that students photocopy the page or pages of the textbook that they used for this notetaking assignment. You will then be able to compare the textbook information to the students' notes.

Enrichment L: This enrichment can be used to evaluate any Cornell notes taken on textbooks. Note that some of the items you can check provide positive feedback; other comments suggest ways to improve notes.

Review Questions

True-False

1. T　2. T　3. F　4. F　5. F　6. T　7. T　8. F　9. T　10. T

Short Answer

1. The five *R*'s are record, reduce, recite, reflect, and review.
2. Answers will vary. They may include:
   - Ask yourself questions about what you have read. Think about the answers, how it can be used and the importance of this new knowledge.
   - Line up the recall columns to get an overview of the outline.
   - Find relationships between ideas.
   - Write a summary.
   - Make additional lists of ideas and/or questions on the back side of your notes.
   - Create other kinds of study tools (flash cards, tapes, etc.).

Notetaking

Answers will vary. However, the notes should include: 1) common characteristics of each intelligence, and 2) occupations or careers associated to each intelligence. The answers explaining/reflecting how their educational experiences would have been different if all seven intelligences were recognized will vary.

Use What You Learned: Culminating Activities

1. Take Cornell notes for this chapter.
2. Take Cornell notes for the next chapter you are assigned.
3. Take Cornell notes on any other textbook chapter. Schedule a time to show your notes to the teacher of that class. Ask him or her to write a brief comment to indicate if your notes appear to have the important details.
4. Select one of your most difficult textbooks. Use SQ4R and the Cornell notetaking system on the chapter.

---

9 Using Cornell for Lecture Notes

PART II includes:	Enrichment M (p. 76)
	Enrichment N (p. 77)

Lecture Notes Profile

1. N　2. N　3. Y　4. Y　5. Y　6. Y　7. N　8. Y　9. Y　10. Y　11. Y　12. Y

The Use of Cornell: Discussion Questions

1. What are the five *R*'s of Cornell?

2. Do you think the five *R*'s that you learned in Chapter 8 can also be used for taking notes from lectures? Why or why not?

3. What system have you used in the past for taking lecture notes? How is it similar to or different from the Cornell method?

9.1   Brainstorming About Lecture Notes

After partners or groups have created lists, compile the lists by writing all the answers on the blackboard. Combine similar answers. Ask students to copy this list. (A writing assignment at the end of the chapter asks students to return to this list to identify techniques used in the chapter to overcome these problems.)

Four Lecture-Notetaking Problems: Discussion Questions

1. Do all the problems listed in Exercise 9.1 fall into one of the four categories?

2. What solutions do you already know for combating weak listening skills? For reconciling differences in speech, writing, and thinking speeds? For selecting and organizing information? For overcoming spelling problems?

Enrichment M: This enrichment provides students with a way to summarize the various techniques for combating the four common problems in taking lecture notes. Answers may vary but should reflect the following.

Weak Listening	*Rate Problems*	*Organization*	*Spelling*
1. Use concentrated listening strategies. 2. Practice. 3. Take a listening class.	1. Talk to the instructor. 2. Use abbreviations. 3. Use symbols. 4. Use shorter sentences. 5. Leave a gap to fill in later. 6. Practice. 7. Tape lectures. 8. Use learning disability services. 9. Keep writing. 10. Mentally summarize. 11. Anticipate next idea. 12. Mentally question.	1. Talk with the instructor. 2. Ask if an outline is possible. 3. Listen for key words. 4. Number ideas. 5. Listen for ordinals. 6. Listen for definitions. 7. Move to a paragraph style. 8. Indicate sidetracks.	1. Read the book before the lecture. 2. Sound out words the best you can; correct later. 3. Take a spelling class.

9.2   Taking Lecture Notes

Read the student's answers to the questions before you look at their notes. Write general comments on their notes (or use the form in Exercise 9.4 for a more formal evaluation). If you feel that other faculty members would cooperate, provide students with a short memo to give to lecturers so that you have feedback from the people giving lectures. A sample memo follows:

> _____ has been learning the Cornell notetaking method to take lecture notes. Would you look at the student's notes and answer the following questions?
>
> 1. Do the notes appear to include the important information presented in the lecture? _____yes _____no
>
> 2. Do the notes show information presented on the blackboard or the overhead? _____yes _____no
>
> 3. What areas, if any, do you see lacking in these notes?
>
> Thank you for your time in providing the student and me with this feedback.

Enrichment N: This enrichment provides students with the opportunity to integrate the memory principles into the Cornell notetaking steps. Answers may vary; ask students to explain their choices. The main answers for each step include:

Record: selectivity, effort, interest, organization
Reduce: selectivity, effort, interest, organization, time
Recite: recitation, concentration, effort, interest, feedback, time
Reflect: association, visualization, effort, recitation, interest, big picture–little picture, feedback, organization,time, ongoing review
Review: all the memory principles

Verbal and Nonverbal Clues: Discussion Questions

1. Each instructor has his or her own style of lecturing. What kinds of verbal clues or verbal patterns have you noticed with some of your instructors?

2. Do intonations, volume of voice, and rate of speech vary from one instructor to another? Give examples.

3. Nonverbal clues can include facial expressions, mannerisms, and body stance. What nonverbal clues have you already noticed with different instructors?

9.3   Observing Clues

Answers will vary.

Students with Learning Disabilities

Being aware of the types of learning disabilities that become apparent during notetaking for lectures is important. You may discover students who were able to take effective notes in Chapter 8 but who are not able to perform well in Chapter 9. Discuss this discrepancy privately with the student.

Students who receive accommodations are entitled to these services without attracting undue attention from the rest of the class. Learning disabilities and accommodations involve student privacy, so do not publicize that some students are receiving notetaking services or taping lectures. If a student is eligible for a notetaker, another student in class (or a former student) could be asked to take notes on NCR (carbonless) paper; two sets of notes are then readily available. If several students are eligible, you may want to contract with a student to take notes; these notes can be set up in a notebook for these students to refer to outside class.

9.4   Evaluating Your Class Lecture Notes

Prepare a short lecture for students to practice notetaking skills. You may want to lecture on upcoming chapters or on specific topics, such as Howard Gardner's multiple intelligence theory, the information processing model, or forms of forgetting.

Many counselors and other faculty members are often willing to visit your class to give a guest lecture. Do not hesitate to ask. Outside speakers often offer valuable variety and interesting topics. Provide the speaker with general guidelines to make notetaking easier for your students. (Clearly indicate headings, use ordinals, control the rate of speech, etc.)

Check your library for possible videos that present topics that could be used for notetaking practice. Always preview the video and make your own Cornell notes. Be aware that some videos present information too quickly, which makes notetaking difficult.

Review Questions

True-False

1. T   2. F   3. T   4. T   5. T   6. T   7. T   8. F   9. T   10. T   11. T   12. T   13. F
14. T   15. F

Short Answer

1. The five steps are record, reduce, recite. reflect, and review. Refer to Chapter 8 for appropriate details for each step.

2. Answers may include:

    - Talking to the instructor about his or her rate of speech
    - Using abbreviations
    - Using symbols
    - Writing shorter sentences that may not be grammatically correct
    - Leaving a gap to fill in later
    - Practicing as often as possible
    - Taping the lecture and using the tape to fill in gaps later
    - Requesting a notetaker (for eligible students)

3. You may want to write in paragraph form when the information is given rapidly and there isn't time to see its organization or when the organizational structure of the information is not yet clear.

Use What You Learned: Culminating Activities

1. Practice taking notes while attending a meeting, watching educational television, or going to a show, lecture, or discussion.
2. Observe friends, family, acquaintances, or employers to identify their specific verbal and nonverbal clues.
3. Use a tape recorder to read a passage from a textbook. Practice taking notes as you listen to the tape. Become more aware of the importance of good organization and pacing for speaking.
4. Return to any of the paragraph examples in previous chapters. Practice taking Cornell notes for these paragraphs.

---

10 Creating Study Tools for Vocabulary

> PART II includes: Enrichment O (p. 78)
> Enrichment P (p. 79)
> Enrichment Q (p. 80)

Vocabulary Profile

1. Y   2. Y   3. N   4. Y   5. Y   6. N   7. Y   8. Y   9. N   10. N   11. N   12. Y

Devising Flash Cards: Discussion Questions

1. What methods do you use to learn new vocabulary words?
2. Do you make vocabulary flash cards for your classes?
3. If yes, how do you know what words and definitions to put on the cards?
4. Are the words you put on flash cards usually words for your receptive or your expressive vocabulary?

10.1 Making Flash Cards

Card 1
- Two kinds of vocabulary (front)
- Receptive vocabulary, expressive vocabulary (back)

Card 2
- Receptive vocabulary (front)
- One kind of vocabulary that consists of words you understand when you hear or read them (back)

Card 3
- Expressive vocabulary (front)

- One kind of vocabulary that includes words you know well enough to use in your speaking and writing (back)

10.2 Making Flash Cards for a Class

Students should have at least five cards. Pay careful attention to the words chosen for the cards; if they are related to one category, a category card should be included.

Enrichment O: This enrichment offers students the opportunity to make flash cards related to this course. Students are required to make one set of flash cards that also includes a category card. This exercise can also be used for extra credit if students decide to make more than one set of cards.

After the cards have been checked and graded, allow ten minutes in class for students to recite their cards to partners. Have the partners give feedback after checking the answers with the information on the cards.

10.3 Making a Vocabulary Sheet

Students should have five terms plus a general category entry. Students could be asked to work with a partner to practice reciting from both sides of the vocabulary sheet.

Extra activity: Enrichment O provides a list of possible topics suitable for developing flash cards. Items from this list or any of the exercises throughout the book could also be used to develop vocabulary sheets. One of these topics could be selected and developed either as a class exercise (model) or as homework. Once the exercise is completed, students can practice in class by reciting from both columns of the vocabulary sheet.

Finding Definitions: Discussion Questions

1. How are important terms brought to your attention in this book?
2. What other methods are used in your other textbooks to draw your attention to important terms?

Strategies for Finding Definitions

As you discuss each strategy, examine the examples in the textbook. Have students circle the definition clues (punctuation, word clues, context clues, and word structure clues). Spending class time working with the examples will facilitate completion of the exercises.

10.4 Finding Definitions

The following words or phrases should be underlined:

Psychology
1. one method of studying intelligence (psychometric) analyzes test scores
2. between firings a brief rest (refractory period)
3. a set of responses (fight-or-flight syndrome) which prepares the animal or person for action in response to danger

Chemistry
1. (physical property) a characteristic that can be observed for a material without changing its chemical identity
2. (law of definite proportions) a pure compound, whatever its source, always contains definite or constant proportions of the elements
3. (gaseous diffusion) process whereby a gas spreads out through another gas to occupy the space with uniform partial pressure

History
1. king (lugal) local governor (ensi)
2. (Indo-European) a large family of languages that includes English, most of the languages of modern Europe, Greek, Latin, Persian, and Sanskrit
3. (liminal) lacked official power, nonetheless played a vital role in shaping the society in which they lived

Enrichment P: This enrichment provides additional practice in finding punctuation and word clues for the purpose of identifying definitions and determining meaning through context.

1. Circled: dash; underlined: how high or low a tone sounds

2. Circled: is called; underlined: an instrument that separates ions by mass-to-charge ratio

3. Circled: came to mean; underlined: emperor

4. Circled: comma; underlined: how we think we should behave or what we regard as an ideal state of being

Answers will vary somewhat. A thematic statement is a declarative sentence placed at the beginning of a speech to tell your audience your main point or points.

10.5   Using Context Clues

Context clues are most often needed for words that are not key terms for the specific subject area; these words are used with the assumption that readers already understand them. Since punctuation and word clues are not given, readers need to strive to get a general meaning through the surrounding sentences. Answers may vary, but the correct answers are as follows:

1. Yes or no answer.
2. Prefects: high military or civil officials in ancient Rome
3. Yes or no answer.
4. Gaul: an ancient region in Europe that is now France and Belgium

1. Yes or no answer.
2. It's important to know that he was an astronomer (Greek) so you understand why he was developing a theory about the earth, planets and the sun.
3. Yes or no answer.
4. Propounded: proposed or put out for consideration

1. Yes or no answer.
2. Aspirant: one who aspires, or has a great ambition or desire, to be recognized, distinctive or honored
3. Yes or no answer.
4. Virtues: moral excellence, righteous quality

Extra activity: Ask students to bring three examples to class of words they encountered in their readings that were unfamiliar to them and that were key terminology for the course. Ask students to copy the complete sentence or sentences that provide context clues. Gather these sentences, and type them up for a class exercise.

Word Structure: Discussion Questions

1. How can you figure out the meaning of some words without using punctuation, word, or context clues?

2. What are some common prefixes you know? (List them on the board.) What are some common suffixes you know? (List them.)

3. Can you pronounce and tell me the meaning of the word *psychoneuroimmunology*?

   Show how word parts can lead to the general meaning of this word:
   Psycho—mind or mental processes
   Neuro—nerves or nervous system
   Immun— ability to fight off disease
   Ology—the study of something

   Using this information, you may infer that the word means "the study of the immune system as it is affected by the mind and the nervous system." A psychology book defines it as "the field that examines the interaction of psychological and physiological processes that affect the ability of the body to defend itself against disease."

Refer to a vocabulary book for other words that may initially be unfamiliar to students but that can be broken apart and defined.

Enrichment Q: This enrichment uses six basic word parts to build additional words and shows students how word parts are an integral aspect of the meaning of many words in English. This exercise can be done with partners, in groups, as a class, or as homework.

Additional exercises for vocabulary development can be developed easily by referring to a vocabulary development book.

Glossaries and Reference Books: Discussion Questions

1. Which of the books that you are using this term have glossaries? How often have you referred to them?

2. How could glossaries help you develop flash cards or vocabulary sheets?

3. Are flash cards or vocabulary sheets more important or less important if a book already has a glossary?

4. Are you comfortable using a hardbound dictionary? Which classes teach more in-depth use of the dictionary?

5. What kinds of thesauruses are you familiar with? Have you used the paperback version that is set up as a dictionary? Have you used the more in-depth version that is set up in numerical categories?

6. What classes have taught you how to use a thesaurus?

7. Have you used a *Franklin Language Master* for quick access to definitions or synonyms? (You may want to bring one into class to demonstrate how easy they are to use.)

Review Questions

Identifying Definitions

w	1.	part of a brand that is a symbol or distinctive design
p, w	2.	means for retaining and accumulating wealth
p, w	3.	a product with no brand at all
p	4.	employees are paid a certain amount for each unit of output they produce
p	5.	the application of scientific principles to management of work and workers
c, w	6.	any false and malicious statement that is communicated to others and that injures a person's good name or reputation, slander
p	7.	the exact words of another
w	8.	measure of variability and tells how the scores tend to be different
c, p	9.	plague, the rat was the vector, or transmitter, of the disease
c	10.	politically devious, corrupt, and crafty

Multiple Choice

1. a   2. c   3. d   4. d   5. a

Short Answer

1. Answers will vary but can include:
   - Shuffle and sort the cards by categories.
   - Create sentences using all the words in one category.
   - Recite from the front of the cards. Sort them into ones you know and ones you need to work on.
   - Recite and spell the terms by working from the back of the cards. Sort them into the ones you know and the ones you need to work on.

2. These ways include punctuation clues, word clues, word structure clues, special print, marginal notes, and chapter features that list the terms to know.

Use What You Learned: Culminating Activities

1. Begin your own system of personalized vocabulary. As you read your textbooks or listen to your instructors, begin recording words that are unfamiliar to you. Make flash cards or vocabulary sheets for these words.

2. Decide which vocabulary system you prefer: flash cards or vocabulary sheets. Return to previous chapters. Make vocabulary study tools for terms you need to learn more thoroughly. Remember to make category cards when possible.

3. Many authors have preferred styles for defining key terms. Look carefully at each of your textbooks. Identify the author's method: punctuation clues, word clues, or context clues.

---

11 Creating Visual Study Tools

PART II includes: Overhead 4 (p. 93)
Enrichment R (p. 81)
Overhead 5 (p. 94)
Enrichment S (p. 82)

Visual Tools Profile

1. Y   2. Y   3. Y   4. Y   5. N   6. Y   7. Y   8. Y   9. Y   10. Y   11. Y   12. Y

Using Visual Tools: Discussion Questions

1. Do you use pictures in any way as you study? If yes, how?
2. Do you use various shapes or colors in any way as you study? If yes, how?
3. Do you take time to visualize or make movies in your head as you read information? If yes, explain your process.

Making Visual Mappings

Overhead 4 is provided for use in discussing how to create and how to study from visual mappings. As exercises are completed for creating visual mappings, allot time to practice studying, reciting, and memorizing the mappings.

Extra activity: Create a class visual mapping so that students can experience the process. An excellent topic is the process of surveying. The following lesson will guide you through the process:

> We have talked about the process of surveying, which has been used to survey three different kinds of information. What are those three? (books, chapters, tests) (Write Surveying in the middle of your board inside a circle. Branch off the circle three times to show each kind of surveying.) What information is important to remember about surveying a book? (List the parts of a book to survey.) Continue until level 3 information and level 4 information are completed for all three kinds of surveying. After the steps for studying from the mapping have been discussed, practice the steps with this class mapping of surveying.

11.1 Mapping for Review Work

Mappings will vary. After the mappings are finished, each group should discuss its mapping with the class, or if the mappings were done on standard or legal-sized paper, they could be copied for the class. When you examine the mappings, check the levels of information for accuracy. Each main idea should branch off the center shape. Check also that key words, not full sentences, are used and that the printing is horizontal. Allow time in class for students to practice the steps for studying from the mappings.

11.2   Creating Mappings from a Textbook

Mappings will vary. You may want students to show you their textbooks if you question the levels of information on the mapping.

Enrichment R: This enrichment relates back to an example in Chapter 7 that discussed the concept of sign mind and design mind. Gabrielle Rico describes the design mind as the creative part of the mind. She recommends clustering (visual mappings) to generate ideas. This enrichment exercise provides students with the opportunity to use visual mapping for brainstorming. Their ideas will vary greatly. The following are given only as suggestions.

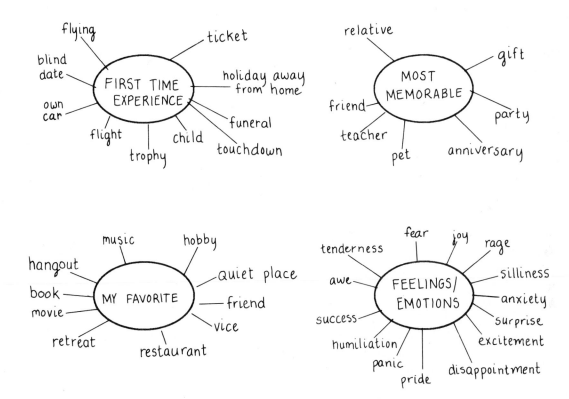

How to Create Hierarchies

Make an overhead of the four steps for creating hierarchies. The following two activities can be used to model hierarchies. The first activity demonstrates how mappings can easily be converted to hierarchies. The second activity is used to add details to a hierarchy already presented in this chapter.

Extra activity: Refer back to the class visual mapping on surveying (or to the mappings generated in Exercise 11.2). Model in class how to convert the same information into a hierarchy format.

Extra activity: Provide students with a piece of legal-sized paper. Refer to the hierarchy example in this chapter for the twelve principles of memory. Have students copy the hierarchy on paper and then add level three information. They can refer back to Chapter 4 if needed. Compare the supporting details each person chose to add to the hierarchy. Note the different ways students organized the details on the paper.

11.3   Turning Mappings into Hierarchies

When you examine the visual mapping for Chapter 10 (page 163), level one and level two information should be as follows. Level three information will vary.

Making Category Grids

Overhead 5 is provided for use in discussing how to create and how to study from category grids. As exercises for creating category grids are completed, allot time to practice studying, reciting, and memorizing the information in the grid boxes.

11.4   Categorizing the Kinds of Leadership

The grid should contain information similar to the following:

	Responsibility	*Tasks Given*	*Communication Flow*
Authoritarian	Has it all	Tasks are assigned to workers.	Top to bottom
Laissez-faire	Waives responsibility and gives it to subordinates	Subordinates do what they want.	Horizontal
Democratic	Has final responsibility but delegates authority	Workers help determine work assignments.	Upward and downward

Extra activity: Challenge students to find information in their other courses that would be appropriate for category grids. Have them create a category grid to present to the class or to turn in for extra credit.

11.5   Drawing Your Time Line

Time lines will vary. This exercise provides an excellent opportunity for students to learn more about each other. Have students form groups of two or three to share their time lines. Comment on choices made for organizing and visually presenting the information on their time lines.

Enrichment S: This enrichment discusses highlights in historical mathematics that led up to our current technology. The information is used to develop a time line. (This exercise can also be used to review marking and Cornell notes.) Note the creative ways students will find to present the information and the dates on the time line.

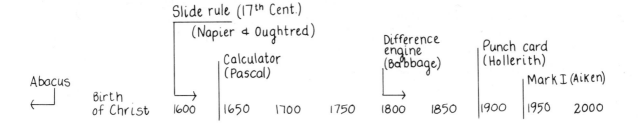

Review Questions

Multiple Choice

1. d   2. a   3. d   4. b   5. c   6. c   7. a   8. b   9. d   10. b   11. a   12. d   13. b
14. b   15. d

Visual Study Tools

The information can be presented in a variety of ways. Regardless of whether a mapping, hierarchy, category grid, or time line is used, the following levels of information should be included.

Five Stages (Generations) of Computers

1. First generation (1946–1958)
    - relied on glass vacuum tubes to control internal operations
    - vacuum tubes generated a lot of heat; computer was huge and required special air conditioning

2. Second generation (1959–1964)
    - tiny electronic transistors replaced vacuum tubes
    - computer size smaller; transistors more reliable, faster, and needed less maintenance
    - programmed with FORTRAN and COBOL languages

3. Third generation (1965–1971)
    - started using integrated circuits, silicon chips with network of transistors
    - faster, more reliable, greater storage capacity, and compatibility with other components
    - remote terminals communicated with central computer

4. Fourth generation (1971–present)
    - large-scale integrated circuits with silicon superchips with thousands of transistors
    - smaller computer
    - IBM and Apple personal computers

5. Fifth generation (future)
    - simulate human decision making
    - may not need to be programmed to complete a task
    - hope to create artificial intelligence to duplicate the processes of the human brain

Use What You Learned: Culminating Activities

1. Make at least one kind of visual study tool for every chapter you study in each of your courses for the rest of the term. The more you practice, the easier and more effective visual study tools become for you.

2. Choose a topic that might be assigned in a writing class for an essay. Write the topic in the center of your paper. Brainstorm! Think of as many different aspects of the topic as you can. Create a mapping by surrounding the topic with possible ideas to explore. For example, what would you put on a mapping that had one of these topics?

   A memorable person in history
   My personal moment of success
   A person I greatly admire
   Essential values for being human

3. Create a category grid to reflect some of your experiences in college. Create a grid to compare and contrast one of the following:

   Three different teachers
   Three different subjects or courses

   To create this grid, you will need to identify the three subjects. Then you will need to identify the categories to place at the top of each column. Complete the grid with appropriate information.

---

12 Creating Multisensory Study Tools

PART II includes: Overhead 6 (p. 95)

Multisensory Profile

1. Y   2. N   3. Y   4. Y   5. Y   6. Y   7. Y   8. Y   9. Y   10. Y   11. Y   12. Y

Three Basic Modalities: Discussion Questions

1. What is your learning-style preference?

2. What study tools do you find you can use effectively to learn new information? Do they match your learning modality? How do you know?

3. What study methods have you tried to use but were not able to use effectively? Why do you think this is so?

Overhead 6 provides you with Strategies for Visual Learners, Strategies for Auditory Learners, and Strategies for Kinesthetic Learners. Students who know their modality strengths can use the appropriate list for making study tools to learn new information.

12.1   Assessing Your Visual Skills

Answers will vary. Discuss the answers and the clarity of visual recall from one student to another. Students with strong visual skills will often be able to provide more detailed answers.

Auditory Learners: Discussion Questions

1. How can auditory learners use oral language to help them study?
2. What are some ways reciting can be used when you study?
3. How could the use of a tape recorder benefit auditory learners?
4. Have you ever used rhymes or tunes to help you learn? Explain.
5. Have you ever used talking calculators or computers? Explain.

12.2   Assessing Your Auditory Skills

Read the following directions to students. Do *not* repeat any of the information since this evaluates auditory ability. After both parts have been completed, have students compare drawings. Show on the board or overhead what each drawing should be like if the directions were followed accurately. Students with strong auditory skills will usually be able to complete the drawings. Students with weak auditory skills may show signs of frustration trying to follow the directions. (Simply state that this exercise is like an experiment and will not be graded.)

Part I

1. Place your pencil on the left edge of your paper. Find the middle point of the left edge of the paper. We will begin drawing from this point. Listen to the directions carefully. I will *not* repeat any of the steps.
2. Move your pencil upward to begin drawing a mountain. Continue until you have drawn three mountains that extend across the entire paper.
3. In the first full valley between mountain one and mountain two, draw a half of a circle. The second half of the circle will not be seen because it sets behind the valley.
4. Draw five lines that extend upward and outward from the half circle.
5. Draw a wavy line across the very bottom of the paper, and extend that line across the entire page.
6. About two inches above the wavy line, draw a straight line that goes across the entire page.
7. In the lower right corner, draw a sailboat that has one sail in the shape of a triangle. The point of the sail is aimed to the right.
8. In the left-hand corner directly above the straight line, draw a square. Place a triangle on top of the square. The triangle should point upward.
9. In the middle of the paper directly above the line, draw three separate triangles that point upward.
10. Place your pencil on the middle of the bottom line of the first triangle. Draw a short vertical line downward. Repeat this for the other two triangles.
11. Let's compare your final pictures.

Part II

1. In the center of your paper, draw a circle. Make a dot to show the center of the circle.

2. Draw a square in the center of the circle. The dot in the center of the circle should also be the center of the square.

3. Draw a vertical and a horizontal line through the circle. The lines should cross at the dot and should extend to the edge of the circle.

4. Draw a straight vertical line on the right-hand side of the circle. The line should touch the edge of the circle and extend above and below the size of the circle.

5. The line you just drew is the beginning of a large triangle. Finish drawing the triangle so that the circle is placed inside the triangle.

6. Compare your drawings.

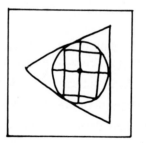

Extra activity: Demonstrate in class how to make a study tape. You can use a visual mapping, hierarchy, set of Cornell notes with the recall column, or marking from previous chapters. Review the correct way to study from the study tool; turn on the tape recorder and speak in full sentences. Add appropriate transitions to provide the necessary organization or to connect ideas together smoothly.

Encourage another student to try making a review tape. Review tapes could be assigned or made available for extra credit.

12.3 Assessing Your Sensory Skills

The variety of strategies students will use for solving this problem is incredible. Some students will make mathematical equations. Others will actually do the walking. Some may take turns making their steps by saying, "Left-right-left."

List all the possible answers on the board. List the different problem-solving methods used. Note the modality (visual, auditory, kinesthetic) used to solve the problem.

Answer: The child will take *six steps*. They will both finish on the *left foot*.

12.4 Using Multisensory Skills

1. A   2. A   3. K   4. A   5. V   6. A   7. A   8. V   9. K   10. V   11. K, A   12. K, V

For examples, answers will vary.

12.5 Working in Threes

The first two levels of information should look like this:

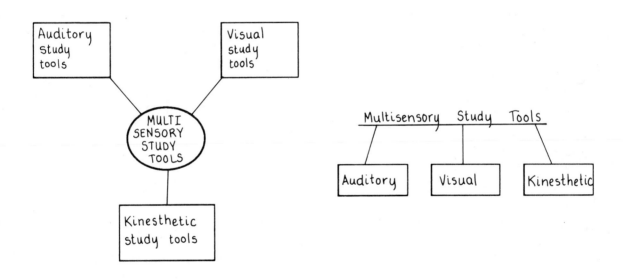

Level three answers will vary.

Accommodations

If you are not familiar with the concepts discussed under this heading, check with your college counseling department, affirmative action office, office for students with disabilities, testing office, or administration for more information. Seek information about procedures, eligibility requirements, and accommodations for students with learning disabilities; obtain a copy of the Americans with Disabilities Act (ADA) now in effect.

Review Questions

True-False

1. T   2. F   3. T   4. T   5. T   6. F   7. T   8. T   9. T   10. T

Short Answer

1. The three modalities are visual, auditory, and kinesthetic.
2. Answers will vary.

Identifying Modalities

1. a   2. a   3. k   4. a   5. k   6. v   7. a   8. k, v   9. a   10. v, k

Use What You Learned: Culminating Activities

1. Make a list of your favorite and most effective study tools for reciting, reflecting, and reviewing information. Each time you sit down to study, make a conscious effort to use at least one of these tools.
2. Make a study tape either as you recite from other study tools or as you prepare for an upcoming test.

---

13 Creating Mnemonics

PART II includes:	Enrichment T (pp. 83–84)
	Overhead 7 (p. 96)

Mnemonics Profile

1. Y   2. Y   3. Y   4. Y   5. N   6. Y   7. Y   8. N   9. Y   10. Y   11. Y   12. Y

Mnemonics: Discussion Questions

1. What information do you remember learning at home or at school that was taught by using a mnemonic?
2. Have any of your teachers in college provided you with mnemonics to remember course information? If yes, explain.
3. What acronyms (a word made from letters of other words) are you already familiar with? (Example: MADD—Mothers Against Drunk Driving)
4. Do you think it is worth the time to memorize and practice a mnemonic such as SAVE CRIB FOTO? Why or why not?

13.1 Creating Acronyms

1. D = distractions   A = attention   T = tuned in   E = emotions
   I = interest   A = ask   N = nonjudgmental

2. The letters will have to be rearranged so that they can be used: R O D T D O N. These can be rearranged as DON'T ROD or as ROD, DON'T.

13.2 Brainstorming Acronyms and Acrostics

1. The letters to use are: *D, D, I, I* (or *E*), and *R* (or *F*). Use only five letters since there are five theories. These are the possible letter combinations: DDIIR, DDIIF, DDIER, and DDIEF. DDIER can be rearranged to make the acronym DRIED (*d*ecay, *r*etrieval failure, *i*nterference, incomplete *e*ncoding, *d*isplacement). Answers for acrostics will always vary, but the acrostic should consist of a sentence five words long.

2. *RWSP* are the letters to use. Since there are no vowels, an acronym is not possible. Make an acrostic.

3. *MVEMJSUNP* are the letters to use, and they must be in order. Since they do not make words, create an acrostic.

4. Answers will vary depending on which key word was selected for each of the five steps. Ask students to explain their mnemonics and the key words they used to create them.

Extra activity: Ask students to bring one or more lists of items that they have to learn in another class. Brainstorm as a class to create mnemonics for remembering this information. Remind students that there is no need to make a mnemonic if the information can be learned and retrieved from memory without difficulty.

13.3 Drawing Cartoons and Pictures

Drawings will vary. Have students show their drawings to a partner, a small group, or the class.

13.4 Creating Mnemonics

1. The hints were *e*valuate, *v*isualize, *a*ffirm, *b*reak into steps, *a*sk for help, and *t*ell others.

2. The letters to use are *TSAQ* or *NSAQ*. An unusual acronym could be SAT Q. Or a sentence could be made. Answers will vary.

3. The letters to use are *NPVAAPCI*. An acronym could be NAACP VIP or NAP, PA VIC. Answers will vary for all other kinds of mnemonics.

4. The letters to use are *HURCP*. An acronym could be CHURP (misspelling, however). Answers will vary for all other kinds of mnemonics.

5. The letters to use are *RDIP*. The acronym is DRIP. Answers will vary for other kinds of mnemonics.

6. The letters to use are *RAO*. The acronym is OAR. Answers will vary for other kinds of mnemonics.

Extra activity: Discuss the *stacking* example in the book. Have students practice visualizing and reciting from the bottom to the top. Add one item at a time. Challenge students to rehearse until they can "see and say" the items in the stacking without looking. Later in the week, without advance notice, see how many students can still see and say the items in order.

Extra activity: Follow the directions in the text to help students memorize the *twelve pegs*. Then, remove the visual pegs, and challenge them to visualize the pegs clearly. With an overhead transparency of the pegs, ask students to give you a list of twelve tasks that need to be done. Draw them one by one on the pegs. After every three or four drawings, turn off the overhead, and have students visualize and name what has been created. Continue until all twelve are done. Challenge students to see who can name all twelve tasks in order. Without advance notice, later in the week see how many students can still name all twelve tasks.

Note: This activity can also be done with concrete items. Gather up a variety of odds and ends, and place them in a paper bag. Have students pull out one item at a time. Find a creative way to draw that item with the peg. Continue taking items from the bag and adding them to the peg system. Practice visualizing and naming. This is an excellent exercise to challenge mental abilities, strengthen concentration, and use visualization skills.

13.5 Using Loci

Ask students to visually walk through the rooms and tell the topic that was placed in each room. Ask for one or more volunteers to give a short speech based on the loci system and the floor plan used in this exercise.

13.6 Checking Your Memory

1. Each letter names one of the Great Lakes: Huron, Ontario, Michigan, Erie, and Superior.
2. You should feed a child BRAT: bananas, rice, applesauce, and toast.
3. DATE IAN represents concentrated listening strategies.
4. The words mean parentheses, exponents, multiplication, division, addition, and subtraction.
5. Turn it left.
6. They point up.
7. Mount Fuji is 12,389 feet.
8. These sentences should be checked because of correct spelling:

   I had chocolate cake for dessert.
   The principal called me about my son.
   I did not receive it.
   The principles of accounting are complex.
9. It is north.
10. The first four items were hot dogs, cabbage, shampoo, and milk.
11. Clean the bathtub.

Review Questions

Short Answer

1. A *mnemonic* is any memory trick or system used to assist the memory. The term comes from Greek and means "to remember" or "to be mindful."

   Acrostics are sentences made from the first letters of key words in the information you want to remember. An example would be the sentence to remember the mathematic order of operations: Please excuse my dear Aunt Sally.*

   An *acronym* is a word or group of words that is made by using the first letter of key words in the information you want to remember. An example would be the word HOMES.*

   Loci is a type of mnemonic that is good for general, rather than academic, use. Items to be remembered are placed in familiar rooms in a floor plan that is visualized. As you walk through the rooms in your mind, you remember the items you placed in the rooms.

   Stacking is a type of mnemonic that is good for general, rather than academic, use. Items to be remembered are stacked in order from the bottom to the top of a pile; practice visualizing the items that have been stacked before more items are added.

2. Mnemonics can assist memory by giving small clues to help you remember information that was difficult to remember by itself. The extra clues in mnemonics help trigger the recall of information stored in your memory. Also, creating mnemonics can be fun and make studying interesting.

3. The steps for making an acrostic are the following:
   - First, list the items you need to remember.
   - Second, underline one key word per item.
   - Third, identify/underline the first letter of each key word, and write it on your paper so that you can see it clearly.
   - Fourth, make a sentence by starting words in the sentence with the letters listed in the step above. Unless the items have to be in order, you can rearrange the letters.
   - Fifth, practice memorizing and translating the mnemonic.

4. The twelve pegs are pencil, swan, clover, chair legs, hand, elephant's trunk, flag, hour glass, balloon on a stick, ball and bat, ladder, and eggs.

5. No. Sometimes you won't have any vowels to use and so you can't make words. If the information has to be in order and the letters in order don't spell a word, you cannot make an acronym.

6. Answers will vary. These are possible answers:

Charleston	Picture the person dancing the Charleston.
Hatfield	Picture a hat in a field.
Mandle	Picture a handle in the shape of an *M*.
Seymour	Picture the person with his or her hand on the forehead straining to "see more"; the person holds the cat Seymour in the other arm.
Vineberg	Picture a vine growing on an iceberg.

7. Answers will vary. A possible answer: Specific time lines have steps and rewards.

---

* Well-developed definitions include a second sentence with expanded information (p. 291). These sentences are examples of expanded information but are not necessary at this point for a correct answer.

Translating Mnemonics

1. The pictures represent the following mnemonics in this order:

stacking	association	cartoon
peg system	acronym	rhymes
acrostic	loci	story line

2. In the following, acronym, acrostic, and association can be interchanged. Stacking and story line can be interchanged.

peg	cartoons	association
acronym	acrostic	loci
stacking	rhymes/rhythms	
story lines		

Enrichment T: This enrichment contains an article about the stages of sleep. Students use this excerpt to apply the study techniques learned thus far in the text. You can break students into groups, or you can assign one or more of the following:

1. Read paragraph by paragraph. Use your textbook marking skills, or make separate Cornell notes.

2. Create vocabulary flash cards or vocabulary sheets for the important terms in this article. Remember to include a general category entry.

3. Create a visual study tool for this information. You can create a visual mapping or a hierarchy.

4. Complete the category grid for this information.

5. Create a study tape for this information.

6. Create a mnemonic to remember the five stages of sleep.

Use What You Learned: Culminating Activities

1. Nine mnemonics were presented in this chapter. Use any four to create mnemonics for information being studied in any of your other classes. Present the mnemonics to the class.

2. Practice using the stacking method, the peg system, or the loci system the next time you go shopping or have a series of tasks to complete.

---

14 Taking Tests with Less Stress

PART II includes: Overhead 8 (p. 97)

Test Strategies Profile

1. N   2. Y   3. N   4. Y   5. N   6. Y   7. N   8. N   9. N   10. N   11. Y   12. Y

Test Anxiety: Discussion Questions

1. Have you ever suffered from test anxiety? Explain what happened.
2. What do you feel are the reasons for test anxiety?
3. How does test anxiety affect a student's performance?
4. What other situations create anxiety attacks that are similar to test anxiety attacks? What do all these situations have in common?

14.1   Recognizing Anxiety

After students have brainstormed, compile their information on the blackboard or overhead projector. A suggested culminating activity involves returning to this list to summarize strategies that can be used for each indicator of test anxiety.

14.2   Getting Ready

After students have formulated their lists, compile them. Overhead 8 can be used for this purpose. Answers should include the following, although students may add other answers as well.

Emotionally Ready	*Physically Ready*	*Mentally Ready*
family cooperation	good night's sleep	materials organized
friends' support	healthy breakfast	study schedule made
affirmations	supplies or materials available	summary notes made
positive self-talk	physical needs taken care of	feedback used
visualizations		questions anticipated
relaxation techniques		review sessions attended
praise		test explained
encouragement		old tests accessed

14.3   Finding Out About a Test

Answers will vary.

14.4   Reflecting After a Test

Have students use this exercise on a test they have recently completed. This same exercise can be used after a chapter or a unit test for this course. Answers will vary.

Review Questions

Multiple Choice

1. b   2. d   3. a   4. d   5. c   6. c   7. d   8. c   9. b   10. a

Short Answer

1. *Anxiety* is excessive stress or an excessive reaction or response to events or situations that disrupt your normal pattern or routine. Anxiety robs you of the ability to recognize the source of stress, gain control, and search for solutions.

   Assisted response is a test-taking technique that involves using other parts of the test to help you answer questions to which you don't immediately know the answer. You skim through the rest of the test looking for key words that trigger your memory for the correct answer.

   Cramming is a last-minute survival technique used to learn large amounts of information. It is the result of being underprepared for a test. Cramming often increases test anxiety.

   Immediate response is what you do when you read a test question and immediately know the answer. Immediate response is the payoff for effective studying and can boost your confidence for the rest of the test.

   Natural stress is the normal reaction or response to events or situations that threaten to disrupt your normal pattern or routine. It may involve physical, emotional, or behavioral reactions.

2. Any three of the following are acceptable answers:
   - Anticipate questions based on your notes.
   - Anticipate questions based on class lectures.
   - Anticipate questions based on your textbook notes.
   - Anticipate questions from the study tools you created.
   - Work with a study partner to create questions for each other.
   - Ask the instructor about the test.
   - Ask former students about the test.

3. Any four of the following are acceptable answers:
   - Survey to find the types of questions on the test.
   - Survey to see if questions are on the back of the test.
   - Survey to find out where to place answers.
   - Survey to see the point values of different test questions.
   - Survey the length of the test so that you can budget your time.

4. Any three of the following are acceptable answers:
   - Determine which kinds of questions you missed the most.
   - Look to see if you made any careless mistakes.
   - Determine the source of the information you missed (lecture, textbook, handouts, overhead).
   - Determine which parts of the test you earned the most points on, and then determine why you scored better on those points.
   - Evaluate if you spent enough time studying.
   - Determine which study strategies worked and which didn't.
   - Evaluate your use of the twelve principles of memory; determine which ones you need to use more effectively.

5. Any three of the following are acceptable answers:
   - Jot down information you think you will need and don't want to forget.
   - Become an active learner. Circle the direction words and underline key terms to keep your mind and eyes focused on the test itself.
   - Whisper as you read the questions.
   - Use a blank piece of paper to block off the rest of the test and to keep your eyes from jumping around.
   - Ignore other students; focus on yourself.

- Use quick relaxation or positive self-talk techniques.
- Use the four stages of answering questions; temporarily skip the ones you don't know and answer the ones you do know.

Use What You Learned: Culminating Activity

1. Make a mapping to show the steps you should use when you survey a test.
2. Return to Exercise 14.1. Brainstorm possible strategies from this chapter to combat each of the test-taking problems identified in this exercise.

---

15 Developing Strategies for Objective Tests

PART II includes: Enrichment U (p. 85)

Objective Test Profile

1. Y   2. N   3. N   4. Y   5. Y   6. Y   7. N   8. Y   9. Y   10. Y   11. N   12. N

Types of Test Questions: Discussion Questions

1. What kinds of questions have you encountered on tests in college?
2. Which kinds of questions are easiest for you to answer? Which are the most difficult?
3. What specific strategies do you already know for answering different kinds of test questions?

Types of Test Questions

Many students don't realize that some kinds of questions are more difficult to answer because they require different levels of thinking and memory skills. Discuss the differences among recognition, recall, and recall-plus questions:

Recognition: You need to recognize the information that is presented to you.

Recall: You have to retrieve information from your memory because all the information is not included in the question.

Recall plus: In addition to retrieving information from your memory, you have to organize and express it in a meaningful way.

15.1   Answering True-False Questions

1. F   It does not give class test dates.
2. F   The three areas are school, leisure, and work.
3. T
4. F   The answers should not be given in the recall column.

5. T
6. T
7. F   Philosophers are not considered kinesthetic.
8. T

15.2   Using Definition Clues

The underlining may vary. The following words should be circled:

1. F   Circled: states that
2. F   Circled: is defined as
3. F   Circled: is
4. T   Circled: also referred to as
5. F   Circled: is
6. F   Circled: is
7. T   Circled: involves
8. F   Circled: refers to
9. T   Circled: are also called
10. T   Circled: are

15.3   Finding Negatives

The underlining may vary. The following words should be circled:

1. T   Circled: not
2. T   Circled: not
3. F   Circled: unacceptable
4. F   Circled: but
5. F   Circled: imbalanced
6. T   Circled: nonproductive
7. F   Circled: not, irrational
8. T   Circled: unprepared
9. T   Circled: irregular
10. T   Circled: no

Use the foregoing answers to emphasize that negatives do not necessarily mean a true-false question will be false. Negatives simply suggest the importance of reading carefully.

15.4   Finding Modifiers

The underlining may vary. The following words should be circled:

1. F   Circled: only
2. T   Circled: some, all
3. T   Circled: often
4. F   Circled: every
5. F   Circled: always
6. F   Circled: everyone, always
7. F   Circled: all
8. F   Circled: always best, most productive, no one
9. F   Circled: always
10. T   Circled: sometimes

Enrichment U: This enrichment provides extra work in identifying 100 percent and in-between modifiers. Students are also asked to write their own true-false questions using these modifiers.

1.	IB	11.	100%
2.	100%	12.	IB
3.	100%	13.	IB
4.	100%	14.	100%
5.	IB	15.	IB
6.	100%	16.	IB
7.	IB	17.	100%
8.	IB	18.	100%
9.	IB	19.	IB
10.	100%	20.	IB

Questions will vary.

15.5   Using Relationship Clues

Underlining may vary slightly from the answers below. The following words should be circled:

1. F   Circled: increases; underlined: procrastination, use time management
2. T   Circled: because; underlined: reciting, utilizes auditory, provides feedback
3. F   Circled: so that; underlined: massed practice, can learn masses of information quickly
4. T   Circled: causes; underlined: too much information, recall column, read instead of recite
5. F   Circled: since; underlined: not necessary, take notes, graphs, charts, or pictures, always easy to remember
6. T   Circled: because; underlined: principle of selectivity, important, put into memory
7. T   Circled: so; underlined: major ideas, underline, stand out from, details
8. F   Circled: because; underlined: terminology, obvious, don't need to write

15.6   Answering Multiple-Choice Questions

1. b   2. d   3. c   4. a   5. d   6. d   7. b   8. d   9. d   10. b

15.7   Answering Matching Questions

1. d   2. i   3. a   4. l   5. b   6. j   7. c   8. h   9. e   10. g

Note that two choices are not used.

Review Questions

True-False

1. T   2. T   3. F   4. F   5. T   6. F   7. T   8. T   9. F   10. T

Short Answer

1. The two strategies are to underline key words and circle red flag words.
2. Any of the following answers will be correct:

<table>
<tr><td>*100 Percent*</td><td>*In Between*</td></tr>
<tr><td>all, every, only</td><td>some, most, few</td></tr>
<tr><td>always, absolutely</td><td>sometimes, often, usually</td></tr>
<tr><td>everyone, everybody</td><td>may, seldom, frequently</td></tr>
<tr><td>best</td><td>some people, few people, most people</td></tr>
<tr><td>adjectives with *-est*</td><td>adjectives with *-er*</td></tr>
<tr><td>none, never</td><td></td></tr>
<tr><td>no one, nobody</td><td></td></tr>
<tr><td>worst</td><td></td></tr>
<tr><td>least, fewest</td><td></td></tr>
</table>

3. Any of the following answers will be correct: causes, affects, effects, because, since, reasons, increases, decreases, result, creates, produce.

4. Any of the following answers will be correct: is, are, which is, defined as, also, also known as, called, or, referred to as, means, involves, states that.

5. The four kinds are definition clues, negatives, modifiers, and relationship clues.

6. Paired association is the linking of two items of information when they are initially learned.

Application of Skills in True-False Questions

1. D   Circled: is
2. M   Circled: usually
3. R   Circled: because
4. N   Circled: not, no
5. M   Circled: all
6. R   Circled: lead to
7. M, N   Circled: all, without
8. R, N   Circled: can result in, irreversible
9. R, M   Circled: because, more
10. M   Circled: reasonably good

Application of Skills in Multiple-Choice Questions

1. b

    Underlining for key words may vary. The following should be circled: a. unnecessary, c. seldom, d. never

    F   The reflect step is an unnecessary step of Cornell.
    T   The reflect step promotes critical thinking.
    F   The reflect step seldom shows relationships of ideas.
    F   The reflect step never uses the recall column.

2. d

    Underlining for key words may vary. The following Red Flag words should be circled: b. never, c. because

    The following explains how distractors can be identified:

    A   makes sense and is a true statement, but d is more inclusive.
    B   is false. It has the Red Flag Word NEVER.
    C   is false. It has a Red Flag Word BECAUSE.

Application of Skills in Matching Questions

1. b   2. d   3. a   4. g   5. e   6. f   7. c

2. Students should first have read column A because it has the shorter items. This helps them become familiar with the choices more quickly.

3. Answers will vary.

4. Answers will vary

Use What You Learned: Culminating Activities

1. Locate some of your previous tests. Analyze each of the types of questions. Look for red flag words and key words that would have helped you correctly answer any of the questions you missed.

2. To prepare for your next test, work with a partner to write your own objective test questions. Practice writing the correct answers.

3. Make a list of ten objective test questions already used on any previous tests for any of your classes. Bring your questions to class so that it can analyze them for red flag words.

---

16 Using Educated Guessing

Educated Guessing Profile

1. N   2. Y   3. N   4. N   5. N   6. N   7. N   8. N   9. N   10. N   11. Y   12. Y

Educated Guessing: Discussion Questions

1. Do you feel it is okay to guess on a test? Why or why not?

2. Do you have any techniques you use to guess answers? If yes, explain your system.

3. Have you noticed if certain teachers use more true or more false answers on tests? Have you noticed any patterns for frequent answers to multiple-choice questions? Explain.

16.1   Guessing at True or False

1. T   There are no clue words; take a wild shot guess.
2. F   Notice the 100 percent words "all," "only," and "one."
3. F   Notice the 100 percent word "always."
4. T   Notice the in-between modifier "can result."
5. T   Notice the in-between modifiers "often," and "seldom."
6. F   Notice the relationship word "because."
7. T   There are no clue words; take a wild shot guess.

8. F   Notice the 100 percent word "only."
9. F   Notice the 100 percent words "for certain."
10. T   There are no clue words; take a wild shot guess.

The modifiers are all, only one, always, can result, often, seldom, only, and for certain.

16.2   Guessing at Multiple Choice

1. d   (D) is the most inclusive.
2. a   (A) and (B) start out as look-alikes, so choose one. (A) is more inclusive.
3. c   (A) has the 100 percent word *never*. (B) has an unfamiliar word, *histogram*. (D) tells about the time of the trauma, but the prefix *post-* means after. (C) is the wild shot guess.
4. a   Eliminate the highest and lowest dates. The choices are between (A) and (B). Guess.
5. d   (A) is ridiculous; death is not a gift. (A) also has a 100 percent modifier (always). (B) is ridiculous. (C) is ridiculous; rivers don't conquer lands or declare countries. (D) makes logical sense.

16.3   Using the Eight Strategies

1. c   (B) and (C) are the middle numbers; use a wild shot guess.
2. d   (D) is most inclusive.
3. b   (A) and (D) have 100 percent words; (C) is silly; (B) has an in-between modifier.
4. c   wild shot guess.
5. a   (A) is most inclusive, and A looks alike with B.
6. b   (B) and (C) are look-alikes; (B) is more inclusive.
7. d   (C) and (D) are look-alikes; (D) is longer.
8. a   (C) and (D) have 100 percent words; (A) is more logical and inclusive.
9. c   (C) and (D) are look-alikes, but (D) has a 100 percent word. (A) has a 100 percent modifier.
10. b   (B) is most inclusive.

Review Questions

Fill in the Blanks

1. 100 percent   2. 100 percent   3. wild shot guess   4. middle   5. negatives, definition
6. in-between   7. false   8. true   9. true   10. highest, lowest

Short Answer

1. Educated guessing should be used only as a last resort after you have already tried immediate, delayed, and assisted response. It should also be used if you run out of time and do not want to leave the question unanswered.

2. It does not always work; it is not guaranteed. Teachers can intentionally write tests so the strategies don't work. More than one guessing strategy may be possible for a question, and you may not choose the one that will be correct.

3. Eliminate options with 100 percent words, foolish or insulting answers, and unfamiliar terms. Eliminate the highest and lowest numbers in a range of numbers. Choose one of any two look-alike options. Choose numbers in the midrange of a series of numbers. Choose options with in-between modifiers. Choose options that are most inclusive or that state, "All of the above." If you have to completely guess, choose (c).

4. First, guess false if there is a 100 percent modifier in the question. Second, guess false if there is a relationship word such as "since," "so," "because." Third, guess true if there is an in-between modifier. Fourth, guess true if you have no clues and have to take a wild shot guess.

5. In multiple choice, the wild shot guess is used by guessing the answer (c). This seems to be where many teachers put the correct answer; they want you to read through the choices before you see the correct answer. In true-false, the wild shot guess is to choose true. Many teachers want to leave students with correct information, so they write true sentences more often than write false sentences.

Use What You Learned: Culminating Activities

1. Have each student write ten true-false and ten multiple-choice questions for any information discussed this term in class. Compile the questions (edit as needed and eliminate duplicates). Make copies for students. These are excellent review tools for students as they prepare for the final exam.

2. Have students locate previous true-false and multiple-choice tests from any of their classes. Cover up the correct answers. Try to answer by using educated guessing strategies. Determine how many questions would have been correct based on the application of these strategies. (The results will often depend on the teacher's test-writing skills.)

---

17 Developing Strategies for Recall and Recall-Plus Tests

> PART II includes: Enrichment V (pp. 86–87)

Recall and Recall-Plus Profile

1. N   2. Y   3. N   4. Y   5. N   6. Y   7. Y   8. N   9. N   10. N   11. N   12. Y

17.1   Filling in the Blanks

1. red bow   2. stem   3. Recall   4. flex-   5. Spaced   6. copyright   7. DATE IAN   8. Suffixes

17.2   Making Lists

The key words underlined will vary.

1. The steps are survey, question, read, record, recite, and review.

2. Any four of the following answers are correct:
   - Assess your reading skills. Take a reading class if needed.
   - Read the paragraph out loud.

- Find definitions for unfamiliar words.
- Find the topic sentence of the paragraph.
- Look for supporting details for the topic sentence.
- Discover the organizational pattern for the details.
- Review your notes from the preceding paragraph.

3. These types are peg system, acronyms, stacking, story lines, cartoons, association, rhymes, acrostics, and loci.

4. Any three of the following answers are correct: raised eyebrows, tilted head, hand gestures, body stance, pauses to glance at notes, writing on the board or overhead.

17.3   Writing Definitions

Answers will vary. Check each answer to see if it has the term, the category, the definition, and some form of expansion.

17.4   Writing Opening Sentences

The words that should be circled and underlined are shown below.

Answers for the opening sentence will vary. Have students write their opening sentences on the board for the class to critique. The sentences with details used to expand the opening sentence will vary because they will be based on the opening sentence.

1. Circled: discuss; underlined: two strategies, anxiety attack, while . . . taking a test

2. Circled: name; underlined: three reasons, notetaking from lectures, is more difficult than, from a textbook.

3. Circled: discuss; underlined: three different ways, can be used

4. Circled: explain; underlined: principle of feedback, study from flash cards

17.5   Understanding Direction Words

1. Circled: explain why—I should give reasons time management can reduce stress.

2. Circled: summarize—I should discuss the main points of six principles of memory without giving specific details.

3. Circled: compare—I should show the similarities and differences between hierarchies and mappings.

4. Circled: contrast—I should show the differences between short-term and long-term memory capabilities and functions.

5. Circled: analyze—I should identify the different parts of the information processing model and then tell which principles of memory are used in each part of the model.

17.6   Writing an Essay

Answers will vary. Inform students how you will grade their essays. I suggest the following:

Five points for following the direction word and limiting the essay to the topic given in the question

Five points for a strong thesis sentence and summary

Five points for each main idea developed into a paragraph with sufficient and accurate supporting details (set a maximum number of points before the essay)

Five points for writing skills: overall organization, transition from one idea to another, grammar, spelling, punctuation, use of course terminology, and expressive vocabulary or word choice

The following essay questions were presented in this chapter. This list can be reproduced to help students select a topic for Exercise 17.6.

1. Explain why the use of effective time management skills can reduce stress.
2. Summarize any six of the twelve principles of memory.
3. Compare the organizational structures of hierarchies and mappings.
4. Contrast the capabilities and functions of short-term memory and long-term memory.
5. Analyze the information processing model in terms of the principles of memory used in each part of the model.
6. Why is metacognition beneficial to the college student?
7. Discuss the characteristics of each of Howard Gardner's multiple intelligences.
8. Time management, concentration, notetaking, and textbook reading skills are all necessary study skills for college students. Explain why each of these study skills is essential for success in college.
9. Many study skills that help you become a more effective, successful student were discussed this term. Select the four study skills that you feel are most important for your personal success. Discuss the key strategies for each of the four study skills that you selected.
10. Discuss the study skill strategies that will lead you to greater personal success in school.

The following questions were adapted from the chapter questions for listings, definitions, and short-answers. These questions can be additional options for your essay assignment.

1. The SQ4R is a system for effectively reading and learning information in textbooks. Discuss in order each step of SQ4R.
2. If you read a paragraph and don't understand what it means, do not move on. Seven strategies can help you understand paragraphs. Summarize any four of these strategies.
3. The acronym PASS CAR, AL represents the nine kinds of mnemonics. Define each of these nine mnemonics.
4. Many verbal and nonverbal clues help students recognize important information. Discuss three verbal and three nonverbal clues that help you identify important ideas during a lecture.
5. Discuss the three levels of information that can be included on a mapping.
6. Explain why visual mappings are effective study tools. Include reference to the memory principles involved in learning from the mappings.
7. Explain how you study from flash cards, Cornell notes, highlighting, and visual mappings or hierarchies.
8. Discuss strategies you can use to deal with test anxiety before a test and during a test.
9. Discuss the reasons notetaking from lectures can be difficult; then, discuss solutions to improve lecture notetaking skills.
10. Discuss the three ways to use surveying when you study.

11. Explain how to use the principle of feedback when you study.

No Review Questions

Since this is the last chapter and it will usually be taught at the end of the term before the final exam, no review questions have been included in the student text. But review questions are available in Enrichment V.

Enrichment V: This enrichment provides students with review questions for Chapter 17.

Fill in the Blanks

1. Recall, long   2. Recall-plus   3. category   4. expand   5. summary, thesis

Listing

1. Answers may vary but can include any six of the following: discuss, tell, name, identify, what are, describe, explain, explain why, explain how, how, when, compare, contrast, define, trace, summarize, evaluate, critique, analyze.

2. The six steps for essay writing are:
   - Identify the direction word.
   - Write a strong thesis statement.
   - Make an outline, mapping, or hierarchy to plan the main points for your essay.
   - Expand your thesis sentence into paragraphs.
   - Summarize your main ideas.
   - Proofread for mechanical errors.

3. Proofreading should include checking spelling, grammar, word usage, and sentence structure.

Definitions

1. *Direction words* are words in test questions that indicate the kind of answer that is expected. Discuss, explain, compare, contrast, and trace are five examples of direction words.[*]

2. *Recall-plus questions* are the highest level or most difficult type of test questions. These questions require you to recall information from memory and organize it in written form to express your ideas or understanding. Definitions, short answers, and essays are all recall-plus level questions.[*]

3. The *thesis statement* is a sentence that clearly states the main point for an entire essay. The thesis statement is placed in the first paragraph of an essay and is then expanded and developed into the paragraphs of the essay.

Short Answer

1. You can use assisted response. Look back through the test for other items that could be included in the listing. If you can't find the exact words or items needed, but you have a general idea, write a synonym or a short phrase to try getting partial points for your general understanding.

---

[*] These sentences may vary. Check that students have expanded the first sentence of a definition by including one or more sentences with details.

2. Study by looking and reading the back sides of the cards. After you have read a definition, say and spell the word you think is on the front of the card. Turn the card over to check your accuracy.

3. You can create an organizational plan by writing a basic outline, creating a visual mapping, or devising a hierarchy. Each of these should show the main ideas and the most important supporting details that you want to include in your essay.

4. If you run out of time and can't finish an essay question, include a list of the important ideas you did not have time to develop into paragraphs. You can also include your outline, visual mapping, or hierarchy.

5. A strong, focused opening sentence lets the reader know immediately that you understood the question and know the direction your answer should take. Such a sentence also helps keep you on track and focused on the topic and directions.

Use What You Learned: Culminating Activities

1. Write five or more recall and recall-plus test questions to prepare for the final exam. This helps you anticipate test questions and gives you practice writing answers. Bring your questions to class so that they can be compiled and copied for all students to use.

2. Locate previous tests. Identify the different levels of test questions used on the tests. Are there certain kinds of questions you miss more often? What strategies have you learned from this chapter for dealing with those kinds of questions more effectively now?

3. Make a hierarchy or visual mapping of all the important points you learned in Part IV of this textbook (Chapters 14–17).

PART II
Enrichment Exercises and Overhead Masters

Enrichment A   Chapter 1

Auditory Activity

Break into groups of three to five people. Discuss each of the following questions with everyone in the group. Record your answers.

1. Who in the group can recite something that she or he memorized in school as a child?
    Names: _____
    (Each person recites part of what she or he remembers.)

2. Who in the group says the alphabet by singing the alphabet song?
    Names: _____

3. Who in the group can sing a few phrases of a current rap song?
    Names: _____
    (Each person recites a few appropriate phrases.)

4. Who in the group can close his or her eyes and "hear" the quality of the teacher's voice?
    Names: _____
    (Can each person repeat exactly what the teacher said?)

5. Who in the group can close her or his eyes and "hear" a parent's exact words?
    Names: _____

6. Who in the group likes to write poetry that rhymes?
    Names: _____
    (Can each person recite a few lines of poetry?)

7. Who in the group can tap out the rhythm of "The Star-Spangled Banner" without singing it out loud?
    Names: _____
    (Each person tries it.)

8. Who in the group can close his or her eyes and "hear" the sounds of a rapidly running river, ocean waves, a bulldozer moving rock, or a siren?
    Names: _____

9. Each person gives directions on how to get from school to a particular place in town. Whose set of directions was easy to follow?
    Names: _____

Based on the preceding information, who in the group do you think is a strong auditory listener?

Enrichment B   Chapter 1

Summarizing the Group Process

Exercises throughout this book recommend working in groups. Please answer the following questions about your last experience working in a group.

1. What are the names of the members who worked in your group?

2. Did every member of your group have the opportunity to give at least one answer?

3. Could you have contributed more answers? Why or why not?

4. Did you sometimes feel yourself dominating the group?

5. Were all answers accepted with respect and without criticism?

6. Did your group stay on task and not wander off the subject? Why or why not?

7. Did you enjoy the group process? Why or why not?

8. How could the group process have been improved or have been more effective?

Enrichment C   Chapter 2

Pie of Life Checklist

The following checklist can be a springboard for finding ways to achieve a more comfortable balance in the three main areas of your life. Check the statements that are true for you. Consider what actions will lead to necessary changes.

_____ I have "empty leisure time" that I could use more constructively for studying, working, or beginning new goals.

_____ I could spend less time watching television, playing music, talking on the phone, sitting idly, daydreaming, or sleeping.

_____ My socializing time is a little excessive. I could spend less time going to movies, going out with friends, or partying.

_____ I could schedule quality time with my friends and plan those times more carefully.

_____ I could reduce the number of hours I spend working on my hobby, getting involved in group activities, or volunteering my time with organizations.

_____ I could determine how many hours per week I want to spend on specific leisure activities and then not exceed that number.

_____ I could get started with my studying and stay focused longer by having my supplies, assignments, notebooks, and work area better organized.

_____ I could decrease my workload at home by planning chores and errands more efficiently.

_____ I could use goal setting and time management principles to get jobs done quickly and more efficiently.

_____ I could discuss my needs with household members and elicit their help in sharing chores more fairly.

_____ I could discuss fewer work hours or better work hours with my employer.

_____ I could look for a different job with better hours and pay.

_____ I could explore other sources of financing or financial budgeting so that I could get by with fewer work hours.

_____ I could find ways to study that don't waste so much time.

Enrichment D   Chapter 2

Goals and Affirmations

Write *Y* if the following goal is well written. It should be clear, specific, and realistic, and it should include a time line. Write *N* if the goal is missing one or more essential elements.

_____   a.   I will organize an ideal study area at home by 5:00 this Sunday.

_____   b.   I hope to find a part-time job sometime soon.

_____   c.   I want to do better on my math test Friday.

_____   d.   I want to learn ten new Spanish phrases by the end of class time this Friday.

_____   e.   I will bench-press one hundred pounds in my weight-training class by the end of this term.

Write *Y* if the following affirmation is well written. Write *N* if the affirmation is missing one or more key elements.

_____   a.   I control my temper around my youngest son.

_____   b.   I should vacuum the house every day.

_____   c.   I will not watch television in the afternoon.

_____   d.   I listen and follow directions accurately.

_____   e.   I am organized and it shows in the way I keep my notebook and my study area.

Write a well-defined goal for school, home, work, or leisure. This could include a small task you need to complete. Be specific. Set a target date. Identify the steps involved. Plan a reward. Then write an affirmation that helps you work to achieve this goal.

Enrichment E (part A)   Chapter 2

Analyzing a Time Management Schedule

TIME	MON.	TUES.	WED.	THURS.	FRI.	SAT.	SUN.
8–9:00	I get the day going. ——————→					Sleep	Sleep
9–10:00	Drive to school. Stop in Cafeteria for coffee. ——————→					Sleep	Break-fast
10–11:00	Algebra class	P.E.	Alg. class	P.E.	Alg. class	Family	Church
11–12:00	lunch	class	lunch	class	Study French	Chores &	
12–1:00	French class	lunch	French class	lunch	Fr. Class	House-work	↓
1–2:00	Eff. L. class	Stay in cafet.	Eff. L. class	Stay in cafet.	Eff. L. class	Lunch	Lunch
2–3:00	← Recreation – Go jog ——————→				lunch	Do things with the Kids	↑ Family
3–4:00	← Go home, do errands, house, get Kids			clean the ——→			Time
4–5:00	← Prepare dinner ——————→						↓
5–6:00	← Family dinner time ——————→					Dinner	Dinner
6–7:00	← Talk with family, t.v. ——————→					T.V.	Study Eff. L.
7–8:00	Church	T.V.	Reading	T.V.	Social	T.V.	Study Algeb.
8–9:00	night –	Study Algebra	Night	Study French	Social	T.V.	Study Fr.
9–10:00	meeting	Study Eff. L.	Class	Study Eff. L.	Social	Social	Bed
10–11:00	← Study Reading – Do Assignments →					"	Bed

Enrichment E (part B)   Chapter 2

Analyzing a Time Management Schedule

Study the Time Management Schedule and answer the following questions.

1. What classes is this student taking?

2. Are there sufficient hours of studying set aside for each class? Explain your answer.

3. Are there times earlier in the day that could be used for studying? If so, when?

4. Do you think the student chose wise time blocks to study for each class? Why or why not?

5. Are there study blocks seven days a week? If not, what recommendations would you make?

6. Is this student using marathon studying? If so, what recommendations would you make?

7. Have flex study hours been included? If not, where would you recommend that they be placed?

8. Are there some times scheduled to work on hobbies or personal goals? If so, when?

9. Does the person seem to have a comfortable balance among school, work, and leisure? Explain your answer.

10. Is there sufficient time scheduled for meals, sleep, and some form of exercise? Explain your answer and any recommendations you may have.

11. Does this student make wise use of consistent patterns? Explain your answer.

12. What general comments can you make about this student and this weekly time management schedule?

Enrichment F   Chapter 2

Weekly Time Management Checklist

Consider the following checked items when you make a new weekly time management schedule.

Study Blocks

_____   Do you have enough study blocks set aside to study for each class? (Use the 2:1 ratio when it is appropriate.)

_____   Do you specifically label "Study" and name the class?

_____   Are your study blocks spread throughout the week?

_____   Are you spending some time studying on weekends?

_____   Do you avoid marathon studying so that you do not study more than three hours in a row?

_____   Do you avoid studying late at night?

_____   Do you include flextime in your schedule?

Fixed Activities

_____   Do you schedule time for three meals each day?

_____   Do you schedule sufficient time to sleep each night?

_____   Do you keep a fairly regular sleep schedule throughout the week?

Balancing Your Life

_____   Do you plan time specifically to spend with your family?

_____   Do you plan sufficient time to spend with friends and get involved in social activities?

_____   Do you plan time for exercise, hobbies, or special interests such as clubs, organizations, and recreational teams?

_____   Do you plan specific time to take care of household chores and errands?

_____   Do you plan time to work on specific goals?

Will the Schedule Work?

_____   Can you "walk through each day" in your mind and see that your schedule is realistic and possible?

_____   Are your peak energy times used wisely?

_____   Do you feel that your life will be more balanced if you follow what you have planned on your weekly schedule?

Enrichment G   Chapter 4

Schemas

Schemas are mental pictures or categories that can help you store information in long-term memory. Some schemas in your memory are well developed because of your experiences and background knowledge. Other schemas may be small or nonexistent.

Different schemas are written in the following circles. Search your memory to find information that you already know about each schema. Surround each circle with words, pictures, facts, or ideas that are related to the topic inside the circle. You will notice that some schemas are well developed and that others are considerably weaker.

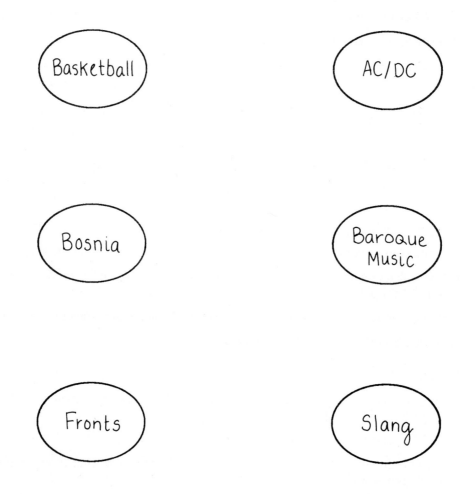

Compare your schemas to another person's. Did you have similar information, or did you interpret the topics differently?

Enrichment H   Chapter 4

Twelve Principles of Memory

Break into groups of four. If your group has less than four, one or more students will take two turns.

Activity 1

1. Begin with twelve pieces of paper or twelve index cards. Write one memory principle on each piece of paper or card.

2. Mix up the pieces of paper and place them face down so that the principles can't be seen. Each person selects four pieces of paper.

3. Take a few minutes to mentally rehearse what you know about the four principles you selected. Try to include the following:
   - The name of the principle
   - The definition or description of the principle
   - Reasons the principle is important for memory
   - Examples of how the principle can be used when studying

4. Follow the order of the principles as listed here. The person who has the principle recites to the group what he or she knows about the principle. Continue until all twelve principles have been reviewed.

   Selectivity
   Association
   Visualization
   Effort
   Concentration
   Recitation
   Interest
   Big picture–little pictures
   Feedback
   Organization
   Time
   Ongoing review

Activity 2

1. Collect the twelve pieces of paper. Mix them up again.

2. Each person selects one memory principle and then has ten minutes to write as much information as he or she remembers about that principle.

Enrichment I   Chapter 4

Memory Checklist

_____   Selectivity: I carefully select the important ideas and supporting details. I spend my time studying this information.

_____   Association: I take time to associate the new information to the information I already know.

_____   Visualization: I make pictures and movies in my mind of the information I am learning. I practice seeing these pictures without looking.

_____   Effort: I willingly apply effort to the process of studying and learning.

_____   Concentration: I use concentration techniques when I study. I strive to keep my attention focused on the material I am studying.

_____   Recitation: I practice information by saying the information out loud and in complete sentences. If I am not able to recite, I use this feedback to study the information further until I can explain it in my own words.

_____   Interest: I take the responsibility to make the information I am studying interesting. If I have no genuine interest in the subject, I create some.

_____   Big picture–little pictures: I actively look for big ideas, categories, or concepts. I also focus on little pictures, the details that together support the big picture.

_____   Feedback: I use feedback in my study methods by questioning and quizzing myself as I study to be sure that I really understand the material.

_____   Organization: I rearrange or organize information so that it is easier to understand and put into memory. This may include making notes, making additional study tools (flash cards, lists, mappings, tapes), or creating mnemonics.

_____   Time: I use my time management skills so that I am able to schedule enough time for studying, rehearsing, and making appropriate study tools.

_____   Ongoing review: I take time to continually review information that I have previously learned. I actively practice retrieving information from memory.

Enrichment J   Chapter 6

Benefits of SQ4R

Activity 1

If you read a textbook without using SQ4R, you see the information only once. When you do all the steps of SQ4R, you see and work with the information more than six times. List and briefly explain the number of times you see and work with information when you use all the SQ4R steps. The first one is done for you.

I work with the information when I:

1. Survey—look at specific parts of the chapter.

Activity 2

Memory is boosted when you use the auditory, visual, and kinesthetic channels into your memory. Which of these channels is used for each step of SQ4R?

Survey uses _____.

Question uses _____.

Read uses _____.

Record uses _____.

Recite uses _____.

Review uses _____.

Activity 3

The SQ4R system will be weakened if you omit one or more of the steps. Brainstorm a list of the benefits or advantages of each step that would be lost if the step was omitted.

Enrichment K   Chapter 7

Pharaohs and Pyramids

The focal point of religious and political life in the Old Kingdom was the pharaoh, who commanded the wealth, resources, and people of all Egypt. The pharaoh's power was such that the Egyptians considered him to be the falcon-god Horus in human form. The pharaoh was the power that achieved the integration between gods and human beings, between nature and society that ensured peace and prosperity for the land of the Nile. The pharaoh was thus a guarantee to his people, a pledge that the gods of Egypt cared for their people.

The king's surroundings had to be worthy of a god. Only a magnificent palace was suitable for his home; in fact, the very word *pharaoh* means "great house." The king's tomb also had to reflect his might and exalted status.

The religious significance of the pyramid is as awesome as the political. The pyramid helped the pharaoh ascent the heavens after death. The pyramid provided the dead king with everything that he would need in the afterlife. His body had to be preserved from decay if his *ka,* an invisible counterpart of the body, was to survive. So the Egyptians developed an elaborate process of embalming the dead pharaoh and wrapping his corpse in cloth. As an added precaution, they carved his statue out of hard stone; if anything happened to the fragile mummy, the pharaoh's statue would help keep his ka alive.

To survive in the spirit world the ka required everything that the pharaoh needed in life: food and drink, servants and armed retainers, costly ornaments, and animal herds. In Egypt's prehistoric period, the king's servants and herdsmen and their flocks were slaughtered at the tomb to provide for the ka. To remind the ka of daily life, artists covered the walls of the tomb with scenes ranging from agricultural routines to banquets and religious festivities, from hunting parties to gardens and ponds. Designed to give joy to the ka, these paintings, models of furniture, and statuettes today provide an intimate glimpse of Egyptian life, 4,500 years ago.

Enrichment L   Chapter 8

Comments on Your Cornell Notes

The following checked items are comments about your textbook notes.

Record Step

_____   You clearly showed and underlined the headings. Well done!

_____   You need to identify and underline the headings.

_____   Your notes will be easier to study because you remembered to leave a space between headings.

_____   Your notes will be less crowded or cluttered if you leave a space before you begin a new heading.

_____   Your notes show accurate and sufficient details. Good work.

_____   Consider using numbering to show the different details under a heading.

_____   You need to write more; some important details are missing.

_____   Phrases often lose meaning over time. Try to use more complete sentences to explain details.

_____   You either copied or referred to specific page numbers to remind yourself of important graphs, pictures, or charts. Good!

_____   Be sure to include information about graphs, pictures, or charts in your notes.

_____   Strive for neater penmanship.

_____   Remember to write on only one side of the paper.

_____   Remember to number each page of your notes.

Reduce Step

_____   Use a two-and-one-half-inch recall column.

_____   Your headings and questions are placed directly across from the same information in your notes. Well done!

_____   Remember to move the heading into the recall column.

_____   Try placing questions or key words directly to the left of the information in the notes.

_____   Your key words or questions are effective.

_____   You are giving yourself too much information or all the answers. You will end up reading the information rather than reciting.

_____   You will need more key words or questions in the recall column to guide you when you recite.

_____   Try using your recall column to see if the key words or questions you wrote are sufficient to help you recite.

_____   Remember that you can add information to the recall column if you feel more is needed when you are reciting.

Other

_____

_____

_____

Enrichment M   Chapter 9

Notetaking Problems and Solutions

Four common problems were identified for taking lecture notes. In the following columns, summarize the techniques recommended for solving the problem shown at the top of the column.

Weak Listening	Rate Problems	Organization	Spelling

Enrichment N   Chapter 9

Cornell and the Principles of Memory

The Cornell notetaking system is so effective because it uses the principles of memory to move information through the information processing model. In the following chart, list the principles of memory that you feel are at work in each step of the Cornell system. You may use a principle more than once.

Principles of Memory (SAVE CRIB FOTO)

- Selectivity
- Association
- Visualization
- Effort
- Concentration
- Recitation
- Interest
- Big picture–little pictures
- Feedback
- Organization
- Time
- Ongoing review

Steps	Principles of Memory
Record	
Reduce	
Recite	
Reflect	
Review	

Enrichment O   Chapter 10

Making Flash Cards

Use the skills you have learned in this chapter to make and study from flash cards related to this course.

Make a category card and definition cards for any *one* of the following. Then practice reciting the cards from the front and the back.

1. The information processing model (Chapter 4)

2. The twelve principles of memory (Chapter 4)

3. The SQ4R reading system (Chapter 6) and the five *R*'s of Cornell (Chapter 8)

4. The theories of forgetting (Chapter 4) and Howard Gardner's seven intelligences (Chapter 8)

5. The organizational patterns used in paragraphs (Chapter 6)

6. Concentration techniques to deal with distracters (Chapter 3)

Enrichment P   Chapter 10

Finding Definitions

In the following sentences, circle the punctuation clue or the word clue used to signal a definition for the word in italics. Then underline the definition.

1. *Pitch*—how high or low a tone sounds depends on the frequency of sound waves

2. An instrument, such as one based on Thomson's principles, that separates ions by mass-to-charge ratio is called *a mass spectrometer.*

3. His title *imperator,* with which Rome customarily honored a general after a major victory, came to mean "emperor" in a modern sense of the term.

4. Our important social attitudes are anchored by our *values,* how we think we should behave, or what we regard as an ideal state of being.

Read the following excerpt carefully. Highlight or underline words or phrases that help you form a definition for the term *thematic statement.* Write your own definition of the term after the paragraph.

> The third lens in your mental microscope focuses on your *thematic statement.* The thematic statement should bring the heart of your message into sharp detail. It should specify precisely what you want your audience to learn or accept, and it should identify the main point or points you will develop in your speech. You should be able to condense these ideas without strain into a single declarative sentence. Often the thematic statement is worked into the beginning of your speech as a preview of what will follow.

_____

_____

_____

_____

_____

Enrichment Q   Chapter 10

Word Parts

Use this list of word parts to help you define the terms that follow:

auto: self   *geo:*   earth
bio: life   *graph:*   written record
biblio: book   *ology:*   study of

Biography means _____.

Autobiography means _____.

Geography means _____.

Geology means _____.

Bibliography means _____.

Biology means _____.

What other words can you think of that use the root *graph* or *graphy*? List them here. After each word, use your knowledge of word structure to write a definition for the word.

_____   _____

_____   _____

_____   _____

What other words can you think of that use the root *ology*? Write them here. After each word, use your knowledge of word structure to write a definition for the word.

_____   _____

_____   _____

_____   _____

If you are not sure of the meanings of any of the words you listed, check a dictionary.

Enrichment R   Chapter 11

Mappings for Brainstorming

Often in writing classes you are asked to generate ideas or topics to write about. Visual mappings can help you get ideas flowing.

Assume you are asked to write a narrative, a personal story about a significant event. Four possible topics follow. Brainstorm by writing as many possibilities as you can around each topic. Draw lines from the topic to your ideas (level two information).

- What are some interesting first-time experiences you have had?
- What things or which people are memorable to you?
- Who or what are some of your favorite people or things?
- What are some emotions or feelings that could be tied to a specific incident?

Suggestions for level three information are below each mapping. Add level three information to your mapping.

First -Time Experiences

My Most Memorable

(Name a feeling or reaction to each experience.)

(Add a feeling, mood, or emotion to each event.)

My Favorite

Feelings, Emotions

(Add a feeling mood, mood, or emotion to each item.)

(Attach an event or incident to each feeling.)

Enrichment S   Chapter 11

Making a Time Line

Work with a partner. Read the following excerpt. Identify the important dates or time periods and the significant events. Then create a time line; add pictures and color if you like.

Early Technological Developments

Since the beginning of recorded history, people have had difficulty calculating answers to mathematical problems. One early mechanical calculating device, the *abacus,* was developed by Chinese merchants before the birth of Christ. Composed of several wires, each strung with ten beads, the abacus enabled the merchants to calculate solutions to mathematical problems and then store the results.

In the seventeenth century, the slide rule was developed through the work of John Napier and William Oughtred. And the first real mechanical "calculator" was developed in 1643 by the Frenchman Blaise Pascal. Pascal's calculator added or subtracted numbers by using a series of rotating gears, or wheels. . . .

In the early 1800s, Charles Babbage, a British mathematician, designed a machine that could perform mathematical calculations and store the intermediate results in a memory unit—the forerunner of today's computer. Babbage called this device the *difference engine.* . . . Babbage is often called the father of modern computer technology.

In the late 1880s, Dr. Herman Hollerith was commissioned by the U.S. government to develop a system that could process the 1890 census data. His punch card system reduced the time required to process the 1890 census data to two and a half years. . . . Based on his experience with the government project, Hollerith founded the Tabulating Machine Company to manufacture and sell punch card equipment to businesses. Later, the Tabulating Machine Company changed its name; today it is known as International Business Machines (IBM).

In 1944 Howard Aiken of Harvard University, in collaboration with IBM and the U.S. War Department, embarked on a joint project to manufacture the Mark I computer. It is not a true electronic computer because it utilized electromagnetic relays and mechanical counters to perform mathematical calculations. Nevertheless, this device opened the door for the development of the electronic computer.

Enrichment T (part A)   Chapter 13

Stages of Sleep

Read this excerpt carefully. Follow the directions provided by your teacher.

Probably the most important technological step toward expanding research on sleep came in 1919 when Hans Berger, a German psychiatrist, developed the *electroencephalogram,* or EEG. . . . The EEG provides a record of the electrical activity of the brain. . . .

When researchers used EEGs to measure brain activity during sleep, they found several distinctive patterns of brain waves. . . . The amplitude (variations in height) and the frequency (speed) of these waves changed systematically throughout the night. William Dement and Nathaniel Kleitman (1957) used these systematic changes in brain waves, combined with activity of muscles and the eyes, to identify six stages of sleep: stage 0, which is a prelude to sleep, four stages of quiet sleep, and rapid eye movement sleep.

Stage 0 and Quiet Sleep During stage 0, you are relaxed, with eyes closed, but awake. The EEG . . . shows a mixture of brain waves, including some alpha waves (rhythmic brain waves that occur at a speed of about 8 to 12 cycles per second). During stage 0, there may be considerable tension in the body and your eyes move normally. The next stages, stages 1 through 4, are called *quiet sleep,* or slow-wave sleep, because all of them are accompanied by slow brain waves, deep breathing, a calm and regular heartbeat, and reduced blood pressure.

As you drift from stage 0 to stage 1 sleep, your eyes move more slowly and begin to roll. The EEG frequency becomes irregular, and alpha waves begin to disappear. . . . After a few minutes in stage 1, you enter stage 2 sleep. In this stage, the EEG shows sharply pointed waves called *sleep spindles.* There are also occasional *K complexes,* which are special waves with high peaks and deep valleys. As you gradually enter stage 3 sleep, spindles and K complexes continue to appear, but they are mixed now with *delta waves,* which are much slower (0.5 to 0.3 cycle per second) and have much higher amplitude. When delta waves occur more than 50 percent of the time, you have entered stage 4, the deepest level of sleep, from which it is most difficult to be roused. It takes about a half an hour to reach stage 4 from stage 1 sleep.

REM Sleep After thirty to forty minutes in stage 4, a sleeper begins to retrace the journey, returning through stages 3 and 2 to stage 1. Then begins an extraordinary stage known as *REM* (for rapid-eye-movement) *sleep,* or active sleep. As in stage 1, the EEG during REM resembles that when you are active and awake, but now your heart rate, respiration, blood pressure, and other physiological patterns also resemble those occurring during the day. At the same time, you begin rapid eye movements beneath closed lids. Paradoxically, while the brain waves and other measures resemble those of a person awake, muscle tone decreases to the point of virtual paralysis. Sudden, twitchy spasms appear, especially in your hands and face.

What is going on during this *paradoxical sleep?* Because of the rapid eye movements, it looks as if the sleeper is scanning some private, internal world, so researchers began waking people up during REM. In about 80 percent of these awakenings, the people said they had been dreaming. In contrast, reports of dreams occurred in only 7 percent of the time when non-REM sleep was interrupted.

A Night's Sleep During the night, most people travel up and down through these stages of sleep four to six times. Each complete circuit takes about ninety minutes. . . . During the first half of the night most of the time is spent in deeper sleep (stages 3 and 4) and only a few minutes in REM. The last half of the night is dominated by stage 2 and REM sleep, from which sleepers finally wake up.

Enrichment T (part B)   Chapter 13

Stages of Sleep

1. Label the rows Stage 0, Stage 1, Stage 2, Stage 3, Stage 4, and REM.
2. Label the columns name of sleep, eye movement, vital signs, muscles, and brain waves. (Vital signs include breathing patterns, heart rate, and blood pressure.)
3. Complete the grid with key words.

Stages of Sleep

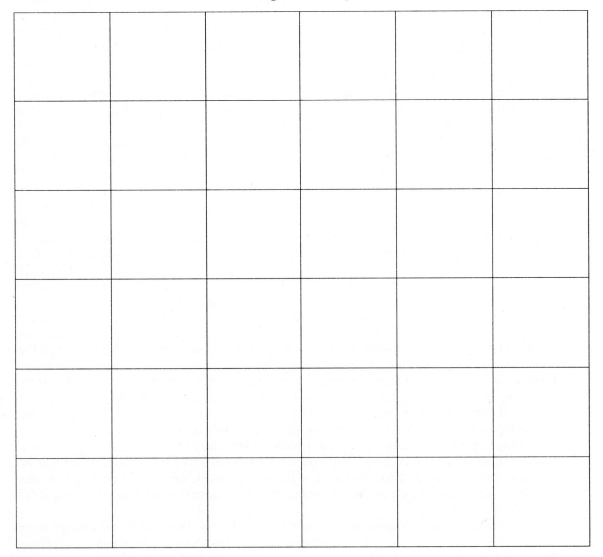

Enrichment U   Chapter 15

Kinds of Modifiers

Work with a partner. Decide if the following words are 100 percent or in-between modifiers. Write 100% if the word is an absolute that doesn't allow for exceptions. Write IB if the word is not an absolute.

_____	1. often	_____	11. none
_____	2. never	_____	12. frequently
_____	3. always	_____	13. sometimes
_____	4. worst	_____	14. every
_____	5. many	_____	15. most
_____	6. best	_____	16. few
_____	7. some	_____	17. all
_____	8. generally	_____	18. without exception
_____	9. usually	_____	19. occasionally
_____	10. no	_____	20. perhaps

Select any six modifiers from the preceding list. Use them to write six true-false questions that cover any information you have learned in this course.

1. _____

2. _____

3. _____

4. _____

5. _____

6. _____

Enrichment V (part A)   Chapter 17

Test-taking Practice

Fill in the Blanks

Write one word in each blank to correctly complete each sentence.

1. _____-level questions require you to retrieve information from _____-term memory.

2. There are many possible correct answers for _____-_____ questions.

3. A definition answer should begin by naming the term and then identifying the _____ that the term belongs in.

4. In a short or definition answer, after you have written the opening sentence, you then need to _____ it into two or more sentences.

5. The _____ sentence or paragraph in an essay should reflect the same information or ideas presented in the _____ sentence.

Listings

1. List six different direction words often found in recall-plus questions.

2. List the six steps to use for writing an essay.

3. List the things you should check when you proofread written answers.

Enrichment V (part B)   Chapter 17

Test-taking Practice

Definitions

Write a definition for each of the following terms:

direction words

recall-plus questions

thesis statement

Short Answer

1. Tell what strategies you can use if you don't have an answer for all the spaces in a listings question.

2. How should you use flash cards to prepare for a fill-in-the-blanks test?

3. Name three or more methods you can use to create an organizational plan before you begin to write an essay.

4. What should you do if you run out of time and can't finish answering an essay question?

5. Why is a strong, focused opening sentence important for short answers and essays?

Overhead 1   Chapter 4

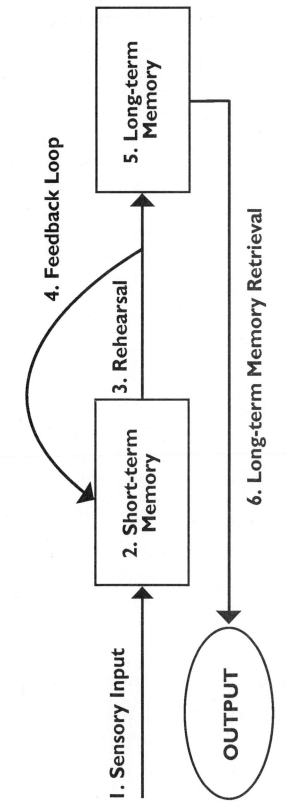

THE INFORMATION PROCESSING MODEL

5. Long-term Memory

4. Feedback Loop

3. Rehearsal

2. Short-term Memory

6. Long-term Memory Retrieval

1. Sensory Input

OUTPUT

Overhead 2 (part A)   Chapter 8

Cornell Notes

Maslow's Hierarchy of Needs	Maslow's Hierarchy of Needs
Who's maslow?	1. Concept of hierarchy of Needs — Abraham Maslow (psychologist)
Define "need"	2. <u>need</u> = personal requirement
"wanting"... "order of importance"	3. Maslow assumed people are "wanting" beings who seek to fulfill needs in their order of importance.
<u>Physiol. Needs</u> What are they?	<u>Physiological Needs</u> 1. Most basic level to survive
	2. Food, water, clothing, shelter, sleep
How are they satisfied by business?	3. Usually satisfied through adequate wages
<u>Safety Needs</u> What are they?	<u>Safety Needs</u> 1. Required for physical + emotional security
Business satisfies by....?	2. Satisfied through job security, insurance, pensions + safe working conditions
<u>Social Needs</u> What are they? Satisfied how?	<u>Social Needs</u> 1. Requirement for love + sense of belonging 2. Work environment, informal organizations, friends + family satisfy soc. needs
<u>Esteem Needs</u> What are they?	<u>Esteem Needs</u> 1. Require respect, recognition, sense of accomplishment + self worth
Satisfied how?	2. Accomplishments, promotions, honors and awards satisfy this need
<u>Self-Realiz. Needs</u>	<u>Self-Realization Needs</u> 1. Need to grow, develop + be what we're capable of
What are they? difficult....	2. Most difficult to satisfy
Satisfy How?	3. Varies w/ individual; examples: learning new skills, new career, be the best

Overhead 2 (part B)   Chapter 8

Cornell Notes

Summary
"ladder of needs"
motivated
 	
order ?
 	
Why is it Δ
important for
motivation &
management ?
	Summary
	1. Maslow suggests we move up the
	   ladder of needs and are motivated
	   by the lower needs first
	2. Do not need to completely satisfy needs
	   on a lower level in order to start
	   work on needs of higher level
	      Ex. majority phy. & safety needs
	         met (but not all), will work
	         on social needs next
	3. Maslow's hierarchy provides useful
	   way to view employee motivation
	   & as a guide for management.
	      — Am. business able to satisfy
	         worker's basic needs, but
	         higher level needs more of a
	         problem
	      — Satisfying higher level needs
	         Varies from one employee to
	         another

Which levels do businesses Satisfy ?	
5 levels of needs?	Self- Realization Esteem Social Safety Physiological MASLOW'S HIERARCHY OF NEEDS

Overhead 3   Chapter 8

COMBINING SQ4R and CORNELL

BEGIN THE SQ4R STEPS:

1. SURVEY: Do an overview for the chapter.

2. QUESTION: Write questions for each heading.

3. READ: Read one paragraph.

4. RECORD: Take Cornell notes on separate paper.

5. RECITE: Recite the important information in the paragraph.

6. Continue to read-recite-record to the end of the chapter.

CONTINUE THE CORNELL STEPS:

7. REDUCE: Make your recall column.

8. RECITE: Cover your notes and recite from your recall column.

9. REFLECT: Do one or more reflect activities.

10. REVIEW: Review your notes, complete the chapter questions and the questions you made in the Q step of SQ4R.

Overhead 4   Chapter 11

VISUAL MAPPINGS

How to Create Mappings

1. Write the topic in the center of your paper.
2. Write the main ideas or the main headings; use lines to connect them to the topic.
3. Add major details to support the main ideas.
4. Add any necessary minor details.

How to Study from Mappings

1. Visualize and recite the topic in the center of your paper.
2. Visualize and recite the main ideas.
3. Check your accuracy by looking at your mapping.
4. Return to the first main idea. Without looking at your paper, recite the major and minor details associated to that main idea.
5. Check your accuracy by looking at your mapping.
6. Continue until you have recited all the main ideas, major details, and minor details.
7. Use reflect activities.
8. Use ongoing review.

Overhead 5   Chapter 11

HIERARCHIES

How to Create Hierarchies

1. Write level one information (the topic) on the top line of the hierarchy.
2. Draw lines downward from the topic to show level two information (the main ideas).
3. Under each main idea, branch downward again for level three information (major details).
4. Add level four information (minor details) under the major details if needed.

How to Study from Hierarchies

1. Visualize and recite the topic written on the top line.
2. Visualize and recite the main ideas on level two.
3. Get feedback by looking at your hierarchy to check your accuracy.
4. Return to the first main idea on level two. Recite the level three and level four major and minor details.
5. Get feedback by looking at your hierarchy to check your accuracy.
6. Continue until all the main ideas have been recited.
7. Use reflect activities.
8. Use ongoing review.

Overhead 6   Chapter 12

MULTI-SENSORY STRATEGIES

STRATEGIES FOR VISUAL LEARNERS

1. Visualize pictures and movies in your mind.
2. Make visual mappings, hierarchies, category grids and timelines.
3. Add pictures to your study tools.
4. Add colors to your study tools.
5. Copy and write information on flash cards or vocabulary sheets.
6. Use non-verbal clues.
7. Record directions and important information.

STRATEGIES FOR AUDITORY LEARNERS

1. Talk out loud, recite and work in study groups.
2. Use tapes to make study or review tapes.
3. Add rhymes or tunes to your studying.
4. Use computerized technology with speech synthesizers.

STRATEGIES FOR KINESTHETIC LEARNERS

1. Use your hands to work with objects or manipulatives.
2. Use large muscle movements as you study by pacing, working on a chalkboard, learning by doing or using drama or dance.

Overhead 7   Chapter 13

PEG SYSTEM

1 = pencil
2 = swan
3 = clover
4 = legs
5 = hand
6 = trunk

7 = flag
8 = hourglass
9 = balloon on a stick
10 = ball and bat
11 = ladder
12 = eggs

Overhead 8   Chapter 14

GETTING READY FOR A TEST

EMOTIONALLY READY	PHYSICALLY READY	MENTALLY READY

PART III
Part Tests and Answer Keys

Part I Test

Name_____ Date_____

(Total possible points: 75)

True-False *(1 point each)*

To help keep your mind focused, underline the key words in the true-false questions before you answer them. Write *T* if the statement is TRUE. Write *F* if it is FALSE.

_____ 1. A syllabus gives you the teacher's name, office hours, course expectations, and the system used for grading.

_____ 2. A well-planned time management schedule should include time to rehearse and practice retrieving information from long-term memory.

_____ 3. If you are using less than the 2:1 ratio for one of your classes, you are not meeting the expectations of college-level courses.

_____ 4. The slackening off process begins in the third week of the term.

_____ 5. The checkmark technique can help you reduce both internal and external distractors.

_____ 6. The red bow technique helps you reduce internal distractors.

_____ 7. The emotional *E* words *easy* and *effortless* are used to increase motivation and success.

_____ 8. Self-talk uses statements that reinforce negative beliefs about self-image and the ability to succeed.

_____ 9. The feedback loop in the information processing model is directly related to at least one of the twelve principles of memory.

_____ 10. The memory principles of selectivity, effort, recitation, and visualization should be used when information is processed on the rehearsal path of the information processing model.

_____ 11. The ability to store information in schemas in long-term memory is greatly increased when the principles of big picture–little pictures and organization are used in the learning process.

_____ 12. The technique of chunking should be used when you plan for long-range assignments.

_____ 13. Flex blocks on a time management schedule provide you with time for unexpected social events or chores.

_____ 14. Studying for more than three hours in a row should always be avoided because then there is not enough time for ongoing review.

_____ 15. Learning to see life as a positive, exciting process can lead to less stress and a willingness to take risks so that you can remain in your secure comfort zone.

Multiple Choice *(1 point each)*

Read each question carefully with all the options. Cross out the options that you know are incorrect. Select the best option that remains. Write the letter of the best option on the line.

_____ 1. The STSR steps for writing goals are
   a. self-motivation, time, steps, and review.
   b. short-term, tell, self-motivation, and reward.
   c. specific, time line, steps, and reward.
   d. start, take action, use self-talk, get results.

_____ 2. External distractors can include
a. sunshine, noises, and lighting.
b. smells, noises, and worries.
c. negative self-talk, clutter, and people.
d. checkmark technique, spider web technique, and framing.

_____ 3. You are using your learning resources when you
a. are aware of your preferred learning modality.
b. select learning strategies that use your strengths.
c. plan your study blocks during peak energy hours.
d. do all of the above.

_____ 4. Creating study tapes, reciting, and working in study groups are effective study strategies for
a. kinesthetic learners.
b. all kinds of learning styles.
c. visual learners.
d. auditory learners.

_____ 5. When you need to take time from one type of activity to find time for another type of activity, you are using the
a. memory principle of ongoing review.
b. memory principle of concentration.
c. increase-decrease method.
d. STSR method.

_____ 6. If you have difficulty completing goals, the memory phrase *EVA, BAT* suggests that you
a. visualize and use affirmations.
b. breathe by threes and use feedback.
c. chunk the goals and use fifty-minute time blocks.
d. do all of the above.

_____ 7. In a well-developed time management schedule, you will not
a. plan to study your most difficult subjects first.
b. include time for personal hobbies or recreation.
c. avoid studying on weekends.
d. create patterns for the week that are easy to follow.

_____ 8. If you do not quiz yourself as you are learning new information, you are not using the memory principles of
a. feedback and recitation.
b. interest and cramming.
c. ongoing review and schemas.
d. organization and time management.

Matching *(1 point each)*

Read through the items in the left column.

Begin with the first item in the right column. Try to match it to an item in the left column. If you see the match, write the letter on the line. Cross off the item on the right so that you do not use it again.

If you do not see the match right away, skip the question. Go back to it after you have made all the matches that you are sure are correct.

_____	1.	Principle of association
_____	2.	SAVE CRIB FOTO
_____	3.	Short-term memory
_____	4.	Long-term memory
_____	5.	Long-term retrieval
_____	6.	2:1 ratio
_____	7.	RAVES
_____	8.	Perfect place
_____	9.	Framing
_____	10.	Mental storage box

a. a storage center where learned information is imprinted
b. a formula for the number of study hours based on the number of hours in class
c. a memory principle that relates new information to existing schemas
d. a memory phrase for techniques to help you mentally prepare to study
e. a technique used to help create visualizations
f. a memory phrase for the twelve principles of memory
g. a relaxation technique that uses breathing and visualization
h. a concentration technique that helps you temporarily remove internal distractors
i. a temporary storage center for sensory input
j. a process that requires ongoing review

Short Answer

Use your own paper to answer each of the following questions. Be sure to clearly number your answers.

1. Define each of the following terms: *(1 point each)*

    goals
    trading time
    learning styles
    concentration
    schemas

2. Discuss the seven suggested techniques to use in achieving concentrated listening. (The memory phrase *DATE IAN* can help you remember these techniques.) *(7 points)*

3. Discuss the recommended techniques for reciting. Explain how reciting should be done. *(5 points)*

4. Describe an ideal study area that has few distractions. *(5 points)*

5. Explain the stages involved in learning new information. Include details to explain each stage. *(10 points)*

6. Select and then list any five principles of memory. After each principle, explain how you can use this principle of memory when you study. *(10 points)*

Answer Key for Part I Test

True-False

1. T 2. T 3. F 4. F 5. T 6. F 7. F 8. F 9. T 10. T 11. T 12. T 13. F 14. F 15. F

Multiple Choice

1. c 2. a 3. d 4. d 5. c 6. a 7. c 8. a

Matching

1. c 2. f 3. i 4. a 5. j 6. b 7. d 8. j 9. e 10. h

Short Answer

1. *Goals* are well-defined plans aimed at achieving a specific result.

   Trading time is a time management technique that allows you to switch the time of two different activities. This gives you the flexibility to handle unexpected situations and still allows you to complete your commitments for the day.

   Learning styles are general ways people learn and remember information. These styles, also called modalities, comprise visual, auditory, and kinesthetic.

   Concentration is a mental process that requires you to direct your thoughts to one subject or issue at a time.

   Schemas are clusters of related information that are organized and stored in long-term memory. The size and number of schemas increase as you learn more new information.

2. Additional sentences to expand the definition with details are recommended. Give 1 point per technique.

   (D) Eliminate distractors.
   (A) Pay attention to the development of ideas.
   (T) Stay tuned in even when information is difficult.
   (E) Monitor your emotions so that you don't overreact.
   (I) Create an interest in the topic being discussed.
   (A) Ask questions at the appropriate time.
   (N) Be nonjudgmental about the speaker's appearance, mannerisms, and speech patterns.

   (For further details, refer to Chapter 3.)

3. For effective reciting, you should use your own words to speak in complete sentences to explain the information as clearly as possible. Imagine yourself trying to explain the information to a friend who is not familiar with the subject. Pay attention to areas that you are not able to clearly explain. Go back to the source of the information to check your accuracy and be reminded of important details. (See the principle of recitation in Chapter 4.)

4. An ideal study area should be a place with minimal or no distractions. It should be a quiet area or an area with a minor noise level. The table and chair should be comfortable and the appropriate size. The work surface and the surrounding walls should be uncluttered. Two or more sources of lighting should be present. Necessary supplies should be readily available. (Refer to Chapter 3 for more details.)

5. New information that is being learned moves through the six stages of the information processing model. The six parts of the model should be discussed: sensory input, short-term memory, rehearsal, feedback loop, long-term memory, and long-term memory retrieval. (Refer to Chapter 4 for details.)

6. Answers will vary. Give 2 points for each answer in which there is a clear correlation between the memory principle and how it is used in studying. (See Chapter 4 for details of each memory principle.)

Part II Test

Name_____   Date_____

(Total possible points: 75)

True-False   *(1 point each)*

To help keep your mind focused, underline the key words in the true-false questions before you answer them. Write *T* if the statement is TRUE. Write *F* if it is FALSE.

_____   1.   The purpose of surveying is to get acquainted with material before you begin thorough reading.

_____   2.   Active learning takes place when you read out loud, recite information, and take notes.

_____   3.   When you read a textbook, you should read a paragraph or short section, stop to check your comprehension, and then take notes before you begin reading again.

_____   4.   The only words in a paragraph that you need to fully understand are the terms in special print.

_____   5.   The topic of a paragraph is usually included in the main idea sentence.

_____   6.   If you read carefully, you will always be able to find the topic sentence in the beginning of the paragraph.

_____   7.   Clue words such as "first," "next," "after," and "finally" are often found in paragraphs organized chronologically.

_____   8.   When you take notes from a textbook, you basically copy main ideas and details word for word so that your notes are accurate and useful for studying.

_____   9.   When you use the third step of the Cornell system effectively, you get immediate feedback that indicates how well you understand the new material.

_____   10.   The recall column in Cornell notes should provide you with key words, your own study questions, and answers to the study questions you create.

_____   11.   The fourth step of the Cornell system encourages you to think about, reorganize, and use new activities to work with the information you are learning.

_____   12.   In the Cornell system, the left-hand column should remain blank while you are taking notes during a lecture.

_____   13.   When you combine SQ4R with the five *R*'s of Cornell, notetaking begins during the second step of SQ4R.

_____   14.   The differences among thinking, speaking, and writing speeds are less than one hundred words per minute.

_____   15.   Your notetaking speed can often be increased by using abbreviations, symbols, and shortened sentences.

Listings

1.   List the steps of the Cornell system in order.   *(5 points)*

2.   List the steps of the SQ4R system in order.   *(6 points)*

3.   List at least six parts of a textbook that should be examined when that textbook is first surveyed. Include sections in the front and in the back of the book.   *(6 points)*

4.   List any three of the seven strategies for comprehending a paragraph.   *(3 points)*

Marking Text   *(10 points)*

Read the following passage carefully. Use textbook marking skills to underline topic sentences and important details. Circle vocabulary words and use any other marking techniques that seem appropriate.

Sleep Disorders

Almost everyone has trouble sleeping sometimes, especially during times of stress. Sleep disorders can be a temporary annoyance or a long-term, even life-threatening problem.

The most common sleeping problem is *insomnia,* a general term for conditions in which a person feels tired during the day because of trouble falling asleep or staying asleep. About 25 to 30 million Americans are chronic insomniacs. Besides being tiring, insomnia is tied to mental distress. In one study, people with insomnia were three times as likely to display a mental disorder as those who had no sleep complaints. Insomnia lasting at least one year also predicted the development of depression and anxiety disorders.

Sleeping pills or alcohol may relieve insomnia temporarily, but they can also be dangerous, especially if taken together, and sleeping pills are highly addictive. Several psychological approaches can help insomniacs—including biofeedback, relaxation training, stress management, and psychotherapy. Insomniacs may also be able to alleviate their problem by going to bed only when they are sleepy and getting out of bed whenever they cannot sleep. Skipping caffeine late in the day and keeping a regular schedule also may help.

Sleeping too much can be a problem, too. People suffering from *hypersomnia* not only sleep longer than most people at night but also feel tired and take one or more naps during the day. More disturbing, however, is a daytime disorder called *narcolepsy*. Its victims switch abruptly and without warning from an active, emotional waking state into several minutes of REM sleep. In most cases, the decreased muscle tone causes the narcoleptic to collapse on the spot and remain briefly immobilized even after awakening. The exact causes of hypersomnia and narcolepsy are unknown, but narcolepsy appears to have a genetic basis.

Sleep apnea is a disorder in which people briefly stop breathing while they are asleep. This awakens them, and they resume breathing. Because apnea episodes can occur hundreds of times per night, sufferers do not feel rested in the morning. Usually they have no recollection of their night awakenings. The problem is much more common in men. It seems to be a disorder of the brainstem and of the automatic nervous system's control of breathing. One effective treatment is to wear a mask over the nose that provides a steady stream of air.

Cornell Notetaking   *(15 points)*

Use your textbook markings to make Cornell notes on the preceding passage. After you have finished taking notes, complete the recall column.

Short Answer   *(5 points each)*

Select any three of the following questions to answer. Write your answers on your own paper. Use complete sentences in your answers.

1. Define each of the following terms:

    supporting details
    marginal notes
    nonverbal clues given during a lecture
    indexes
    glossary

2. Why is marking textbooks and taking notes from textbooks important? Discuss the value of using these notetaking systems.

3. Explain the steps to use for studying from highlighted notes.

4. What techniques can you use to maintain concentration on a lecture when your thinking speed is much faster than the instructor's rate of speech?

5. Reflecting and reviewing are important processes to use when you study. Both SQ4R and Cornell use the step of review. Discuss at least four different activities that can be done during a reflect or a review step.

Answer Key for Part II Test

True-False

1. T   2. T   3. T   4. F   5. T   6. F   7. T   8. F   9. T   10. F   11. T   12. T   13. F   14. F   15. T

Listings

1. Give 5 points if the steps—record, reduce, recite, reflect, and review—are correct and in order. Deduct 1 point for each incorrect step and/or for the steps listed out of order.

2. Give 6 points if the steps—survey, question, read, record, recite, and review—are correct and in order. Deduct 1 point for each incorrect step and/or for the steps listed out of order.

3. Give 1 point for each correct answer. Any six of the following are correct:

title page	copyright page	table of contents
introduction	appendix	glossary
bibliography	index	

4. Give 1 point for each correct strategy. Any three of the following strategies are correct:
   - Assess your reading level or reading skills.
   - Read out loud.
   - Find definitions of unfamiliar words.
   - Find the topic sentences.
   - Look for details to support the topic sentence.
   - Discover the organizational pattern used in the paragraph.
   - Review the notes on the previous paragraph.

Marking Text

If students underlined the topic sentences, underlined the majority of the supporting details, and circled the key terms, give all 10 points. Reduce the number of points based on the amount of information omitted. (To be objective, set your standards before you begin grading.)

Paragraph 1: Sleep disorders can be a temporary . . . problem.

Paragraph 2: The most common sleeping problem is insomnia, a general term . . . staying asleep.

   Details: 25 to 30 million Americans, tiring, mental distress, lasting at least one year, depression, anxiety disorders

   Circle: insomnia (possibly chronic insomniacs)

Paragraph 3: Implied: A variety of techniques are available to deal with insomnia.

   Details: sleeping pills, alcohol, temporarily, dangerous, psychological approaches, biofeedback, relaxation, stress management, psychotherapy, bed only when . . . sleepy, out of bed whenever . . . cannot sleep, skipping caffeine

   Circle: (Possibly general vocabulary terms: biofeedback, psychotherapy, alleviate)

Paragraph 4: Sleeping too much can be a problem, too.

   Details: hypersomnia, sleep longer, feel tired, naps, daytime disorder, narcolepsy, switch abruptly, without warning, REM sleep, decreased muscle tone, collapse, briefly immobilized, causes of hypersomnia . . . unknown, narcolepsy . . . genetic basis

   Circle: hypersomnia, narcolepsy (possibly REM sleep, genetic basis)

Paragraph 5: Sleep apnea is a disorder in which . . . are asleep.

Details: awakens, resume breathing, hundreds of times per night, not feel rested, no recollection, more common in men, disorder of brainstem, automatic nervous system, effective treatment, mask, steady air

Circle: sleep apnea (possibly automatic nervous system)

Cornell Notetaking

To receive all 15 points, the notes should:

1. Be neat and well-organized
2. Have main ideas shown differently from details
3. Have ideas numbered
4. Reflect similar information that was underlined
5. Have key words or questions (not answers) in the recall column
6. Have pages numbered if more than one page was used

Short Answer

1. Give 1 point per definition.

   Supporting details are key words, phrases, definitions, facts, statistics, or examples used in paragraphs to explain, support, or develop the topic sentence.

   Marginal notes are notes written in the margins of a textbook. These notes can be questions, lists of information, summaries, comments, or key words.

   Nonverbal clues given during a lecture are body movements such as facial expressions, hand gestures, and body stance as well as pauses and writing on the board or overhead. These body movements can signal important points in a lecture.

   Indexes, found in the back of the book, are alphabetical listings of important names, events, or concepts found within the book. Page numbers are given to help you quickly locate information. There may be an author index and a subject index.

   A *glossary* is a minidictionary found in the back of a book. It provides limited definitions; it defines words only the way they were used in the book.

2. Marking textbooks and taking notes are important so that you have reduced information to study. To do both processes, you must selectively pull out the information that is important to learn. By working with reduced amounts of information, you have more time to study. Your notes are valuable because they are what you spend most time studying. (See Chapter 7.)

3. Reread only the marked information. Then string the information together to form your own sentences. Recite and write this information in your own words. (See Chapter 7.)

4. First, keep writing and taking notes so that you stay actively involved. Second, mentally summarize the information that has been presented. Third, try to anticipate the next point that will be made. Fourth, mentally question the information. (See Chapter 9.)

5. Reflect and review activities can include reviewing the recall columns by lining them all up to see the overall organization, taking time to think about relationships and associate information to other information you know, writing summaries or making lists of important ideas or questions, and making other kinds of study tools, such as flash cards. (See Chapters 9 and 10.)

Part III Test   Name_____   Date_____
(Total possible points: 75)

Multiple Choice *(1 point each)*

Read each question carefully with all the options. Cross out the options that you know are incorrect. Select the best option that remains. Write the letter of the best option on the line.

_____ 1. To get the most benefit from your vocabulary study tools, you should
    a. recite the information.
    b. use reflect activities.
    c. use reciting, reflecting, and reviewing activities.
    d. ask a friend to quiz you with your cards.

_____ 2. The goal of visual study tools is to
    a. create more work.
    b. study without reciting.
    c. create strong images in your mind.
    d. learn to draw better.

_____ 3. Visual images are strengthened when the picture is
    a. uncluttered.
    b. colored or shaded.
    c. logically organized.
    d. all of the above.

_____ 4. In a hierarchy on information from a chapter, main ideas in the hierarchy
    a. should reflect only chapter headings.
    b. may include your own categories as well as headings.
    c. should show all important terminology.
    d. should always include pictures.

_____ 5. The basic modalities that can be used in multisensory study tools are
    a. visual, fine motor, and auditory.
    b. kinesthetic, auditory and visual.
    c. auditory, bodily, and kinesthetic.
    d. none of the above.

_____ 6. Tape-recording information is beneficial when used to
    a. replace the need to take notes in class.
    b. add missing lecture details and summarize review work.
    c. review vocabulary words and definitions.
    d. do all of the above.

_____ 7. Sorting and reorganizing flash cards to create mappings, category grids, or time lines are activities that would be especially beneficial to
    a. auditory learners.
    b. visual learners.
    c. kinesthetic learners.
    d. all of the above.

_____   8. When information is difficult to remember and you need extra clues to trigger your memory, consider making
  a.   mnemonic devices.
  b.   acronyms for the difficult information.
  c.   a peg system if there are less than thirteen items.
  d.   an acrostic with key words.

Finding Definitions   *(2 points each)*

Circle any word or punctuation clues that can help you find the definitions of the words in italics. Then underline those definitions. (If there are no word or punctuation clues, then just do the underlining.)

1. Working from the assumption that all change, positive or negative, is stressful, Thomas Holmes and Richard Rahe developed in 1967 the *SRRS* (Social Readjustment Rating Scale).

2. Epicurus (340–270 B.C.) based his view of life on scientific theories. Epicurus put forth a *naturalistic theory of the universe.* Although he did not deny the existence of the gods, he taught that they had no effect on human life. According to Epicurus, the principal good of human life is pleasure, which he defined as the absence of pain. He concluded that people should avoid all undesirable, violent emotions.

3. In 1916 Gilbert Newton Lewis proposed that the strong attractive force between two atoms in a molecule resulted from a *covalent bond,* a chemical bond formed by the sharing of a pair of electrons between atoms.

4. The church hierarchy, or leaders, encouraged *coenobitic monasticism*—that is, communal living in monasteries.

5. Our important social attitudes are anchored by our *values,* how we think we should behave or what we regard as an ideal state of being.

6. Alcohol dependence or abuse, commonly referred to as *alcoholism,* has been implicated in half of all the traffic fatalities, homicides, and suicides that occur each year.

Category Grid of Multisensory Learning   *(12 points)*

Complete the following grid. Give specific characteristics of each kind of learner, and name at least three specific study methods that would be effective because they use the learner's strengths.

Kind of Learner	Characteristics	Three Study Methods
Visual		
Auditory		
Kinesthetic		

Visual Study Tools *(10 points each)*

From the following three options, choose two of the options. If you wish, you can begin by making a list of your ideas. Then convert the list into a mapping or a hierarchy.

1. Make a hierarchy or a mapping to show the different kinds of visual study tools you can create to use when you study.

2. Make a hierarchy or a mapping to show the different kinds of mnemonics you can create to use when you study.

3. Make a hierarchy or a mapping to show different methods for finding the definitions of words in paragraphs.

Short Answer

Read the following selection carefully. Then answer the questions that follow.

Approaches to Psychology

Psychologists use many theoretical approaches in their attempts to understand why an individual or a certain group of people behave or respond as they do. Among the most significant approaches in psychology today are those known as the biological, psychodynamic, behavioral, humanistic, and cognitive approaches.

The *biological approach* places special emphasis on the electrical and chemical activity of the brain and on the actions of hormones. This approach tries to explain people's behaviors, emotions, mental disorders, and memory on the basis of what happens biologically within a person. Wilhelm Wundt was one of the early psychologists who used the biological approach to understanding people.

Sigmund Freud created a theory to explain mental disorders and personality. This theory also led to a form of therapy called psychoanalysis. This *psychodynamic approach* holds that all behavior and mental processes reflect constant and often unconscious struggles within each person. These struggles usually involve conflicts between the impulse to satisfy instincts or wishes and the restrictions imposed on the individual by society.

John Watson urged psychologists to study what they could directly observe. He encouraged psychologists not to rely on people's thoughts or feelings, which could be easily distorted. This *behavioral approach* assumes that behaviors grow out of patterns of rewards and punishments. Experiences mold individuals.

Carl Rogers and Abraham Maslow, both well-known psychologists, believed that people are not controlled by instincts, biological factors, or rewards and punishments. People control themselves. According to this *humanistic approach,* each person has an innate tendency to grow toward his or her own potential and chooses how to think and act based on his or her perception of the world.

The *cognitive approach* emphasizes the importance of thoughts and other mental processes but also focuses on how the brain operates—how it takes in information, processes information, and uses information to modify behavior. Psychologist William James, as early as 1890, used this approach to try understanding how learning and memory help people get along in the world.

1. What are the five approaches to psychology? (*2 points*)

2. Could you create an acronym to remember these five approaches? Why or why not? (*2 points*)

3. Create and write down your own acrostic for the five approaches to psychology. (*3 points*)

4. Return to the selection. Circle all the words you would put on vocabulary cards. List any category cards that you would include in your flash cards. (*4 points*)

5. Once you had your vocabulary cards created, how would you study from these flash cards? Give specific details. (*4 points*)

6. Draw a category grid that could show the important information to learn about the approaches to psychology. Label the rows and the columns in your grid. You do not need to fill in the boxes with information. (*3 points*)

7. Create a visual mapping or a hierarchy to show at least two levels of information from the selection. (*5 points*)

Answer Key for Part III Test

Multiple Choice

1. c   2. c   3. d   4. b   5. b   6. b   7. c   8. a

Finding Definitions

1. Circle ( ). Underline Social Readjustment Rating Scale.

2. This word is defined only through context clues. Underline principal good of human life is pleasure, absence of pain, and life should avoid all undesirable, violent emotions.

3. Circle: ,. Underline a chemical bond formed by the sharing of a pair of electrons between atoms.

4. Circle: —. Underline communal living in monasteries.

5. Circle: ,. Underline how we think we should behave or what we regard as an ideal state of being.

6. Circle referred to as. Underline alcohol dependence or abuse.

Category Grid of Multisensory Learning

Give 2 points per box (cell) for accurate information. Answers will vary but could include some of the following.

Visual	Strong visual memory Good at remembering pictures or graphs Ability to remember colors Good at visualizing	Making hierarchies, grids, mappings, time lines Using color-coding Adding pictures or cartoons Putting everything in writing; copying Using nonverbal clues
Auditory	Strong auditory memory Good ear for language Good vocabulary Sense of music, tones, rhymes Good expression of ideas	Reading out loud Reciting often Participating in discussions and study groups Making review tapes Singing, making jingles Using exaggerated voice Using computer voice synthesizers
Kinesthetic	Hands-on experiences Movement	Handling objects Making manipulatives Using exaggerated movements Pacing while studying Working at a chalkboard Typing or using a computer Making large wall charts

Short Answer

If students do not have time in class to complete this test, the article on approaches to psychology and the short-answer questions could be used as a take-home test since the answers require students to apply skills.

1. Give 2 points for a list of all five (biological, psychodynamic, behavioral, humanistic, cognitive) and 1 point for a partial list.

2. No. There are no vowels, so an acronym cannot be made.

3. Answers will vary. Give all 3 points for a sentence that has words beginning with the letters *b, p, b, h,* and *c.* Deduct 1 point if the sentence has more than five words.

4. Give 1 point if the five approaches are circled. Give 1 point if the names of psychologists are circled. Give 1 point if other unfamiliar words are circled. (Answers will vary but may include psychoanalysis or innate.) Give 1 point if at least one category card is listed; it can be for either "five psychological approaches" or "psychologists."

5. Give 4 points for an answer with sufficient details that include studying from the fronts and the backs.

   To study from the front of the cards, read the word, recite the definition, check your accuracy, sort cards into piles of cards you know/need to study, review missed cards, and use ongoing review.

   To study from the back of the cards, read information, name and spell/write the term, check your accuracy, and sort the cards into ones you know and ones you need to study.

   Additional ideas include reflecting with the cards and sorting by categories, group, or cluster cards to make mappings on a table or elsewhere.

6. Give 1 point if the rows are labeled correctly with the five approaches. Give 2 points if the two columns have meaningful labels. Answers will vary, but could include: "Believed" or "Characteristics," "Psychologists."

7. The visual mapping or hierarchy should have psychological approaches as level one. The five approaches should be shown as level two.

Part IV Test

Name_____ Date_____

(Total possible points: 75)

True-False *(1 point each)*

To help keep your mind focused, underline the key words in the true-false questions before you answer them. Write *T* if the statement is TRUE. Write *F* if it is FALSE.

_____ 1. When you need to use assisted response, the test itself can be a source for missing information or answers.

_____ 2. Test anxiety can stem from underpreparedness and from past experiences with people or school.

_____ 3. Stress is a reaction or response to an event that threatens to disrupt your normal routine.

_____ 4. "I can't do this even if I try" is an example of procrastination.

_____ 5. Cramming is one method for overcoming the feeling of being underprepared before an exam.

_____ 6. Synonyms or related phrases can sometimes earn some points on a test when they are used in fill-in-the-blank or listing questions.

_____ 7. You should use assisted response on tests before you try delayed response.

_____ 8. When you analyze graded tests, you should focus all your attention on the mistakes you made and on why you didn't know the answers as an immediate response.

_____ 9. Objective test questions include true-false, matching, definition, and short answer.

_____ 10. In a true-false question, it is important to read the question carefully so that you will notice modifiers, negatives, and items in a series.

_____ 11. Red flag words are important because they indicate that an answer will be false.

_____ 12. Multiple-choice options that have negatives or words with negative prefixes will always be distractors.

_____ 13. The words "cause," "produce," "create," and "decrease" are 100 percent modifiers often found in true-false questions.

_____ 14. Multiple-choice questions should be read as a series of true-false questions before the best answer is selected.

_____ 15. A war and the year it was fought are an example of a paired association.

Red Flag Words *(2 points each)*

Circle all the 100 percent modifiers, in-between modifiers, definition clues, relationship clues, and negatives in the following true-false questions.

1. All matter exists in only one of three physical forms: solid, liquid, or gas.

2. The term *vapor* is often used to refer to the gaseous state of any matter that normally exists as a liquid or a solid.

3. The term *states of matter* means the three forms of matter, which are solid, liquid, and gas.

4. The natural sweetener Sorbitol is the best sweetener for diabetics to use because it does not cause rapid fluctuations in blood sugar level.

5. After an arrest, the police are required to read the Miranda rule, which states the constitutional rights of the individual.

Matching *(1 point each)*

Read through the items in the left column.

Begin with the first item in the right column. Try to match it to an item in the left column. If you see the match, write the letter on the line. Cross off the item on the right so that you do not use it again.

If you do not see the match right away, skip the question. Go back to it after you have made all the matches that you are sure are correct.

_____ 1. Compare

_____ 2. Define

_____ 3. Trace

_____ 4. Evaluate

_____ 5. Analyze

_____ 6. Discuss

_____ 7. Explain why

_____ 8. Explain when

a. discuss chronologically
b. identify the parts
c. discuss the time of an event
d. show likenesses and differences
e. give reasons
f. tell about a topic
g. give the definition
h. justify your opinion

Short Answer

1. Discuss at least four strategies or activities that you can do at the beginning of a test to reduce test anxiety. *(4 points)*

2. Describe effective strategies to use in studying for a test that you know will have a large number of fill-in-the-blank and definition questions. *(4 points)*

3. Use what you learned in Chapter 17 to define each of the following terms: *(3 points each)*

    paired association
    open-ended questions
    thesis sentence

4. Assume that you read a test question and didn't know the answer. What test-taking strategies should you use *before* you resort to educated guessing? *(5 points)*

Essays *(10 points each)*

Use your own paper to write essay answers to any two of the following questions. Each essay will be graded on accurate content, sufficient details, clear organization that includes a thesis statement and clearly defined paragraphs, and acceptable grammar and spelling.

1. Metamemory is the process of understanding the abilities of your own memory system, the different kinds of tasks involved in learning, and the strategies you use most effectively to learn new information. Discuss how you use these three aspects of metamemory when you study.

2. One source of test anxiety is underpreparedness. Discuss specific strategies that you can use to reduce test anxiety by being well prepared for tests.

3. Discuss specific techniques that you can use to get emotionally, physically, and mentally prepared for tests.

4. The memory principle of selectivity has been discussed frequently throughout this course. Explain how the principle of selectivity is used in surveying, notetaking, making study tools, and studying for tests.

Answer Key for Part IV Test

True-False

1. T   2. T   3. T   4. F   5. F   6. T   7. F   8. F   9. F   10. T   11. F   12. F   13. F   14. T   15. T

Red Flag Words

Give 2 points per sentence if all the red flag words are circled. Give 1 point if only some of the red flag words are circled or if some words are circled that are not red flag words.

1. All, only one
2. is, refer to, any, normally
3. means, which are
4. best, because, not
5. which states

Matching

1. d   2. g   3. a   4. h   5. b   6. f   7. e   8. c

Short Answer

Give 4 points if the answer is well developed and includes an opening sentence and at least one additional sentence with accurate details.

1. Answers may vary. The following strategies may be included:
   - Use affirmations or positive self-talk about the test in front of you.
   - As soon as you get the test, jot down important information that you want to remember.
   - Get your mind on the test by listening carefully to the directions given by the teacher.
   - Survey the test before you begin working. Note the kinds of questions, the length of the test, where to place answers, and if questions are on the back of the test.
   - Quickly plan your time. Be sure to allow enough time for essay questions.
   - Read directions carefully. Underline and circle important words to help keep your mind focused on the test.
   - Read the questions in a whisper if you start to panic.
   - Cover the rest of the test with paper or your hand so that your eyes stay focused on the question at hand.

2. Answers will vary but should include the following general concepts:
   - For fill-in-the-blank questions, study from the back side of your flash cards or from the left column of your vocabulary sheets. You need to practice retrieving the exact vocabulary words from your memory and spelling them correctly.
   - For definition questions, practice from the front of your flash cards or from the right column on your vocabulary sheets. Practice giving good definition answers by naming the term, identifying the category of the term, giving the specific definition, and then expanding the definition with at least one more sentence.
   - Recite and review frequently. Make piles or lists of words that need further review. Use ongoing review.

3. *Paired association* is a method of learning information by linking two items together when you study. For example, an author may be linked to his or her literary works or a term may be linked

to its definition. When you think of one part of the pair, it should be immediately associated with the second item in the pair.

Open-ended questions are types of test questions that have many possible right answers. Correct answers are derived by using information from several different sources or chapters or by applying knowledge to a new situation. Answers will be correct as long as they are logical. Rote memory of specific answers is not possible because such a list was probably not developed prior to the test.

A *thesis sentence* is a type of sentence used to directly state the main point of an essay. The thesis sentence also indicates directly or indirectly what main ideas will be developed or proven in the essay.

4. Answers will vary but should include the following main points:

- You should first use delayed response. This means that you read the question carefully a second time. You quickly look for key words and do a memory check to see if you can recall where and when you learned the information. You may want to create a question for yourself to help you locate the answer in your memory.
- If you can't get an answer from delayed response, put a checkmark next to the question and leave it for now. Move to the next question.
- After you have answered all the questions you can, return to the unanswered questions. Use the rest of the test to search for possible answers. Look at the key words in the question. Scan through the rest of the test looking for that word or for a category of information related to that word.
- Only after you have exhausted these steps do you use an educated guessing strategy.

Essays

For better results, consider providing students with the essay questions in advance. Students can then plan and practice writing their essays prior to the test. For the test itself, they could be allowed to bring in a list of ideas, an outline, or a visual mapping of the essay.

Answers will vary. To receive the full 10 points, students should meet the criteria given in the essay question directions. You should establish the following point system, or a similar system, before you begin grading:

- Accurate content, 3 points
- Sufficient details, 4 points
- Thesis statement, clearly defined paragraphs, 2 points
- Acceptable grammar and spelling, 1 point